Ethnicity, Hunter-Gatherers, and the "Other"

Ethnicity, Hunter-Gatherers, and the "Other"

Association or Assimilation in Africa

Edited by Susan Kent

Smithsonian Institution Press

Washington and London

Copy editor: Peter Donovan
Production editor: Duke Johns
Designer: Brian Barth

Library of Congress Cataloging-in-Publication Data
Ethnicity, hunter-gatherers, and the "other" : association or assimilation in Africa /
edited by Susan Kent.
    p.   cm.
   Includes bibliographical references and index.
   ISBN 1-58834-060-0 (alk. paper)
    1. Ethnicity—Africa. 2. Hunting and gathering societies—Africa. 3. Herders—
Africa. 4. Traditional farming—Africa. 5. Assimilation (Sociology)—Africa.
6. Africa—Ethnic relations. I. Kent, Susan, 1952–
GN645.E8338 2002
305.8'0096—dc21   2002021018

British Library Cataloguing-in-Publication Data available

Manufactured in the United States of America
09 08 07 06 05 04 03 02   5 4 3 2 1

⊛ The paper used in this publication meets the minimum requirements of the
American National Standard for Information Sciences—Permanence of Paper for
Printed Library Materials ANSI Z39.48-1984.

For permission to reproduce illustrations appearing in this book, please correspond
directly with the owners of the works, as listed in the individual captions. The
Smithsonian Institution Press does not retain reproduction rights for these illustrations individually, or maintain a file of addresses for photo sources.

This book is dedicated to all hunter-gatherers with the hope that they will be allowed to decide their own path, their own future.

Contents

six
Dangerous Interactions: The Repercussions of Western Culture,
Missionaries, and Disease in Southern Africa
Susan Kent   150

seven
Solitude or Servitude? Ju/'hoansi Images of the Colonial Encounter
Richard B. Lee   184

eight
Cultural Contact in Africa, Past and Present: Multidisciplinary
Perspectives on the Status of African Foragers
Alison Brooks   206

nine
The Complexities of Association and Assimilation:
An Ethnographic Overview
Alan Barnard and Michael Taylor   230

ten
Why the Hadza Are Still Hunter-Gatherers
Frank Marlowe   247

eleven
Putting Hunter-Gatherer and Farmer Relations in
Perspective: A Commentary from Central Africa
Axel Köhler and Jerome Lewis   276

Illustrations

Tables

Acknowledgments

There are a number of people who made this book possible. I thank Scott Mahler, acquisitions editor at the Smithsonian Institution Press, for considering, and then publishing, *Ethnicity, Hunter-Gatherers, and the "Other": Association or Assimilation in Africa*. Mary McNeeley compiled the book-wide bibliography and did other important editorial tasks. Of course, there would be no book without the authors' contributions. Equally important were our informants, field assistants, and others who helped us collect the data that we share here with the readers. All of these individuals deserve our thanks and appreciation.

one

Interethnic Encounters
of the First Kind

An Introduction

Susan Kent

In today's world of shrinking ethnic boundaries, intergroup relationships have often promoted assimilation. At the same time, hunter-gatherers have been in contact with neighboring non–hunter-gatherers around the world for centuries. The nature of these interactions and the validity of cultural autonomy has been questioned. In *Ethnicity, Hunter-Gatherers, and the "Other"* the universality of the assimilation of one society by another is examined among past and present hunter-gatherers throughout Africa, with an emphasis on southern Africa.

The so-called revisionist anthropologists claim that all southern African hunter-gatherers, including those occupying the Kalahari Desert, lost their hunter-gatherer culture circa 1,500–2,000 years ago when the first Bantu-speaking agropastoralists entered southern Africa (perhaps most notable, Wilmsen and Denbow 1990). Some anthropologists suggest that hunter-gatherers, or at least highly egalitarian ones, are somehow more vulnerable to assimilation than other groups. Are there, in fact, particular qualities of egalitarian forager societies that make them more likely to forgo their own cultures to become enslaved ethnic minorities? The debate about hunter-gatherers' autonomy is ultimately not based on whether one small group (the Ju/'hoansi; !Kung) can be classified as hunter-gatherers or if one specific region—the Kalahari—supported hunter-gatherers until the end of the twentieth century. Instead, the debate based on intercultural boundary maintenance and includes both emic and etic identities. Exploring hunter-gatherers' boundary maintenance will allow us to better understand southern African foragers, in addition to contemporary or former foragers worldwide and through time.

I invited the most qualified, experienced archaeologists, ethnohistorians, and ethnographers, who have studied and thought about hunter-gatherers for decades, to write on these issues and more. In each of the following chapters, authors deal with aspects of hunter-gatherer autonomy, or its loss, based on their own long-term research projects. Although this is not a book on the construction of ethnicity as a theoretical concept, it is necessary to explain how the term *ethnicity* (and *ethnic group*) is used by the authors. The term is used to refer to different homogenous cultures rather than subcultures within a larger pluralistic one.

The authors' specialized in-depth knowledge and long-term fieldwork are invaluable in resolving the controversies about the nature of hunter-gatherers and their interactions with "others." Alan Barnard and Michael Taylor in Chapter 9 present a thoughtful commentary on the previous chapters. Alison Brooks provides an insightful discussion of the biological and prehistoric markers of hunter-gatherers and their interactions with "others" in the Kalahari, Central Africa (Pygmies), and East Africa (Hadza). Because all modern hunter-gatherers interact with other cultures, I also asked Frank Marlowe, and Jerome Lewis along with Axel Köhler, to write commentaries on the Hadza and on the Pygmies respectively. These commentaries allow readers to examine the same issues that have been raised by the southern African hunter-gatherer research among the East and Central African foragers. One note concerning the following chapters: the data-rich chapters provide concrete information from which readers can evaluate authors' discussions. The use of several forms and spellings of group names and places is inevitable when dealing with nonliterate groups. Within chapters consistency does not and cannot extend beyond a local region, group, or time period, and therefore interchapter variability occurs.

I have never understood why those scholars who claim that the Kalahari hunter-gatherers are merely a destitute pastoralist ethnic group at the bottom of their Bantu-speaking neighbors' hierarchy, do not claim the same for hunter-gatherers living in Central or East Africa (also see Brooks, Chapter 8; Barnard and Taylor, Chapter 9; Marlowe, Chapter 10; and Köhler and Lewis, Chapter 11). If East or Central African hunter-gatherers are viewed as full-time, autonomous twentieth-century hunter-gatherers, why not those of the Kalahari? This and other intriguing questions are discussed in the following chapters.

ETHNICITY, ETHNIC GROUPS, AND HUNTER-GATHERERS

A number of anthropologists and sociologists question the utility of the terms *ethnic, ethnic group,* and *ethnicity* (Romanucci-Ross and DeVos 1995:18; Banks 1996; papers in Lamont and Fournier 1992; Levine 1999). Though the public often believes that ethnicity is biologically determined, in actuality it is a very subjective concept (Banks 1996). There are several difficulties in anthropologists' conceptions of ethnicity and ethnic groups. One problem is that ethnic groups are usually identified on the emic level by participating group members. Barnard (1996) defined an emic perspective as one that the group members use to identify and understand their world (i.e., from the group's own perceptions). In contrast, the etic perspective is one in which a group is perceived by any person different from the culture or ethnic group (Barnard 1996:180). When studying hunter-gatherers, anthropologists often identify southern African Basarwa (Bushmen or San, as they are also known) based on some anthropologist's etic view (such as on Wilmsen's view [1989]). In contrast, most groups are identified as an ethnicity based on the group's emic perspective. Their ethnic identity is therefore recognized as such on both the emic and etic levels (i.e., there is usually congruence between the etic and emic views of classifying a group, but it is not an absolute).

The question becomes, who do you believe? Is it more valid to look at what the group participants say (emic view) or what particular anthropologists state (etic view)? Only some Western outsiders perceive the Basarwa as impoverished Batswana Bantu-speakers. That is, many anthropologists' etic view concurs with the emic view, but not the so-called revisionists/political economists. However, since they are a vocal and influential group, we need to adjudicate their arguments before examining the focus of this book, boundary maintenance and intercultural relations.

The revisionist debate comes down to several issues. One is, are the twentieth-century Basarwa full-time hunter-gatherers with a twentieth-century hunter-gatherer culture, as they themselves assert (see Lee, Chapter 7)? Or are they, as the revisionists assert, a disenfranchised, subjugated minority ethnic group within the pluralistic Batswana Bantu culture—a group that has not been full-time or even part-time hunter-gatherers since the Late Stone Age several thousand years ago? When the emic view, in this case the Basarwa's, and some anthropologists' etic perspectives do not agree, which etic perspective should we use—that of anthropologists who agree with the Basarwa emic view or that of anthropologists whose own etic view differs? We will return to this, but first we need to distinguish culture and cultural groups from ethnicity and ethnic groups.

IDENTIFYING ETHNICITY

Ethnic groups are most commonly defined within pluralistic societies, such as the United States where there are Italian-Americans, Asian-Americans, and others. Many of these ethnically diverse groups have lived in North America for numerous generations and are no more culturally Asian, African, or German than are their neighbors. "Ethnicity" and "ethnic group" are commonly used to distinguish slightly different groups, all of whom share a basic common culture, from the multitude of other groups within a pluralistic society. Such ethnic groups may be composed of individuals who are physically, religiously, linguistically, or traditionally different. The groups use these differences to distinguish themselves from others in the society (Barth 1998; DeVos 1995). As noted by Barth (1998), ethnic groups are not distinct, separate cultures, but are parts of a large heterogeneous society, a definition with which I agree.

Once self-identity is established, ethnic groups take on an aura of permanence and history, as well as a sense of belonging fostered by their perceived differences from their neighbors. Ethnic group members need to have an "other" from whom they can contrast. This is why, I suggest, ethnic groups are commonly found in heterogeneous societies. In fact, I question whether ethnic groups can even exist without an "other" from whom to differentiate themselves. Can a single ethnic group encompass an entire culture? I and others suggest not, because to us ethnic groups are parts of a society, not a whole (e.g., see papers in Romanucci-Ross and DeVos 1995; for the latter, see Barth 1998:12). That is, an ethnic group is not synonymous with a culture; they represent different entities. Therefore, Basarwa and Bantu-speakers are not different ethnic groups but are different cultures.

In many respects, the public understanding and use of the terms *ethnicity* or *ethnic groups* is similar to that of race (e.g., Pieterse 1996). Each is thought to be a biological distinction when both are actually learned social constructions that separate people into groups (e.g., African American, Euroamerican, Asian American). In fact, there is more genetic variation within the African American "race" than between African Americans and Euroamericans (Cartmill 1998; Templeton 1998). Races, like ethnic groups, then are socially and not biologically determined. Thus, ethnic groups are no more "real" than are "races." We know this in theory, but sometimes forget it when viewing ethnicity, boundaries, and separate autonomous cultures. In some discussions, as in Hemphill, Lukacs, and Walimbe (2000), it almost seems as if they have forgotten that culture is completely taught and is not genetic. The existence of "pure" ethnic groups or "pure" cultures is as fallacious as is the existence of "pure" races, an important fact to remember when discussing Basarwa and other hunter-gatherers' intercultural interactions.

Ethnicity is based on how people feel about themselves and how other groups perceive them, not solely on how they are observed to behave by outsiders (DeVos 1995:25). "Defining oneself in social terms [i.e., by ethnic group] is a basic answer to the human need to belong and to survive" (DeVos 1995). This need to socially inter-connect and belong is what I refer to as sociality. Barth (1998:6) describes ethnic groups as "the social organization of [intra]cultural difference." The term *ethnic group* implies a relationship based on perceived autonomy, social interaction within and between groups, or intracultural dominance and subjugation. Marxists and an-thropologists from related theoretical orientations, such as political economy, often view ethnic groups as primarily based on domination, and/or unequal economic development and modernization (see discussion in Pieterse 1996:38). If based on modernization, ethnic groups have a relatively shallow depth of only 200–400 years. While neo-Marxists will disagree, I think ethnic groups are social groups first, and economically or politically dominated groups second. It is a mistake to claim that ethnic interaction inevitably involves hostilities and domination, even if at this point in time, ethnic groups tend to be violent in many parts of the world. The modern world is able to explain modern issues, such as current ethnic violence, but I suggest that it cannot explain all non-Western past ethnic behavior.

Boundary maintenance is an essential topic for the study of the relationships be-tween hunter-gatherers and others. The identification of members within an ethnic group is supposedly the result of objective criteria, such as biology. Ethnic group boundaries are actually more fluid, as can be illustrated by an Italian-American who may go back and forth between ethnicities depending on circumstances, such as being American in Italy, Italian-American in some parts of North America, and just Italian in other parts (Roosens 1995). Ethnic membership, then, is usually based on subjective, nonempirical, arbitrary, and emotional emic principles or issues, often in ways that outsiders cannot understand. Ethnic groups can be composed of people who do not feel they fit or belong with another group, using perceived "racial" or genetic reasons to justify separation, such as some Native Americans who do not see themselves as Euroamericans, regardless of the actual percentage of Indian or Euro-american ancestry. They set themselves off from Euroamericans as biologically different, using the percentage of presumed Indian ancestry, rather than cultural cri-teria. As Roosens (1995:122) notes, "the social determination of ethnic identity can be far removed from the actual biological basis, even though this biological distance is publicly known."

A good example of the subjective nature of ethnic groups occurred when I was a graduate student conducting participant-observation fieldwork on a remote part of the northern Navajo Reservation in North America. I lived in a hogan and/or ra-mada, depending on the season, with a number of families, but I spent most of my time with two unrelated families. At one point, about five or six Navajos and I were sitting outside talking when one brought up his disgust of "white people." Both the men and women then went into great detail regarding everything they hated about Euroamericans. Although we were friends who slept in the same hogan, I began to feel uncomfortable. Finally, I interrupted to say, "wait, but I'm an Euroamerican." They all stared at me somewhat startled for a moment because they had never considered that I was different. Then one Navajo responded, no, I really was an Indian, but just was not cognizant of it. The others all agreed with this view and claimed that I was unaware of my Indian heritage and therefore I did not identify myself as Indian. They said that they knew that one of my great-grandparents had married an Indian. Because I tried to be totally honest in all matters concerning the people with whom I worked and lived, I told them how much I like Navajos and Indians in general, but that my father (who was born in Germany) and mother who was first generation, were not related to any Indians. No, they insisted I was not an Euroamerican. I believe they thought this because I did not act like other Euroamericans they had known. They asserted that I was biologically part Indian and was simply unaware of some past relative who had a child with a Cherokee (one of the least well-defined Native American groups because of so much biological and cultural intermixing with non-Indians).

In this case, my informants knew I was culturally not Navajo because my purpose in living with them was to try to learn their culture. Because I did not act as most Euroamericans they had encountered, but was clearly not Navajo, they decided I must unknowingly be biologically Native American. That explanation satisfied my informants, but not me. I could not personally accept their identification because I did not identify myself as Native American. I was not brought up thinking of myself as part of that group. In this case, the emic view included me as an unknowing Indian based on presumed biology, while the etic view (my view as an outsider) did not agree. Native peoples, and other ethnic groups, usually internally agree on what constitutes their ethnic group and what boundaries are maintained.

Changes in ethnicity often do not seem "real" or "natural" if they are assumed after one is an adult. I was included in the Indian group by my Navajo friends for subjective reasons, even though I did not reciprocate their perceived identification of myself as a Native American. The same can be said about cultures. According to DeVos and Romanucci-Ross (1995:367), "To be subjectively genuine, changes in identity must start sufficiently early to make the assumption of a particular behavior feel internally natural to the individual." In contradiction to many people's conception of ethnic groups as objective, empirical realities, then, the Navajo example supports Roosens's and others' claims that ethnicity and biology do not necessarily co-occur.

In order for individuals to feel as if they belong to, and are accepted by a specific ethnic group, there has to be an emic-etic two-way interplay. If both emic and etic perspectives are the same, a person can assimilate, even as an adult, as the following example from my fieldwork in the Northwest Coast of North America demonstrates. A biologically Euroamerican woman married a Lummi Indian (Salish-speaking former hunter-gatherers). They lived on the Lummi Indian Reservation in Washington State. She identified herself as an Indian, and was also identified by the Lummi as Indian. Thus, her etic view agreed with the Indians' emic view. I attended a closed ceremony where this Euroamerican woman, who had blond hair and blue eyes, was present. Since the ceremony was not open to the public, I asked who she was. I was told that she was the local Coastal Salish minister's wife. Her husband held culturally mixed religious services that blended Christianity with Coastal Salish beliefs and rituals. She was, according to my Lummi informant, part Cherokee, which, to them, explained her Euroamerican physical appearance. It turned out that the Euroamerican woman adopted the newly reconstituted Coastal Salish culture, was beginning to learn spirit dancing, and embraced the Lummi culture more than many of the Christian Lummi, who deliberately were not present at the traditional ceremony. This is an example of what happens when both emic and etic views coincide. My interpretation is that the minister's wife wanted to be Native American so she would be accepted by her husband and her Coastal Salish neighbors. She was accepted as Native American because the community allowed her to identify herself as an Indian (Cherokee).

These two examples differ from the experiences of "hippies" with Native Americans. Especially during the 1970s, there were young Euroamericans who wanted to be Indian for mistaken romantic reasons, but they were not accepted as such by Native Americans. They were ridiculed by both other Euroamericans and by Indians. Thus, there needs to be some consistency, some attribute(s) that all agree is necessary to be eligible for membership in an ethnic group (a commonly presumed or actual connection). This is equally true for membership within a particular culture—one cannot be accepted as belonging to a specific culture without some attributes that are agreed upon from the emic and etic perspectives. The emic views of the participants in different ethnic groups or cultures are one mechanism used to maintain their boundaries and to set them apart from one another, particularly when the boundary is mutually distrustful and/or antagonistic.

As noted above, there are times when the terms *ethnicity* and *ethnic groups* are used to pertain to an entire culture or society (Banks 1996; Romanucci-Ross and DeVos 1995). However, I prefer to keep ethnic groups and societies with different cultures separate. In southern Africa, I view four distinctly different protohistoric cultures (not ethnic groups): Basarwa hunter-gatherers, of which there were at least five and probably more discrete cultures, the Khoi (also known as Khoe Khoe, Khoi Khoi, and Khoe) herders, the Bantu-speakers, and the Europeans. The former two societies were small-scale and probably did not have minorities or ethnic groups; they were homogeneous. The latter two were larger and more sociopolitically complex with hierarchies built into their social and political systems. One can suggest that the different Bantu-speaking groups (e.g., Batswana—the dominant group—and Bakgalagadi, Bayei, Bapedi, Bakalanga, Herero Basotho, etc.) are separate ethnic groups within the larger Bantu culture. Similarly, the British and Afrikaners are separate ethnic groups within the larger South African European culture.

Cultural and ethnic boundaries are not necessarily the same. As a generalization, cultural boundaries are more rigid and impermeable than ethnic ones. For example, it would be much easier for a Northern Irish Catholic to switch to the Protestant side of their long-standing ethnic conflict, than it would be for one of them to switch to a different, non-Western culture. Wilmsen (1989 and elsewhere) views all southern African hunter-gatherers as a disadvantaged ethnic group within the wider Bantu society when, in fact, they form a distinct culture (see following chapters; also see chapters in Kent 1996c). Based on the belief that the Basarwa represent a single ethnic group rather than distinctively different cultures, Wilmsen and Denbow (1990) portray Basarwa boundaries as very fluid, which is a characteristic of ethnic-group boundaries, not of cultural boundaries. Several anthropologists including myself have also characterized the Basarwa as flexible societies (Barnard 1996; Kent 1996a; Silberbauer 1996). However, the flexibility we wrote about pertains to the internal Basarwa cultures—their religion, economy, and other parts of their culture—not necessarily to their boundary maintenance. Because Basarwa cultures have lasted longer than that of the Khoi (Khoikhoi) herders and other societies that once inhabited southern Africa, perhaps we should view Basarwa cultural boundaries as more resistant than many other groups that are now culturally extinct.

The fact that cultures have been able to live next to each other without one invariability enslaving the other can be seen by the diversity of distinct cultures in Africa prior to European contact. Since no society is isolated, all those cultures had frontiers and therefore, all had boundaries and boundary maintenance. The unique characteristics of Western imperialism and colonization obscured many cultural boundaries in Africa and elsewhere, often through programs explicitly designed for culture-cide (see Chapter 6). Not all expanding societies had such policies. Concomitantly, the archaeological record substantiates intercultural trade and boundary maintenance in most of southern Africa until the appearance of European colonialists. The archaeology does not indicate hunter-gatherer subjugation prior to European contact (Sadr, Chapter 2; Kent, Chapter 3).

In order for ethnic groups to exist, there needs to be contact with "others" and the magnitude of that contact is often intense and competitive in multiethnic societies. We have no evidence, as the following chapters show, that intercultural interactions throughout southern Africa were consistently hostile until European contact. There are regions around the world where intercultural relations remained nonviolent, sometimes as trade partners and sometimes in symbiosis. For example, symbiotic relations occurred between hunter-gatherers and farmers in the American Southwest (Kent, Chapter 3; Spielmann 1982), and among various groups of African Pygmies and villagers (Köhler and Lewis, Chapter 11). Because forced incorporation into Western culture occurred throughout the twentieth century, does not automatically mean it occurred similarly or as often in or out of Africa with all the diverse hunter-gatherer societies that existed until the end of the twentieth century. That is, not all hunter-gatherer cultures were destroyed by contact with their non-Western neighbors.

ASSOCIATION AND HUNTER-GATHERERS

Southern African foragers did not immediately give up their autonomy when pastoralists entered the region, nor were they barely able to provide for themselves and their families. The belief that once hunter-gatherers saw the immigrating pastoralists or colonizing Europeans they gleefully gave up their impoverished "scrounging for food" way of life is unlikely. There is little reason for these individuals to eagerly become inferior, low-status pastoralists without cattle. Hunter-gatherers were definitely seen by colonizers as dirty, destitute, impecunious, grubby, semi- or nonhuman beings (see Chapter 6, this volume). The question is whether or not this characterization was an objective, nonethnocentric description or one conceived of by European colonists and agreed upon by their agropastoralist neighbors.

The conception of hunter-gatherers as particularly vulnerable to outside cultures is not supported by the archaeological or historic data. Hunter-gatherers did not happily acquiesce to assimilation and domination because their lifestyle was so marginal that they welcomed a "superior" new subsistence source (e.g., as is demonstrated in Sadr, Chapter 2; Guenther, Chapter 5; Kent, Chapter 6; and Lee, Chapter 7). What lure did the agropastoralists have to entice hunter-gatherers to abandon their own culture, even when it meant perpetual poverty and low status? Kalahari hunter-gatherers did not have many possessions because of their mobility, lack of storage practices, and strong sharing ethos. This, coupled with the absence of some kind of animal transportation, prohibited the accumulation of goods. There were coveted objects that the hunter-gatherers wanted from the Europeans, such as guns, horses, tobacco, and salt. However, with the exception of a few items such as iron and pottery, the incoming Bantu-speakers did not have such different technology or objects to make the hunter-gatherers envious.

Once foragers began to become sedentary and/or had access to some means of animal transportation, they wanted to accumulate possessions, particularly the exotic ones brought by the Westerners. Since the Bantu-speakers brought only a limited amount of new possessions, the local people would not have been quite so awed by the sheer number of exotica. The extreme discrepancy of wealth and possessions was not as pronounced or visible between the groups prior to Western colonization. For example, out of principle and fear of retaliation for the havoc they caused, many colonists did not trade horses or guns with hunter-gatherers, even though they did with the Bantu-speakers and Khoi (Chapter 6, this volume). This situation made hunter-gatherers more vulnerable than the Khoi or Bantu-speakers, and severely hampered their ability to fight for their land or way of life. The Europeans' arrival, not the Bantu's, therefore was destructive to all native groups (Chapter 6).

MYTHS OF THE KALAHARI

Were the many different now extinct groups of hunter-gatherers that once inhabited southern Africa always hungry, always forced to seek out the little unappealing food available and, therefore, vulnerable to assimilation (i.e., opposite to the earlier view of the Basarwa as the original affluent society [Sahlins 1974])? Westerners sometimes look at a foreign landscape and declare it unfit or inhospitable for human habitation because it does not lend itself to Western types of subsistence practices, even if it is suitable for other types of non-Western use. For example, the Kalahari Desert is not the barren wasteland some believe. In fact, the Kalahari is not a desert at all—the mean annual precipitation for much of the middle to northern Kalahari is approximately 500 mm, which technically classifies the region as semiarid (Thomas and Shaw 1991:90). Most of the rain falls between November and April and there is an 18-year cycle of rainfall fluctuations (Thomas and Shaw 1991). The oscillation consists of wet and drought periods that can last from days to years or decades (Thomas and Shaw 1991:91). Finally, the vegetation community of much of the Kalahari is an open-tree savanna. Acacia trees and various types of grass and bushes are common, along with the range of wild animals characteristic of a savanna ecosystem.

The Kalahari has undergone and probably will continue to undergo severe droughts every 18 years or so. These droughts affect the range and distribution of game and, as a result, the well-being of humans who prey on these animals. Drought usually disperses the game, making them harder to hunt, and forcing people to compete with the wild animals for moisture-containing plants. The last very bad drought in the Kutse area (near the Central Kalahari Game Reserve) ended in 1988 and people suffered greatly from it. However, that drought not only affected the hunter-gatherers, but it also affected farmers and herders throughout much of southern Africa, even in regions not considered to be marginal to humans. Kutse Basarwa still hunted during the drought, challenging as it was, as my data show for the 1987 dry season (also see Tanaka 1980 who observed Xade during a particularly bad drought). The Central Kalahari Basarwa lived in areas with no surface water for two to three months out of a year. Although this seems extremely harsh for Europeans, it was not equally harsh to hunter-gatherers, who used wild melons for their liquid needs. Silberbauer (1998, personal communication) said that the G/wi Central Kalahari Basarwa located their sites near melon patches and/or would abandon an area based on the availability of melons and not on the availability of water.

My intention here is not to question whether the Kalahari is a harsh and uninviting environment in which to live, but rather to ask if the Kalahari is uncommonly more difficult and unpredictable compared to most other habitats. I suggest that the perception of the Kalahari as extremely harsh is based on Westerners' perceptions and the way in which Westerners use land. My second question is, does the Kalahari environment evoke more anxiety and vulnerability than other semiarid and more arid environments in which farmers and pastoralists live? I suggest not. Cycles of droughts are probably just as detrimental to small-scale horticulturalists as they are to hunter-gatherers, if not more so. Yet, we emphasize the difficulties for hunter-gatherers more than for societies with different subsistence practices that lived throughout southern Africa. The Kalahari experiences good and bad years, which are not completely dissimilar to areas inhabited by horticulturists and hunter-gatherers elsewhere in southern Africa and the world in general.

The very fact that the Kalahari was able to sustain large herds of animals until the Westerners' arrival shows that it is not the desolate habitat that most anthropologists think it is. In other words, even if harsh to Westerners, any land that can support such a large number and diversity of small and large animals as we know the Kalahari did for thousands, if not millions, of years, can at the same time also support human hunter-gatherers who were not necessarily always marginal or on the brink of extinction. Their hunter-gatherer culture allowed them to utilize the available resources without destroying them, unlike the Western or most precolonial Bantu-speaker cultures. These latter cultures were not ideologically or materially adapted to thrive in this specific environment without causing much anxiety concerning the environment and its exploitation. The same was not invariably true for all other cultures, especially not for the mobile hunter-gatherers.

Other parts of southern Africa occupied by hunter-gatherers, such as the Little Caledon River area of South Africa or Lesotho, had year-round springs and rivers, abundant vegetation, and large herds of animals before the encroachment by Europeans (see Chapter 6, this volume). These regions are not environmentally marginal no matter how one wants to calculate marginality. I suggest it is a misnomer to label southern Africa in general (with exceptions perhaps in parts of Namibia), and the Kalahari in particular, as marginal, desolate, bleak environments. The semiarid Ghanzi area in the Kalahari described by Guenther (Chapter 5) has year-round surface water that, with the advent of boreholes, provided a favorable environment for farming and raising cattle, which is one reason Europeans and Bantu-speakers moved there during the nineteenth and twentieth centuries. This is also why the rate of change at Ghanzi was so much more rapid than elsewhere in the Kalahari. The less well-watered parts of the Kalahari were considered marginal or uninhabitable for the Europeans and Bantu-speakers who brought exotic domesticated plants and animals with them that were not adapted to semiarid conditions, a concern not shared by the local hunter-gatherers. For the Basarwa, "it is not scarcity that is the central factor (although scarcity may obviously occur) but rather the need for flexibility in order to cope with variations in abundance and the difficulties of predicting the location and abundance of crucial resources from one year to the next" (Hall 1988:142–143).

Marginal environments imply resources that are hard to obtain due to their scarcity or to the large amount of work necessary to procure or process them. The people I studied at Kutse as one example, did not have refrigeration, guns, horses, or a meat trade with Bantu-speakers and did not subscribe to the Protestant work ethic. Men and women only acquired enough meat and plants to sustain themselves and their sharing network for a few days. They spent much of the day visiting nearby camps, gossiping, and taking naps. Sometimes they would work on making an arrow or grind tobacco while visiting or entertaining visitors at their camp, but not always. In fact, they would tease me that I worked far too hard because I was always writing things down, even when I was not interviewing (recording my time-allocation observations). They thought I was actually foolish when I trudged to different camps during the hot summer season. From their perspective, no work was important enough to spend all day in the hot sun without shade. If people thought the occasional government wage job, when available, was too demanding (such as smoothing out the sandy tract near the game reserve), they quit with no stigma or complaints from their spouse, even though that was the only source for money. These people, in other words, did work, but they did not, by any means, expend all their time, discussions, or efforts on just getting by. They were not the "original affluent society" nor did they spend most of their time procuring or worrying about food.

The above indicates that southern African hunter-gatherers did not occupy such uninhabitable regions that they were forced to abandon their culture at the first opportunity to stave off starvation. Such years did occur, but primarily after the impact of colonization, the introduction and proliferation of foreign technology, and the successful raising of domesticated animals, particularly cattle. The drilling of boreholes (wells) allowed cattle and horses to live deep in the Kalahari, permitted sedentarization, and prompted a concerted effort to change the hunter-gatherers' way of life by missionaries, government officials, and others. One example is Xade where Sugawara (Chapter 4) states that guns, horses, cattle, boreholes, and a meat trade caused overhunting and abuse of the land. Note that the first four items (guns, horses, cattle, and boreholes), and perhaps cattle or the meat trade, were not available at Xade prior to the arrival of Europeans and their material culture. These changes greatly altered the Xade hunter-gatherer way of life, including social relations, sharing, politics, and other realms. Elsewhere in the Kalahari, Yellen (1977) reported the absence of springbok in the Dobe area by 1969, as a result of the degradation of land by Herero Bantu-speakers' cattle. However, at least until the abandonment of Kutse in 1997, springbok were common and actually one of the favored species to acquire.

There is little doubt that hunter-gatherers traded with the Bantu and later, the Europeans. Trade goods are found at prehistoric and historic archaeological sites (see Chapters 2 and 3, this volume). Sadr (Chapter 2) shows that hunter-gatherers living on the easternmost margin of the Kalahari were autonomous until a little over 100 years ago. As I suggested above, contact or association do not always equate with assimilation or "culture-cide." Most hunter-gatherers were not destitute, had objects to trade (hides), and coexisted as autonomous cultures with neighboring Bantu-speakers. The arrival of the Europeans was, I suggest (Chapter 6), the catalyst for the major transformations of the precontact multicultural habitation of southern Africa. The Batswana moved from South Africa during the 1800s to escape the chaos created by the Zulu wars. The Zulu wars in turn were the result, or at least were facilitated by Western technology, particularly guns, and horses they acquired from the colonists. The Zulu were expansionists before the arrival of the Europeans, but combining this with superior weapons and animal transportation, and the disruption already caused by colonialization, allowed them to disturb the entire cultural makeup of southern Africa as groups fled from them and their destruction.

We can speculate that depending on the cycle of droughts, the physical boundary of the Kalahari probably varied so that parts that are considered to be the Kalahari Desert today (such as Tsodilo Hills or Molepolole), were during years of good rain attractive to Bantu-speakers as a place where they could graze their cattle. We can also see that particularly well-watered parts of the Kalahari, such as Ghanzi, attracted European farmers who used the local hunter-gatherers as laborers (Guenther, Chapter 5). However, this was not a pan-Kalahari occurrence. There were few European or Bantu settlements in the Kalahari until boreholes were dug in the early twentieth century. The precise time depends on where because change in the Kalahari was not uniform or at the same rate. Whereas the fringes of the Kalahari probably moved around a bit depending on the climatic cycle, the interior of the Kalahari itself (such as the Central Kalahari region) could not be settled by Bantu agropastoralists with cattle and horses because of the lack of surface water for two to three months a year. As a result, some groups remained autonomous hunter-gatherers until the late 1960s and others until 35 years later.

Guenther (Chapter 5) describes the consequences of the arrival of Bantu-speakers and Boers in the Nharo area of the Kalahari. I suggest that the migration of both Europeans and Bantu-speakers was, at least partially, stimulated by the general colonization of South Africa. As land became more scarce due to the colonization of South Africa, people moved to new areas to live. For example, the Batswana moved to the Molepolole fringe of the Kalahari in Botswana when previously, before the Zulu wars, they had lived in South Africa. Similarly, some Afrikaners moved to the Ghanzi area to escape the rules and regulations of the colonial British South African government. They were able to move to Ghanzi because of the favorable water resources (Guenther, Chapter 5). However, the motivation for their move—the turmoil of colonial South Africa—was, I propose, not present prior to European contact.

ASSIMILATION AND HUNTER-GATHERERS

Every long-term encounter with different cultures does not result in assimilation. In fact, boundary maintenance may be amplified by encounters with the "others." That is, genocide and culture-cide or assimilation are not inevitable outcomes of intercultural relations. According to Barth, "Interaction in such a social system does not lead to its liquidation through change and acculturation [or assimilation]; cultural differences can persist despite inter-ethnic contact and interdependence" (1998:10), as well as intercultural contact, I would add. Perhaps because colonization on such a large scale is relatively recent, we sometimes are blinded to other types of intercultural relationships where autonomy is maintained for both groups. Instead, we assume and generalize that all intercultural interactions are destructive to one of the participants. Boundary maintenance can be subtle or not. Agropastoralists and some anthropologists' conceptions of Basarwa as marginal, regularly unable to provide for themselves and family, childlike, unreliable, ignorant, and unsophisticated are not shared by the Basarwa. When you ask the Basarwa, or at least the ones I worked with, they are equally unflattering about the Bantu-speakers. Even when the first Western explorers skirted the Kalahari, some would have perished had the native peoples not shown them what plants provide liquids as well as other survival skills. However, instead of producing awe and admiration of the Basarwa culture that was so much better adapted to the Kalahari than their own, the explorers saw the Basarwa as inferior and ignorant because they lacked guns, horses, clothing, and other European cultural material. Basically, anyone not Western was inferior. This ideology of superiority and other traits of Western culture described in Chapter 6 (this volume) promoted violence, and in some cases the extermination (culturally and sometimes physically) of hunter-gatherers throughout much of southern Africa.

It is necessary to go out of one's way in order to not perceive hunter-gatherers from the conception of Western colonists or Bantu agropastoralists. Neighbors, such as the Bantu and Basarwa, do not always think well of each other. Negative and stereotypical perspectives of "others" are a common means of maintaining cultural boundaries. Perpetuating such views often helps one group show their neighbors the vast perceived or real differences between "us" and "them." Ironically, while considering the Basarwa "backwards" and generally ignorant, Bantu-speakers still come to Kutse expressly to consult a Mosarwa (singular for Basarwa) sucking doctor. Bantu-speakers' shamans do not use the same methods. Despite the Basarwa being perceived as inferior, their healing techniques are considered to be very powerful and sometimes better than the Bantu-speakers' curers. It is a mistake to generalize about an entire culture, in this case the Basarwa, by what their non-Basarwa neighbors think of them. This boundary maintenance technique is also used in Central Africa. Villagers often feel superior to their Pygmy neighbors (Köhler and Lewis, Chapter 11). Unfortunately the Bantu perception of the Basarwa is the dominant view presented in most popular, and in some scholarly, literature. Even more unfortunate, it appears as if the Xade Basarwa are acquiring the Bantu-speakers' negative image of themselves (Sugawara, Chapter 4). This did not happen at Kutse, where I worked prior to its abandonment.

THE NEED FOR CONTEXT

One of the major problems in African hunter-gatherer research is interpreting data out of context. Uncritical use of data, and most significantly, the lack of awareness of the data's context, can invalidate interpretations. These invalid interpretations are sometimes used to fuel theoretical debates. It is a mistake not to examine inconsistencies in interpretations by various Kalahari anthropologists. The assumptions of each researcher and other critical issues need to be addressed before using one person's interpretations.

The three most important contexts that must be studied before making interpretations are: (1) historical context, (2) temporal context, and (3) cultural context and its variability. Failure to acknowledge the impact of these contexts obscures rather than elucidates. It also encourages ad hominem accusations that degenerate into debates about who is "right" and what is the "true" interpretation. This becomes detrimental to all forager research. As Megaw and Megaw (1996:176) wrote, there is "an emerging consensus that ethnicity, and the perception of ethnicity depend on context."

One way to determine if a generalization is valid, such as the Basarwa have not been full-time hunter-gatherers for thousands of years, is to look for inconsistencies in the supporting arguments. For some reason, revisionists use different standards of autonomy. Proponents of revisionism state that the twentieth century Basarwa are not autonomous because they have different artifacts (including iron) than the Late Stone Age hunter-gatherers had. However, twentieth-century Bantu also have different artifacts than had the Iron Age agropastoralists, a fact that does not cause the revisionists to deny them their autonomy. That is, no one claims that twentieth-century Bantu are not "real" agropastoralists because their material culture has changed through time.

Other inconsistencies also occur. Numerous anthropologists have translated the major texts Wilmsen (1989) used to support his position that the Basarwa have been enslaved, or at least dominated by Bantu-speakers. All reviewers of Wilmsen's translations that I am aware of state categorically that Wilmsen (1989, 1996) misinterpreted the German, sometimes at key parts of the journals (Lee and Guenther 1991, 1993; Harpending 1991; and others). Wilmsen (1989) bases much of his evidence of a loss of Basarwa autonomy on the writing of Passarge, particularly his revisionist belief that the Dobe area was occupied by subservient Basarwa who had lost their hunter-gatherer identity and way of life thousands of years ago. Guenther (Chapter 5), however, shows how the social and political ideology of Passarge skewed his perceptions and resulting writings on the Basarwa. These biases were compounded by the general ethnocentric views of the Basarwa common at the time of Passarge's explorations and writing. Raum (2000:668) as another example states that Wilmsen's "translations subvert the original meaning" of Passarge and that "More instances of faulty translations could be adduced, if space permitted. As an introduction to Passarge's valuable texts this book [Wilmsen 1996] may be of interest to novices but should hardly prove sufficient for experts." Numerous other anthropologists have also described the many mistakes made in translation, even if Passarge's writing were not biased (Guenther 1999; Lee and Guenther 1993; Harpending 1991).

Also inconsistent are Wilmsen and Denbow's (1990) interpretations of the archaeological record in which they contend that prehistorically, Bantu-speakers enslaved the Kalahari Basarwa. Sadr's (1997) interpretation of the same data instead verifies the Dobe researchers' contention that the Dobe Basarwa had been autonomous hunter-gatherers during the periods Wilmsen and Denbow said they were not (also see Yellen and Brooks 1988, 1990; Lee, Chapter 7; Brooks, Chapter 8).

More inconsistencies abound because of overgeneralizing and using data out of context. Some researchers have unquestioningly adopted one stance over another without exploring the context of either. Sugawara (Chapter 4) portrays the Xade Basarwa as almost the opposite of the Kutse Basarwa, with whom I worked, and the context of the studies explains why. Particularly at odds is cultural autonomy, self-identity, and subsistence, all of which become understandable once the context is known. However, anthropologists could point to Xade as evidence that the Basarwa are a downtrodden group under pressure from the Bantu-introduced economy and politics, as depicted by Sugawara in Chapter 4. They might generalize that the significant changes in sharing and other practices at Xade are equally valid for all Kalahari Basarwa, neglecting the context of the data. Kalahari researchers and consumers of their research then would inaccurately conclude that the portrayal of the Xade of the 1990s is valid for all Basarwa and for all time, including 40 years ago when Silberbauer (1981) studied Xade. Without any context of the data, it is not recognized that both Sugawara and Silberbauer's views of Xade are correct for the particular time period during which they studied. Neither is wrong unless one ignores the context of time, history, and change—Sugawara's interpretations (Chapter 4) are accurate for the 1990s and Silberbauer's are correct for the 1950s.

Not only have there been rapid, but unequal, rates of change throughout the Kalahari that need to be taken into consideration when evaluating the appropriateness of the data, but the conditions during which a study was conducted also need to be recognized. For example, Tanaka's (1980) initial research occurred during a severe drought whereas Silberbauer's included drought and nondrought years. Therefore, Tanaka's (1980) work exemplifies a period when the people at Xade were under extraordinary ecological stress that is not reflected in Silberbauer's research, which provides information on more common, or at least varied, conditions. Often such differences provoke asinine accusations between researchers, each one claiming to have the correct view.

Different local histories and circumstances also can lead to dissimilar, although still valid, interpretations. For example, Silberbauer collected his data during drought and nondrought years on and off over a period of approximately 10 years. Tanaka (1980), who studied Xade a few years later, visited after a borehole had been drilled. The presence of a borehole, particularly during a severe drought, allowed more people to aggregate for longer periods of time than would have been possible before, as well as making the area attractive to Bantu-speakers who needed the water source for their livestock. The differences between Silberbauer's and Tanaka's accounts are primarily attributable to the drilling of the borehole and its repercussions along with the presence of a severe drought during the latter's fieldwork. Tanaka's (1980) study is an excellent description of a stressed group during an especially difficult period. Silberbauer's (1981) study is an excellent description of a group over a period of drought and nondrought years. Once the data are contextualized, it becomes apparent that the differences do not result from one person being wrong and the other right. Instead, both are correct, given the context of the data.

Without context, the Kutse, Xade, Ju/'hoansi, and Nharo data also appear to contradict each other. However, during the same time period (mid 1980s to the mid 1990s), Kutse and Xade experienced a very different history of contact and acculturation. At the same time that Xade had a school, store, Christian minister, a few Western-styled houses, health clinic, and government offices, Kutse had none. A nurse came to Kutse from the largest nearby village once a month for one morning to distribute medicine and inoculate children. The closest store, government office or local chief, and school were all located in the village with the clinic, almost a day's walk away. Xade Basarwa used guns and horses to hunt and participated in a formal meat trade with the Bantu. At the same time, there were no horses, guns, or meat trade at Kutse and sharing networks were still intact during my fieldwork (Kent 1993, 1995, 1996b). These differences have enormous ramifications in the amount and direction of change at Xade versus Kutse. Change at Xade included new sharing patterns, amount and type of hunting, and kinship relations in a village of hundreds of Basarwa who live next to and not far from Bantu-speakers' formal government schooling, clinic, and store.

The differential impact caused by dissimilar contact histories provides the necessary context to allow researchers and readers to contextually place each study. Examining the Dobe data, we see that toward the end of the 1960s, Ju/'hoansi were beginning to interact with the growing numbers of Herero Bantu-speakers who moved to Ngamiland during the early twentieth century to escape the German war in Namibia (Lee 1993). Just across the border of Botswana into Namibia, Ju/'hoansi living at the borehole at Chum!kwe (Tsumkwe) underwent dramatic culture change as the result of enlisting in the South African military (Gordon 1992). Because of their reputation as hunter-gatherers, the military hired them to track and fight against South Africa's enemies, such as the African National Congress (ANC). Many were also taken north to Angola by the South African military to fight in the war there. The disruption at Chum!kwe caused by very rapid culture change resulted in malnutrition, drunkenness, fighting, poor health, unemployment, and cessation of hunting and gathering (e.g., Kent and Lee 1992).

I question why anyone would expect the same rate and history of contact with different cultures in a region as vast as southern Africa. Certainly in the New World, the rate and impact of change varied by location and history. For example, the Northwest Coast Indians' culture of North America was transformed by Euroamericans at least a century after most Native Americans and/or their culture had vanished on the eastern coast. Similarly at Xade in Botswana, change became particularly fast-paced at the end of the 1960s when a borehole was drilled. The borehole permitted the aggregation and sedentism of a large number of people, including Bantu-speakers with cattle and horses. In contrast, the first major thrust of rapid change for the Kutse Basarwa occurred almost 30 years later in 1997–1999, when the government began their relocation program. The community of Kutse was, as a result, abandoned along with the inhabitants' traditional way of life. Various groups of Bantu pastoralists and Khoi herders did not "infringe on the traditional areas of Bushmen in the northeast [of Namibia] until after the introduction of firearms"

(Gordon 1992:28). Autonomous hunter-gatherers occupied the Caledon River region South Africa, and Lesotho almost a century after the hunter-gatherer way of life was extinct in the Cape area (Chapter 6, this volume).

Another example of ignoring the context of the data that has resulted in misunderstanding, mistaken conclusions, and acrimony is the cultural diversity in the Kalahari. Scholars commonly think that there is one Kalahari hunter-gatherer culture that is exemplified by the Ju/'hoansi. However, the Central Kalahari Basarwa (as those from Xade and Kutse) are quite different in many ways. Their languages are mutually unintelligible, and are as similar as English is to Russian or Arabic (Barnard 1994 personal communication; Lee 1996 personal communication). Depending on the researcher, Ju/'hoansi and G/wi are in different language families or, at least, in different subfamilies (Barnard 2001, personal communication). Gender relations, politics, settlement patterns, and other realms of culture also differ (Kent in prep). Lumping the Ju/'hoansi with the Central Kalahari Basarwa is incorrect. Nonetheless, because most anthropologists do not contextualize their data, the Ju/'hoansi are often presented as the only Kalahari hunter-gatherers. Diversity must be pointed out, not hidden. Knowing the context of the Bantu-speakers, Europeans, and the Kutse and Xade Basarwa data allows us to understand their cultural differences, rather than disagree about differences among anthropologists.

The next question that needs to be addressed is why hunter-gatherers would align themselves with culturally different, arrogant Bantu neighbors in the first place. After all, the hunter-gatherers were looked down upon as ignorant and assigned menial tasks. Why did the first Mosarwa (singular for Basarwa) voluntarily work for the "others?" Patricia Draper and Nancy Howell presented a paper at the 1998 American Anthropological Association that explored why the first individual Ju/'hoansi worked or lived near Bantu-speakers. They investigated kin networks, thinking that people with few kin might not enjoy the backup strategy of living with one's far-flung kin in times of need. Although logical, their study was inconclusive. One reason for the ambiguity of their results may have been due to what Barnard (1992) calls the Basarwa's "universal kinship" system in which kin are loosely defined. Sometimes even the anthropologist is incorporated within the system. At Kutse, friends are classified as kin, even if they speak different dialects and are from different Kalahari locations (Kent 1995). Fictive kin are often called "cousin," which means unspecified distant kin.

Since kin recognition is so flexible, anyone can become a relative. Therefore, almost anyone can be incorporated as generic kin, extending kin networks when necessary during emergencies. I suggest that those who initially voluntarily worked and lived with Bantu-speakers did so because, regardless of the number of kin they had, they were malcontents. As a result, they may have had a wide kin network but those relatives were not very friendly or encouraging toward them. They were not socially well-adjusted and therefore had less to lose socially or psychologically by working for a Bantu family. I suggest that a well-adjusted person with close friends, even without relatives, would not opt to work for or live near insolent neighbors in a submissive relationship.

DISCUSSION

We tend not to study boundary maintenance. This is unfortunate because boundaries are what separate us from "others." Even the cultural conservatism among some hunter-gatherers can act as a boundary enhancer in ways not fully explored by anthropologists (Marlowe, Chapter 10; Barth 1998; Banks 1996 for those who have studied intercultural boundaries).

In anthropology it is crucial to determine how to classify people into meaningful categories, such as hunter-gatherers. Does emic or self-identity supercede etic or outsider's identity? Or, put another way, does learning supercede biology when identifying the culture of a person? This question refers back to the Navajo examples I gave. The Euroamerican hippies who wanted to be identified as Native Americans and therefore saw themselves as such (the etic perspective), were not accepted by Native Americans (emic perspective). Most people would not classify them as American Indian at least partly because of the emic view of Native Americans, but also because of the perceived belief that culture is biological. In order for people to be classified as Indian, a certain percentage of their ancestral genes must come from Indian origins. Usually emic and etic identifications are the same. However, when they are not, is the emic classification of a people more valid than the etic, or vice versa? Should an etic identification by the Basarwa's neighbors be privileged over the etic view of an anthropologist or the Basarwa's emic perspective?

Another example from Kutse further illustrates the necessity to either use the emic perspective when identifying a group or expressly state that the following is one's personal view, based on an etic or outsider opinion. After the revisionist debate became acrimonious in anthropology journals, I asked one of my main informants how he classified himself. After stating he was a hunter, I played devil's advocate and told him about Wilmsen's claims, specifically those stating that no Basarwa at that time (early 1990s) were full-time hunter-gatherers. He argued a bit about how someone could think that they were anything but hunter-gatherers. Then he said, "Look, you can call me a Mosarwa or you can call me a 'Bushman'; I don't care because they are the same. But I am a hunter [I hunt; I go hunting]. That is what I am. That is what I do." My informant's claims to be a full-time hunter are empirically supported by my long-term, multiyear time-allocation studies (Kent 1993; 1996b). Thus, from an emic and my own etic perspective, Kutse Basarwa were full-time hunter-gatherers until they were relocated in 1997.

Interestingly, most Bantu also see the Basarwa as hunter-gatherers, which is why the government has implemented expensive programs to try to change them into being the very agropastoralists that the revisionists claim the Basarwa already are and have been for 2,000 years! If the Basarwa are no longer foragers and have not been for centuries, why does the government need to expend energy and resources to change them from their hunting and gathering life? I was told of a nearby Bantu chief who refused to put a Kutse man in jail for poaching on the game reserve, even though the government game scouts caught him in the act of butchering the gemsbok he had speared. The chief said you cannot lock up a Mosarwa (singular for Basarwa) for hunting because Basarwa are hunters and gatherers; that is their way of life. One cannot put a man in jail for hunting when he is a hunter-gatherer. It is ironic, then, that the only people I have encountered who do *not* identify Basarwa as hunter-gatherers are the Western revisionist anthropologists! Other anthropologists, neighboring Bantu groups, and the Basarwa themselves (i.e., both foreign and local etic views and the emic view) all perceive the Basarwa as hunter-gatherers, who, depending on where in the Kalahari one refers, existed as such until the middle to end of the twentieth century.

Societies, including the culture of hunter-gatherers, pastoralists, farmers, and others are based on shared social, symbolic, and other abstract ideas. They also are based on a self-perceived inclusion of all those who hold fictive or biological ancestry and origins (DeVos 1995:18). This leads to the question, what is the reality of culture and biology? If African hunter-gatherer infants were brought to the United States the day they were born, and never taught anything of their biological roots or parents' culture, would they still be hunter-gatherers (or more specifically, G/wi or G//ana)? For example, a man in his 30s-40s who lived at Kutse was very young when his Mokgalagadi (singular for Bakgalagadi) Bantu father died. His Mokgalagadi mother remarried a Mosarwa man. She also died while the boy was very young. He was raised by his Mosarwa father and, later, Mosarwa stepmother. When I questioned him about his cultural identity, he claimed he was a Mosarwa and *not* a Mokgalagadi, even though he was taller and had darker skin than most Basarwa. I then asked whether his parents were both Bakgalagadi and he answered yes, but that he is a Mosarwa. Everyone asked in the Kutse community reaffirmed his claim to be a Mosarwa. The fact that he was a Mosarwa sucking doctor was further proof to them that their identification was correct. He moreover usually spoke in Sesarwa (the language of the Basarwa). He was taught, and today participates, in the Mosarwa culture even though Westerners, including anthropologists, would use biology to classify him as a Mokgalagadi and designate him as not a "true" or "real" Mosarwa hunter-gatherer (also see Marlowe, Chapter 10 for an example from the Hadza foragers in Tanzania). How can this be if culture is taught and not biological?

Did such examples of intermarriage and association with the Bantu threaten Basarwa autonomy, as is commonly assumed? I would say not. Intermarriage probably occurs at most cultural boundaries, and we know intermarriage has occurred with the G//ana, G/wi, and Bakgalagadi at Xade (Sugawara, Chapter 4). While some anthropologists claim the G//ana, for example, are not "true" hunter-gatherers because they intermarried with the Bantu, the same is not said of the Bantu who intermarry with the Basarwa. That is, why are G//ana who intermarry with Bantu not true hunter-gatherers while the Bantu married to the G//ana retain their agropastoralist culture and identity? The cause, I suggest, is the confusion of genes and biology with culture and learning. Intermarrying can contribute to change or the breakdown of a society if the offspring are taught to view culturally mixed marriages as such, or it can strengthen the culture if parents emphasize and instruct their children in that culture. Arguments about intermarriages resulting in "not real" hunter-gatherers harks back to a time when there was a belief in cultural and racial purity. Since culture is taught and learned, intermarriages can result in one culture or the other being adopted or blended. Villager and Pygmy groups intermarry, just as the Hadza and various other groups throughout Africa, without losing their cultural identity or autonomy. Intermarriage, by itself, does not destroy an autonomous society (see Marlowe for intermarriage among the Hadza, Chapter 10). At Kutse there were more Basarwa women married to Bakgalagadi men (Bantu-speaking) than vice versa, but not exclusively so. In some cases, their children were raised as Basarwa (i.e., learning hunting and collecting skills as did the person in the previous example). In other cases, children were raised as Bantu-speakers (i.e., living in a town where children attend school and are preoccupied with small livestock). Children in mixed marriages are often raised as Bantu when their fathers are Mokgalagadi because of the Bantu society's patrilineality, which is not present in Basarwa culture. However, this then does not "dilute" the hunter-gatherer or the Bantu culture. Unless a society is on the brink of extinction, or with a severely unbalanced sex ratio, marriages in which children adopt their father's identity do not necessarily jeopardize their mother's culture.

Just because two groups are associated through marriage, trade, or other means, does not automatically imply domination and subjugation. Two societies can coexist as associated but autonomous, unless one is imperialistic, intent on conquering and converting all people different than themselves. Barth (1998:10) noted that "ethnic distinctions do not depend on an absence of social interaction and acceptance, but are quite to the contrary often the very foundations on which embracing social systems are built. Interaction in such a social system does not lead to its liquidation through change and acculturation; cultural differences can persist despite intercultural contact and interdependence." I suggest that it is the Western anthropologists who make association invariably a case of domination and subjugation. They do so because nation-state imperialism has been common during the past few centuries. However, the frequency of colonization and other inherently unequal situations are recent in many parts of the world and did not occur everywhere at the same time, making views of all intergroup relations based on the imperialist model inappropriate.

Although anecdotal, the following example shows that the Central Kalahari Basarwa are not as meek as many portray them to be. Between 1997 and 2000, an unknown number of Central Kalahari Basarwa were forcibly relocated, at gunpoint according to residents, to a large government settlement. In 2000, I was told that over 100 people had illegally returned to their previous communities located within the Central Kalahari Game Reserve. They were willing to give up the clinic, school, and drinking water from government-run boreholes, and free government food and supplies (consisting of maize meal, sorghum, tea, salt, sugar, cooking oil, as well as matches, soap, etc.). I was told that the returnees said they got along fine without the government-supplied services and provisions previously and could do it again (government-provided food and petrol-driven boreholes for this group had only started circa late 1970s or early 1980s).

Their assertions do not sound like they come from a totally oppressed group enslaved by the Botswana government, or by other Bantu. Their comments do not sound like people who are happy to be assimilated into Bantu hierarchies, even in 2000. These are twentieth-century hunter-gatherers desperately trying to resist the Botswana government relocation project so that they can preserve their hunting and gathering culture, even if that means being cut off from all Bantu-provided services, medicine, and food. If these Basarwa were the impoverished assimilated people portrayed by some anthropologists, they would not have stood up to the Bantu-speakers, or knowingly broken laws that prohibit hunting in the Central Kalahari Game Reserve so that they could return to their communities and preserve their way of life. Whether the Botswana government will forego their settlement plans and allow the Basarwa who want to hunt and gather to continue as foragers remains to be seen. Unfortunately, I am not optimistic that there will be twenty-first-century full-time Kalahari hunter-gatherers who will be allowed to exist in association with, but not dominated by, their Bantu neighbors.

CONCLUSIONS

As anthropologists, we should know that data without context is misleading at best. Archaeologists certainly recognize the limitations of artifacts—their data— without a detailed study and knowledge of the objects' context. Ethnographers must also do so. Without accounting for context, conclusions can be reached that are misleading or incorrect. Time periods, ecological change, rapid culture change, or other unusual conditions must all be taken into account before formulating interpretations.

A reason for the resistance to the recognition of autonomous hunter-gatherers by some anthropologists may stem from the popularity of the neo-Marxist theoretical orientation of political economy. This perspective characterizes almost all intercultural or interethnic relationships as ones of domination, subjugation, and inequality. Some political economists find the theoretical orientation so compelling (political imbalances, wealth discrepancies, etc.) that they unintentionally perceive inequality within egalitarianism and are unaware of the amount of cultural diversity or temporal variability in history. Interpretations that are then based on faulty data or data taken out of context, even if they support the desired conclusion, tend to be incorrect. If correct, these interpretations are so for the wrong reasons and therefore are still misleading. The difficulty in applying revisionism to non-Western societies is that, like Marxism, it is based on Western society. In the case of hunter-gatherers neo-Marxism is inappropriate, I suggest, because the Western nation-state colonization is a relatively recent development, only 400 to 600 years old. The seductive lure of this theoretical perspective and its power to explain events that have occurred since colonial and modern Western imperialism makes some anthropologists less critical of data and their context than is usually acceptable. This is particularly true for the many people who do not understand the extent and nature of multiculturalism in southern Africa, past or present.

Are the Basarwa particularly vulnerable to assimilation because they live in the Kalahari? There are regions in which farmers suffer from droughts, insects, and other problems that exceed those in the Kalahari and yet they are not characterized as marginal. Usually when anthropologists refer to an area as inhospitable, they implicitly mean inhospitable for the particular subsistence strategies employed by Westerners. These include large-scale agriculture and animal husbandry. The image most Westerners have of the Kalahari "Desert," in other words, is a myth. It is a semiarid savanna that has its bad years, even lean years, just like other environments. At the same time, it is a scattered wooded savanna (at least in the Central Kalahari region and north) that supported a large number and variety of small and large wild animals and plants before the intrusion of boreholes (wells) and livestock (cattle are particularly destructive to local habitats and often outcompete indigenous species). The Kalahari, therefore, was capable of sustaining the Basarwa and did not make them more vulnerable to assimilation.

Instead of writing twentieth-century Basarwa off as "not real or pure" hunter-gatherers, we should look at their boundary maintenance. Instead of asserting that there are no hunter-gatherers, contra empirical observations, historical accounts by explorers and missionaries, and informants' interviews, we should be studying the different methods used to preserve a particular way of life in a multicultural social environment. Boundary-amplifying mechanisms are utilized to maintain views of "us" and "them," and these are what anthropologists should be studying. Comments I heard at Kutse, such as all Bakgalagadi Bantu-speakers are rich but stingy, exaggerate the cultural differences between Bantu-speakers and Basarwa by leveling a substantial insult against all Bantu-speakers. Sugawara (Chapter 4) discusses the negative perceptions and generalizations of Bantu-speakers toward the Xade Basarwa, which are mechanisms of boundary maintenance among the Bantu-speakers.

It is ironic that of all disciplines, anthropology has practitioners who still claim and/or write as if culture were genetic. Barnard (1989) also argued that anthropologists in general (including some Kalahari specialists) expect a much greater degree of "purity" in their hunter-gatherers than in any other kind of people, including the local Bantu agropastoralists. Why is purity so important to anthropologists? The belief that the Basarwa cannot be hunter-gatherers because their culture has changed over the 2,000 years since the Late Stone Age is inconsistent with the assumption that the Bantu-speakers are still full-time agropastoralists even though their culture has also changed over the same 2,000 years (e.g., Schrire 1980, 1984). Incongruities like these often point out problems in interpretations. Instead of dismissing all modern Basarwa as too "impure" to be studied as hunter-gatherers, we should be examining their culture, both in terms of thoughts and behavior, to determine how boundary maintenance was perpetuated for such a long period of time when elsewhere in southern Africa hunter-gatherers and Khoi cultures have been extinct for centuries. The reason, I think, people focus on cultural purity arises from the assumption that the more biologically "pure" a group, the more likely they are to continue practicing a precontact lifestyle.

Archaeologists, like ethnographers, also overgeneralize about the attributes of, for example, autonomous pastoralists or hunter-gatherers. As shown in Chapters 2 and 3, archaeologists assume that only hunter-gatherers hunted and therefore any wild meat at Bantu-speakers' camps must have been, and is identified as, hunted by the Basarwa who exchanged it for exotic items or as tribute. Archaeologists likewise often interpret wild animal bones at prehistoric Bantu sites as a sign of hunter-gatherer tribute or slavery (Chapter 3, this volume). Such stereotypic thinking reinforces ideas of what Bantu and Basarwa do, but it is not accurate. For example, Bakgalagadi also hunted wild animals (Schapera 1984; Solway 1986). Hunting, thus, was not the exclusive domain of the Basarwa. The fact that modern Bantu-speakers hunted until recently does not make them less pastoralists because they hunted game and collected some wild plants. The same is true for the Basarwa—because Basarwa have a few head of small livestock does not necessarily disqualify them as hunter-gatherers.

Why is the idea of autonomous hunter-gatherers so hard to accept? Because, I suggest, the Western public sees ethnicity, culture, and race as biologically "real," even when all the data show that they are social constructs no more or no less real than any other learned classification (e.g., Hemphill, Lukacs, and Walimbe 2000). Westerners presume a biological ancestry that may or may not be empirically correct since culture and ethnicity are social, not biological, categories. In addition, highly egalitarian societies are the most unlike Western culture. Some researchers find it difficult to use models that are not oriented toward hierarchical societies. In most cases, models that emphasize power differentials, gender asymmetry, economic inequality, and similar traits do not fit highly egalitarian societies and they should not be applied to understand such cultures.

Anthropologists must be very careful not to presume that boundary maintenance is static or similar through time. The following chapters show how the boundaries between hunter-gatherers and Bantu-speaking agropastoralists were probably quite different and had dissimilar ramifications than the boundaries that existed between European colonists/missionaries and hunter-gatherers. Advanced technology in and of itself did not make colonists view hunter-gatherers as nonhuman, or at best as inferior humans. In other words, Westerners' possession of more sophisticated technology aided, but did not cause, them to spread their ideas about "others" through colonization. As the old saying goes, guns do not make wars, people do (however, for a different perspective, see Marlowe, Chapter 10). How and why these boundaries changed through time and between different societies are just some of the topics explored in the following chapters. As Lee states in Chapter 7, to uncritically accept the idea that the Basarwa are cattle-less, subjugated peasants dominated by all their neighbors as they have been for centuries, denies them that combination of cultural traits that are unique to the Basarwa and result from their hunter-gatherer traditions, and do not result, as the revisionists claim, from their undesirable position in the Bantu-dominated hierarchy.

Will there be Basarwa hunter-gatherers in the twenty-first century? I am not optimistic, because of policies now being enforced by the Botswana government. The Basarwa culture may not be intact even in a decade or two. It is, therefore, crucial not to ignore the culture of hunting and gathering that the Basarwa have managed to continue almost to the beginning of the twenty-first century. While it is important not to deny the Basarwa or any group their cultural past for any reason, it is particularly imperative when their future appears to be so bleak. I hope I will be proven wrong. However, unless southern African governmental policies concerning the Basarwa are quickly and substantially revised, I see the disappearance of a type of society that managed to endure in southern Africa for centuries after it had become extinct throughout much of the world as an impending and incalculable loss to all humanity and cultural diversity. As the Native Americans and other conquered societies demonstrate throughout the world, the destruction of a culture creates a void in people that is only filled with hopelessness and pain. I truly hope that is not the fate of the twenty-first-century Basarwa.

The following chapters specifically explore the prehistory, history, and present of hunter-gatherers. Authors seek to understand boundaries and interactions in new ways and show that the Basarwa have not been enslaved for the past 2,000 years. The Basarwa are finally given their due for having an autonomous hunting and gathering culture that existed until the present time; they are accorded respect and admiration for being able to modify, adapt, and endure centuries of contact with "others." Hunter-gatherers throughout Africa and the rest of the world provide a fascinating and insightful contrast to us, the "others," and the last thing we, as anthropologists, should do is to ignore, deny, or not recognize the fascinating insights they, as a group, can provide for the understanding of humankind through the millennium.

ACKNOWLEDGMENTS

I am most grateful to Alan Barnard and Mat Guenther, who provided important feedback about this chapter. Leona Ripley and Mary McNeeley corrected the grammar. I also am thankful to Scott Mahler, acquisitions editor of Smithsonian Institution Press, who, by publishing this book, gave us authors a chance to present our views to readers.

two

Encapsulated Bushmen
in the Archaeology
of Thamaga

Karim Sadr

The question of when Kalahari Bushmen became encapsulated in the Bantu farmers' world has been the focus of fierce debate among a small group of anthropologists and archaeologists for some time now. On one side of the debate, researchers have argued for a pan-Kalahari encapsulation of Bushmen since the earliest contact with farmers some 1,500 years ago (Denbow 1984, 1990; Wilmsen 1989; Wilmsen and Denbow 1990). On the other side, the position has been that in the deepest Kalahari at least, Bushmen were until very recently independent foragers (Lee and Guenther 1991, 1995; Solway and Lee 1990; Yellen 1990a, 1990b; Kent 1992).

A question that arises is how does one actually distinguish encapsulated or subjugated Bushmen from independent hunter-gatherers in the archaeological record? How does the material detritus of independent foragers who interacted and traded with farmers differ from that of subjugated ex-foragers who were dependent on farmers for their livelihood? A number of recent archaeological studies have addressed the issue of interaction between farmers and foragers in southern Africa (Klatzow 2000; Mazel 1986; Sampson 1995; Jolly 1995; Wadley 1996, 2001; Thorp 1996; Van der Ryst 1998). The material signature of encapsulated foragers,

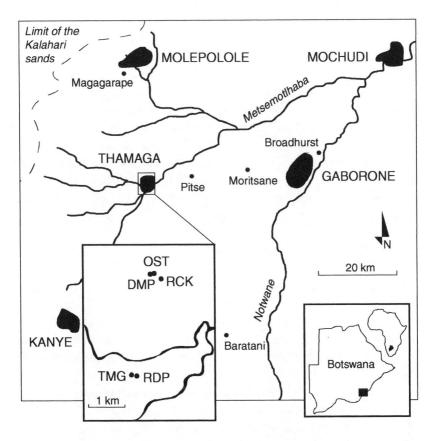

Figure 2.1. Map of southeastern Botswana with place names mentioned in text. OST= Ostrich Shelter, DMP=Damp Shelter, RCK=Rocky Shelter, TMG=Thamaga 1, RDP= Radiepolong.

however, has not been explicitly described (but see Voigt et al. 1995:37–38 and Walker 1995:62 for some ideas on this).

The area around Thamaga in southeastern Botswana (Fig. 2.1) provides a first glimpse of how such material culture might differ from that of independent hunter-gatherers. The Thamaga area contains many rockshelters and evidence for hunter-gatherer occupations from 4,500 years ago until the recent past (Robbins 1985, 1986). The area is also rich in Iron Age sites of farmers and herders (Campbell et al. 1991, 1996). Most importantly, there is a rich historical and ethnohistorical record that documents the presence of subjugated Bushmen here during the past few centuries (cf. Schapera 1953; Okihiro 1976). It follows that any rockshelters around Thamaga occupied by Bushmen in the last few centuries will provide the archaeological signature of a subjugated ex-forager population.

Five excavated rockshelters around Thamaga show very clear differences in the composition of the material remains dating to the last few centuries and those from earlier periods. They show that although contact with farmers commenced about 2,000 years ago, at first this contact had little effect on the traditional way of life of the hunter-gatherers. The material remains of Precontact and Early Contact periods are nearly identical. Some time during the last few centuries, however, the material culture of the local foragers was transformed. This change apparently signals the transition from an independent hunter-gatherer way of life to one of dependency upon the farmer-herders of the area. The reasons for this change are still under investigation. This paper will deal only with how autonomy, interaction, and trade can be distinguished archaeologically from subjugation, assimilation, and dependence in the rockshelter occupations of the Thamaga area.

SETTLEMENT HISTORY OF THAMAGA

The village of Thamaga lies about 40 km off the southeastern edge of the Kalahari sand cover, in the thin stony soils of the Metsemotlhaba River valley in southeast Botswana (Fig. 2.1). The Metsemotlhaba (sandy water) is a seasonal drainage that ultimately reaches the Limpopo via the Notwane River. At an elevation of about 1,000 m, Thamaga receives annually 500–550 mm of rain. This supports a tree and bush savanna with a mixture of broadleaf deciduous trees as well as acacia thorns. Current land use is agricultural and pastoral (Silitshena and MacLeod 1994). As recently as the mid-nineteenth century, this landscape contained abundant herds of buffalo, elephants, and other wild game (Livingstone 1857; Cumming 1850).

Thamaga is located in Kwena tribal territory, now called the Kweneng District. The Kwena, whose current capital Molepolole lies 30 km north of Thamaga, were the first important Tswana-speaking tribe to settle in what is now Botswana. On the basis of oral histories, Schapera dated their arrival here to around 1720 (1980:83, 1953:15). In earliest times, the Kwena may have numbered no more than a hundred souls (Okihiro 1976:65).

The Kwena were not the first Bantu-speaking herder-farmers to settle this area. Oral histories indicate ancestors of the non–Tswana-speaking Bakgalagadi people had settled in the Molepolole area sometime in the late fifteenth century (Okihiro 1976:128–129). The Bakgalagadi apparently mingled freely with the resident Bushmen (Schapera 1953:14). The Kwena, it seems, had a different attitude. After a period of conflict, they subjugated the Bakgalagadi (Mautle 1986:20–21), assimilated some, and pushed the rest out of the better agricultural zones of the hardveld and into the Kalahari sands (Schapera 1953:14; Okihiro 1973:104, 1976:138).

The Bushmen of the area were likewise subjugated, at least as far as the Kwena were concerned. Schapera (1953:37) states that all people occupying the country when the Tswana arrived were considered serfs and parceled out in local groups among the chiefs (see also Mackenzie 1871:128–133). The hunter-gatherers, however, seem to have considered themselves neither serfs nor permanent subjects (cf. Kirby 1939:188; Mackenzie 1871:132): they served when it suited them and left when they felt like it (see also Sugawara's chapter, Köhler and Lewis's chapter, this volume). Throughout this paper then, "subjugated Bushmen" should be understood to refer to a part-time condition seen through the eyes of the herder-farmers. The condition only became permanent when Bushmen groups were tightly surrounded (encapsulated, in its original sense, see Woodburn 1988:36) and hence unable to withdraw from the farmers' world.

Oral histories compress time. The archaeological record indicates that farmers settled in southeast Botswana long before the fifteenth century when the Bakgalagadi are thought to have arrived. By A.D. 600 there were Early Iron Age sites with two separate pottery styles. The Baratani facies is found at sites such as Baratani some 40 km southeast of Thamaga, and Pitse, 10 km east of Thamaga (Fig. 2.1). The Broederstroom facies is found at Magagarape near Molepolole. These sites were long-occupied villages and contain evidence for iron working, agriculture, and pastoralism (Campbell et al. 1996, 1991). The Baratani facies may represent populations who came from the Congo-Angolan coast as part of the Kalundu tradition or the Western Stream of Bantu migrations (Denbow 1990: Huffman 1989). The Broederstroom facies, on the other hand, may have ultimately come from East Africa as part of the Urewe tradition or the Eastern Stream of Bantu migrations (Huffman 1998:58).

Later sites dating from A.D. 1000–1400, such as Moritsane and Broadhurst, contain a different style of ceramics known as the Eiland tradition (Campbell et al. 1991; Denbow 1981). This period is here referred to as the Middle Iron Age. These sites contain kraals and many were located on hilltops (Caister 1982:87). Their occupants may have been involved peripherally in the Indian Ocean trade via more complex societies such as Toutswe in east central Botswana and Mapungubwe in the Limpopo River valley of South Africa (van Waarden 1998). It has been suggested that sites with Eiland pottery were occupied by ancestral Bakgalagadi (Campbell et al. 1991:289).

About A.D. 1300 yet another pottery style, the Moloko, appeared in the area. Sites of this period are referred to as Late Iron Age. The makers of the Moloko pottery were herder-farmers and are sometimes equated with Sotho-Tswana speakers (e.g., Campbell et al. 1991:289). The equation of pottery styles with language groups is of course a contested issue (see for example Hall 1987:20–24), but the traditional potters of Molepolole still produce wares not unlike those of the archaeological Moloko tradition. The equation of Eiland pottery with Bakgalagadi, however, is more poorly documented (Campbell et al. 1991:289).

In comparison with the Iron Age settlement history, that of the later Stone Age of this area is less well known. For several millennia until four or five thousand years ago, the Kalahari and its margins may have been too marginal for occupation by hunter-gatherers (Walker 1995:59–60). Rockshelter sites, such as Robbins's Thamaga 1, show that Late Stone Age hunter-gatherers reoccupied this landscape only about 4,500 years ago (Robbins 1986). The excavations reported below show intermittent occupation of the rockshelters around Thamaga until about 100–150 years ago.

THE KWENA IN THE NINETEENTH CENTURY

It is of central importance in this study to document that during the last few centuries the Bushmen of the Thamaga area were indeed considered subjects by the Kwena farmer-herders. If this can be clearly established, then the material remains in the rockshelters dating to the last few centuries must be those of subjugated Bushmen. To this end, a closer examination of recent history is in order.

Before 1820 the Kwena were a rich and prosperous tribe. The Difaqane—the upheavals resulting from various developments, including Shaka's Zulu wars—put an end to that (Ngcongco 1982; Hamilton 1995). Until the early 1840s the Kwena were harassed and invaded by Sotho and Nguni people. After 1842 Chief Sechele began reconsolidating the Kwena at the same time as English traders and missionaries began to appear on the scene (Okihiro 1973:104). In 1845 the famous missionary and explorer Dr. David Livingstone settled among the Kwena, bringing with him Christianity, Western medicine, trade, and protection against Boer expansionists (Livingstone 1857; Okihiro 1973:107). Three years later Livingstone opened the way to Lake Ngami and with it the interior to European ivory hunters (Schapera 1953:15). For a while now the Kwena capital became the most northerly entrepôt of the Cape trading network, supplying ivory and ostrich feathers to the European market (Parsons 1977:119). This trade brought many guns to the Kwena, with which they successfully defended themselves against the Boer attack of 1852 (Ramsay 1991). Their success resulted in a population boom as refugees put themselves under Sechele's protection: in 1849 he had only 3,620 followers, but by 1897 there were 20,000 at his capital (Ramsay 1991:201). In 1885, to safeguard the by-then economically vital "Road to the North," Britain imposed her protection on what came to be known as Bechuanaland (Ramsay 1991:202; Tlou and Campbell 1984:145–147).

Before the Protectorate, three phases can be distinguished in Kwena foreign trade relations (Okihiro 1973:105–106). The products from their Kalahari hinterland played a major role in each phase. In the eighteenth century the Kwena exported desert products, notably animal hides that they made into karosses, to other Tswana-speaking tribes to their southeast. In exchange they received iron implements, which were then used to buy cattle from the Khoekhoe in the south. This southward inter-Tswana trade was replaced by a period of indirect trade with Europeans, the axis of which was to the north and northeast, ultimately connecting with the Portuguese on the east coast of Africa. The major traffic during this phase was in ivory for glass beads. In the early 1840s this network was supplanted by direct British trade, with the traffic again heading south and involving mainly ivory for guns, but also including brass and copper wire, knives, hatchets, and clothes in exchange for karosses and ostrich feathers. This was the most intense phase of foreign trade for the Kwena: guns made hunting vastly more efficient, while the British ox-wagons could haul greater volumes at a time. The Kwena in this phase controlled access to the Kalahari and thereby to the ivory in the north (Okihiro 1973:105–106). After the 1860s the Ngwato (an early offshoot of the Kwena, occupying the lands to the northeast of Kweneng) began challenging the Kwena as trade masters of the Kalahari (Parsons 1977:119).

THE KWENA AND THEIR SUBJECTS

Although throughout this period the desert dwellers were exploited primarily for labor in hunting (e.g., Kirby 1939:268), closer inspection shows that the relations between Kwena masters and their Bushmen and Bakgalagadi subjects evolved through different, overlapping phases. In the earliest phase of contact with the Kwena, avoidance and conflict were the rule (Mautle 1986:20). Even until 1852 some Bakgalagadi avoided Kwena oppression by hiding deep in the Kalahari (Okihiro 1976:142). Here, they were nevertheless subject to surprise visits by Tswana who would simply take with impudence their supplies (Livingstone 1857:56; Lye 1975:184; Mackenzie 1871:130). Such dreaded visits forced the Bakgalagadi and the Bushmen to hide their residences far from water, where they would often conceal their supplies in pits filled with sand and covered with a hearth (Livingstone 1857:59; Wilmsen 1997:153).

The next (in some cases the first) phase of relations was a tributary one. All the people who occupied the country when the Tswana arrived were deemed subjects[1] (Schapera 1953:37; Hitchcock 1978:107–108). The Tswana chiefs would receive in tribute whatever their subjects produced or acquired. Schapera (1953:26) mentions the brisket of every big game, one tusk per elephant, and the skin of every lion or leopard hunted. The Tswana chiefs would also use their serfs as desert guides in hunting expeditions, and would occasionally give gifts of tobacco, spears, or knives (Hitchcock 1978:103; Livingstone 1857:56; Mackenzie 1871:128). In similar arrangements, the Ngwato apparently obtained ivory from their desert dwellers in exchange for glass beads (Parsons 1977:118). Andrew Smith, who traveled to Ngwato territory during this period, mentioned that the Bushmen "have always been the hunters of the

Bechuana" (Kirby 1939:268). Nonetheless, emphasizing that the hunter-gatherers considered themselves independent, he states further that they stole cattle and only resorted to the Ngwato when they were hungry, but otherwise lived apart in small parties here and there (Kirby 1939:188).

In the third phase, with the intensification of Kwena exports in direct trade with the British after the 1840s, the subjects were given guns and dogs to hunt for their Tswana masters. Mackenzie (1871:131) states that "Public opinion is against putting such dangerous weapons into the hands of the 'lower classes.'" Nonetheless, Tswana masters continued to take their subjects' produce. Mackenzie paints the picture thus:

> When his [Tswana] master arrives he takes possession of the little huts, and receives all skins, etc., which the family have collected.
>   Woe betide the Bushmen should it be found out that they have hidden away part of the produce, or that, instead of keeping the skins for his master, the Bushman has ventured to make with some of them a mantle for himself or his wife! (1871:130)

Intensification of hunting with firearms led, not surprisingly, to the depletion of game animals: in Livingstone's memorably inappropriate simile, "as guns are introduced among the tribes all the fine animals melt away like snow in spring" (1857:170). The decimation of game brought about the fourth phase in Kwena relations with their subjects, who were now deployed as menial workers on cattle posts and fields (Schapera 1953:28; Hitchcock 1978:103; Gadibolae 1985:25). Finally, with the declaration of the Protectorate, the Bakgalagadi were given property rights and serfdom officially ceased (Okihiro 1976:96). The Bushmen, however, were still hunting for and paying tribute to their Tswana masters when the Clifford expedition crossed the Kalahari in 1929 (Ramsay 1989:91). By this time, even the Bakgalagadi seem to have acquired Bushmen clients (Ramsay 1989:92; Silberbauer and Kuper 1966).

There are indications that the Bushmen subjects were treated differently than the Bakgalagadi. Mackenzie (1871:128–129) notes that the relationship between the Bakgalagadi and their masters was much more friendly than between the same masters and their Bushmen. Apparently, however, the Bushmen were more respected. According to Mackenzie (1871:128), "The helplessness of the Bakgalagadi excites the contempt of their owners." Similarly, Livingstone mentions that whereas a few Tswana could domineer an entire village of Bakgalagadi, fear of poisoned arrows would turn them into "fawning sycophants" when dealing with Bushmen (1857:56).

Before Livingstone arrived, Andrew Smith, traveling in this region during the mid-1830s, reported that Bushmen lived just beyond Kwena kraals, traded berries, and occasionally stole cattle, while the Bakgalagadi occupied the desert (Lye 1975:269), presumably trying to avoid contact with the Tswana. Mackenzie, traveling in this area three decades later, praised the ability of Bushmen in herding oxen and in hunting with firearms (1871:99, 137). Indeed, he mentions that by general consent Bushmen were leaders of every hunting party (1871:135). At the same time, however,

> When rival chiefs fight for supremacy in the same tribe, the conditions of the [Bushmen and Bakgalagadi] is wretched in the extreme. They are then scattered and peeled, driven hither and thither, and mercilessly killed, as the jealousy, caprice, or revenge of their masters may dictate. It is quite fair in such a struggle to kill all the vassals, as it would be to lift the cattle, of him who cannot be displaced from his chieftainship. (Mackenzie 1871:133)

THE ROCKSHELTERS OF THAMAGA

The Late Contact Period

All five of the rockshelters excavated near Thamaga in 1996 (Fig. 2.1) appear to contain terminal occupations dating within the last few centuries. These occupations may thus fall partly or wholly within the oral historic period, when Bushmen were subjects of Kwena masters. They provide a good indication of what the remains of dependent, largely assimilated Bushmen may look like in the archaeological record.

Of these five shelters, three—Ostrich, Damp, and Rocky—are located on Thamaga Hill, a large granite outcrop in the middle of the village. At the northern foot of the hill there is a scatter of Eiland potsherds and other artifacts indicating the remains of a small village or hamlet occupied during the Middle Iron Age, ca. A.D. 1000–1400. On top of the hill there are scatters of Moloko potsherds, stone alignments, and patches of burnt mud-walling. They are the remains of a Late Iron Age settlement. In this region sites with Moloko pottery date to about A.D. 1300–1850.

Ostrich Shelter, so named because of a faint yellow painting of three ostriches on the boulder forming its back wall, is a rockshelter located near the north base of the hill, overlooking the Middle Iron Age settlement. Two square meters were excavated here revealing some 30–50 cm of artifact-bearing deposits atop decomposing bedrock (Fig. 2.2). The excavated area was riddled with pits that had been dug from various levels of the occupation. They put in mind the caches mentioned by Livingstone (see above). Two charcoal samples from hearths were dated. The upper yielded a result of 140 ± 60 B.P. (Beta 107601) and the lower dated to 290 ± 50 B.P. (Beta 107602). At two standard deviations the upper one calibrates to A.D. 1655–1950, while the lower one, due to the nature of the calibration curve (Talma and Vogel 1993), comes in three intervals from A.D. 1475–1675, A.D. 1775–1800, and A.D. 1945–1950.

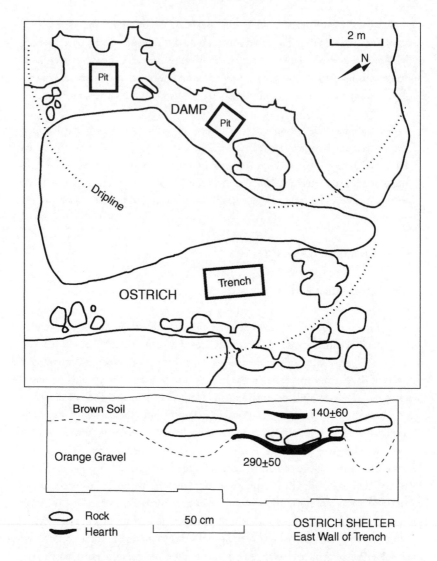

Figure 2.2. Plan and profile of Ostrich and Damp shelters. Blackened areas on profile mark radiocarbon samples and the numbers give the estimated age of the samples in years before present.

Several diagnostic potsherds of Moloko type, as well as a small iron axe, a metal bead, and three glass seed beads make up the inventory of objects presumably obtained from herder-farmers. Several Late Stone Age artifacts confirm that the rock-shelter occupants were indeed descended from the erstwhile hunter-gatherer population of the area. In addition to the rock art, there are 10 complete and 4 broken or unfinished ostrich eggshell beads, 1 microlithic segment, and 2 typical Late Stone Age thumbnail scrapers. Most of the eggshell beads are very small and within the range of Late Stone Age hunter-gatherer bead sizes from Botswana (Tapela 1998).

Just behind the rock forming the back wall of Ostrich Shelter, several immense boulders have collapsed to form a large chamber (Fig. 2.2). Two pits were dug here in what we called Damp Shelter. It is possible that the cultural debris is part of the same occupation as in Ostrich Shelter. No dates are available, but the excavation brought to light 20 Moloko sherds and 1 Eiland sherd. The last was lying practically on the surface and may have been collected from the immediate vicinity where Eiland sherds are not uncommon. One green-on-cream glass bead was also found.

A small pit was also excavated in Rocky Shelter high on the eastern flank of Thamaga Hill. Again, no dates are available, but the excavation did yield 9 diagnostic Moloko potsherds. It seems probable the site was occupied more or less at the same time as Ostrich and Damp Shelters.

These three sites share a number of similarities that provide the material signature (or archaeological marker) for an ex–hunter-gatherer population now dependent on and largely assimilated into the dominant herder-farmer culture of the area.

All three of these sites have a lot of potsherds, very few flaked stones, and very few bones (Table 2.1). Sheep make up a significant proportion of the faunal sample from Ostrich Shelter (Table 2.2, Ina Plug, personal communication). The ceramic pots probably did not arrive empty. Indeed, both the sheep bones and the vessels may represent rations obtained from herder-farmers (cf. Hitchcock 1978:315–316; Sampson 1995). Given the negligible quantities of remains pointing to hunting, skin processing, or craft manufacture (Table 2.3), it seems likely that the payment for the pots and their original contents, perhaps even the sheep and the odd metal and glass artifacts, would have been labor. The historical record suggests that this could have been as professional hunters or as menial laborers in the settlement, fields, and cattle posts of the herder-farmers living at the base of Thamaga Hill.

Radiepolong and Thamaga 1, the two remaining excavated shelters, are located 4 km to the south of Thamaga Hill. The materials from the terminal occupations at these sites suggest a population less assimilated and less dependent on the herder-farmers. There are fewer exotic objects such as pottery, metal, or glass, and many more traditional items such as stone tools (Tables 2.1 and 2.3).

Slightly over 5 m² were excavated at Radiepolong, a small shelter formed by a giant granite boulder (Fig. 2.3). This shelter is on the same outcrop and only a few hundred meters to the east of Thamaga 1, the site originally excavated by Larry Robbins in the 1980s. Although at Radiepolong (as well as most of the other excavated shelters) there is no visible natural stratigraphy, the vertical distribution of artifacts and bones allow the delineation of three major occupation periods (Fig. 2.3). At Radiepolong the boundary between the terminal occupation (the Late

Table 2.1

The Material Signature at Rockshelters near Thamaga

Site	Potsherds	Lithics	Grams of Bone	Volume of Deposit (m³)	Potsherds as Percentage of Total Sherds and Lithics	Lithics (g/m³)	Bones (g/m³)	Potsherds (g/m³)
The Late Contact period (terminal occupation)								
Thamaga 1	13	235	67	0.15	5.2	1,516	432	87
Radiepolong	182	1,982	495	0.79	8.4	2,499	624	230
Rocky Shelter	50	8	0	0.18	86.2	44	0	278
Damp Shelter	288	46	54	0.42	86.2	109	128	686
Ostrich Shelter	336	33	236	0.63	91.0	52	374	1,622
The Early Contact period								
Radiepolong	63	6,607	1,449	0.89	0.9	7,415	1,626	71
Thamaga 1	4	1,303	209	0.12	0.3	10,768	1,727	33
The Precontact period								
Radiepolong	0	1,488	847	0.49	0	3,036	1,728	0
Thamaga 1	0	255	19	0.04	0	6,375	475	0

Table 2.2

Details of Bones from the Rockshelters near Thamaga

Site	Bone Fragments	Identified Bones[a]	% Livestock
The Late Contact period (terminal occupation)			
Thamaga 1	68	7	0
Radiepolong	975	129	2.3
Rocky Shelter	3	0	0
Damp Shelter	209	85	0
Ostrich Shelter	361	29	27.6
The Early Contact period			
Radiepolong	3,435	396	0.5
Thamaga 1	382	17	0
The Precontact period			
Radiepolong	1,651	162	0
Thamaga 1	37	2	0

[a]All bones identified by Ina Plug, Transvaal Museum, Pretoria.

Table 2.3

Details of Formal Stone Tools from Rockshelters near Thamaga

Site	Scrapers	Segments	Other Backed[a]	Other Tools[b]
The Late Contact period (terminal occupation)				
Thamaga 1	1	3	1	1
Radiepolong	45	12	4	31
Rocky Shelter	0	0	0	0
Damp Shelter	3	0	0	0
Ostrich Shelter	2	1	0	1
The Early Contact period				
Radiepolong	165	28	13	64
Thamaga 1	16	9	2	15
The Precontact period				
Radiepolong	20	2	3	9
Thamaga 1	0	0	0	1

[a]Includes backed pieces and backed bladelets.

[b]Includes adzes, miscellaneous and broken retouched pieces.

Contact period) and the preceding Early Contact period is clearly visible in a sharp drop-off in bone and lithics, and a sharp increase in ceramic artifacts.

The terminal occupation at Radiepolong has yielded one radiocarbon date of 200 ± 60 B.P. (Beta 107603), which at two standard deviations calibrates to A.D. 1535–1545 and 1635–1950. Diagnostic pottery is rare at Radiepolong. Of the 11 Moloko sherds, however, 10 occur in the terminal occupation and the last lies just under the boundary separating the Early from Late Contact. It may have been trampled down, but it should also be kept in mind that in the absence of natural stratigraphy the boundary between occupation periods is nowhere razor sharp.

In comparison with the broadly contemporary terminal occupations on Thamaga Hill, Radiepolong's terminal occupation contains more lithics, fewer ceramics, and a bit more bone (Table 2.1). As Table 2.2 shows, there are proportionally fewer domestic animal remains than in the rockshelters overlooking the Late Iron Age settlement at the base of Thamaga Hill. The impression gained is of a population not as dependent on herder-farmers. This may have been an effect of distance from the main herder-farmer settlement in the area, although it cannot be ruled out that the terminal occupation at Radiepolong was slightly earlier, and the interaction with herder-farmers somewhat different, than at the Thamaga Hill shelters. Two pieces of metal wire, one of which has a decorative device attached, and two glass beads (a seed bead and a larger green-on-white) were recovered in the Late Contact period layers of Radiepolong. In addition, a gunflint recovered

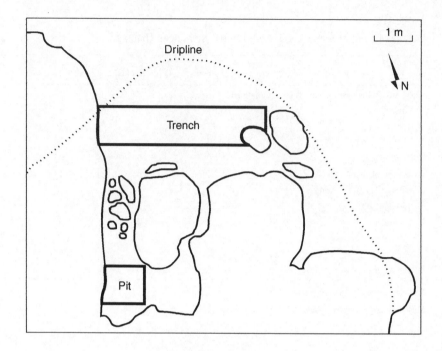

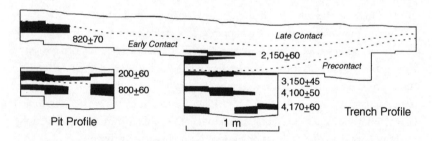

Figure 2.3. Plan and profile of Radiepolong Shelter. Blackened areas on profile mark radio-carbon samples and the numbers give the estimated age of the samples in years before present.

from the top of the terminal occupation may point to the services offered by the rockshelter occupants in return for the pots and exotic artifacts.

Our square meter excavated at Larry Robbins's site of Thamaga 1 (Fig. 2.4) provided a very similar picture. Robbins's excavations were conducted in 10-cm spits that cut through the boundaries between occupation periods. All our excavations were carried out using Sampson's (Sampson et al. 1989:7) method, which allows artifacts to be plotted horizontally to within 25 cm and vertically to within about 2.5 cm of their original positions. This method provides a sharper resolution of cul-

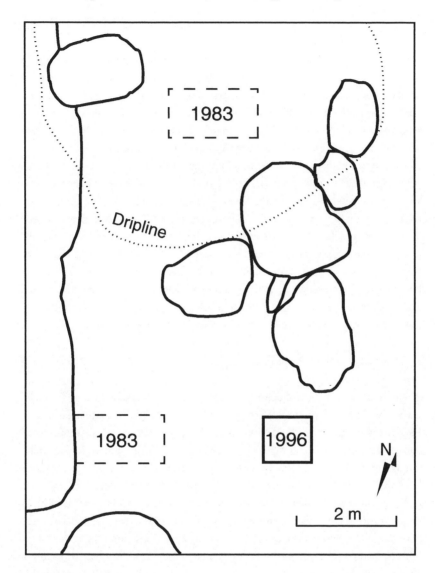

Figure 2.4. Plan of Thamaga 1.

tural stratigraphy. At Thamaga 1 the terminal occupation is undated and our test pit did not intercept any diagnostic sherds, although Robbins's pits contain Moloko sherds in the top few layers. Otherwise, however, the material signature of the terminal occupation at Thamaga 1 is just like Radiepolong's: lithics and bones are more numerous and pottery less so than at the shelters on Thamaga Hill (Table 2.1). Robbins (1986:7) reports sheep or goat remains in the Late Contact layers of

Thamaga 1. Our small pit did not intercept any domestic animal remains (Ina Plug, personal communication).

Overall, the terminal occupations at these five shelters exhibit the material remains of an ex–Late Stone Age hunter-gatherer population to varying degrees assimilated and dependent for subsistence on the dominant herder-farmer population of the area, who may have been the historically known Kwena. The material signatures seem to even distinguish between a more highly dependent population living right on the farmer-herders' doorstep, and their less assimilated cousins (or immediate predecessors) still living in the bush. Or perhaps we are seeing two ends of a seasonal round. In modern times, Bushmen have been known to spend part of the year attached to farmers and the rest in pursuit of a more traditional hunter-gatherer way of life (Silberbauer 1960; Silberbauer and Kuper 1966; Vierich 1977; Hitchcock 1978). In either case, it is of interest to note also a possible change in settlement patterns that took place in the transition from Early to Late Contact periods. We found no Early Contact period occupations on Thamaga Hill, despite the presence of a Middle Iron Age settlement at the base of the hill. For reasons as yet unknown, during the Middle Iron Age herder-farmer settlements did not attract hunter-gatherers as they did in the Late Iron Age.

The Early Contact Period

The material signature of the Early Contact period rockshelter occupations is dramatically different from that of the Late Contact period. The artifacts from the Early Contact layers at Radiepolong and Thamaga 1 show an independent Late Stone Age hunter-gatherer occupation. The Early Contact hunter-gatherer material signature differs from the earlier Precontact occupation in degree but hardly in kind, the latter difference being restricted to the presence of a few potsherds. The potsherds indicate contact and interaction, but there is no evidence at all of subjugation, assimilation, or dependence on herder-farmers during this Early Contact period (see also Smith and Lee 1997; Lee's chapter in this volume).

At Radiepolong, the end of the Early Contact period is well dated. Two dates on charcoal gave results of 800 ± 60 B.P. (Beta 107604) and 820 ± 70 B.P. (Beta 107605) (Fig. 2.3). At two standard deviations they respectively calibrate to A.D. 1065–1075, 1155–1295, and to 1035–1295. The beginning of the Early Contact period at Radiepolong dates to over 2,000 years ago. A sample of ostrich eggshell from near the base of this period was dated to 2150 ± 60 B.P. (Pta-7388), calibrated at one standard deviation to 189–40 B.C. A date of 2,000 years was also obtained by Dr. William Downey from a soil sample collected from the middle of the Early Contact layers and dated at the Thermoluminescence Laboratory of the University of Botswana. Since the earliest Iron Age settlements in southeastern Botswana only date to the sixth century A.D.

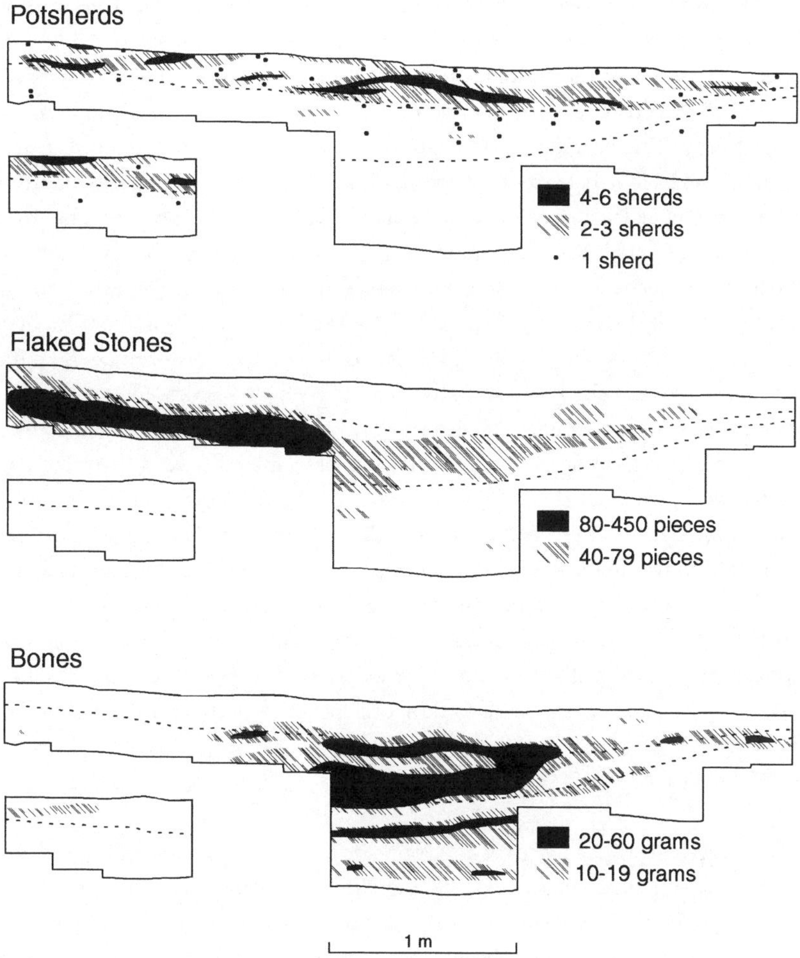

Potsherds

■ 4-6 sherds
⧫ 2-3 sherds
• 1 sherd

Flaked Stones

■ 80-450 pieces
⧫ 40-79 pieces

Bones

■ 20-60 grams
⧫ 10-19 grams

|_____ 1 m _____|

Figure 2.5. Distribution of pottery, stone, and bone in the Radiepolong section. The contours are based on counts per 12,500 cm³, or a rectangular 'box' of deposits measuring 25 cm wide by 5 cm tall by 100 cm deep.

(Campbell et al. 1996, 1991), it is assumed that the earliest contact at Radiepolong was at long distance and probably took place through intermediaries.

There are 63 potsherds in the Early Contact period. Of these 4 are definite Eiland types. Another 4 definite Eiland sherds are found in the succeeding Late Contact period. Three of these, however, are right at the boundary between Early and Late Contact. The third is practically on the surface, in a zone of known disturbance extending down into the Early Contact layers. The association between Eiland pottery and at least the upper phases of the Early Contact period seems adequately clear.

Aside from this pottery, there is little to indicate contact with, much less assimilation into, herder-farmer economies. There is a very small proportion of domestic faunal remains in the middle and upper parts of the Early Contact layers (Table 2.2). But overall, the material signature of the Early Contact period is much more similar to that of the Precontact period than to the Late Contact (Table 2.1 and Fig. 2.5). Lithics, unlike in the Late Contact period, are very numerous (the paucity of lithics in the Precontact layers, as shown in the middle profile on Fig. 2.5, is odd, but may be due to the limited area of excavation into Precontact deposits). Bone is as numerous as in the Precontact layers. Potsherds are few in the Early Contact period and all but absent in the Precontact. The two sherds in Precontact layers, at the far right of the profile shown at the top of Figure 2.5, occur in a very rocky zone where the boundary between the Pre- and Early Contact layers was smeared as a result of difficult excavation conditions. They probably belong to the Early Contact period.

Other classes of artifacts echo this pattern of similarities between Early and Precontact occupations (Fig. 2.6). Ostrich eggshell is rare in the Late Contact but common in the Early and Precontact periods (Fig. 2.6, upper middle profile). Artifacts associated with traditional ritual and exchange among Late Stone Age hunter-gatherers, such as ochre, specularite, quartz crystals, petrified wood, and mica, occur mostly in the Early Contact period and rarely in the Late (Fig. 2.6, lower middle and bottom profile). The absence of these materials in the Precontact period is odd. Again, it may be due to the small amount of deposits excavated from this period.

SUMMARY AND CONCLUSION

The evidence from the five excavated rockshelters near Thamaga indicates that a dependent, largely assimilated ex–hunter-gatherer population can be recognized archaeologically by the paucity of traditional and prevalence of foreign remains related to craft production and subsistence technology (see also Kent's Chapter 3, this volume). In this case the low numbers of lithics and bones, and the high numbers of ceramics, provide the clearest markers, although less clearly the same trends can be seen in ostrich eggshell versus glass beads, metal objects, and traditional exotics such as crystals and pigments. It appears that the differences in the relative quantities of ceramic, stone, and bone can perhaps even distinguish between relatively more or less assimilated populations. At Thamaga, there is a clear material distinction between ex–hunter-gatherers living on the edge of herder-farmers' villages (the equivalent of "Farm San" perhaps, see Guenther 1976; Sampson 1995; Vierich 1977) and those still living in the "bush."

The material differences between such assimilated groups and independent hunter-gatherers (even if clearly in contact with herder-farmers) are vast and easily visible in the material remains. In occupations attributable to independent hunter-

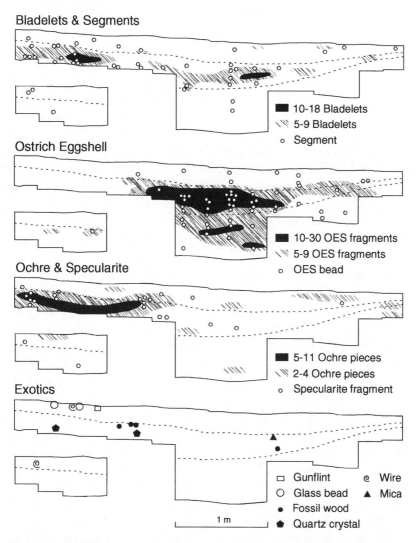

Figure 2.6. Distribution of other artifacts in the Radiepolong section. The contours are based on counts per 12,500 cm³, or a rectangular 'box' of deposits measuring 25 cm wide by 5 cm tall by 100 cm deep.

gatherers, the lithic index is unmistakably high, objects related to traditional exchange and ritual are common, and foreign exotics are rare—and in this case restricted to ceramic vessels, perhaps even only potsherds. Independent hunter-gatherers in contact with herder-farmers leave a material signature very much like that of Precontact hunter-gatherers. Assimilation and dependence radically change the hunter-gatherers' material inventory. The same general pattern has been observed in the Seacow River Valley in the contact between Bushmen and Trekboers (Voigt et al. 1995:37–38). Compared with the Thamaga rockshelters, sites such as Cae Cae in the deepest Kalahari show no material change indicative of subjugation (Wilmsen 1978; Sadr 1997:fig. 3). The material signature there is more similar to that of the Precontact and Early Contact layers at Radiepolong.

As clear as the above explanation of the material remains seems, the discussion will be incomplete without considering alternatives. Two come to mind. First, that the material changes seen in the Radiepolong sequence represent not changes in the nature of contact, but in the intensity of occupation. In other words, it could be argued that the high lithic and bone index in Precontact and Early Contact layers represent simply a more intensive occupation than in the lithic and bone-poor layers of the Late Contact period. The very high ceramic index, however, makes this argument untenable: if it were just a question of fewer man-days of occupation, ceramics should also be fewer in the top layers. For an ephemeral hunter-gatherer occupation, there are simply far too many pots in the top layers.

This gives rise to the second alternative explanation: that the terminal occupants of the rockshelters were not ex–hunter-gatherers at all, but the herder-farmers themselves. This is a more complex alternative and relates to the ethnic identity of the rockshelter occupants (cf. Wadley 2001). There is no way of knowing what language the terminal occupants of the rockshelters spoke, nor what they looked like or how they dressed or how they behaved in public. In short, we can't be sure which culture—Bushman, Bakgalagadi, or Kwena—they felt themselves to be part of. We can, however, see continuity in aspects of their material culture that connects them with the Late Stone Age indigenous hunter-gatherers of the area. The clearest among these lines of continuity is in the places occupied. Another line of continuity is in the typical Late Stone Age hunter-gatherer artifacts such as segments, scrapers, and small ostrich eggshell beads, which are found even in the top layers of the shelters. These suggest that no matter how culturally and genetically mixed the last occupants of the shelters were, they probably considered themselves at least in part descended from the aboriginal hunter-gatherers of this region.

The point at which the ex–hunter-gatherers were evicted or became fully assimilated (and thus indistinguishable archaeologically from the farmers) must date to just after the terminal occupations in the rockshelters. The elders of Thamaga, who have lived there since 1935, cannot remember Bushmen in these parts (Gopolang 1997). The local Bushmen must therefore have disappeared sometime after the mid-nineteenth century when flintlocks were introduced to this area (as indicated by the presence of a gunflint in the terminal layer of Radiepolong—see Fig. 2.6, bottom profile) and before the early decades of the twentieth century. Perhaps the official abolition of serfdom in early Protectorate times (Schapera 1970:89–90) marks the point at which the Bushmen disappeared from Thamaga.

ACKNOWLEDGMENTS

This research was funded by the Archaeology Unit and the Research and Publications Committee of the University of Botswana. The Office of the President of Botswana kindly permitted the research. I wish to thank all the students who helped with the excavations and analyses. Earlier versions of this paper were presented in various fora and distributed among the other contributors to this volume. For fear of leaving anyone out I will just say that I am extremely grateful to all who made helpful comments.

NOTE

1. Schapera (1953:37) prefers to call them serfs instead of subjects. Mackenzie (1871:128) used also other terms such as slaves and vassals. Andrew Smith said the Tswana consider Bushmen their servants (Kirby 1939:271). None of these terms adequately describe the relationship that existed between the Tswana masters and their Bakgalagadi and Bushman subjects. This relationship is known as *bolata* in the Tswana language (after Gadibolae 1985; *bothlanka* after Guenther, this volume). There seems to be no exact equivalent in English. However, a good idea of the nature of *bolata* can be gained from Mackenzie (1871:128–133).

three

Autonomy or Serfdom?

Relations between Prehistoric Neighboring Hunter-Gatherers and Farmer/Pastoralists in Southern Africa

Susan Kent

Throughout prehistory and in different regions of the Old and New Worlds, hunter-gatherers lived adjacent to or within areas inhabited by farmers and/or pastoralists. Theories of their interactions range from enslavement of the hunter-gatherers in southern Africa to trade in the North American Southwest. The southern African hunter-gatherers are portrayed as impoverished pastoralists, who lost their cattle and were forced to hunt and gather only because of their poverty. In contrast, Plains hunter-gatherers in North America are seen as autonomous people who participated in intercultural trade with their neighbors. Southern African foragers are thought to have existed as enslaved peoples forced to work for their more socially/politically complex agropastoralist neighbors for thousands of years. While no doubt such scenarios did occasionally occur, how common were they in southern Africa before Western colonization? Can these scenarios be extended to all southern African foragers, including those of the Kalahari, for the pre, proto-, and historic periods?

During the 1980s and 1990s, revisionism swept southern African archaeology, as well as hunter-gatherer ethnography (discussed in Kent 1992, 1998a, 1998b). Partly

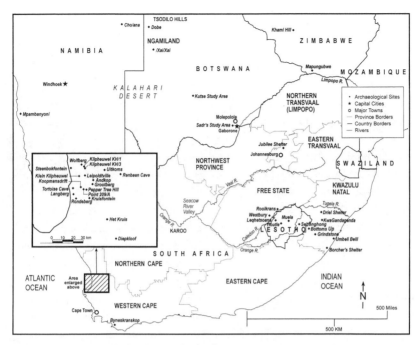

Figure 3.1. Archaeological sites in southern Africa.

because of the elegance of the writing by the main proponents of revisionism, many anthropologists uncritically accepted it. Therefore, a number of southern African prehistoric forager sites were interpreted as evidence of hunter-gatherers' passive servitude to the incoming Bantu agropastoralists. Originally Wilmsen and Denbow (1990) reserved their depiction of enslaved hunter-gatherers as far back as 1,000–2,000 years to those of the Dobe area in the Kalahari Desert (Fig. 3.1). However, as a result of the popularity of revisionism, many archaeological sites located outside the Kalahari are now interpreted, or reinterpreted, as having been occupied by hunter-gatherers dependent on their herding neighbors. A loss of cultural autonomy is invariably assumed, but rarely demonstrated (Sadr 1997; Brooks, Chapter 8, this volume). The same is true of an assumed longing for the agropastoralist way of life by the apparently grubby, hungry, unhappy, indigenous hunter-gatherers, a condition I refer to as "pastoralist-envy," with apologies to Freud.

One problem is that this portrayal of hunter-gatherers by Wilmsen (1989), and other revisionists (Motzafi-Haller 1998), is consistent with agropastoralists' perceptions, but *not* with the perceptions of hunter-gatherers. My own work among Kalahari hunter-gatherers during the 1980s and 1990s shows that hunter-gatherers looked down on agropastoralists, just as agropastoralists looked down on them. In Chapter 1, I suggest that such antagonistic perceptions of neighbors are a boundary-maintenance mechanism and not a valid view of either group. Therefore, it is essential not to rely on one group's belief in their superiority without examining both group's views (also see Köhler and Lewis, Chapter 11, for the same concerning African Pygmies).

Some anthropologists working in southern Africa have, in my opinion, uncritically accepted a static model of domination perpetuated by Bantu-speakers (Motzafi-Haller 1998). There are archaeologists who apply this immutable model to the past without developing methods that would distinguish trade from tribute and autonomous interactions from enslavement. By reevaluating the archaeological and ethnohistoric data, we can examine these models of interactions between culturally distinct groups in southern Africa. The models can then be used to interpret intercultural relations in the Kalahari where autonomous hunter-gatherers may have persisted until the last few years of the twentieth century.

Archaeologists studying southern Africa commonly describe a client-patron relationship between hunter-gatherers and agropastoralists at sites with relatively small amounts of pottery, domestic animal bones, crops, and sometimes iron, along with stone tools and wild faunal remains (e.g., Wilmsen and Denbow 1990). It is less common to question the archaeological visibility of different modes of intercultural interactions, or the ability of archaeologists to distinguish autonomous trade from domination or enslavement. The specific types of evidence that can be used as signatures of different types of intercultural interactions are even less commonly determined (see Sadr 1997, this volume for a discussion on the material correlates of intercultural interactions).

All of this leads to one fundamental question. Do artifacts reflect culture? I think so, but few anthropologists have directly tested their assumption that assemblages of objects at sites can indicate assimilation or enslavement. This assumption is based on another untested belief, that continuous contact between different cultural groups inevitably results in the conquest of a less complex society by a more complex one. Without rigorous testing, it is not appropriate to believe that more socially and politically complex societies always assimilate, and in southern Africa enslave, less complex groups. Jolly (1996:277) describes the Bantu-speakers as "the dominant pastoralists" and states that "hunter-gatherer societies in southern Africa and elsewhere have been closely enmeshed with neighboring farming communities for hundreds and sometimes thousands of years." My question is, why assume this? Whether implicit or explicit, there is an assumption that all southern African hunter-gatherers throughout prehistory were highly egalitarian and eager to forego their own culture. The process of assimilation and domination is often thought to be unidirectional—the conquest invariably going from agropastoralists to hunter-gatherers. Yet, we know that the converse did occur—change was bidirectional, as exemplified by some Bantu-speaking groups who incorporated clicks into their language (e.g., the Xosha). While hunter-gatherers were not isolated or unfamiliar with agropastoralists prior to European contact, they also were not so attracted to them that they willingly gave up their own culture to acquire a disadvantaged position among the Bantu. This view of hunter-gatherer assimilation cannot be reconciled with the early explorers' descriptions of three culturally distinct societies in South Africa: (1) hunter-gatherers, (2) Khoi herders (also known as Khoikhoi, Khoekhoe, and Khoe), and (3) Bantu agropastoralists (e.g., Guenther Chapter 5, Kent Chapter 6).

What the prehistory, ethnohistory, and ethnography of southern Africa document, I suggest, is the relatively unusual circumstance necessary to create the all-encompassing culture change that occurred between A.D. 1700 and 2000. The unprecedented circumstance in southern Africa was Western colonization and the rise of nation-states (also see Guenther, Chapter 5). The enormous influence European colonization had on local groups is often not taken into account when reconstructing southern African prehistory. European impact, however, was not felt similarly everywhere and was not uniform. It is no coincidence that hunter-gatherers continued to be viable in the areas not heavily populated by Europeans. In fact, Europeans did not try to colonize parts of southern Africa, including the Kalahari where hunter-gatherer cultures persisted until the end of the twentieth century.

As noted by Mitchell (1996:291), some anthropologists see hunter-gatherers as "*tabula rasa* until the advent of such [agropastoralist] interaction." Perhaps more common is the implicit assumption that even if hunter-gatherers had an identity separate from their neighbors, they passively allowed themselves to be incorporated into a disadvantaged position in a more complex society. If so, we should see much more repetitiveness in site structure, material culture assemblage, and faunal and botanical remains between those areas once inhabited by Bantu-speakers and assimilated hunter-gatherers. Instead, most Bantu-speakers' sites are quite distinct from hunter-gatherer camps. Those sites that are more ambiguous are often so because of a confusion of the material culture of autonomy and trade with that of serfdom and tribute. In addition, we do not have the techniques to reliably distinguish a hunter-gatherer site from a site at which pastoralists hunted and gathered. While it may be difficult, it is not impossible to distinguish trade between autonomous societies from domination, tribute, or enslavement. How do autonomy and domination appear in the archaeological record?

MATERIAL CULTURE AND INTERGROUP INTERACTIONS

Anthropologists of all subdisciplines need to tackle questions of culture change, trade, tribute, intercultural relations, autonomy, dependence, differential rates of change, and similar topics before they attempt to distinguish trade between autonomous societies from domination or enslavement. However, archaeologists are in an even more difficult position than other anthropologists. Archaeologists need to determine different types of interactions based on the material culture excavated from sites. I think enough studies show that we can differentiate cultures by noting subtle variations in their material culture assemblages. The problem, instead, is the absence of studies that examine material cultural assemblages specifically to determine the type of interaction occurring between past societies (this is beginning to change, e.g., Rogers 1990; Smith 1987; Stein 1998; and others).

A number of archaeologists have cautioned against using absolute counts of foreign objects at a site to determine the nature of interaction between groups (Kent 1983; Rogers 1990; Stein 1998; Smith 1987). More sophisticated methods than absolute counts are feasible when data are from historic sites. That is why most of the studies on culture change, acculturation, and assimilation pertain to the historic period or to ancient civilizations that had writing. These methods, however, can rarely be applied to prehistoric nonliterate groups where no written documents, observations, or descriptions are available. Nonetheless, I am optimistic that subtle changes in the material culture of groups can provide insights concerning the nature of prehistoric interactions. Even if somewhat simplistic, absolute counts can be employed to examine common assumptions. For example, we can test the supposition that even small amounts of Bantu or European artifacts or domestic animal bones at a hunter-gatherer camp signify assimilation and clientele relations, if not serfdom.

Enslavement reflects a domination of not only a people's labor and ideas, but of their material culture, architecture, and subsistence. Not all anthropologists agree that cultural autonomy versus assimilation can be measured by the ratio of one group's artifacts found at another group's site (see Saunders 1998; Singleton 1998). The lack of agreement, I suggest, emanates from two problems common with these types of studies: an absence of ethnoarchaeological research that examines different patterns of intergroup interactions, and the tendency to focus on one particular class of objects, such as ceramics or animal and plant remains. By using all artifact categories, in addition to the botanical and faunal remains, and architecture, it is possible to ascertain the amount and type of intercultural interaction.

THE ETHNOARCHAEOLOGY OF DOMINATION

To study the different types of material culture reflective of the extremes of interaction (i.e., assimilation and association), I selected three distinct contemporaneous hunter-gatherer groups that had different types of interactions with neighboring farmers/agropastoralists. I compared these groups with a non–hunting-gathering society where there is no ambiguity; they were completely enslaved by a dominant group. On one end of the continuum of autonomy discussed here are the Kalahari hunter-gatherers, in the middle are the Efe Pygmies, and on the opposite end are African American slaves in the eighteenth and nineteenth centuries. The absolute

Table 3.1

Material Culture at Recently Abandoned Hunter-Gatherer Camps

	Efe Pygmies	Ju/'hoansi	Kutse
Percentage of villager/neighbors' objects	58.87	1.00	26.81
Percentage of villager/neighbors' object categories (hunting gear, clothing, pots, etc.)	73.08	27.73	37.21

Table 3.2

Frequency of Domesticated Animal Bones

	Kutse Hunter-Gatherers[a]	Early Iron Age Bantu Agropastoralists[b]	North American Slaves[c]
Percentage of domestic animal bones	10.4	93.8	81.5

[a]From abandoned Kutse camps.

[b]From KwaGandaganda, South Africa (Whitelaw 1994).

[c]From Kingsmill Quarter site, Virginia, USA (McKee 1987).

number of objects acquired directly by individuals (through hunting, gathering, scavenging, or by their own manufacture) was compared to the number of objects given, lent, or bought from the other group (in the case of the foragers, their non–hunter-gatherer neighbors and in the case of the African American slaves, their Euroamerican masters; Table 3.1; Fig. 3.1). The number of object categories, using similar categories for each group was compared (Table 3.1). A brief discussion of material culture and intercultural relationships is presented.

North American Slavery Material Culture

One way historic North American slave autonomy was undermined was by denying slaves their own material culture. When African slaves were first imported to North America, they had autonomy and status similar to European indentured servants, with one important difference—their period of servitude never ended. Through time there was a visible reduction in the amount of artifacts produced or controlled by local slaves, primarily Colonware pottery and various types of modified objects (Handler 1989). Fewer slave-made and controlled artifacts corresponded with an increase in the domination and oppression of African Americans by Euroamericans. As African American slaves were increasingly acculturated and exploited through the centuries, their material culture changed accordingly (Wheaton and

Garrow 1985). Slave-produced objects were replaced with European/Euroamerican made and used artifacts (Handler 1989; Wheaton and Garrow 1985:251). By the 1800s, almost all artifacts were acquired in some way from the dominant Euroamerican population (i.e., given, purchased, etc., Moore 1981).

The plantation architecture of slave quarters during the late eighteenth and early nineteenth centuries was not similar to the architecture common in West or Central Africa. Houses were often square or rectangular, small, wooden structures, with one or two rooms that significantly differed from the round mud or grass huts common to West or Central Africa (Moore 1981). I suggest that Western-influenced architecture was forced on the slaves as another means to subjugate them. By not permitting the construction of African house forms, masters were able to further distance slaves from their previous autonomous African culture. Masters, I suggest, used slave housing to emphasize the dependency of slaves on their masters for basic needs such as shelter. Architecture also was a reminder of the vast economic, social, and political differences between impoverished slaves who lived in small simple structures and their masters who lived in large, opulent houses. I do not mean to imply that the plantation owners necessarily consciously required slaves to live in one- or two-room houses for the reasons given here, because poor whites also lived in similar houses. However, denying them their traditional African architecture was one more visible way to show who was in control and who was not. In other words, housing was one less means available for slaves to convey a cultural difference between themselves and their Euroamerican owners. The same was true for banning or discouraging African religions or public and group dances and meetings, although Euroamericans were not entirely successful in doing so.

Further control was imposed by prohibiting native African languages (in addition, most slaves were from different tribes whose languages were mutually unintelligible). There were many other subtle forms of control masters had over their slaves. At the same time, African Americans slaves resisted the complete domination of their masters by using their modified version of Christianity (e.g., beliefs in magic). For example, "Anecdotes emphasizing satire and the mocking of masters, Euroamerican complaints of enslaved African Americans unwillingness to work, and traditional religious practices may all have been part of [slaves' resistance to domination]" (Garman 1998:153). There was a reflexive relationship wherein masters attempted to force their domination and slaves retaliated with various forces of resistance. In other words, even African American slaves were not the passive subjugated people that many anthropologists believe hunter-gatherers were in southern Africa.

Faunal remains found at plantation slave quarters were primarily from pig, sheep/goat, and cattle, in that order (McKee 1987:34–35). Botanical remains from both slave quarters and their masters' or overseers' houses included rice and maize. While wild plant and animal remains may have been a little more common at slave quarters than at nonslave quarters, they also were present at the overseer and plantation owners' houses (Wheaton and Garrow 1985). Exceptions occurred (e.g., Otto 1984), however, in general wild animals were usually supplemental to both groups' diet rather than a staple (Wheaton and Garrow 1985). At the Kingsmill slave quarters, 81.46 percent of all identifiable bones were from domesticated animals (Table 3.2). I suggest that game was not significantly more common at slave quarters because they did not have the luxury of free time to hunt.

At the Hermitage Plantation, a higher percentage of "undesirable" parts of the domestic animal were found at the slave quarters than at the master's house (Thomas 1998). However, what twentieth-century archaeologists believe to be "undesirable" pieces of meat may not have been the same for eighteenth- and nineteenth-century slaves. In fact, there are today some animal parts that are regional favorites associated with an ethnic group, which would be considered "undesirable" by people living in other regions of North America. Therefore, I question the ability of archaeologists to know what were considered "undesirable" animal parts.

Perhaps the most notable feature of North American slave-master interactions is that, whether intentional or not, slaves were not permitted their own material culture, partly as the visual effects of overall domination by another group (Wheaton and Garrow 1985). I suggest this was an attempt to exert more complete control over African American slaves. It was one way the dominant Euroamerican masters denied slaves their cultural autonomy. This can be found in other parts of the world where slaves were completely dominated by a different ethnic or cultural group. In southern Africa, there are few sites interpreted as forager occupations that have a similar virtual absence of hunter-gatherer artifacts (exceptions do occur in areas excavated by Hall and Smith 1998; Sadr, Chapter 2, or Wadley 1996).

While African American slaves were not completely passive in their position and anthropologists have demonstrated the presence of goods being made and sold in a market by and for slaves (Singleton 1998; Thomas 1998), their actual autonomy was limited. At the same time, African American slavery is a clear case of one group being dominated, assimilated, and enslaved by another. The material correlates of this type of intergroup interaction are quite distinct and are visible in the archaeological record. Specifically, there is an overwhelming amount of the dominant group's mundane material culture mixed in with a few indigenous objects that were permitted or, if not, had been hidden from their masters. Further discussion of the material culture of slavery is beyond the scope of this chapter.

Central African Pygmy-Villager Interaction and Material Culture

Efe Pygmies have a symbiotic relationship with their farming neighbors. Efe women spend six months or more working in the gardens of the Lese in exchange for domesticated plants (Fisher 1986; for other Pygmy groups, see Köhler and Lewis, Chapter 11). Most carbohydrates in the Efe diet are procured this way. Efe men and women assist villagers in clearing and planting new gardens. The "bulk of their caloric intake is in the form of cultivated food acquired in exchange from Balese villagers. Metal tools, cooking utensils and clothing and manufactured items are also acquired from villagers" (Peacock 1985:45–46). Efe men hunt for the Lese, and much of the meat is given away for clothing, metal, and other nonforest products. "Over half of the meat eaten by Lese comes from Efe to whom they give cultivated food or material goods in return" (Bailey 1985:44). Each Efe group considers itself to belong to a Lese villager, a relationship that is often, although not necessarily, inherited from father to son. Both groups speak languages from the same linguistic family (Hewlett 1996:219). Efe and Lese also perform certain ceremonies together, such as boys' initiations (Hewlett 1996). The Efe spend approximately seven months of the year living near the villagers. During the other five months, they rarely travel more than an eight-hour walk away from the villages (Bailey 1985:46). Efe and Lese intergroup interaction is very intricate and is essential to both groups. Unlike the North American slaves, the Efe maintain some group and cultural autonomy, but not as much as many Kalahari hunter-gatherers.

The material culture assemblage of the Efe reflects a strong interdependency on Lese villagers (Table 3.1). Over 50 percent of Efe artifacts are Lese in origin, meaning they were either borrowed, lent, or purchased from the villagers, rather than collected, acquired, or manufactured directly by the Efe. Another perspective is gained by viewing the number of artifact categories from one group present at another's camp (such as a hunting gear, clothing, pots, etc., Table 3.1). Again, the Efe material culture categories are dominated by categories acquired directly from the Lese villagers, but not to the same extent as were the categories of material culture of the African American slaves. At the same time, the Efe build houses that are culturally distinct. They live in round grass huts that contrast significantly from the village wood and mud rectangular houses. Only acculturated Pygmies build rectangular grass huts, which still differ architecturally from the large structures inhabited by the villagers. In contrast, the African American slaves' houses differed from their masters' more in size and complexity than in substance.

Ju/'hoansi and Central Kalahari Hunter-Gatherer/Agropastoralist Interactions and Material Culture

Two different Kalahari hunter-gatherer groups—Ju/'hoansi from Ngamiland and Central Kalahari Basarwa from Kutse—illustrate some of the cultural diversity present among southern African foraging societies. The Ju/'hoansi (formerly known as !Kung) did not interact much with either Europeans or Bantu-speakers until the twentieth century (Lee, Chapter 7 and 1979; Lee and Guenther 1991, 1993). Contrary to what has been claimed (Schrire 1980), the Ju/'hoansi never represented a marginal impoverished pastoralist group under the domination of the Bantu-speaking Batswana. Their autonomy is visible both culturally and material cultur-ally (Tables 3.1, 3.2). Ju/'hoansi were autonomous with a distinctive culture, includ-ing a distinct language, that differed from that of their nonforaging neighbors. Beginning in the early 1970s, some Ju/'hoansi moved in order to be closer to nearby Herero Bantu agropastoralists' camps, as is described by Draper (1975a, 1975b). By the 1990s, the Ju/'hoansi could no longer be described as hunter-gatherers. Instead they practiced an opportunistic mixed subsistence strategy, which was influenced by their interactions with the Herero or Batswana Bantu speakers (Draper and Kranichfeld 1990; e.g., hunting for Bantu-speakers with borrowed horses and guns; earning wages with which to purchase food, etc.).

A different group of hunter-gatherers representing several central and eastern Kalahari dialects lived at Kutse, a recently sedentary community. They interacted with Bantu-speaking Bakgalagadi for 1,000 to 2,000 years. However, instead of the foragers adopting the Bantu culture, the Bakgalagadi, whose totem was the hyena (Okihiro 1976), adopted much of the Kalahari hunter-gatherer culture (Kent, in prep.). Interestingly, the first group of Bakgalagadi that moved to the Kalahari pos-sessed only small livestock, as cattle were unable to live without year-round water. Like the hunter-gatherers, they relied heavily on hunted game for meat and wild plants for vegetables. Later waves of the Bakgalagadi were goat and cattle agropas-toralists, with different totems than the hyena. They established large villages on the periphery of the Kalahari, such as near Molepolole or Tsodilo Hills, Botswana. I suggest that these cattle pastoralists were able to use the Kalahari year-round only after boreholes were drilled in the early to mid-twentieth century and not before. The village Bakgalagadi tried to dominate all local Kalahari peoples, including the rural Bakgalagadi of the hyena totem. I have proposed elsewhere (Kent 1998a) that village Bakgalagadi and hunter-gatherers were autonomous societies interacting through trade. Cultural boundary-maintenance mechanisms kept the groups sep-arate. Cultural autonomy was maintained several ways, one of which was mutual ethnocentrism—each harboring beliefs that the other was inferior. Basarwa hunter-gatherers and village Bakgalagadi maintained distinctively different archi-tecture, spatial patterning, language, beliefs, sociopolitical organization, sharing ethos, and material culture. These different traits helped maintain cultural bound-aries and reinforced their autonomy. Because intergroup interaction is not static, Bantu-speakers and hunter-gatherer interactions changed dramatically after Euro-pean contact. Changes varied by location and group. These changes were much less substantial in the Kalahari and did not affect the Nharo until the early to mid 1900s, the Ju/'hoansi until the 1980s, and Kutse until the 1990s.

A comparison of a similar number of recently abandoned Kutse, Ju/'hoansi, and Efe camps demonstrates that the nature of interactions between groups is directly reflected in their material culture and faunal remains. The percentage of Ju/'hoansi functional categories directly obtained from agropastoralists was 27.73 percent. This figure is well below the 73.08 percent of the villager's categories found at the Efe Pygmies' camps. Also unlike the Efe material culture assemblage, only 1.00 percent of the absolute numbers of objects at abandoned Ju/'hoansi camps in the 1960s were directly Bantu in origin. Similarly, Kutse camps only contained, on average, 37.21 percent of Bantu categories and 26.81 percent of Bantu-acquired objects (Tables 3.1, 3.2). Furthermore, both the Ju/'hoansi in Yellen's study (1977) and the Kutse Basarwa in my study occupied very different types of houses compared to the dominant village Bantu-speakers (grass huts or small windbreaks versus mud huts, respectively). Bantu and Basarwa also had different subsistence procurements, languages, and religious ideologies.

Another method used to dominate groups is forcing them to adhere to mobility and settlement patterns that resemble those of the dominant society. Mobility is particularly discouraged by oppressors because it allows individuals to escape domination, taxes, forced labor, and other forms of subjugation. North American slaves were not permitted to leave or stay as they pleased, whereas, until 1998, Kalahari hunter-gatherers were free to live wherever they wanted. I am not aware of any evidence of foragers being forced to live near pastoralists in southern Africa so they could be watched and controlled by Bantu-speakers. In contrast, European colonists did try to resettle indigenous peoples near missions and move them off of desirable land. The view that in most parts of southern Africa foragers were autonomous until colonization by Europeans is reinforced by their mobility patterns, material culture assemblages, wild animal and plant remains, and architecture. Colonization primarily occurred only in the areas deemed suitable for habitation by the encroaching settlers who sought good farmland and pastures (as in the Ghanzi area, see Guenther, Chapter 5). Consequently, indigenous Basarwa groups practicing a very different type of subsistence in areas perceived as unfavorable by the Europeans and Bantu-speaking agropastoralists were spared the subjection suffered by hunter-gatherers elsewhere (e.g., see Chapter 6). Later, after the incursion of European colonists, foragers occupying specific regions unpopular with Westerners, and their economy and technology also remained autonomous. Other evidence for continual autonomy includes the fact that many foragers maintained their distinct languages long after European contact (by contrast, African American slaves were forced to learn English). Autonomy in ideology/religious expressions is evident in the rock art depicting hunter-gatherer motifs dated after the Bantu arrival in southern Africa (however, there are many unanswerable questions surrounding the rock art in southern Africa; for example, it is not definitely known when rock painting died out).

I agree with many of the criticisms of material culture studies used to study inter-group interactions (Stein 1998). However, not all are universally valid or germane to the data presented in this chapter because intercultural interactions have many dimensions, not all of which are visible in the material culture alone. I concentrate in Chapter 6 on changes in the social, political, economic, religious, and ideological realms of cultures resulting from different types of intercultural interactions. In this chapter I focus on changes in material culture and subsistence as a result of intercultural relationships. Below, and with few exceptions, I suggest that the southern African archaeological record does *not* support interpretations of enslavement or even client relationships between most hunter-gatherers and herders, until the colonization by Westerners. Even after European contact, hunter-gatherers residing outside the Cape Province led a relatively autonomous existence (but not totally isolated or uninformed). One example is Sadr's (Chapter 2) description of autonomous forager and agropastoralist interaction in eastern Botswana only a hundred years ago.

As noted in Chapter 6, the nature of interactions between hunter-gatherers and Bantu-speakers prior to Western colonization is not well known. Whether the Bantu had slaves and if the slavery was as extreme as European/Euroamerican slavery is questionable. Since much of the ethnohistoric literature discusses the Batswana and other Bantu groups domineering the Bakgalagadi, serfdom did not necessarily extend to the more mobile hunter-gatherers. I suggest that the selling of hunter-gatherers and Khoi herders into slavery may have been a response to the European's needs and use of slaves. The first Dutch settlers imported slaves from other parts of Africa until they realized how much easier and less costly it was to enslave the local peoples (Kent, Chapter 6). The settlers employed Bantu and Khoi to obtain slaves for them. In addition, the influx of exotic Western goods increased the Bantu's need for tribute and trade items used to procure the desirable objects. As a result, hunter-gatherers (and Bakgalagadi) were forced into servitude to meet the colonists' demands for forced labor and to allow dominant native groups to obtain the new intriguing material culture introduced by the Europeans.

Agropastoralists forcing specifically hunter-gatherers into slavery is not supported by the archaeological record in most areas. Its validity, I suggest, is questionable prior to European colonization. Instead, I propose that the majority of hunter-gatherer and agropastoralist societies interacted either autonomously through trade or similarly to the Pygmy-and-villager symbiotic relationship. Perhaps most important is to recognize the diversity of intergroup interactions that occurred prehistorically and historically in southern Africa. Even though the material expression of domination, symbiosis, and autonomy were detailed above based on only four separate examples, there are a variety of hunter-gatherer societies around the world that interacted with horticultural, pastoral, or other societies without being enslaved, as the following examples demonstrate.

NON-AFRICAN HUNTER-GATHERER/FARMER INTERACTIONS

Through the study of the Indian Birhor, we can see the importance of examining material culture between culturally distinct groups more critically than has been done in southern Africa. While the Birhor foragers of northeastern India were dependent on neighboring villagers' cultigens (Smiley 1979/1980), analogous to the Efe, their symbiotic relationship was not visible in the Birhor material culture assemblage. Wild products collected by the Birhor were exchanged for villager-produced objects and food (Smiley 1979/1980:158). Instead of showing a symbiotic relationship, abandoned Birhor camps were dominated by objects traded from villagers (Smiley 1979/1980). One reason for this domination was merely preservation. The farmers' material culture was more durable than the hunter-gatherers' and had a higher chance of being preserved in the archaeological record. Differences in preservation incorrectly suggested a dependence by the hunter-gatherers on the farmers' objects without showing the equal dependence of the farmers on the foragers (Smiley 1979/1980). The actual symbiotic forager/villager relationship was masked by differential preservation. This is relevant to prehistoric southern Africa where Bantu-speakers' ceramics, iron, and architecture were much more likely to preserve than hunter-gatherers' material culture. In addition, sedentary people tend to have significantly higher frequencies of artifacts than more mobile peoples, again skewing the numbers of objects associated with each group (Kent 1993). I posit that the problem of preservation, and the differences in object abundance associated with sedentary versus mobile peoples, is not unique to the Birhor. In southern Africa, the material culture and architecture of the hunter-gatherers also are less archaeologically visible than those of the sedentary Bantu-speakers and Europeans. This creates the false belief that dependency was always unidirectional, or even that foragers had been culturally exterminated in many regions (Kent 1990).

Cultural preservation and boundary maintenance in multicultural regions throughout the world has similarities. Both Birhor and African hunter-gatherers were perceived as inferior by farming/pastoralist villagers. Just as the Bantu and later the European colonists conceived of African hunter-gatherers, Birhor hunter-gatherers were thought to be wild or primitive savages. This was one means to maintain separate cultural boundaries. Village farmers looked down on the Birhor hunter-gatherers while at the same time needing their wild products from the forests (Smiley 1979/1980). The shamanistic skills of the foragers were requested by villagers, despite their disdain of the former (Smiley 1979/1980). Birhor hunter-gatherers manipulated the cultural constraints on interaction with the farmers and used mobility to maintain and reinforce their cultural integrity (Smiley 1979/1980:159). I suggest that the same strategies, particularly mobility among those who were nomadic, were used by the southern African hunter-gatherers to maintain their cultural boundaries and to avoid complete domination. African American slaves, in contrast, could not use mobility to escape their masters and maintain an autonomous existence (although, of course, some did try to run away).

It is fallacious to think that whenever two groups with different cultures interact, one automatically dominates, acculturates, or overpowers the other, even if one group believes they do. The spread of Western culture modified prehistoric intergroup boundary maintenance and control. It is beyond the scope of this chapter to list every hunter-gatherer society that has survived immigrating groups in prehistory. Many maintained their autonomy, as is visible in the diversity of their built environments, material cultures, behaviors, and ideologies *until* domination and colonization by a nation-state. By presenting a few examples, I hope to have demonstrated that many of the assumptions about southern African hunter-gatherer and agropastoralist interactions are suspect or at least cannot be proven with the data currently used to assert claims of dependence or enslavement. What then can we infer about prehistoric pastoralist and hunter-gatherer intercultural relations in southern Africa?

Although obviously not totally comparable to North American slaves dominated by Euroamericans, serfdom in southern Africa would, I anticipate, have a similar material culture signature. There would be, I suggest, an overwhelming number of nonforager artifacts and categories, as well as a majority of domesticated versus wild animal and plant remains at enslaved or assimilated hunter-gatherers' sites. In contrast to North American slave quarters where most bones found were from domesticated animals, only 10 percent of the identifiable faunal assemblage at abandoned Kutse camps was from domestic animals, primarily goat/sheep (Table 3.2). The absence of any domesticated animal bones at the highly mobile Ju/'hoansi summer camps located away from boreholes was partly because the summer camps were not located where Ju/'hoansi would have had access to domesticated animals. I suggest that the percentage of wild faunal remains at the Ju/'hoansi winter aggregated camp would have resembled the percentage at Kutse. That is, the Kutse pattern of 90 percent of all bones from wild fauna is more generalizable to autonomous hunter-gatherer sites than the Ju/'hoansi figure of 100 percent. Compare this figure to clearly agropastoralist sites, such as the Khami Hill Ruin site in Zimbabwe where 90.17 percent of all bones came from domesticated species (Thorp 1984:270), or the Early Iron Age site of KwaGandaganda where 98.83 percent of all bones were from domesticated species (Whitelaw 1994:43). Had hunter-gatherers been enslaved, I would expect frequencies over 60–70 percent of domesticated animal and plant remains for each category. One reason is that slaves are usually too busy working for their masters to have time to hunt or collect wild plants.

The wild animal bones located at pastoralists' sites and the increase in the number of lithic scrapers found at both forager and agropastoralist sites through time are not indicative of slavery or even of symbiosis. Changes in the frequency of scrapers at agropastoralist camps do not necessarily imply hunter-gatherers forced into servitude scraping hides at their neighbors' sites. It is possible that processed hides were the medium hunter-gatherers used for trade. Nowhere is there evidence that the hides were obligatory for hunter-gatherers to give to their neighbors. In fact, the presence of a relatively small percentage of agropastoralists' objects and domestic animal remains at forager sites supports the trade explanation for the increase in scrapers more than it does the slave or assimilation explanations. The common belief that hunter-gatherers provided all, or even most, of the game for the agropastoralists is not supported by the data. There is no evidence to suggest that agropastoralists did not hunt. To the contrary, agropastoralists have been ethnographically documented to hunt wild animals in southern Africa (e.g., Schapera 1984; Solway 1989, personal communication). Ethnohistoric records document that Khoi herders also hunted for their own game meat. As a result, there needs to be some empirical counterargument before assuming that Khoi or Bantu neighbors were *not* responsible for the introduction of much of the wild fauna remains at their sites. There is no reason to assume that only hunter-gatherers prehistorically scraped hides of domestic or wild animals using stone scrapers. There is nothing prohibiting agropastoralists from tanning and scraping hides of domestic or wild animals themselves.

We can also examine what is *not* present at camps, as well as what is. For example, I would expect more evidence of iron and other objects originating from the pastoralists at prehistoric assimilated hunter-gatherer sites. Sites occupied by assimilated people should closely resemble those to whom they assimilated. In several rockshelter sites thought to have been inhabited by hunter-gatherer serfs of the Bantu-speakers, none to very little iron is found (Tables 3.4–3.7). The few pieces of iron located at prehistoric hunter-gatherer sites can be accounted for by occasional intercultural trade (Wiessner 1977, 1990). The above shows that sites inhabited by assimilated or enslaved former foragers should have more pottery, iron, domestic animal bones, and cultivated plant remains. Even the Efe, who had an integrated symbiotic relationship with villagers, had over 50 percent of their objects originating directly from the Lese. How do we translate this information so that it is useful in interpreting the archaeological record of southern Africa?

INTERPRETING ETHNOHISTORIC INTERCULTURAL RELATIONS

If we try to determine who the early Western explorers in the 1600s and 1700s were describing when they wrote of local peoples in southern Africa, there should have been at least three or four different cultural groups as possibilities: (1) the Khoi herders, (2) hunter-gatherers, (3) Bantu-speaking agropastoralists, and (4) a combination of Khoi and hunter-gatherers unknowingly undifferentiated. The latter undifferentiated group was larger than many anthropologists suspect because in some cases Europeans could only distinguish the Bantu-speakers as distinct from all other native groups, who they often categorized as a single culture. Sometimes physical similarities and the use of a click language were sufficient to erroneously group Khoi herders with hunter-gatherers. I do not think the ambiguity of the naming of cultural groups is taken into consideration enough when anthropologists read the early explorers and missionaries' narratives. Hesse (1997:7) noted: "it is clear that the terminology used to describe the new members of the Berlin Lutheran congregations in the Western Cape, changed from to time. Also, the terminology used by individual missionaries changed from time to time." During the 1860s, a cultural appellation was sometimes used to designate people as impoverished, low social/political status, native peoples (Hesse 1997:6–8). The "term 'Hottentot' was used to describe people of a lower economic or social status. Prietsch thus described the village next to his new mission station . . . as a 'Hottentot village' since the dwellings consisted of huts; not houses. Thus, people were also classified in ethnographic terms by their material culture" (Hesse 1997:7).

Therefore, the terms *Hottentot* and *Bushmen* in ethnohistoric documents did not, according to Hesse (1997), necessarily specify the culturally and economically distinct groups of hunter-gatherers and Khoi herders. However, many anthropologists assume the labels did specify separate groups. Stuart suggests that "it may be that the history of the Cape has been written with too much of an acceptance that missionary accounts portrayed 'what actually happened'" (1995:116). Until 1815 there was no specific reference to hunter-gatherers who were all referred to as "Hottentots," particularly if they worked on a farm, in the administrative surveys of indigenous peoples, or in official legislation (Szalay 1995:99). As early as 1828, Cape hunter-gatherers "were already considered Hottentots, from whom they were by now indistinguishable" (Szalay 1995:103). This makes distinguishing the Khoi and hunter-gatherers problematic when archaeologists rely on the ethnohistoric sources for their evidence of impoverished herders who lost their stock or hunter-gatherers who had acquired stock (e.g., see Bollong and Sampson n.d.).

As a consequence of the known unreliability of the use of terms that are today cultural markers—"Hottentot" for Khoi herders and "Bushmen" for hunter-gatherers—anthropologists must first prove, rather than just assume, how the term *Bushman* was being used by each explorer. After all, unless Khoi herders had their stock with them or were living in Khoi dwellings, how would an explorer differentiate between Khoi on a hunting or collecting trip (we know Khoi hunted) and autonomous hunter-gatherers? Explorers and missionaries would have had to have been fluent in the different languages to be able to distinguish the groups correctly. To which group did an explorer refer when he chronicled that people were hunter-gatherers who had adopted goats versus Khoi who had lost their goats (as some of the explorers claimed)? I suggest that anthropologists cannot know. Why then take the colonizers' cultural labels literally?

It can be misleading to uncritically accept ethnohistorical sources as correct and to then use them to interpret the archaeological record. For example, in a letter written in 1779, Gordon described people "whom he called 'inlanders' and Bushmen" (Bollong, Smith, and Sampson 1997:278). It is impossible to know whom Gordon referred to as "inlanders" or "Bushmen." Another example is Dunn's description of the use of pots in Bushmanland in 1872 made by "pure Bushman people," who were still using "their own pottery" (quoted in Bollong, Smith, and Sampson 1997:279–280). What "own" signifies to Dunn cannot be determined. The term might mean simply that the "Bushmen" were using non-Western pottery, such as pottery traded from the Bantu and now "owned" by the Bushmen.

There is limited ethnographic evidence to support the claim that the ceramic pots were an important marker of intercultural trade. An / Xam-speaking former hunter-gatherer said that pots were used in gift exchanges (Bleek and Lloyd 1911:375). Trade or gift exchange was observed throughout the nineteenth and twentieth century among culturally different groups in South Africa. That pots were mentioned in his group's folklore only indicates that pots were present, not who made the pots or how they were obtained. I do not imply any static customs through thousands of years, but Kutse hunter-gatherers in the Kalahari reported that they never made pottery; it was always obtained from local Bakgalagadi through trade, usually of hides (Kent 1988–1995 fieldnotes). What this means is that archaeologists cannot assume what the presence of dissimilar pottery styles at sites mean, but must demonstrate that their favored inference is the one best supported by the data (i.e., test multiple, competing hypotheses, not just one). Until archaeologists can distinguish between ceramic types as denoting different cultures (i.e., pastoralist-made pots or hunter-gatherer-produced pots), or functional differences (used for different tasks or types of cooking, etc.), ceramic variability cannot be reliably interpreted.

In many cases, though not necessarily all, I think that we cannot demonstrate what the explorer meant or to which group he was referring. I suggest saying we do not know the cultural affinity of many of the people referred to as Khoi or Bushmen by early explorers is better than saying we do know when we are really just guessing. I recommend that anthropologists not use the cultural epithets employed by early explorers, missionaries, and others, unless there is some way to know what the terms and categories meant to the individual authors, and whether the labels were accurately applied.

PREHISTORIC HUNTER-GATHERER SITE INTERPRETATIONS IN SOUTHERN AFRICA

Employing the method described by Sadr (1997), it may be possible to distinguish the sites of autonomous hunter-gatherers who had little to no interaction with their

Bantu neighbors from those of hunter-gatherers who had some relationship with "others" but not necessarily an adversarial or inferior one. Sadr suggests (1997:107–108) that the number of ceramics to the number of lithics plus sherds differs significantly at hunter-gatherer sites compared to agropastoralist sites. Known hunter-gatherer sites that were occupied by autonomous foragers not living near agropastoralists tend to have high formal tools and low ceramic indices compared to the same indices at herder-hunter sites, probably Khoi, and to Iron Age sites, probably inhabited by Bantu-speaking agropastoralists (Smith et al. 1998).

The difficulty with these indices is that we do not know why such variation should exist. There is no theoretical basis for the correlation between autonomy and the percentage of formal tools. Is the relationship causal or spurious? Perhaps a better measure is the percentage of sherds in the artifact assemblage. Based on ethnoarchaeological and ethnohistorical research, slaves would have a very high percentage of their oppressors' artifacts, hunter-gatherers in symbiotic relationships would have a high percentage of their partners' artifacts, autonomous foragers in direct trade relationships would have a moderate to low percentage, and those in indirect trade relationships, a very low percentage.

Sites located at /Xai/Xai and Dobe, large pans far into the Kalahari, about 140 km from Tsodilo Hills, were interpreted by Wilmsen and Denbow as showing that Ju/'hoansi hunter-gatherers and their ancestors were poor pastoralists lacking cattle (Wilmsen and Denbow 1990; Denbow 1984, 1986). Sadr (1997), reanalyzing the published data using his indices, demonstrated that the sites were inhabited by autonomous hunter-gatherers who occasionally had direct or indirect trade with agropastoralists. Brooks and Yellen also interpret these sites as documenting the long history and prehistory of autonomous foragers occupying these areas (Yellen et al. 1987). Even if the few bones purported to be from a cow by Wilmsen and Denbow (1990 and elsewhere) at a few sites found near Dobe, really are from a cow, what do 3 bones from domestic stock mean when they are found amidst hundreds of wild faunal remains? There are far too few domesticated animal remains at these sites to indicate that the Ngamiland hunter-gatherers were anything other than autonomous foragers, with occasional and minimal interaction with agropastoralists, probably in the form of indirect or direct trade. The few possible cow bones (none are definitely identified as *Bos*) and the presence of a few nonlocal objects do not validate the revisionists' scenario that foragers abandoned hunting and gathering at Dobe and elsewhere to become serfs of the agropastoralists thousands of years ago. According to Smith (1996:13), the /Xai/Xai sites have, at most, a few possible cattle bones, no goat remains, only small numbers of potsherds and pieces of iron, and large numbers of stone tools. Obviously, if there were such a profound economic transformation from autonomous foragers to enslaved herders, there should be archaeologically visible changes in the artifacts at sites through time (Sadr 1997).

However, when restudied, the artifacts from /Xai/Xai showed that "the pivotal site in Denbow and Wilmsen's argument about Bushman encapsulation, shows hardly any material change from its oldest to youngest levels" (Sadr 1997:109).

There are probable agropastoralist sites within what today are the margins of the Kalahari. It is likely that the border of the Kalahari shifted through time, depending on the drought cycle (Chapter 1) and on yearly rainfall (Yellen et al. 1987; Smith 1996; Lee, Chapter 7). In fact, only sites in the well-watered areas of Tsodilo Hills of Botswana or on the fringe of the Kalahari contain cattle and goat bones, iron and copper tools, glass trade beads, and some stone tools (Smith 1996). I suggest that there is no reason to suspect that the Tsodilo Hills sites, with many domestic animal bones and Bantu-associated artifacts, represent assimilated foragers *and not* agropastoralists herding deeper into the Kalahari during periods of favorable climatic regimes.

THE INTERRELATIONSHIP BETWEEN SOUTHERN AFRICAN PREHISTORIC HUNTER-GATHERERS AND AGROPASTORALISTS OUTSIDE OF THE KALAHARI

Early and Late Iron Age Bantu sites throughout Botswana and South Africa are distinctly and unambiguously agropastoralist sites, with evidence of iron smelting, corrals, social and gendered division of space, and an abundance of domestic animal bones and plant remains (e.g., Hall 1998). Hunter-gatherer sites are in sharp contrast to the larger, more architecturally and spatially segregated Early and Late Iron Age Bantu sites. As noted above, sites occupied by assimilated peoples are similar to those of the group to whom they assimilated. The reason that the agropastoralist sites are so startlingly different from the hunter-gatherer sites is because they reflect occupations by distinct, autonomous cultures. If not, the artifact assemblages would look more similar to one another.

Enslaved peoples are often not permitted their own distinct material culture as a means of domination, as discussed above. The percentage of sherds in the total artifact assemblage and the number of formal tools and/or scrapers in the lithic inventory may reflect the nature of interaction as archaeologists purport (e.g., Sadr 1997; Smith et al. 1991). However, I do not understand the basis for using the percentage of scrapers to formal tools or to the entire lithic assemblage as an indicator of forced labor by dominated hunter-gatherers who processed hides for the agropastoralists (Table 3.3). The differences could likely represent different time periods or the same group performing different activities. In contrast, the percentage of sherds reflects the intensity of the interactions because it represents trade between autonomous or symbiotic cultures. Moreover, ceramics also are items that could potentially be used in an asymmetric power relationship, as we saw above with the case of the African

Table 3.3

Objects from Middle Stone Age (MSA) Sites

Artifacts	Wolfberg WB/9 Open Koppie MSA	Sehonghong Rockshelter Level MSA 9	Sehonghong Rockshelter Level MSA 6	Sehonghong Rockshelter Level MSA 5	Sehonghong Rockshelter Level MSA 3
Total number of flaked lithic artifacts, including flakes	1,192	4,864	4,646	13,316	1,435
Number of formal tools	22	11	17	15	8
Percentage of formal tools in the entire flaked artifact assemblage	1.85	0.23	0.37	0.11	0.56
Number of scrapers	5	5	8	5	3
Percentage of scrapers in formal flaked tools	22.73	45.46	47.06	33.33	37.50

Wolfberg is in South Africa and Sehonghong is in Lesotho (Wolfberg data from Manhire 1987; Sehonghong from Carter, Mitchell, and Vinnicombe 1988).

American slaves' Euroamerican-dominated culture. An increase in the percentage of scrapers at forager sites has also been interpreted as evidence of hunter-gatherer tribute payments to agropastoralists. Similarly, the presence of an increase in scrapers at some agropastoralist sites has been suggested to represent subservient foragers forced to process hides at the Bantu encampments.

To assess these statistics as measures of subjugation, I examined a number of sites. Table 3.3 lists the indices at a Middle Stone Age site where there cannot have been dominated hunter-gatherers or tribute. We know that Bantu agropastoralists, Khoi herders, and cattle were not present during the Middle Stone Age in South Africa and, therefore, there are no ceramics or domesticated faunal remains at these sites. The percentage of scrapers to formal flaked tools ranges by site and occupational level from 22.7 percent to 47.1 percent (Table 3.3). The percentage of formal tools to the total lithic assemblage ranges from 0.2 percent to 1.9 percent. More recent, but still before the arrival of Bantu-speakers, formal tools from the Late Stone Age levels at Tloutle Rockshelter make up from 0.5 percent to 0.8 percent of the entire stone tool assemblage (last 2 columns in Table 3.4). The percentage of scrapers to formal tools in the pre-Bantu, Late Stone Age levels ranges from

90 percent to 91 percent. These figures change dramatically during the Iron Age when the first agropastoralists migrated into southern Africa.

At the nearby Muela Rockshelter site and at the most recent level at Tloutle, the percentage of scrapers to formal tools ranges from 54.8 percent to 61.3 percent (Kaplan 1993; Mitchell 1993). If the frequency of scrapers represents tribute or forced labor, the percentage of formal tools should be the opposite of what it is at both sites. The sharp drop in scrapers, from 90 percent or 91 percent before the agropastoralist appearance in southern Africa to 55 percent to 61 percent after their arrival, also casts doubts on the interpretation that the percentage of scrapers is indicative of forced hide preparation. Fewer scrapers in the formal tool category contradicts the revisionist assumption that hunter-gatherers were dominated by agropastoralists almost 2,000 years ago. The lower percentage of scrapers at these sites does not indicate that hunter-gatherers had a client or similarly disadvantaged relationship with agropastoralists.

The sherds present in the postcontact levels at these rockshelters obviously were acquired in trade. However, the significance of trade and interaction with the Bantu was slight. The number of sherds is so few, from 0.01 percent to 0.4 percent of the assemblage, that it is clear they were acquired by autonomous hunter-gatherers. The paucity of other nonlocal objects, such as glass and iron, ranged from none to 23 pieces, which again indicates either indirect or direct trade (Table 3.4).

The frequency of scrapers varied so much among the 19 stratigraphic levels at the Late Stone Age preagropastoralist site of Byneskranskop that I question whether it was seasonality or site function that substantially impacted their distribution, rather than tribute or serfdom. The top level at Byneskranskop is Early Iron Age, which is the period when the agropastoralists first settled in southern Africa. Their interaction with hunter-gatherers was trade between autonomous societies (probably in some cases, including Khoi herders). Autonomy is demonstrated in the top level at Byneskranskop where the percentage of sherds in the assemblage is only 0.03 percent, again an indication of trade and not domination.

Although not every Iron Age hunter-gatherer site can be examined here, most do not indicate enslavement or even a disadvantaged client-patron relationship. For example, dates "from both the Borchers Shelter and Umbeli Belli [archaeological sites located in the Natal, South Africa] . . . indicate that hunter-gatherer occupation and exploitation of the coastal belt continued up to at least the eighteenth century, [even though] . . . Umbeli Belli is occupied almost contemporaneously with the Later Iron Age site of Mpambanyoni" (Cable 1984:76). Table 3.5 shows that the percentage of scrapers to formal tools at the four rockshelter sites Cable excavated ranges from 32.6 percent to 64 percent. Scrapers make up over 60 percent of the formal tools at the Bottoms Up site, which some may argue indicates dependence. However, the preagropastoralist levels at Tloutle and Byneskranskop

Table 3.4

Two Lesotho Rockshelter Sites

Artifacts	Muela Layers 1–3	Muela Layers 4–5	Tloutle Mid–Late Holocene[a]	Tloutle Early Holocene	Tloutle Terminal Pleistocene
Total number of flaked lithic artifacts, including flakes	23,782	8,613	122,833	33,286	1,194
Number of formal tools	445	108	647	167	10
Percentage of formal tools in the entire flaked artifact assemblage	1.87	1.25	0.53	0.50	0.84
Percentage of scrapers in formal flaked tools	54.83	59.26	61.36	91.02	90.00
Ostrich eggshell beads	14	4	144	—	—
Ostrich eggshell fragments	5	5	494	594	21
Number of ceramic sherds	21	1	524	1	—
Bone points, shafts, and tools	12	1	17	1	—
Percentage of sherds in total lithics and ceramics	0.09	0.01	0.43	N.A.	—
Glass, metal, plastic / ochre, or other pigment	23 / —	— / —	2 / 20	— / 2	— / —
Number of domesticated fauna bones / percentage of bone assemblage	[b]	[b]	65 / 2.94	— / 0.0	— / 0.0

[a]Surface artifacts were not included for the Tloutle Rockshelter because the author indicated it had been disturbed (Mitchell 1993).

[b]Faunal report for Muela Rockshelter was not available.

N.A. = too few objects to calculate a meaningful percentage.

Muela data from Kaplan 1993; Tloutle data from Mitchell 1993.

had 60 percent to 91 percent scrapers. In the assemblages of Grindstone and Umbeli Belli, sherds are, respectively, 1.44 percent and 6.18 percent, very small to suggest anything but independent trade (Table 3.5). The percent of formal tools at the sites excavated by Cable (1984) range from 1.3 percent to 7.6 percent, the lower figure being less than that at the Wolfberg Middle Stone Age site (Manhire 1987), when there were no Bantu in the region. These figures show that the percentage of formal tools in an assemblage is not related to time period, the presence of agropastoralists, or enslavement/autonomy.

Rockshelter sites occupied after herders migrated to the Western Cape coastal

area in South Africa circa 2,000–1,600 years ago are interpreted as evidence of foragers in a subordinate relationship with pastoralists (Jerardino Wiesenborn 1996:47,
51). The material culture, faunal remains, and settlement pattern changes occurring
after 2,000 years ago in the Western Cape are thought to have been caused by the
first series of migrations of stock owners who introduced domestic sheep along
with ceramics to the region. The interpretation of hunter-gatherer subaltern status
is based on the presence of less than 4 percent of 1,687 faunal remains identified as
domestic animals at Tortoise Cave and 1 percent of 500 faunal remains at Steenbokfontein Cave (Jerardino Wiesenborn 1996:169). With one exception, the domestic
animals were all sheep. That means that despite the faunal assemblages with 96 to
99 percent wild animals, hunter-gatherers are seen as subjugated (as based on number of bones and not number of individuals). The 31 sherds from Tortoise Cave are
viewed as further evidence of a client-patron relationship in an assemblage that includes 1,702 lithic artifacts, pieces of worked and decorated ostrich eggshells,
modified wood, cordage, chunks of pigment, ornaments made of various materials,
and worked marine shell (Jerardino Wiesenborn 1996). No sherds were uncovered
at Steenbokfontein Cave.

In another attempt to study the complex relations in southern Africa, Thorp
(1997) examined two post–European-contact rockshelter sites in the Eastern Free
State occupied during the mid-1800s. She proposes that Westbury Rockshelter was
occupied by autonomous foragers whereas Rooikrans was occupied by subservient
hunter-gatherers dominated by agropastoralists. The main reasons for her interpretations are the larger number of ceramic sherds and species of domesticated plants
at Rooikrans than at Westbury (Thorp 1997:252). The artifact assemblage and botanical remains, examined from the perspective presented in this chapter (and entire
book), indicate autonomous foragers. Beyond the extreme differences in the number of objects, probably indicating a longer occupation at Rooikrans than at Westbury, the sites are fairly similar. For example, the percentage of formal tools in the
rest of the lithic assemblage ranges from 3.9 to 5.7 percent at Rooikrans and 5.1 to 8.3
percent at Westbury (Table 3.7). Perhaps because of the differences in overall assemblage size, the percentage of scrapers is higher at Westbury than at Rooikrans. This
is counter to what would be expected if Rooikrans were occupied by clients processing hides for agropastoralist patrons. While Rooikrans has more species of domesticated plants, it also has more species of wild plants, another indication, I suggest,
of the longer occupation at Rooikrans (Table 3.9). As discussed in Chapter 6, the
Eastern Free State and Lesotho were areas in which hunter-gatherers retained their
autonomy longer than those living in the Cape because of later colonization. Missionaries and others describe the foragers as free people fighting against the colonists
for their land and wild animals. To me, the sites demonstrate the varied pace of
change after colonization and the autonomy of hunter-gatherers until they were

Table 3.5

Rockshelter Sites from the Natal Region of South Africa

RockshelterArtifacts	Borchers Layers 1+2	Borchers Layer 3	Bottoms Up	Grindstone	Umbeli Belli
Number of flaked lithic artifacts, with unworked flakes	29,277	13,763	3,564	686	11,020
Number of formal tools	524	196	147	52	138
Number of scrapers	303	98	94	17	68
Percentage of formal tools in the entire flaked artifact assemblage	1.79	1.42	4.13	7.58	1.25
Percentage of scrapers in formal flaked tools	57.82	50.00	63.95	32.69	49.28
Ostrich eggshell beads	—	—	—	30	3
Ostrich eggshell fragments	—	—	—	—	—
Number of ceramic sherds	5	—	3	10	726
Bone points, shafts, and tools	33	48	—	—	—
Percentage of sherds in total lithics and ceramics	0.00	—	0.00	1.44	6.18

All data from Cable 1984.

killed during the latter part of the 1800s (there were no autonomous foragers described in the area at the beginning of the 1900s). As Mazel (1981:89) wrote, Iron Age peoples in the southern Natal, South Africa, probably had "never posed any threat to San [hunter-gatherer] lifestyles, which may have persisted undisturbed until the arrival of the Whites." It was the arrival of Europeans, I suggest, that ushered in the demise of many hunter-gatherer societies in southern Africa, a topic discussed in Chapter 6.

The implicit assumption many archaeologists have is that hunter-gatherers cannot live next to a more sociopolitically complex group without being assimilated and/or enslaved. Whereas this certainly has occurred at times throughout the world, the question here is whether the data support the prevalent view that it occurred in southern Africa. For example, Smith (1998) describes the differences between two shell middens located near the coast of South Africa as demonstrating what he refers to as an almost universal marginalization of hunter-gatherers by agropastoralists. There are a number of assumptions in his proposition. One is that the coastal hunter-gatherers 3,000 and 300 years ago at the Witklip site were socially/politically less complex than the agropastoralists at the Kasteelberg site occupied between approximately 1,800 and 800 years ago. Nonegalitarian complex coastal hunter-gatherers are known ethnographically and archaeologically, which makes that assumption questionable. Smith's (1998) second assumption is that the presence of many sheep and seal bones and ceramics at Kasteelberg represents the omnipotent agropastoralists' settlement while the few sheep or seal bones and the predominance of antelope bones and tortoise remains, with few sherds present, represents the oppressed hunter-gatherers at the Witklip site. The conclusion reached is that foragers voluntarily acquiesced to agropastoralists' need for herders because they were unable to compete with the more wealthy cattle-owning Bantu, and that change through time can be interpreted as "the indicators of increased peripheralization of the hunter" (Smith 2001:123).

At other sites, foraging groups in the Western Cape who stored shellfish are interpreted as possibly having "undergone, to varying degrees, relatively fast assimilation into the incoming pastoralist society practicing a food-producing economy" (Jerardino Wiesenborn 1996:169). In addition the pastoralists could have induced ecological and social stress among the foragers. The interactions of other hunter-gatherer groups with pastoralists in the Western Cape Province were characterized as "involving loosely defined clientship with stock-owning groups, intermarriage, conflict and/or avoidance with pastoralist groups" (Jerardino Wiesenborn 1996:170).

If Iron Age agropastoralists usually won most battles with hunter-gatherers, despite having similar weapons, there should be more evidence of conflict than there is. Agropastoralist skeletons from five Iron Age sites in Zambia, Botswana, and South Africa indicate a relatively low amount of trauma. The low frequency of trauma that is present can occur from numerous causes not related to feuding, warfare, or violence of any kind. For example, at Mapungubwe only one individual out of 109 skeletons had evidence of trauma (Henneberg and Steyn 1955). Although based on nonrepresentative sample sizes too small to reliably interpret and on four sites from Zambia and Botswana spanning 400 years (from A.D. 900 to A.D. 1300), Murphy (1996) suggested that 25 percent of the men and 9 percent of the women had evidence of trauma (total number of individuals is 21). However, 14 of the total 35 skeletons could not be sexed and therefore were not included in her calculations of trauma (Murphy 1996:89). Perhaps a more reliable measure of the frequency of trauma is to compare the number of individual skeletal elements with and without evidence of traumatic injury. Only 0.4 percent of a total of 936 elements had injuries indicative of trauma (calculated from Murphy 1996:216; table 5.20). As the data indicate, I do not think southern Africa was enmeshed in continuous conflict as it was after colonization. The upheaval brought by the European settlers was because of the reasons I discuss in Chapter 6, none of which are relevant to intercultural relations prior to Western incursion.

Some archaeologists suggest that hunter-gatherer autonomy existed until the latter part of the Late Iron Age. Wadley (1996), for example, separates her excavations

Table 3.6

Subservience and Autonomy at Rooikrans and Westbury

Artifacts	Rooikrans Rockshelter		Westbury Rockshelter	
	Number	Percent	Number	Percent
Lithic tool categories (adze, scrapers, backed tools, borers, and size category differences)[a]	25		15	
Number of flaked lithic artifacts				
Level 1	371		27	
Level 2	2,039		18	
Level 3	1,206			
Percentage of formal tools/all flaked tools				
Level 1		5.7		6.8
Level 2		3.9		7.0
Level 3		4.9		
Number of scrapers				
Level 1	10		21	
Level 2	49		22	
Level 8	32			
Percentage of scrapers/formal tools				
Level 1		47.6		81.5
Level 2		63.6		78.6
Level 3		57.1		
Ground stone tools				
Level 1	2		1	
Level 2	7		5	
Level 3	3			
Species of domesticated plants[b]	4		2	
Species of wild plants	5		2	
Number of ceramic sherds	511		97	
Estimated ceramic vessels	30		"a few"	
Number of sherds divided by total number of lithics and ceramics	8.1		8.6	
Domestic animals	Present		Present	

Comparison of objects from two rockshelters located in southern Africa. Rooikrans is interpreted as representing hunter-gatherer subservient clients dominated by Bantu-speakers in contrast to autonomous hunter-gatherers at Westbury rockshelter. All data from Thorp 1997.

[a]Not all necessarily imply different functional usages, but categories were counted the same for both rockshelters.

[b]I did not know whether the gourd found in levels 2 and 3 at Rooikrans Rockshelter was a domestic or wild plant and therefore did not include it in these figures.

at Jubilee Shelter in the Eastern Free State, South Africa into Early Iron Age (1,840–1,350 years ago) and Late (less than 1,350 years ago). The percentage of scrapers in formal tools varies between 54 percent and 90.2 percent just within the Early Iron Age period (Table 3.6). While Wadley (1996) suggests that the Late Iron Age component of the site represents foragers in a client relationship with patron agropastoralists, the number of sherds in this level is extremely small, only 4.8 percent of the entire artifact assemblage (Table 3.6). To further complicate the task of identifying different cultures, the Late Iron Age part of Jubilee Shelter is located only 500 m from an agropastoralist site. It is impossible to know unambiguously whether the sites were occupied at the same time or a decade apart, but either way the end result would be the mingling of artifacts. Certainly direct co-occupation is not evident from any part of the artifact inventory, making it difficult to interpret (Table 3.6). Were these autonomous hunter-gatherers staying near an agropastoralist site during trading expeditions, or were agropastoralists reoccupying Jubilee Shelter to hunt and gather near their own site? Because of the continuity of the objects at Jubilee, I suggest the last occupation of the site represents autonomous foragers who came for short periods to trade with the agropastoralists. This would explain the lack of domesticated plant and animal remains, ceramics, iron, and other products that if acquired in trade, were taken to the region the foragers inhabited. It also would explain the multiseasonal occupation of the site, which apparently differed from the seasonal site occupations during the Early Iron Age (Wadley 1996).

In many other Late Iron Age rockshelter sites with preserved faunal remains there are few definitely identified domestic animal bones, suggesting that herding appears to have been introduced in parts of South Africa relatively late, perhaps 1,000 years later in the Free State and parts of the North Cape (Klein 1979:47). At sites located elsewhere, domestic sheep/goat bones are more prevalent, indicating more interaction, but *not necessarily* enslavement (e.g., Diepkloof Rockshelter, Parkington and Poggenpoel 1987). At sites such as Diepkloof, cultural affinity is still very difficult to establish because Late Stone Age lithic artifacts are virtually absent (Wilson 1996). How do we know that the site was not occupied by Khoi herders or even by Bantu agropastoralists who we know hunted wild animals, in addition to keeping livestock?

With a few exceptions, it is surprising how few Khoi sites have been identified as such. Most sites that are not Bantu are classified as hunter-gatherer, ignoring the fact that Khoi herders occupied parts of South Africa for at least 2,000 years. Most problematic is the visibility of both hunter-gatherer and Khoi sites. We know that the two groups were present sometimes in the same or adjacent areas. The little variation that does exist among supposed hunter-gatherer sites representing different degrees of autonomy may actually be the difference between hunter-gatherer and Khoi sites. That is, archaeologists might unintentionally be conflating hunter-gatherer and Khoi sites and mislabeling variability in ethnicity as variability in autonomy.

Table 3.7
Artifacts from Three Stratigraphic Levels at Jubilee Shelter

Artifacts	1840–1550 B.P.	1350 B.P.	<1350 B.P.
Lithic tool categories (adze, scrapers, backed tools, borers, and size category differences)	6	4	3
Number of flaked lithic artifacts, including unworked flakes	9,181	353	1,889
Number of scrapers	295	7	54
Percentage of formal tools in the entire flaked artifact assemblage	3.56	3.68	3.28
Percentage of scrapers in formal flaked tools	90.21	53.85	87.10
Ostrich eggshell beads	251	—	33
Ostrich eggshell fragments	1,650	16	354
Number of ceramic sherds	121	9	95
Bone points and shafts	157	8	49
Percentage of sherds in total number of lithics and ceramics	1.30	2.49	4.79
Bone ornaments	6	—	—

All data from Wadley 1997.

The earlier sections on the ethnoarchaeology of domination indicate different patterns of material culture change than those recorded for Iron Age southern Africa. For example, little evidence of major social/political changes is visible in the upper Rose Cottage artifacts. Although ceramics and some domesticated faunal remains are present (Wadley 1992), the Rose Cottage lithic assemblage does not indicate assimilation. While Wadley (1992) suggests that the wood species used at Rose Cottage are more variable (implying less targeted species selection), this may only mean a change in selection of firewood and species distributions. Neither of these indicates serfdom in and of themselves. Even in the early 1920s, hunter-gatherers were identified in the Eastern Free State, although by then they had only the remnants of their former culture. In my opinion, the archaeological data indicate that autonomous, but not isolated, hunter-gatherers persisted in the Caledon River, South Africa/Lesotho area until the turn of the nineteenth century.

Rather than question the ability of the artifact assemblage to reflect social/political change, I suggest more careful use of the ethnohistoric sources. It is difficult to reconcile claims by so many archaeologists that their prehistoric sites indicate hunter-gatherer clients or slaves of the agropastoralists, with the numerous ethnohistoric observations of hunter-gatherers in Botswana, South Africa, and Lesotho (Kent,

Chapter 6, this volume). For example, "By 1860 the missionaries stated emphatically that the only place where Khoisan ('Hottentotten,' 'San' or 'Buschmännern') was to be found, was in the Orange Free State [South Africa]" (Hesse 1997:6). Missionaries in Lesotho also recorded the presence of hunter-gatherers from the 1840s to the 1890s, although during the later date most were not autonomous and procured food through stealing domestic animals, raiding for other foodstuffs, and dependence on handouts from colonists and Bantu-speakers (How 1962). Their existence as hunter-gatherers until the end of the nineteenth century is testimony that their ancestors had been a viable society prior to European colonization. That is, hunter-gatherers had not been assimilated centuries before European arrival by the agropastoralists. If they had been assimilated, there would not have been even the remnants of identifiable foragers in southern Africa at the end of the 1700s in some areas, the end of the 1800s in other areas, and the end of the 1900s in parts of the Kalahari.

Perhaps most contentious is the rock art that depicts livestock (Jolly 1996). As Sadr (1997) notes, thus far, there are only untestable assumptions and speculations about the meaning of the art. Any one of the following explanations of the rock art are equally conceivable but impossible to test. Are paintings of cattle merely wishful thinking of what the artists would like to have, or evidence of their being forced to herd for pastoralists? This, of course, just leads to even more difficult questions, such as, if the latter is valid, then why would someone paint beautiful cows next to super-natural figures to illustrate their enslavement? Or does the art betoken autonomous hunter-gatherers who just had a feast, were happily full of beef, and therefore had cattle on their minds when they decided to paint the rocks? Equally possible from a Lévi-Strauss perspective, the cattle could represent the category of "domestic" or "culture" in contrast to wild animals, thereby having symbolic importance in girls' or boys' initiations where "wild" children, without much knowledge of their culture, become enculturated adults. Cattle instead could symbolize "the other"—culturally different pastoralists, and illustrate either danger and fear or friendship and resources. It is even conceivable that an artist painted a relatively unusual animal that is particu-larly valuable in terms of meat but is not often available to the artist. Did the artist use a portentous moment such as a ceremony of some kind for her or his inspiration, or a dream, or a vision during a trance? The problem is that anyone's guess is as valid as mine. I suggest we cannot determine whether the art motifs have anything to do with intergroup interactions because we cannot reliably evaluate any of these conjectures or demonstrate why one scenario is better than another, much less test hypotheses.

OSTRICH EGGSHELL BEADS: AN ARCHAEOLOGICAL CASE STUDY

Some archaeologists support their view of change in hunter-gatherer sovereignty based on a few or even one attribute, such as a change in a single class of artifacts—

ostrich eggshell beads. Later in time, ostrich eggshell beads became larger, particularly at Bantu sites. The appearance of large beads on hunter-gatherer sites after 500 years ago "is coincident with the growth in cattle herd sizes at the Cape" (Smith 2001:123). According to some archaeologists, the change in bead size at hunter-gatherers' sites co-occurring with the growth of cattle herds, implies that hunter-gatherers were forced to labor for their agropastoralist neighbors. No longer able to compete with the agropastoralists, hunters "became clients, not only do they serve important functions necessary for the success of pastoral life, *but they ideologically accept their position as dependent*" (emphasis added; Smith 1998:201).

Change in bead size is not necessarily indicative of domination. Agropastoralists could have copied what was an internal hunter-gatherer change in bead size, or could have received the larger beads in trade with autonomous hunter-gatherers. Foragers may have decided to alter bead size due to cultural aesthetics, to make them a more valuable trade item, or many other alternatives that do not include domination. There is no evidence of domination, only of change in artifacts. In addition to the ostrich eggshell beads, there are relatively few numbers of sherds and domestic faunal remains at these sites (Smith 2001:123 and elsewhere).

What may just be a cultural or temporal marker, the increased size of ostrich eggshell beads, or even a borrowed style from neighboring cultures, is singled out as proof of serfdom or a similar dependent relationship. In many other culture areas around the world, stylistic change of trade items is interpreted as internal change through time or for other reasons, but rarely is the change used as the sole indicator of intergroup conquest. I suggest it is the revisionist theoretical perspective that encourages archaeologists to interpret minor changes in artifact frequencies or types, such as bead styles, as evidence of domination. The faunal assemblage at most sites considered to be those of enslaved hunter-gatherers rarely has a large percentage of domesticated animal remains (see Table 3.10). The same is the case for botanical remains. Even the changes in the lithic inventory are usually relatively small. The number of ceramics within the total artifact assemblage is usually extremely small, often less than 10 percent, and sometimes less than 1 percent of all artifacts. These are not the signatures of domination. At most, they are the signatures of normal internal change over thousands of years and of trade between autonomous societies.

OUT OF AFRICA: PREHISTORIC HUNTER-GATHERER AND FARMER INTERACTIONS IN THE NORTH AMERICAN SOUTHWEST

South African archaeology, and anthropology in general, has been rocked by the intensity of the revisionism debate about the nature of the interactions between hunter-gatherers and agropastoralists. As noted above, much of the revisionist position is argued without sufficient evidence. Data can have multiple interpretations, and those interpretations are often contradictory. For that reason, among others, it is instructive to venture outside of southern Africa and examine what archaeologists elsewhere use as evidence of different types of intergroup interactions.

Sometimes archaeologists are too close to current debates in their area to be able to step back and take a nonpartisan view. It is, therefore, useful to test our interpretations and theoretical orientation in a different culture area to determine the reliability of our inferences. Examining similar phenomena—in this case, hunter-gatherer interaction with farmers who kept domesticated animals and who also hunted—provides a more objective perspective from which to view the southern African archaeological record. In addition, the revisionist radical political economy position has not been as influential in the archaeology of the North American Southwest.

Intercultural Relations between North American Farmers and Hunter-Gatherers

Protohistoric autonomous North American Great Plains hunter-gatherers and Southwestern Anasazi farmers are interpreted as autonomous societies that partook in trade but not in domination. At Plains hunter-gatherer sites approximately 50 percent of all sherds are Rio Grande Anasazi Pueblo ceramics (Spielmann 1982, 1998 personal communication). That is, 50 percent of the ceramics at Plains hunter-gatherer sites are Rio Grande Pueblo glazeware ceramics traded from the farmers and approximately 50 percent are local Plains ware ceramics. A small amount of nonlocal obsidian unretouched flakes (less than 5 percent of the lithics) and occasional pieces of turquoise exotic to the area (but available in the general Anasazi region) were recovered from Plains hunter-gatherer sites. During the same time period bison bones, and particularly bison bone tools, were found at Pueblo sites in the Rio Grande area—a region that bison did not inhabit at the time. For example, at the Anasazi site of Gran Quivira, New Mexico, of all the identifiable bone tools, 27 percent were made from bison bone, 19 percent from deer, and 17 percent from pronghorn antelope (e.g., Hayes, Young, and Warren 1981:156). Calculations of the amount of meat available based on species and the individual skeletal parts present show that at the Anasazi site "bison led native mammals during all periods, followed by pronghorns" (Hayes, Young, and Warren 1981:65). Such distributions of pottery and bison bones would likely be interpreted as evidence of one group dominating another in southern Africa (Table 3.8). However, in the North American Southwest, it is interpreted as trade between autonomous societies by Spielmann (1982) and others (e.g., Hayes, Young, and Warren 1981). Any *southern African hunter-gatherer site with 50 percent of the artifacts from agropastoralists would be identified pro forma as occupied by dominated hunter-gatherers, but not in the North*

Table 3.8

Percentage of Mammal Meat at Gran Quivira

Species	Early Period	Middle Period	Late Period (Early Spanish Contact)
Mule deer	8.94	9.72	4.71
White-tailed deer	1.83	0.97	2.13
Pronghorn antelope	40.21	32.11	17.60
American bison	47.52	54.81	30.57
All others	1.50	2.39	1.28
Total wild mammals	100.0	100.0	56.29
Total domestic mammals	0.00	0.00	43.71
Total mammals	100.00	100.00	100.00

Figures show the percentage of mammal meat available based on faunal remains identified at the late Anasazi site of Gran Quivira in New Mexico (modified from Hayes 1981:180).

American Southwest. The ethnohistoric studies support the Southwestern archaeologists' interpretation of cultural autonomy. Early Spanish explorers and missionaries recorded the presence of a large annual trade "fair" between Pueblo farmers and Plains hunter-gatherers during which time the latter would camp outside the villages of the former. In the American Southwest we know serfdom did not exist. These data, therefore, cannot be interpreted as proof of enslavement.

Particularly interesting is the change in the domestic to wild animal bones ratio during the early historic period circa 1659, when the Spanish first built missions in the Pueblo Anasazi region of the North American Southwest (labeled the Late Period of early Spanish contact in Table 3.8). This period precedes Spanish domination and control that occurred after the Pueblo Revolt in the 1680s. During the Late Period, domesticated animals surpassed bison as the largest source of meat at the site, comprising 43.7 percent of the available meat (Table 3.8). Bison, in contrast, drops to 30.6 percent from 47.5 percent and 54.8 percent during the two earlier prehistoric periods. The percentage of domestic animals in the faunal inventory was even higher after the Spanish reasserted their sovereignty over the descendants of Anasazi Indians. Note that almost half of all mammal meat available at Gran Quivira during the Early Period and over half during the Middle Period was from bison. The Pueblo farmers traded maize and ceramics. Yet, southwestern archaeologists do not interpret the distribution to be indicative of domination or serfdom of either the Plains hunter-gatherers or the Anasazi farmers.

When Europeans did arrive and built missions, but before they conquered the Pueblo Indians or could completely dominate them, just under half of all meat

(43.7 percent) came from domesticated animals brought in by the Spanish (the Late Period). The domesticated animal remains at Gran Quivira were from a period before the complete domination of the Pueblo people by Spanish colonizers. That is, the domestic animal bones date to before the famous Pueblo Revolt of 1680, during which the Pueblo Indians successfully defeated the Spanish, forcing them to withdraw to near the current border of Mexico. In other words, the 43.7 percent of domestic faunal remains date to a period before the loss of cultural autonomy or enslavement of the Pueblo Indians, a time when they were able to defend themselves against the Spanish invaders. Had this occurred in southern Africa, these same percentages and same distribution of Plains bison bones versus locally available fauna at the farmers' sites during the prehistoric periods would likely be interpreted by archaeologists working in southern Africa as hunter-gatherers forced to work for the farmers. After Spanish contact but before Spanish conquest, the introduction of a relatively large number of domesticated species' bones at the expense of the bison and other wild animals, would be interpreted by many southern African archaeologists as evidence of domination and enslavement.

In the case of the North American Southwest, we know that such interpretations are false because we have Spanish missionary records that clearly show that the Plains hunter-gatherers and Anasazi farmers did not have a client-patron relationship, nor a serf-tribute relationship. Neither were the hunter-gatherers slaves of the Anasazi farmers, despite the fact that approximately 50 percent of their ceramics are found at Plains hunter-gatherer sites along with 50 percent of their own local Plains wares. The Spanish recorded trade between autonomous, culturally distinct societies. The North American Pueblo farmer/Plains hunter-gatherer intercultural interactions in which both groups maintained their autonomy are not unique. In fact, I suggest that the subjugation of groups by methods similar to Western-style colonialization was the exception in the past rather than the norm.

Intercultural Relations between North American Plains Hunter/Farmers and Euroamericans

It is possible to determine intercultural relationships from the archaeological record, as the ethnoarchaeological and ethnohistoric studies presented here attest. I propose it is not the data that is in need of correction but rather the interpretations of the data. For example, prior to Western colonization in North America, Arikara Indians of the northern Great Plains maintained their autonomy while indirectly and later directly trading with Euroamericans for almost 100 years. At first, a few Euroamerican goods were acquired through indirect and possibly occasional direct trade. From the initial contact in Period I until Period V (1500–1835), exotic objects consisted of less than 1 percent of the entire artifact inventory (Table 3.9).

Table 3.9

Arikara Indian and Euroamerican Artifacts in Domestic Lodges

Artifacts	Period I A.D. 1500–1680	Period II 1681–1725	Period III 1726–1775	Period IV 1776–1805	Period V 1806–1835	Period VI 1836–1862
Number of Arikara objects	14,569	9,756	16,768	4,966	4,965	30
Number of Euroamerican objects	3	80	108	38	240	147
Total number of objects	14,572	9,836	16,876	5,004	5,205	456
Percentage of Euroamerican objects	0.02	0.81	0.64	0.76	4.61	32.24
Relations	Precontact; Euroamerican objects from indirect trade	Some trade, relations still good	Still good autonomous trade relations	Rejection of Euroamericans and their goods	Increased hostilities and worsening relations—the beginning of a decline in autonomy, while still maintaining a semblance of Arikara culture (no symbolic, client-patron, serf, slave or similar dependent relations)	Too few archaeological data to make interpretations, but a general continuation of Period V relationships

Table shows artifacts located in domestic lodges through time (all data from Rogers 1990:230–233, Appendices 1 and 2).

Rogers (1990:214) commented that for "more than a century after direct contact with Euro-Americans the nature of the interaction continued to be largely controlled by Arikara views of exchange as a social process and Arikara notions of how to place Euro-Americans within a cultural context" (Rogers 1990:211).

Period IV is interesting in that it was a time when the Arikara lost their awe of Euroamericans and the objects they had to trade. While the percentage of the number of Euroamerican objects in Period IV was similar to Period III, the percentage of Euroamerican categories declined significantly. No longer did the Arikara think the Euroamericans were supernatural, as they had in earlier periods. The result was the Arikara rejection of trade goods and, symbolically, a rejection of the Euroamerican fur traders themselves (Rogers 1990). Table 3.9 shows the progression of Euroamerican contact and the beginning of the deterioration of relations. More Euroamerican goods are present in the Arikara artifact assemblage during Period V than the earlier periods, reflecting the beginning of a change in relations.

During the time periods presented in Rogers's (1990) study, the Arikara Indians were not enslaved, forced to pay tribute, or otherwise subjugated. However, Periods V and VI saw increased hostilities and intercultural conflict. Unfortunately, Rogers (1990:221–227) writes that there were too few artifacts dating to Period VI to interpret the intercultural relations in the material culture at excavated Arikara sites. Nonetheless, the increase in the percentage of Euroamerican goods in Period VI is consistent with the growing animosity between the two culturally distinct groups. As the ethnoarchaeological studies above show, objects are culturally manipulated. This means we should be able to determine the nature and differences in the relationships and exchanges between culturally dissimilar groups by examining their artifacts. Rogers's (1990) study shows that changes in the percentage of foreign objects and the percentage of foreign categories of objects at Arikara sites reflect the changing relationship between the Arikara and Euroamericans. The same is true of the material culture at southern African archaeological sites. Even when 32 percent of the material culture was foreign objects, Period VI, the Arikara were not serfs of the Euroamericans. In fact, Rogers (1990:211) writes "An analysis of continuities in individual artifact categories in domestic earthlodges indicated a relatively high level of continuity in Arikara categories, but a relatively low level in Euro-American categories . . . which is not too surprising considering that while economic patterns did change over the nearly 200 years encompassed by this study, the basic patterns of day-to-day life were not altered beyond recognition."

Eventually, there were few to no Arikara artifacts in their material culture assemblages, as they were conquered and assimilated by the Euroamericans. Like the African-American slaves, complete domination of the Arikara is clearly visible in the material culture. Basically there were few to no Arikara artifacts because there were few to no Arikara beliefs or general culture left. The southern African sites discussed above did not exhibit the changes that signify assimilation or serf-dom until late European colonization, depending on the region. I suggest that the percentage of agropastoralist artifacts at hunter-gatherer sites in Africa would be much higher if they were in a symbiotic relationship, like the Efe, and higher still if enslaved, like the African-Americans (Table 3.2).

DISCUSSION

One difficulty I think some anthropologists have in acknowledging autonomous Iron Age or twentieth-century hunter-gatherers in southern Africa stems from a static model of foragers. Late Iron Age hunter-gatherers differed from Early Iron Age and from contemporary foragers. Likewise, Early and Late Iron Age agropasto-ralists differ from contemporary agropastoralists. It would be surprising if Iron Age hunter-gatherers were not different than their predecessors or from contemporane-ous agropastoralists. It seems that almost any change in the South African archaeo-logical record is interpreted as evidence of domination. Even when a faunal assemblage has less than 10–20 percent domestic bones and the artifact assemblage has less than 10–20 percent sherds, they are interpreted as evidence of domination. Any small deviation from one time period to another often is viewed as reflective of enormous cultural changes, such as a loss of autonomy. Instead, difference means a dynamic, evolving society. It does not *necessarily* imply an enslaved one. Difference means adapting to cultural and environmental changes facing a people, not *necessar-ily* assimilation or extermination of a culture. As a consequence, I interpret many changes in the archaeological record as documenting the continuously mutable life of autonomous hunter-gatherers in southern Africa, as they faced both the benefits and the challenges created by groups immigrating into their region. We allow Early and Late Iron Age agropastoralist cultures to change through time without forsak-ing their autonomy. Why can't we do the same for hunter-gatherers?

A second problem is that the majority of hunter-gatherer sites that have been excavated in southern Africa are rockshelter sites, whereas the majority of pasto-ralists' sites are open-air encampments. Archaeologists who study southern Afri-can hunter-gatherers tend to concentrate on rockshelter sites to the exclusion of open-air sites because rockshelter sites usually have better preservation. However, too few open-air hunter-gatherer sites have been excavated to know if all open-air sites are not *in situ* as is presumed, or if many are undisturbed, but just do not have the faunal remain preservation found at rockshelter sites. It seems likely that differ-ent activities and/or seasons, or length of occupations occurred at open-air sites than at rockshelter sites. Are we missing information about the past, by ignoring open-air hunter-gatherer sites? In some cases, as with much of the eastern Free State of South Africa, Late Stone Age open-air sites have not been recorded, much less excavated, while almost all of the Late Stone Age rockshelter sites in the same area have been documented and dug. How can we know if hunter-gatherers were or were not enslaved in a region if we only selectively examine their sites? Examining open-air sites is particularly important since rockshelter sites may have been temporary or seasonal camps until the late historic period when foragers used them to escape from the Europeans and other groups with guns and horses.

A third complication is the tendency to presume that Iron Age foragers were semi- to completely nomadic. There really is little evidence to support this view except in a few regions. Coastal Cape hunter-gatherers, for example, could have been fairly sedentary, particularly those who stored shellfish and perhaps other resources. Hunter-gatherers who were nomadic could have used mobility to escape domination by other societies while sedentary hunter-gatherers may have been more sociopolitically complex with chiefs who could organize their subjects against threats.

A fourth difficulty is the common view that the impact between indigenous hunter-gatherers and migrating Bantu-speakers had to result in conflict, and therefore domination of the more vulnerable hunter-gatherers by the agropastoralists. As was shown with the North American Southwestern Anasazi and Plains Indians, cultures can exist together without one dominating the other. A misunderstanding of the diversity and nature of intercultural relations is not restricted to southern Africa. Elsewhere archaeologists also mistake autonomy with slavery. Although not referring to any single group or geographical region, Cusick stated the issue as "(1) formulations of acculturation . . . tend to portray Western people as active agents and non-Western peoples as passive recipients; (2) . . . [anthropologists] *tend to confuse change in behavior or behavioral systems with change in identity; (3) cultural traits are equated with material culture, and quantifiable changes in material culture over time are equated with acculturation* . . . ; and acculturative frameworks are incapable of accurately predicting what aspects of culture will change in given circumstances" (emphasis added, Cusick 1998:135–136). The result, I suggest, is misconstruing past and present complex and dynamic interactions among the different cultures of southern Africa.

I see no evidence in the archaeological record for forced or even symbiotic interactions between hunter-gatherers and Iron Age agropastoralists. The consequences of agropastoralist contact, I propose, did not destroy hunter-gatherer culture. Agropastoralists and foragers exploited different niches in the same area. Agropastoralists probably took some hunter-gatherer land (although more was probably taken from the Khoi). However, at the same time agropastoralists provided new opportunities for trade in novel iron and ceramics that the hunter-gatherers could now exploit. Independent Iron Age hunter-gatherers and agropastoralists could have occasionally feuded and competed, but in general, were amiable autonomous neighbors who used different resources. If this were not the case, the archaeological record should look different than it does. Assimilated societies have assimilated architecture and assimilated material culture. That is, if southern African hunter-gatherers truly are assimilated Bantu, their camps should more closely resemble those of the agropastoralists, just as African American architecture resembled extremely small Western rectangular houses.

The possibility of a generally compatible land use by both hunter-gatherers and agropastoralists can be indirectly substantiated in several ways. It is unlikely that a large percentage of individual agropastoralists had herds with hundreds, and in a few cases, even more cattle, as occurs today in parts of southern Africa. Contemporary agropastoralist herds abuse the land through overgrazing, making it uninhabitable for both foragers and wild animals. In contrast, precolonial herds were much smaller and less destructive as can be inferred from the many ethnohistoric sources that describe the presence and sometimes profusion of game almost everywhere in southern Africa. In some regions, explorers were impressed by the huge herds of large and small animals (see Chapter 6). These herds were killed after Europeans arrived with guns and horses. The formerly ubiquitous wild animals described by the first Europeans demonstrate that the precontact agropastoralists did not destroy the land to the point that it could not support both game and foragers (and presumably, wild plants). If earlier agropastoralists had been as destructive as their twentieth-century descendants, the large numbers of wild animals and foragers would not have been able to survive to historic contact throughout southern Africa. Thus, the destruction of wild resources almost everywhere today in southern Africa by agropastoralists and Westerners is not appropriate or valid to project into the past, precolonial, time period. This means hunter-gatherers and agropastoralists were not invariably in direct competition for habitat that could only support one group, making the possibility of intercultural competition less plausible and the case for intercultural amity more plausible.

Archaeologists in other regions of Africa are questioning the meaning of a changing material culture and what it signifies in terms of worldview and ideology. For example, DeCorse (1998:369) asks what changes in material culture reveal about changes in the culture of a group of people, in this case the Elmina of Ghana. He states that a "tremendous change in the artifact inventory should not . . . be viewed as an *ipso facto* indicator of changes in worldview. Continuity in the beliefs of the African population at Elmina may be assessed by considering three categories of information: the built environment, the foodways system, and the material indications of ritual behavior" (DeCorse 1998:369). His work concludes that "Collectively, the cognitive context in which artifacts functioned—how the Elmina people thought about the trade materials they used, viewed the buildings they occupied, and conceived their religious life—suggests resilience rather than sequaciousness, continuity rather than change in African beliefs and identity" (DeCorse 1998:369). I suggest that DeCorse's conclusions are relevant to the archaeology of southern Africa.

A basic premise many archaeologists and ethnographers have is that hunter-gatherers, voluntarily or not, gave up their autonomy to acquire the herders' culture because the presence of domesticated animals was too much of an incentive to ignore. "By taking on the cultural markers of the herders" hunters were increasingly involved in herder life at the expense of their cultural autonomy and freedom (Smith 1998, 2001:123). Although they may have acquiesced sometimes, hunter-gatherers were too prevalent ethnohistorically to have been destroyed or assimilated prior to European contact. In general, it often is easier for mobile hunter-gatherers with limited material culture to defend themselves than it is for semisedentary pastoralists who must protect their stock and possessions. Certainly in North America and elsewhere hunter-gatherers were able to coexist with semisedentary or sedentary more socially/politically complex farming societies.

The common conception of inevitable hunter-gatherer serfdom is based on the tendency for most Westerners, be they colonists, missionaries, ethnographers, or archaeologists, to believe that how "others" view hunter-gatherers is a valid picture of them. Smith, as one example, writes that cattle were the source of wealth for the Bantu, and because hunter-gatherers did not have access to this wealth, cultural boundaries were pronounced and eventually led to hunter-gatherer domination. In other words, the agropastoralist definition of wealth, appropriate behavior, inferiority and superiority are adopted by most Westerners. Hunter-gatherer artifact frequencies and ostrich eggshell bead stylistic changes are interpreted as demonstrating the hunter-gatherer position as dependent and "in a virtual feudal relationship" (Smith 2001:123). It is important, I suggest, to understand the intercultural exchange from the hunter-gatherers' perspective.

A fifth concern is the need to remember that there never was a uniform history of interaction between cultures in southern Africa. Archaeological, ethnohistoric, and ethnographic data all show that there was a sometimes-complex interplay of interactions in any one region at any one given point in time. Missionary records in 1860 recorded the presence of hunter-gatherers in the Free State of South Africa, after hunter-gatherers had lost their culture and identity elsewhere in southern Africa, particularly in the Cape area (Hesse 1997:6). Prior to the mid to late 1800s, little change is visible in hunter-gatherer life based on the upper levels excavated at Rose Cottage Shelter in the Eastern Free State, South Africa (Wadley 1992). Alternatively, enormous changes occurred in Namibia where a number of Ju/'hoansi males were enlisted in the South African army to fight against the ANC (African National Congress) or against Namibian independence (Gordon 1992). Participating in army life dramatically changed mobility patterns, ideology, social relations, subsistence strategies, and material culture. However, Botswana is a completely different country with a different history and interaction with Europeans. It is not valid to generalize a similar departure from earlier indigenous lifestyles to all hunter-gatherers anywhere in southern Africa, including Botswana (Kent 1992).

Also important to consider are the differences in the history and nature of contact between native hunter-gatherers and Bantu neighbors throughout southern Africa over the past 1,500–2,000 years. For example, Herero pastoralists today have devastated the Dobe environment, making full-time hunting and gathering difficult for basic subsistence needs (Lee 1993). The Herero migrated to Ngamiland in the early part of this century and were not present in Botswana before. Not until 1969 were some wild animals no longer found near Dobe pan, at least partially due to overgrazing and the presence of the Herero (Yellen 1977). Another example is the belief by some researchers that the dearth of good pasture in the Karoo of South Africa was the result of overgrazing during the historic period or before. Instead, historic rainfall records and recent palynological studies show that the type of vegetation present is likely due to local climatic regimes (Bousman and Scott 1994). This important study suggests that some archaeologists' claims that Iron Age agropastoralists ruined the grasslands with overgrazing, and driving out the game, making it impossible for hunter-gatherers to subsist without resorting to serfdom in order to survive, are not very compelling and, at least in some areas, the data suggest otherwise.

A sixth consideration is that not all regions of southern Africa were equally suitable to European economics, such as parts of the Kalahari in Botswana, where their impact with the indigenous groups was significantly less intense or severe. For at least several centuries, cattle could *not* exist in the central Kalahari due to a lack of surface water for anywhere from two to four months of the year. Therefore, the prehistory of the Kalahari is not analogous to that of other regions in southern Africa. Today Bantu-speaking agropastoralists with their cattle have settled in the central Kalahari but only where a borehole or well has been mechanically dug, such as Xade, described by Sugawara in Chapter 4. Since Westerners did not settle the Kalahari until the later part of the twentieth century, hunter-gatherers living there were less impacted by the problems that occurred during colonization. For example, the devastating epidemics brought by unsuspecting Europeans did not spread as readily in the Kalahari where the population, general way of life, and mobility all countered such epidemic diseases. The epidemiology of disease shows quite clearly that there are certain requirements for the proliferation of specific endemic diseases, and these requirements were not present until hunter-gatherers aggregated in sedentary communities (see Kent, Chapter 6, this volume). While individuals in contact with ill persons can die from being infected, that person would not instigate an epidemic because of the hunter-gatherers' mobility in the Kalahari and their distance from more populated areas. The impact of European colonialists and Bantu-speaking immigrants cannot be generalized elsewhere, including the central Kalahari during the late twentieth century and Ngamiland during the mid-twentieth century.

Table 3.10

Domesticated Animal Remains from Ju/'hoansi, Kutse, Bantu Iron Age, and North American Slave Camps

Site	Percentage of Domestic Animal Bones
Iron Age agropastoralist site, South Africa[a]	93.83
Sinclair site (planter's residence; nonslave), Georgia[b]	80.8
Sinclair site (African American slave quarters), Georgia[b]	88.3
Pike's Bluff (planter's residence; nonslave), Georgia[b]	81.8
Jones (slave quarters), Georgia[b]	81.5
Kingsmill Quarter (African American slave quarters), Virginia[c]	81.46
Gran Quivira, New Mexico, Late Period (after Spanish contact but before Spanish domination)[d]	43.71
Abandoned Kutse sites, Botswana[e]	10.36
Diepkloof Rockshelter, South Africa (circa 45,270–390 B.P.)[f]	6.00[f]
Tortoise Cave, South Africa (circa 18,000–1300 B.P.)[g]	3.9
Tloutle, mid–late Holocene[h]	2.9
Steenbokfontein Cave, South Africa (circa 2,000 B.P.)[g]	0.4

Table shows percentage of domestic animal bones in the identifiable faunal remain inventory at abandoned Ju'hoansi, Kutse, Bantu Iron Age, and North American slave camps. Note figure from historic slave quarters is computed using data in McKee (1987:34).

[a]From KwaGandaganda Iron Age site, South Africa, Whitelaw 1994.

[b]Moore 1981.

[c]McKee 1987.

[d]Hayes 1981.

[e]Kent fieldnotes.

[f]Parkington and Poggenpoel 1987 (note that dune mole rat, bats, and similar species are not included; also note that if fish and lobster are included the value is 5.0 percent; the figures for this site are based on MNI).

[g]Jerardino Wiesenborn 1996 (includes both Tortoise Cave and Steenbokfontein Cave).

[h]Mitchell 1993.

The seventh source of misunderstanding is the questionable, usually implicit, belief that two groups with separate identities and different modes of subsistence cannot exist next to one another without one incorporating the other. As I tried to show above, the data in most cases do not indicate hierarchical or unequal intercultural relations. That is, none of the data clearly demonstrate enslavement. If slavery did occur, in most cases it is not visible in the material culture or faunal remains of either group. Therefore one cannot use the archaeological evidence as proof of subjugation. Instead, many archaeologists use revisionism as proof of inequality. That is, the assumptions underlying revisionism are accepted as fact and are used to explain the past, regardless of the archaeological record. For example, the hunter-gatherer sites described above that contained 90–99 percent wild animal bones and 0.5–6.5 percent sherds out of an artifact inventory of thousands of lithics are interpreted as occupied by serfs or clients forced to work for agropastoralists. In my opinion, this interpretation is based on the revisionist theoretical perspective, not the data. Table 3.10 clearly shows differences between the frequencies of domesticated animals in groups with varying degrees of autonomy. The underlying belief is that hunters are almost always in subservient social positions to herders. When foragers do compete with food producers, they do not compete as equals (Smith 2001:122). This perspective, however, is derived from that of the agropastoralist not the forager (see Brooks, Chapter 8).

Agropastoralists believe that mobile foragers are perpetually poor because they have fewer possessions than many sedentary groups, and, in particular, no cattle. Whereas foragers may wish they had a cow to slaughter for immediate consumption, we cannot assume that all hunter-gatherers since the arrival of the Bantu, wanted cattle as wealth rather than as an immediate feast. The belief in impoverished foragers goes along with the agropastoralist belief that hunter-gatherers are obsequious, culturally inferior, and "primitive." What is not realized by anthropologists who accept such portrayals as valid is that they are basing their conception of foragers on the beliefs of the Bantu, not necessarily on the beliefs of the hunter-gatherers. The Bantu opinions are merely cultural boundary-maintenance mechanisms that may or may not have anything to do with "reality." Their negativism is neither questioned nor challenged by many anthropologists who do not try to learn what the foragers' conceptions are of the "other" (see Chapter 1; Lee, Chapter 7).

Smith (2001) cites early Dutch colonialists who described the foragers as poor, to support the common assumption that the wealthy agropastoralists were powerful, as they would be in Western society where wealth is equated with status and power. The same cannot be projected to very different cultures in the past. Difficult as it is not to impose Western beliefs on non-Western societies, it is essential to ensure that an interpretation is not based on European values. For example, in many Melanesian societies "big men" and "big women" have the least amount of wealth because they gain their status by giving away the most goods, making them poor using Western standards. The chiefs of many North American Northwest Coast Indians have much power and prestige, but not significantly more commodities than others (although they do have elite objects that commoners do not have access to). Whenever Northwest chiefs acquire enough objects to have a surplus, a potlatch or redistribution of the goods occurs, wherein the chief gives away whatever surplus he had acquired. Poverty has a cultural definition that does not translate to all societies. Labeling hunter-gatherers as impoverished evokes a sense of them as vulnerable to Western assimilation, because if foragers were superior or dominant, they would not be poor. Hence, their poverty is perceived as a symptom of being subjugated. Unintentionally, the Western definition of wealth and status is used as a criterion of superiority or dominance. Too often anthropologists unintentionally use their own cultural views, or those of the neighbors of hunter-gatherers, as valid, without knowing or asking what the foragers think. This can be a source of misunderstanding of intercultural relationships as they varied across space and through time in southern Africa and elsewhere.

CONCLUSIONS

Why are there such great differences between American Southwestern and southern African archaeologists' interpretations of the intercultural relationships of hunter-gatherers and farmer/agropastoralists? The reason, I suggest, is because the political economy revisionism orientation currently popular in southern African anthropology was not popular at the time of Spielmann's research in the American Southwest. As crucially important as our theoretical orientations are, it is even more important that they do not blind us to the data and what our analyses reveal. There are, I propose, differences between theoretically informed interpretations and theoretically biased interpretations. I suggest that archaeologists working in southern Africa assume a domination of foragers by pastoralists when in many cases the data suggest otherwise or are too ambiguous to make any reliable inferences.

Changes in material culture during the Middle and Late Stone Age are thought to result from changes in functions, subsistence, environment, and other reasons unrelated to subornation. In contrast, almost any change after the arrival of the Bantu in southern Africa is unquestioningly attributed to the subjugation of the foragers. Sometimes domination is inferred on the basis of low frequencies of what probably were trade items—domesticated animals and plants, ceramics, or large ostrich eggshell beads. There is nothing inherent in bead size or distribution that demonstrates intergroup inequality. Ostrich eggshell bead size only implies change and nothing else. The idea of subservient foragers, then, does not come from the artifacts, but from the archaeologists' interpretations. Archaeologically, enslavement is visible at historic African American sites. Societies dominating others restrict the material culture of a subjugated people as a means of enforcing their power and control, while eroding the cultural identity of the oppressed. If enslaved by the agropastoralists, African hunter-gatherers would not be allowed, and probably also would not have the time, to make and use their own separate material culture. Symbiosis is visible, as at the abandoned Efe sites. Neither is visible on the basis of change in one artifact type, but only on the entire artifact, faunal remain, and botanical remain assemblages.

Dissimilar histories and contacts created variable reactions among the foraging inhabitants throughout southern Africa. These differences, however, are not usually acknowledged or studied, resulting in very misleading generalizations. Those archaeologists who claim the same history for all hunter-gatherers throughout time all over southern Africa also claim that all hunter-gatherers are today merely impoverished pastoralists at the bottom of a strict sociopolitical, economic hierarchy imposed by Bantu-speakers and/or Europeans. Becoming serfs or otherwise being exploited or enslaved is not a situation to which most groups, hunter-gatherers or not, would aspire. This therefore would not have occurred unless they were forced. The prehistory, history, and ethnography do not support such an interpretation prior to the arrival of European colonists.

There is much variation among the remaining hunter-gatherer societies of the last half of the twentieth century in southern Africa. I think it is a safe assumption that there was at least as much diversity in the past, if not more. Sedentary hunter-gatherer groups residing near permanent sources of water may have been less able to deal with invading agropastoralists circa 1,500 years ago or with Europeans of the past 400 years than were the more mobile, egalitarian, and opportunistic groups. Even with the demise of many hunter-gatherer societies, some foragers remained culturally intact through most of the twentieth century.

If any group was seriously threatened by the agropastoralists, I suggest it was the less mobile Khoi who were probably in direct competition over resources important to their animal husbandry. The fact that nomadic peoples who move regularly can potentially avoid a portion of their territory, if absolutely necessary, needs to be considered when trying to understand intergroup interactions when the first agropastoralists migrated to southern Africa.

The archaeological record, I suggest, shows that most hunter-gatherers abandoned an area rather than passively allow Bantu-speakers to force themselves and their families into a lifetime of slavery or even an unequal client relationship 1,000–2,000 years ago. The arrival of Europeans, however, created a very different situation, but only in some parts of southern Africa. The archaeological record in most cases does *not* reflect dominated hunter-gatherers. Enslaved hunter-gatherers would have much higher percentages of domesticated faunal bones and plant remains at their sites because they would not have had time to hunt or collect wild plants for themselves. Even an assemblage of roughly 50 percent of the objects from neighboring peoples does not signify slavery, but, instead, symbiotic exchange, as with the Pygmies, who are culturally and behaviorally intertwined with the villagers. Many southern African archaeological sites interpreted as evidence of a hunter-gatherer–client, agropastoralist-patron relationship do not have the material culture to support such an interpretation. Most archaeologists working outside of southern Africa would not interpret the hunter-gatherer sites as demonstrating anything more than trade between autonomous societies wherein both think they are getting the best "deal" for their exchanges (which is one reason it is important to talk to both groups involved in trade before determining domination).

Approximately 1,000 to 2,000 years ago, depending on the region, the Bantu-speaking newcomers brought with them their different cultures, economies, opportunities, and dangers to the resident foragers who reacted to the invaders in various ways, depending on the time period and groups involved. However, without evidence, it is unproductive to assume that all intergroup interactions inevitably led to domination.

The spread of Western society is completely unparalleled in most respects and in most geographical regions (exceptions include Islam and a few other cultures). Western and similar state-level empire-building nations mixed ethnocentrism with racism, resulting in widespread culture-cide and genocide that was not necessarily a part of all past immigrating societies. Westerners will not interact with other cultures except within a Western culture milieu. That is, Westerners demand that the people they interact with speak their language, know their culture, adhere to their same god, and wear their clothes. What evidence do we have of anything similar when the Bantu agropastoralists immigrated to southern Africa? I propose it is Bantu-centric to interpret prehistoric intercultural relations from contemporary agropastoralists' conceptions of hunter-gatherers. It also is ethnocentric or Eurocentric, and inappropriate, to view prehistory as identical to the history of European expansion.

ACKNOWLEDGMENTS

I sincerely thank Karim Sadr for his valuable comments on a rough draft. I appreciate the many stimulating conversations with colleagues, including Lyn Wadley and Garth Sampson. However, all errors contained within are the sole fault of the author. I also am grateful to Mary McNeeley and Leona Ripley for their editorial suggestions and assistance in putting this volume together. Mary McNeeley also drafted the map contained in this chapter. All errors and shortcomings are mine alone.

four

Optimistic Realism or
Opportunistic Subordination?

The Interaction of the G/wi
and G//ana with Outsiders

Kazuyoshi Sugawara

There are many ways to study the relationship of hunter-gatherers with other people. The question of where to depart from, as well as what to aim for, is dependent on the methodological choice of every anthropologist, influenced by his or her personal history. My point of departure is 'natural history' and observation of everyday behavior, derived from my background of primatology and ethology (Sugawara 1990). Although this methodology may seem to be opposed to the revisionist criticism of evolutionary paradigms in ecoanthropological studies of hunter-gatherers (Wilmsen 1983; Wilmsen and Denbow 1990), I do not intend to reconstruct the evolutionary process of hunter-gatherer societies. Rather, my interest has been concentrated on the understanding of behavioral, as well as communicative, grounds of small-scaled societies that have been characterized as 'egalitarian' in terms of face-to-face interactions (cf. Goffman 1963).

The main part of the following descriptions and arguments is based on the analysis of everyday conversations recorded among a sedentary community of hunter-gatherers belonging to the G/wi and G//ana dialect groups. In order to fully understand a particle of conversation in an indigenous context, accurately interpreting the literal meaning of each utterance is quite necessary but not at all sufficient. Even in a very short conversation, many variables, such as knowledge, belief, memory, and the relationship between the participants, are incessantly activated and realized (cf. Moerman 1988). In this sense, the anthropological analysis of everyday conversation can only establish a bridgehead for understanding the multi-layered reality of the lifeworld of the people. In accordance with this, the description itself has to be multidimensional. For this reason, I shall also use other sources of data such as naming practices, narratives of personal history, and discourses drawn from informal interviews.

As all of these materials are based on oral information, there will always remain a serious methodological difficulty for any attempt to understand the true reality of the social world experienced by the people themselves. Briefly, we don't have any ultimate criterion for judging to what degree the oral 'representation' of any event faithfully maps the *real* event. Of course, a genuinely historical approach is generally equipped with various methods to confirm the coherence of diverse data, or to locate them in the objective world. However, within the limits of ethnographic description, the method that I have chosen to overcome this hindrance is rather indirect. In the following argument, I shall pay more attention to the way in which people explain or interpret an event they have come through, than to the question of "Did it *really* occur?" (cf. Rosaldo 1980). In other words, I shall try to formulate some *scheme of practice* by which they organize their experiences in interactions with the outside.

BRIEF SKETCH OF THE MODERN HISTORY OF THE G/WI AND G//ANA

The G/wi and G//ana are closely related groups belonging to the Khoe-speaking Bushman people (Barnard 1992a), and a large part of them used to live in the Central Kalahari Game Reserve (CKGR), which was demarcated in 1961. Among them, the population living in the Xade area, the mid-western part of the CKGR, has been receiving special attention by Western and Japanese anthropologists. The modern history of the Xade area began in 1958 with the first anthropological survey by George B. Silberbauer, who contributed to the establishment of the CKGR (Silberbauer 1981). The borehole at !Koi!kom drilled under his supervision became the center of the settlement in the 15 years that followed. Just after Silberbauer left, Jiro Tanaka started his investigations in 1967. The primary interest that motivated Tanaka's studies was to elucidate the mechanisms of human ecological adaptation to the natural environment (Tanaka 1980). However, after the Remote Area Development Programme (RADP) was enforced by the Botswana Government in 1979, the population of the Xade area underwent drastic changes. In 1982, Tanaka started organizing a number of research teams in order to systematically study the change

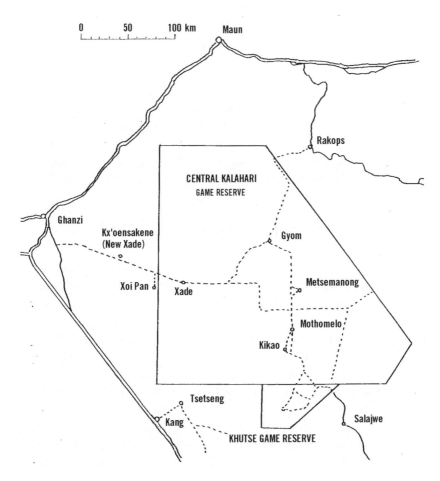

Figure 4.1. Ghanzi district of Botswana.

itself.[1] The G/wi, G//ana, and the Bakgalagadi Bantu-speaking people came to form a large community of more than 600 people, settled around the borehole of !Koi!kom. About half of them were immigrants from other areas of the CKGR or neighboring farms and towns. Since then, the nomadic hunting-gathering life has rapidly transformed, and the people have become dependent on governmental aid (Tanaka 1987; Osaki 1990). In addition, the cash economy has also entered the life of the people, as employment in road construction and the sale of arts and crafts have become commonplace (Tanaka 1991; Ikeya 1996a).

After the settlement, the traditional bow-and-arrow hunting was rapidly replaced by "equestrian hunting," group expedition hunting using horses (Osaki 1984). Gathering, especially of firewood, continued to be carried out by women. Compared with the gathering activity in the previous nomadic life, the burden of one trip became greater and the time necessary for gathering increased (Imamura-Hayaki 1996). While in the 1960s, altogether only several dozen goats were raised by G//ana people in the Xade area (Tanaka 1980), according to the census of 1987–89, the number of goats had strikingly increased to about 2,700 (Ikeya 1993). This rapid growth was mainly due to the distribution of female goats to each household by the government, which started in 1984 (Tanaka 1987), as well as to the purchase by cash obtained through road construction labor and the selling of folk crafts. According to the investigations by K. Ikeya, pursued in the rainy seasons from 1993 to 1995, *tsama* melon, cowpea, and maize were also cultivated in various combinations at 40 fields around the camps (Ikeya 1996b).

THE CATEGORIES OF HUMAN BEINGS

Silberbauer describes the G/wi words that denote the categories of non-G/wi people, and also schematizes the categories of human beings in the G/wi culture, using concentric circles around the 'Ego' (Silberbauer 1981:61–62). As I am following the orthography that was established by a collaborating linguist (Nakagawa 1996), the category names used in this paper differ from those used by Silberbauer. The G/wi and G//ana call themselves /gui-ko and //gana-ko or /gui-khoe and //gana-khoe respectively. Both the derivative morpheme -ko and the noun khoe mean "person." The Nharo are designated as qabe-ko. Not only the G/wi–G//ana and Nharo, but Bushman groups in general are denominated by the inclusive term *Kūa*, the connotation of which may be "company." The Bakgalagadi are called ≠Kebe (≠ibina in Silberbauer's orthography).[2] Less frequently, the G/wi and G//ana also use the synonymous word qhari, but this word might as well refer to the Tswana in general. Finally, Europeans are called /koo.

As the words *Kūa* and ≠Kebe are frequently used as contrasting categories in everyday conversation and as they clearly characterize the relationship between the G/wi–G//ana and the Bakgalagadi, I will use the words *Kūa* and ≠Kebe to roughly indicate these two "ethnic groups."

HISTORICAL RECONSTRUCTION OF THE RELATIONSHIP BETWEEN THE G/WI–G//ANA AND THE BAKGALAGADI: SOME HINTS FROM NARRATIVES AND NAMING CONVENTIONS

Masakazu Osaki (1996) and Kazunobu Ikeya (n.d.) have been examining the history of the relationship between the G/wi, G//ana, and the Bakgalagadi agropastoralists. In this section I will use the available data of naming conventions and narratives of life history as hints for the historical reconstruction.

Naming Conventions

Tanaka and Silberbauer both briefly describe the naming conventions in G/wi–G//ana society. "The !Kung San have definite rules regarding the assignment of names, but the ≠Kade San [i.e., G/wi and G//ana] do not. Some names derive from incidents occurring at the time of birth . . . ; others are simply names of items or everyday phrases. . . . Some names have no meaning at all" (Tanaka 1980:100). "A baby is named by the grandparents or by one of the siblings of its parents in a public announcement. The name usually commemorates some happening or circumstances associated with birth" (Silberbauer 1981:164).

The results of my investigations on G/wi–G//ana personal names differ from the above observations in the following two points. Firstly, according to my interviews, there are few names that "have no meaning at all." Furthermore, most of the names that apparently seemed to be "simply names of items or everyday phrases" turn out to have derived from "incidents occurring at the time of birth." Secondly, I found that babies were most frequently named by their own father.

I conclude that in the G/wi–G//ana society, newborn babies are most usually named by their father after some conspicuous incident that occurred during pregnancy or infancy (Sugawara 1997). Such a naming convention, resulting in a quite low percentage of persons with the 'same name,' stands in sharp contrast to the homonymous method common among the Ju/'hoansi, where personal names are selected from a limited stock and "are repeated over and over from generation to generation" (Marshall 1976:225). On the other hand, among the Nharo one can find many names "that speak about certain circumstances" that occurred at the time of birth. However, the Nharo naming convention is different from that of the G/wi and G//ana, as children are generally named after family members (Visser and Visser 1998:227–229).

A quantitative analysis was carried out of data collected from 202 persons. Six age brackets were distinguished; Old, Middle, Adult, Young adult, Adolescent, and Juvenile (Table 4.1). Most of those belonging to the last category were born after the enforcement of the RADP. Their names are registered on the medical reports of the Xade clinic. Here, even if the mother of a baby tells the nurse a G/wi–G//ana name, the latter will translate it into Setswana. Most of the parents will accept the Setswana name thus suggested. These circumstances are reflected in the conspicuously high percentage (nearly 70 percent) of names with Setswana origin in the category 'Juvenile.' This point indicates that the traditional G/wi–G//ana naming practice in their own language is now rapidly losing significance.

Except for those names for which the original Setswana words could not be ascertained, the anecdotes after which 167 persons had been named could be classified into 11 types (Table 4.2). Most relevant for the subject of this paper is a type of anecdote

Table 4.1

Personal Names with Setswana Origins

Sex/Age	Old	Middle	Adult	Young Adult	Adolescent	Juvenile	Total
Male	2/11	1/10	1/13	5/23	5/19	13/18	27/94
Percentage of male Setswana names	18.2	10.0	7.7	21.7	26.3	72.2	28.7
Female	1/14	0/15	2/22	1/13	1/8	24/36	29/108
Percentage of female Setswana names	7.1	0.0	9.1	7.7	12.5	66.7	26.9
Total	3/25	1/25	3/35	6/36	6/27	37/54	56/202
Total percentage	12.0	4.0	8.6	16.7	22.2	68.5	27.7

In each age bracket, "M/N" indicates the number of personal names with Setswana origins/the number of all names for which the anecdotes were recorded. The age of each person was estimated in 1992, based on relative birth order, appearance, and the status in the life-cycle. The category 'Juvenile' includes those persons estimated as less than 15 years old. As some of them were born after the beginning of research in 1982, their absolute ages are known.

that refers to the relationship with the Bakgalagadi (≠Kebe). Examining the distribution of all the types of anecdotes among the age brackets, only this type was found significantly frequent in the Old/Middle category. This reflects that, compared to recent times, the contact with the Bakgalagadi was of more memorable nature half a century ago.

To give some examples, the anecdotes from which several personal names originated can be summarized as follows:

(N1) /khoo-≠Kebe ("inform of" + "Bakgalagadi," an old man's name): During a gathering trip this man's father found a camp of ≠Kebe, and coming back home, he informed the coresidents of his find.

(N2) !koan ("sort out," an old man's name): This man's father lived close to a ≠Kebe man. During his absence, the ≠Kebe man stole the skin of a bat-eared fox from him. Finding out afterwards, the father openly spoke ill of the ≠Kebe man. Hearing this, the latter took him out of the crowd and beat him up.

(N3) !koan-kua ("sort out" + "Bushman," an old man's name): In a camp, ≠Kebe and Kūa people were living together. The former singled out a few persons from the Kūa and shared their food only with them. The parents of !koan-kua were among those who received no privileged treatment by the ≠Kebe.

Table 4.2

Naming Anecdotes among the Age Brackets

Types of Anecdotes	Old/Middle	Adult/ Young Adult	Adolescent/ Juvenile	Total
Marriage/pregnancy	11 (22.0)	18 (26.5)	10 (20.4)	39 (23.3)
Conflict by *zaaku**	6 (12.0)	17 (25.0)	14 (28.6)	37 (22.1)
Socioeconomic conflict	11 (22.0)	9 (13.2)	12 (24.5)	32 (19.2)
Land name/transaction	7 (14.0)	6 (8.8)	2 (4.1)	15 (9.0)
Interaction with ≠Kebe	7 (14.0)+	1 (1.5)	3 (6.1)	11 (6.6)
Hunting/gathering	5 (10.0)	13 (19.1)	4 (8.2)	22 (13.2)
Others	3 (6.0)	4 (5.9)	4 (8.2)	11 (6.6)
Total	50	68	49	167

Figures in parentheses indicate the percentages in each column. The symbol + indicates that the observed value is significantly higher than the expectation ($p < 0.05$, df = 1).

* *zaaku* means the persistent extramarital sexual relationship.

(N4) *gyio-cue* ("pay" + "migrate," an old woman's name): Her father had a close economic relationship with a ≠Kebe man. When the ≠Kebe man went back to his village, he told her father not to migrate to a different place and he promised to remain. However, during the absence of the ≠Kebe man, the father, agreeing with a proposal of his kinsman, migrated to a place where *tsama* melons were abundant. The ≠Kebe man tracked them and accosted the father, saying, "Why did you migrate? Pay me some compensation."

These anecdotes reveal that there occurred quite a few encounters between the G/wi, G//ana, and the Bakgalagadi in the Central Kalahari, resulting in friendly transactions at least on some occasions. However, they also suggest that the former assumed a subordinate position to the latter. It may not be incidental that both in (N2) and (N3) "Kūa" is the object of the transitive verb "sort out." The essential character of the relationship to the agropastoralist Bakgalagadi, as perceived by the G/wi–G//ana themselves, may have been encoded into these names.

Narratives of Liminal Character

As was pointed out by Tanaka (1980:14), the G//ana have had more contact with the Bakgalagadi than the G/wi, resulting in a considerable rate of mixed blood. In fact, the most influential G//ana people are half Bakgalagadi who already possessed goats and cultivated fields in the 1960s. One of them was appointed as headman of the Xade community when sedentarism began. Even among the G/wi, there are people of mixed blood with the Bakgalagadi, mostly originating from the southwest area of the CKGR near Tsetseng. Ciama,[3] an old man from this group, who died in 1996, was an excellent storyteller, and his narrative recorded in 1994 includes a number of striking anecdotes that are very suggestive for the present subject.

Ciama was a fluent speaker of Setswana and possessed a profound knowledge of the sorcery of the ≠Kebe. In his long narrative he thus organized many cases of his kinsmen and acquaintances' deaths into a consistent 'causal' chain. Only a part of these anecdotes can be summarized below.

(D1) [1940s?] Both Ciama's father Masimo and his father's elder brother Gyiro loved the same girl, but Masimo married her (Ciama's mother). For this reason, Gyiro held a grudge against Masimo, and when Masimo visited him, he served him bean porridge that was poisoned. Coming home, Masimo began to agonize and died the next morning.

(D2) [1968?] Gyiro's eldest son loved the beautiful girl Culozera and married her. However, Gyiro objected to this marriage, saying, "Don't indulge in a Kūa woman. Take a ≠Kebe woman as wife." Obeying his father's order, the son deserted Culozera. When Gyiro visited Culozera's camp, she served him a porridge of *tsama* melon that was poisoned. At midnight Gyiro arrived at his camp and began to agonize. He died the next evening.

(D3) [1975?–1990] The oldest man in Xade, Hororigyo, and a G//ana man named Tsemako, known as the 'greatest goat owner' of the area, both had a relationship with a young woman called Kx'oyakene. This kind of 'shared relationship' called *!naaku* is usually proof of a close friendship. Hororigyo married her, but she soon gave birth to Tsemako's child. /Koa-aba, a man from a different area, visited Xade and stayed for many months. He tempted Hororigyo to abandon the relationship with Tsemako and instead to start a new one with himself. When Tsemako found out about this, he got so angry that he maybe secretly set a magical medicine in Hororigyo's hut. One night, when Hororigyo was drinking in Ciama's hut, /Koa-aba courted Kx'oyakene in his absence. She rejected him and was maybe raped. At midnight, a G/wi woman living near Hororigyo's hut woke from her sleep and witnessed that /Koa-aba sprinkled something (maybe magical medicine) onto Hororigyo's hut. He hurriedly left Xade and never came back again. Several months later, one morning, Kx'oyakene went gathering with her husband. When she was picking //qane berries (*Grewia retinervis*), Hororigyo went ahead and set fire to a grassy area in order to make it easy to collect *tsama* melons. Having picked many melons, he went home alone. Late at night he and his coresidents began to worry about Kx'oyakene who had not yet come home. Ciama practiced divination (/xou) and predicted that she had died, but the others did not believe him. The next morning they tracked her and found her burnt to death. She had been caught by the fire that her husband had set. After the burial, Ciama and another G/wi man witnessed at midnight that Hororigyo in deep grief practiced complicated magical devices on the sand under which his wife had been buried. From then, Tsemako's wives and kinsmen died one after another. In 1990, Tsemako himself died suddenly. All of these deaths were allegedly caused by Hororigyo's sorcery. In 1994, several months before this narrative was recorded, Hororigyo died. According to Ciama's interpretation, he was killed by a very influential Bakgalagadi man who had left Xade three years before but visited again for a short period. It is said that during his stay, Hororigyo was served a cup of poisoned tea.

Ciama concluded the above story as follows, "Medicine is this way. It's bad and ugly. You boast of it, but you yourself will die of it." Considering Tanaka's claim that "[t]he San are basically realistic and rational, having no systematic beliefs about any supernatural powers" (Tanaka 1980:110), these stories seem to be quite fantastic. However, narratives of this kind are quite common in the Bantu culture. Here it is assumed that negative feelings such as anger, grudge, envy, and jealousy will prompt someone to make use of sorcery. Faced with inexplicable misfortune such as illness, disaster, and death, any occasion of social conflict or strange behavior will be retrospectively framed up and reinterpreted as the cause of this misfortune. Although I cannot afford to deepen this issue here, it should be noted that this kind of retrospective interpretation of strange matters is also common among the G/wi–G//ana's cognition of the social world and the natural environment (Sugawara 2001). However, the point is that most of the G/wi–G//ana are hardly acquainted with such a systematic discourse of sorcery. In fact, my research assistants in their early 30s had not known about this story until they assisted me in recording Ciama's narrative.

Thus, Ciama was a liminal person, standing at the border between G/wi and Bantu cultures (cf. Gordon 1992). In everyday context, he was respected as an old G/wi man who was wise, eloquent, and rich, possessing a number of goats, and having been married to three wives. However, he was also often called ≠Kebe and was not unwilling to profess himself to be ≠Kebe. The liminal character of his existence was not only embodied in his fantastic storytelling, but also connected with a peculiar symbolic power. As was referred to in (D3), he was an expert of divination and was often asked to practice rituals on various occasions, such as curing illnesses or purifying the pollution caused by an abnormal delivery or the death of a baby. The clients usually rewarded these practices by presenting a goat, so that Ciama would clearly profit from using his 'symbolic resources' at the interface of the two cultures.

Characteristics of the Economic and Social Transactions with the Bakgalagadi

The life-history narratives of several older men include a number of episodes that hint at the characteristics of the economic and social transactions between the G/wi–G//ana and the Bakgalagadi.

(T1) According to the narrative of Siekua, a G/wi man in his early sixties when interviewed in 1994, he and other G/wi men were often employed as trackers by ≠Kebe hunters, probably in the late 1940s or early 1950s. The ≠Kebe hunters were on horseback and used guns to shoot the game. The G/wi men used to cut the meat into strings, dried it and had donkeys carry the bundles of it back home. This procedure is quite similar to the "group equestrian hunting" common in recent years, except that the use of guns has been strictly forbidden since the demarcation of the CKGR. In former days the G/wi men also followed the tracks of leopards and lions with dogs. They used to eat the boiled meat of leopards, but threw away the lion meat. Although their ≠Kebe employer sold the leopard and lion skins to white farmers at high prices, he did not pay them much money. <<We were sad and wept. "Oh! What is this ≠Kebe man doing? Oh! We ourselves carried it, and skinned it, but he does not share so much money with us.">>[4]

(T2) Probably in 1969–70, Siekua participated in a hunting expedition team composed of five G/wi and three G//ana men. Two of these, one G//ana and one G/wi man, each owned a horse, and so two adolescent G/wi men of the team could ride on horseback. They killed giraffes, elands, and gemsboks, and carried the dried meat to Rakops to sell it to the Bantu-speaking villagers. In this village, a woman who had not received any meat informed the police, as selling wild game meat was prohibited. Four of them—Siekua, two other G/wi men, and one G//ana man—were arrested and put into jail for several months from winter till the beginning of the rainy season. In prison they were supplied with abundant food. <<We worked, worked, worked . . . and returned to eat porridge and meat. We were not hungry. *Aeh*,[5] we were satisfied. We became fat! [Laugh] But my heart was aching, thinking of my children. I was satisfied, but my heart was aching.>>

The above episodes reveal that even in previous nomadic life the G/wi and G//ana had not always adhered to the 'traditional' bow-and-arrow hunting, but were at least occasionally also involved in the "equestrian hunting." This was an important constituent of the transactions with the Bantu-speaking people, even though it was later made illegal within the CKGR.

What made the characteristics of the G/wi–G//ana relationship with the Bakgalagadi ambiguous was the fact that some of the people with mixed blood were categorized as ≠Kebe at least in some social contexts, not only by themselves but also by other people. Such a type of categorization was especially sensitive in the context of marriage or of sexual relationships.

(T3) The G/wi man ≠Noekuchue had continued a sexual relationship (*zaaku*)[6] with Ciama's second wife for many years. <<Ciama accused me [≠Noekuchue], saying, "I am a ≠Kebe, but you keep a *zaaku* relation with my wife. You are a Kūa, but you continue to enter my hut.">>

(T4) A middle-aged G//ana man, Dao//gua, married the daughter of a rich G//ana family with mixed blood. This marriage was promoted by the daughter's mother. <<She said, "Let this man marry my daughter. He is very strong and always kills 'things' [game]." However, my mother objected against this marriage. "Do not let a ≠Kebe woman marry a Kūa man. Even if a Kūa man marries her, the ≠Kebe people will soon deprive him of his wife." She was right. That woman [the mother of the bride] talked and said, "UO!! [an interjection expressing surprise or disagreement] He is Kūa, but he will marry her." She gave Toope [name of the bride] to me.>>

The most striking point is that the locution of "You are (or, 'he/she is') Kūa, *but . . .*" is repeatedly heard, when people talk about their relationship with the Bakgalagadi or the G/wi–G//ana with mixed blood. This locution was, of course, originally addressed to the Kūa by the ≠Kebe. It embodies the negative view the outsiders held of the G/wi and G//ana. Furthermore, as it is repeatedly quoted by the people themselves, this negative characterization seems to have been internalized as the self-image of the Kūa, too. However, the opposite motif of emphasizing the equality between the Kūa and the ≠Kebe can also be seen, for example, in the narrative of the old G/wi man !Kao!kae.

(T5) !Kao!kae and his elder brother //Gaa had a father with mixed blood. Probably in the early 1970s, together with several G/wi men and a ≠Kebe man, they sat around a pot in which they cooked the meat of a kori bustard (*Ardeotis kori*), a large bird. When //Gaa was stirring the meat, a piece dropped out of the pot. He gave it to an older G/wi man sitting there. Then the ≠Kebe man complained. <<He said, "Why did you first give a piece of meat to a Kūa, though you and I, who are ≠Kebe men, are sitting here." My elder brother said, "We all killed a leopard recently. We washed ourselves with the [magical] medicine [which prevented the leopard from biting us], and then we killed the leopard. Therefore, this is just the [meat of] kori bustard for the older Kūa man. He will first eat it, then we will eat." Then he [the ≠Kebe man] got sulky.>> Being resentful for this incident, the ≠Kebe man practiced

sorcery in order to take revenge for the humiliation. Soon / / Gaa suffered from serious diarrhea and died after thrashing about for several days.

In the above story, the brother of the narrator resisted discriminating between
the ≠Kebe and the Kūa by putting emphasis on the collaboration between the
≠Kebe and the Kūa in hunting dangerous animals. This orientation toward equality did not come to a happy ending. Far from it—the rightful, though tiny attempt
to claim equality seemed to be defeated by the supernatural power monopolized
by the ≠Kebe. In spite of this, such an interpretation of the relationship between
the Kūa and the ≠Kebe is not confined to the Kūa's 'inferiority complex' but it is
open to a criticism of their self-image, which was generated and congealed
through interactions with the Bantu-speaking people.

CATEGORIZATION DEVICES AND THE CHARACTERIZATION OF INTERGROUP RELATIONSHIPS IN EVERYDAY CONVERSATION

In the early stages of conversation analysis, when it developed from the discipline
of ethnomethodology, one of its central issues was the question, how the participants categorized those to whom they were referring. Harvey Sacks proposed
the "membership categorization device" (abbreviated as "categorization device" below), which is culturally constructed and invoked unconsciously by the participants (Sacks 1972/1986). Most relevant for the present argument is the device
'ethnic group.' Elsewhere, I analyzed several examples of G/wi conversation and
delineated how the participants differentiated themselves from the Bakgalagadi or
even from the G/ /ana (Sugawara 1991). First, I shall summarize the findings of this
analysis.

Features Differentiating between Ethnic or Dialect Groups

When the Bakgalagadi people are referred to in everyday conversation, much attention is paid to their incomprehensible way of behavior, ranging from such trivial
matters as 'beating a dog fiercely' to apparently farfetched rumors. Examples for the
latter are as follows:

(K1) A rich Bakgalagadi man was said to have killed a daughter of the influential
G/ /ana man !Noaya by sorcery in 1984. He was also said to have evoked the light-
ning by which many of !Noaya's goats were killed in 1985.

(K2) It is said that, a long time ago, a Bakgalagadi man earned much money by selling his own son to the government.

(K3) It is said that, a long time ago, a Bakgalagadi man killed his younger brother by magical medicine.

(K3) is homologous to (D1), Ciama's narration in the above section, though the names of the characters are different. The important point is that the G/wi–G//ana are tempted to put emphasis on the difference between themselves and the Bakgalagadi by insisting that the latter possess mysterious powers or behave in strange manners beyond comprehension. Examples (K2) and (K3) point at the most essential indicator for characterizing 'us' and 'them.' The G/wi and G//ana regard brotherhood as the most reliable tie between individuals, and love for one's own children constitutes the profoundest delight of life. The ≠Kebe, on the other hand, are considered to be cold enough to negate these fundamental values of social life.

I have observed several cases in which G//ana people expressed a sense of superiority over the G/wi. Similarly, the G/wi sometimes make negative comments on the character of the G//ana, for example:

(G1) A G//ana man lived with his G/wi wife in a camp of which all members but himself were G/wi. His mother-in-law complained about her seven-year-old grandson who would often tease his younger brother, saying, "This is the way a G//ana child behaves. He doesn't distinguish his own younger brother [from other children]."

(G2) A young man complained that, though his G//ana-speaking friends had patrolled to inspect his snares for him, they had not set snares again after catching two steenboks. In response to this complaint, a different young man said, "G//ana men don't know how to set snares. Where do they come from?"

The locution of "Where do you come from?" is often used to mock a partner's absurd way of behaving. Such discourse is grounded on the well-known logic of discrimination, that an observed negative trait of behavior shown by a person (or even a child) is to be ascribed to the 'origin' of this person. As soon as the 'origin' is confirmed, the negative trait is generalized into a collective trait shared by a set of people who have the same origin. This logic of discrimination, used to differentiate between the two dialect groups G/wi and G//ana, is basically the same as the logic that serves to differentiate the G/wi–G//ana from the Bakgalagadi.

Transaction and Conflict between Ethnic Groups in the Settlement

The attitude of the G/wi–G//ana toward the Bakgalagadi is characterized by some kind of ambivalence. On the one hand they often backbite the Bakgalagadi for their bad demeanor, while on the other hand they are willing to have various transactions with them. The G/wi sometimes visit Bakgalagadi camps in order to obtain temporary jobs such as processing hides or building fences around the fields. In the following conversation, an old G/wi woman was criticized for her bad manner in offering a service.

Conversation 1[7] (23 August 1989)

An adult woman, //Noeba (nb),[8] and an old man, Siekua (SK), are talking.

> **nb:** She arrived and spoke. She said to them (*mf. dl.*), "Bring your things. Bring those dirty things and let me wash-give." Zubu's mother could not understand and thought, "Oh! How can [this] woman [say such a thing]? We (*f. inc.*) will not brag of ourselves. As if we always receive what ≠Kebe people (*mf.*) spontaneously offer; only when they give their things to us, {we will make-give, make-give}.
> **SK:**   {right word, right word}.

Explanation: The old woman—referred to by the pronoun 'she' in the first line— recently had moved to the camp of the appointed chief, a rich G//ana man of mixed blood. Soon after this she said to the chief and his wife, "Bring your dirty things. I will wash them for you." Listening to this scene at this occasion, Zubu's mother, whose son had married SK's daughter, had been very astonished and told her bad feeling to **nb** afterwards.

Although, strictly speaking, the chief and his wife are not Bakgalagadi but G//ana-speaking, they are often referred to as '≠Kebe' in everyday discourse among the G/wi. Moreover, my research assistant further explained as follows: traditionally, G/wi people used to visit the ≠Kebe with collected plant food. The host would eat the offered food, and, after eating, take out some goods from his house *by himself (kaake)* so as to give them to the G/wi visitor. Receiving them, he or she would repair, wash, sew, or tan those goods and return them to the host. The manner of working in this fashion is condensed in the verb *ts'awa-ma* (translated as "make-give"), which is a compound of the verbs "make" (*ts'aon*) and "give" (*maa*). In fact, this manner of working seems to be idealized by the participants of the above conversation, as is exemplified by SK's eager response, "right word," and it reveals essential features of the socioeconomic relationship between the G/wi–G//ana and the Bakgalagadi. In sum, the modest attitude of the former is valued and the voluntary favor of the latter is expected. Such attitudes and expectations are to be maintained even under the conditions of close everyday contact in the settlement.

Another type of economic transaction between the G/wi–G//ana and the Bakgalagadi can be seen on special occasions, such as when performing rituals. On various occasions, the G/wi–G//ana are willing to ask a Bakgalagadi 'doctor' to carry out a ritual. In the previous section I have already drawn the attention to the peculiar status of Ciama, an old G/wi man, profiting from his 'symbolic resources' at the interface between the two cultures. This is also true for the Bakgalagadi 'doctors.' In spite of their fear of the magical power exerted by the Bakgalagadi, the G/wi–G//ana also feel attracted to it.

However, we should not underestimate the possibility that the relationship between the G/wi–G//ana and the Bakgalagadi may lead to 'negative reciprocity' (Sahlins 1974). If the Bakgalagadi charge high for their homemade beer the G/wi–G//ana have drunk, or when they reward a whole day's work with only this beer, they establish a relationship of negative reciprocity, in which they appropriate the G/wi–G//ana's labor and production or, at best, haggle over it (Sugawara 1988). Furthermore, the relationship between these two ethnic groups is always open to plain conflict and antagonism. Tanaka described an occasion of violence, in which several young Bakgalagadi men assaulted a young G/wi man who was about to marry a G/wi girl of mixed blood (Tanaka 1987). I myself observed an incident of conflict that was not as serious as the case described by Tanaka.

Conversation 2 (21 October 1987)

The old G/wi man SK and an old G//ana man named /Nooso (NS), who is visiting the subject camp, are talking in the early morning.

SK: Yesterday a man killed [hit] our (*m. pl.*) children (*mf. pl.*). And then [he] will catch him [a boy] and take him to prison.

NS: In this way, they will take Gyoba to [prison], too.

SK: That is to say, now those people [Bakgalagadi] have come here. Those people have come here now. When we (*m. pl.*) were living there, their children killed a female goat. We had no responsibility, but Gongore's daughter felt so sad that we paid for the goat.

NS: [I heard that] they (*m. dl.*), Campasi and the other, said and said: "How bad you (*mf. pl.*) are! Your children killed the goat of Guetsa's father. We (*m. dl.*) told you to pay for it, but you have remained silent."

[a number of passages omitted]

NS: Let us go [to the court] and settle this matter.

SK: That's what I say. Let us go to argue with Campasi. Previously, they (*m. pl.*) took //Aon's blanket. He was drinking, hanging the blanket on a donkey's back. They took it. He continued looking for it. I said, "Stop it. I know about them. They will kill you. Do not quarrel with them. And keep silent. If you meet them, do not mention the blanket." [following passages omitted]

Explanation: This conversation was recorded on the day succeeding an incident, where a very influential Bakgalagadi man, nicknamed Campasi, hit the G/wi boy Muretse, who was living in a camp neighboring SK's camp. In the evening preceding this incident, several G/wi boys had quarreled with Campasi's son. One of them had beaten him with a stick, so that he cried and told his father. Getting angry, Campasi rushed to the place, caught the innocent boy Muretse, who had not beaten his son, pushed him down and even kicked him. SK and NS recall various other occasions of conflict that they have experienced with Campasi: (1) Campasi's sons abused one of the goats of 'Gongore's daughter' (a G//ana woman) and caused its death. The sons of SK's kinsmen witnessed this. But, as Campasi made a false statement against these boys, SK and his kinsmen were forced to pay compensation for the goat. (2) Gyoba, Muretse's grandfather's younger brother, was accused that his sons had killed the goat of Campasi's kinsman. (3) Campasi's adolescent kinsmen stole a blanket from SK's son //Aon.

Following the above conversation, Muretse's father visited Campasi's camp and demanded to negotiate this matter in court. About one hour later, the court was held at the center of the settlement, and a lot of people attended. The argument lasted for many hours, but as no reconcilement was attained even in the late afternoon, people became tired of the endless argument and dispersed. Finally, the court was dissolved and never held again on this matter.

A number of interesting points can be drawn from the above course of events. A rather tiny incident, namely the intervention of a Bakgalagadi man in a quarrel among children, uncovers the latent hostility of the G/wi–G//ana against the Bakgalagadi. This might have been accumulated through frequent interactions between them during settlement life. Campasi, who had been prompted by the RADP to migrate from Metse-a-manong to Xade with his large herd of goats, soon obtained a strong political power in his new community. The above conversation shows that the G/wi–G//ana had deepened their antipathy against him every time they underwent an unfair treatment that was made possible by his political power. But this is only one side of the coin. Although many G/wi and G//ana in union expressed their antipathy against the power of a Bakgalagadi man, they did not make any persistent effort to negate the power relationship between themselves and the Bakgalagadi in general. Finally, in order to make their antipathy public, they had to rely on the 'court,' which had been imported from the Tswana institution of *kgotla* under the supervision of the government. But most of the time in the 'court' was spent in confirming the actual course and details of the matter, and an effective consensus hardly ever developed.

COPING WITH THE NEW INSTITUTIONS

As was described by Tanaka (1987), after being given the franchise, the G/wi–G//ana first participated in an election in August 1984. As most of the people were illiterate, they voted by choosing pieces of papers of different colors, each of which denoted a different party. The following conversation was recorded about five years later after the first election, when most people had lost interest in the elections.

Conversation 3 (28 September 1989)

About a week before the new election, a G/wi-speaking old man of mixed blood, /Ade (AD), visited the subject camp. He attempted to talk about the election, but could not attract the attention of the people in the conversation circle. At last, he repeatedly called to two married women, //Gaesi (ga) and her younger sister Gyieka (gk).

AD: Listen to me well!
gk: We (*mf. pl.*) are listening well, certainly!
AD: *Aheh* [Yah].
gk: We are listening well.
AD: *Eheh* [Sure], and then . . .
ga: He [the officer] will give me two [pieces of paper].
AD: And then, you . . . you will put [one of them] in.
gk: You will put the red [paper] in a tiny [envelope], and you will put the black one in that [wastebasket].
ga: *Eheh'i,* Then, you will put the black one in that [wastebasket].
AD: Throw it away.
ga: *Eheh'i.*
AD: You will throw it away.
gk: You know, there are two. When you are given them, you go and take out the 'wildebeest.' Put it in [the wastebasket], and then put the red one in an envelope and give it back again.

Explanation: The red and black papers respectively denote the ruling Botswana Democratic Party (BDP) and the Botswana National Front (BNF), a nongovernmental party. The woman, **gk**, likened the black paper to the wildebeest, a kind of black antelope.

An interesting feature can be noticed in the course of this conversation. Generally speaking, in various types of face-to-face interaction, the G/wi–G//ana people usually seem to give special consideration to the spontaneous action of their communication partners, and they tend to avoid plainly attracting the attention of the latter (Kitamura 1990). In the light of this characterization, AD's behavior of repeatedly calling to the particular participants looks rather curious. In fact, by saying, "We are listening well," **gk** bluntly expresses her antipathy toward the intrusive manner of

AD. However, in spite of such a sign of resistance to the intervening action of the other party, both she and her elder sister reveal quite an uncritical notion of how to vote. They seem to entertain little doubt as to the adequacy of the option of "throwing away the black paper into the wastebasket." Here, voting for the ruling party is regarded as the best way to cope with the extrinsic institutions enforced upon them, regardless of the prospective results of their choice.

Two days before the election, official voting guidance was carried out by a G/wi-speaking man, /Koa≠kebe (KO), who was a member of the settlement's 'Council.' He visited many camps in order to remind the people to bring their identification cards to the election, so that they could be identified in the voting register. The following sample was abstracted from a conversation between him (KO) and an old man, !Kao!kae (KK), living in the neighboring camp.

Conversation 4 (5 October 1989)

KO: When we went to that G//ana camp there, we found that they did not own the cards, so the officer said, "Oh! This way, it won't go well." Thus in order to 'put the card into their ears' [inform them of the card], I'm going around 'together with the time' [looking at a digital watch].

KK: *Nh* [Yes], I understand, my uncle. Indeed, I listened to you well. No complaint. 'When the day is about to end' [I will soon die], you have told me well. Previously I could not understand well, because I'm old. Look! Previously, when you (*mf. pl.*) were living there, they said, "/*Kii* [vote for] the chicken, then you will become rich." But I will /*kii* the other one. When I'm standing with my anus exposed, 'you' (general pronoun) take the feces from my anus to eat them. A man will reject such an unpalatable thing as feces. So, I will not 'put [it] into that (*f.*)' [vote for that party].

Explanation: The chicken is the emblem of the Botswana People's Party (BPP), which did not put up a candidate in the 1989 election. Although the emblem of the Botswana National Front is the key, KK confused the emblem of the BPP with that of the BNF. The metaphor of 'anus' is occasionally used in everyday discourse. The phrase of "suck another's anus" means "intermeddling in another's affairs." In this context, "taking the feces from my anus to eat them" can be interpreted as "doing quite useless and stupid things."

Although KO's status as member of the 'Council' might have obliged him to support the ruling party, he did not explicitly request KK to vote for the BDP. However, as if KK was anticipating the implicit wishes of KO, he stated that he would not vote for the nongovernmental party, using striking metaphors concerning anus and feces. Recalling that these two men are secondary affines and old friends of each other, such a course of interaction is not surprising. Behaving in an unreserved manner, they seemed to smoothly adjust their social relationship to new interests, for example the newly institutionalized election.

The most striking component of this conversation is the usage of the verb /kii. The G/wi–G//ana language, of course, lacks the word 'vote.' The people had to represent the notion of 'voting' by their native word /kii. When used as a noun, /kii can be approximately translated as 'trance dance.' However, in fact, this term is subject to the "indeterminacy of translation" (Quine 1960). Singing and dancing is designated as /kii-sa //nae ya ia, which literally means to "sing and dance (or stamp) the /kii." Moreover, as a verb this term means to "be expert in" some magical practice. For example, ≠aa-sa /kii means to "be good at making the wind (≠aa) blow by magic." Thus, this word probably covers a peculiar semantic field concerning different kinds of supernatural powers (Sugawara 1990:118).

We can imagine that the underlying purpose of 'putting a piece of red paper into a box' is too opaque for the people's practical way of thinking. However, they tried to understand the meaning of this nontransparent, extraneous act by connecting it with an important notion intrinsic to their culture. In other words, by invoking their communal imagination, the G/wi–G//ana managed to adapt to the new extrinsic institution.

The most serious blow the G/wi–G//ana communal imagination had to cope with was the regulation of hunting, especially the prohibition against eland hunting, imposed by the 'extrinsic' government in 1990. Elands are symbolic of female fertility, so that the menarche is celebrated by the eland dance (gyuu-/kii-sa), in which only women can participate (Tanaka 1980). The following conversation exemplifies not only the dissatisfaction with the prohibition, but also the distrust of the government officers who imposed it on the people.

Conversation 5 (19 October 1992)

The old man, SK, his son, //Aon (AO), and his son-in-law, Zubu (ZB) are talking.

AO: They [government officers] said, "Stop killing the eland." But the man passing here tells [us to kill] an eland.

SK: The people will bind that man because of the eland.

AO: I will tell the people to bind him.

SK: They come to tell [us to] work [to kill the eland]. They themselves tell [us to] work.

AO: How is that? Those who tell [us to kill] the eland are ≠Kebe, but [I heard that] they let a man work and pay money to the man. They want kx'ooxo [eat-thing = big game (Tanaka 1996)].

SK: They use us for it.

ZB: They are liars! They say, "Men can live without eating meat." Who doesn't eat meat?

Here, the three men insisted that some of the government officers who visited Xade were so eager to eat the eland meat that they asked the G/wi–G//ana men to poach it. I don't know whether this insistence is true or false. However, the prevalence of such a kind of rumor itself throws light on the asymmetric nature of the relationship between the G/wi–G//ana and the government. The people could not find any formal way to resist the one-way announcement of the prohibition against eland hunting, and in 1990, wildebeest hunting was also prohibited. As for the wildebeest, the hunters at least could utter sarcastic remarks such as "I don't want to eat an animal as black as the ≠Kebe," or "I hate killing wildebeest because when I kill them, they cry *"Yoo, yoo"* like ≠Kebe and make me uneasy." In contrast to this, being deprived of eland meat can be compensated for only by criticizing the hypocritical nature of the claim "Men can live without eating meat," which rationalizes the prohibition of hunting. But this kind of criticism can hardly be made public, since the G/wi–G//ana themselves know very well that they cannot survive in their settlement without the food supplies distributed by the government.

IMAGE OF SELF AS KŪA

As was pointed out at the beginning of this paper, the G/wi–G//ana apply the category name 'Kūa' not only to themselves but also to the Nharo and various groups of 'Bushmen' living in other areas. I have recorded a number of conversations in which they emphasize how lifestyle and physical characteristics of the Kūa differ from those of the ≠Kebe.

Conversation 6: Excerpt (4 November 1992)

Four men were talking about the growth difference of Kūa and ≠Kebe children. On the one hand, when the parents go out for hunting and gathering, the Kūa children are often left in the camp. When they are hungry, they eat edible grasses their mothers have collected, and when they are finished, even eat up their roots. Their stomachs are filled with fibers. Thus, they grow very slowly. On the other hand, the ≠Kebe children eat delicious and nutritious food such as maize, milk, and yogurt. Thus, they grow very fast, as boiled milk foams abruptly. So, even if a Kūa boy and a ≠Kebe boy are of the same age, the latter soon becomes taller and boasts of his superiority, saying, "I'm older than you."

The above remarks reflect the fact that the average height of the 'Bushmen' is far shorter than that of the Bantu. Furthermore, the following remark of my research assistant is even more striking: "In *bara* [the harvest season], I went to Ghanzi. I was sitting in a snack bar and was surprised to see two white women, cheerfully laughing, pushing each other's shoulders, and even pressing one's face to the other's shoulder. I was astonished, thinking, '*Eheh'i*, we Kūa are ugly, while those white people are beautiful, but they behave in the same way as us.'"

I was shocked to find that my assistant felt such a sense of self-depreciation, all the more because I had often been impressed with his graceful movements when we walked in the bush.

The image of self as *l'être-pour-autrui* is generated and congealed through the experience of being stared at by the other (Sartre 1943). Above all, being photographed is the most inescapable way in which the image of self is objectified by the other's eye. In the rainy season of 1983–84, a South African cameraman nicknamed Poro visited Xade together with his wife and a Nharo interpreter. In order to photograph the 'traditional' hunting-gathering life, he employed a number of G/wi men and women and made them live in an artificial camp at Kaochuwe, the homeland of my subject group, about 50 km south of Xade, for more than three months. Three years after Poro had left, in a conversation circle, a G/wi woman, //Gaesi (ga) told some other people about the quarrel she had experienced with him on the final day of their life at Kaochuwe.

Conversation 7: Excerpt (13 October 1987)

Several men and women had been discussing the demeanor of a Japanese researcher. This topic of conversation concerning the trouble in which a /koo-bi (white man, or Japanese man) was involved may have reminded a woman, **ga**, of her experience with another 'white man.'

On the very day we had been allowed to go back home, the sun obstructed it. The sky was bright with no cloud. He said, "Yesterday, there were so many clouds in the sky that I could not take good photos. Today, we will not migrate." At midday like now, he told us (*f. pl.*) to stand up and sing. In the blazing sunshine, we kept standing, clapping and singing. One of the women began to weep, saying, "This [such a miserable experience] may be the omen that my child has died. Oh! White man, do not treat me so badly." He told me, "Hang the /kaa [*Coccinia rehmannii;* its big root is edible] on your forehead and go over there together with this woman. Then, walking across to the other woman standing there, come back here together with her." I carried my load and sat down holding my knees in the shadow of his hut. He came to ask me, "Why are you here?" "Because it is cool and comfortable here." We argued, argued, and argued. Then he lost his temper. "Stand up and go back to your own hut. This woman speaks to me badly, though the men speak to me more nicely." I said, "Hey, Poro. The men will die, because they can drink nothing but your saliva. Because I left my children at Xade, I myself have died in my heart. I am a dead person." "Go back to your hut." "I hate going back to the hut which I have once thrown away. Because we have quarreled so much, you must not take a photo of me. Only if I sleep, you may photograph me." He told the interpreter, "Go to her hut over there and deprive her husband of the trousers I have given him." I said, "Stand up and deprive your wife of her skirt, and then deprive my husband of his trousers."

All of Poro's acts that aroused **ga**'s anger have a common character. That is, the persistent effort to revive the 'traditional' way of life could not help forcing upon the people a manner of behaving that was incongruous with their ordinary sense of practice: singing in blazing sunshine, approaching another woman and soon returning without any purpose, going back to a hut which one has already closed and left, and so on. Above all, the white man's most striking act was his attempt to deprive **ga**'s husband of the gift he had once offered him. Moreover, attempting to take off the clothes that cover somebody's lower half of the body, can be very naturally perceived as an act of hurting this person's human dignity not only in the G/wi community, but also everywhere else.

According to **ga**'s story, she boldly and persistently had opposed to the outsider's attempt to confine her to an immobile image of 'traditional life.' We can suspect that this story only reflected an image of self that was idealized by herself, as we have no means to know to what degree her depiction of the past argument was faithful to the actual event. However, even if this suspicion may be true, the fact that she was quite eager to present this image of self in front of her companions should not be underestimated, because through the repetition of this kind of self-presentation, the people are provided with an opportunity to reorient their attention toward their own lifestyle and reality as Kūa. At the same time, through the recurrent reenactment of conflict between them and the outsider, the people can sharpen their sense of criticism toward the values forced upon them by the latter.

What, then, do the G/wi themselves regard as the most essential value embedded in their own reality of life? It has often been argued that the trance dance is the most essential core of Bushman culture (e.g., Guenther 1986b). As was discussed in the preceding section, the fact that voting is designated by the G/wi term /kii also exemplifies that the trance dance constitutes an important part of the G/wi cultural imagination. Some excellent G/wi–G//ana dancers maintained that they had been taught by qabe-ko (Nharo) masters. They hereby pay their respect to the Nharo, assigning to them not only the ability to propagate their skills, but also to teach them new dancing repertoires.

On the other hand, the G/wi sometimes talk about a strange Kūa group called ≠qx'ao//an living in a distant region in the direction of sunset, maybe beyond Ghanzi (a town about 180 km northwest of Xade). A ≠qx'ao//an man is said to be able to incarnate himself into a lion by pulling off his human skin like a snake and, instead, wearing lion skin. When incarnated as a lion, he will kill and eat people, while as a human dancer he exerts an extraordinary power to heal the sick. Undoubtedly, this ≠qx'ao//an is synonymous with the ≠au//ei (or ≠Au//eisi, a southern !Kung group [Barnard 1992a:46–47]), who "are greatly feared for their supposed fierceness and ability to transform themselves into lions and prey upon people" (Silberbauer 1981:61).

This stereotype of ≠qx'ao//an strikingly coincides with the "liminality position" between 'animal/supernatural' and 'human/natural,' which, Robert Gordon argues, frames the image of Bushmen held by the Bantu neighbors, as well as the European colonists (Gordon 1992:213). But, the point is that the G/wi attribute such supernatural powers not to themselves but to other Kūa groups with whom they rarely encounter. In other words, the G/wi have not passively internalized the image that was pressed on them by the outside. Interacting with the ≠Kebe and /koo-bi (white men), the G/wi seem to be conscious of their marginal status. However, projecting further marginality onto the alien Kūa group in the direction of sunset, their cultural imagination firmly grasps their own image as 'human being' (khoe).

THE DISCOURSE ABOUT THE 'RELOCATION'

In 1986, the cabinet of the Botswana government decided to relocate the people living in the CKGR to new places outside the reserve. Eleven years later, in May 1997, the first wave of people began to migrate from Xade to the new settlement Kx'oensakene, or New Xade. In the course of four months until September 1997, all the residents of Xade successively left their homes. As the political process and background of this "relocation program" was described by Ikeya (n. d.) and other researchers, I will not comment on the course of events during these 11 years. I will only describe some of the discourses about the "relocation" in order to deduce several distinctive patterns of G/wi–G//ana behavior and thought that molded their negotiations with the government.

From 1987 to 1992, the government held many public meetings at the 'court' of Xade, in order to persuade the people to agree with the relocation program, but it was persistently opposed. A typical argument founding their opposition can be summarized as follows. A long time ago, some G/wi–G//ana men persuaded a white man, George B. Silberbauer, to make a borehole at !Koi!kom. In a meeting held in 1987, an old G//ana man designated this borehole as "the water which I made by my mouth," meaning that the borehole belongs to him and his people, while the Tswana never contributed to the establishment of it. Therefore, the government has no right to expel the people from Xade. Eleven years later, at the new settlement, I recorded the discourse of an old G/wi man, which was based on a logic quite similar to this.

The derivation of the new settlement's name, Kx'oensakene, is not clear, but it literally means "look for life." A patterned discourse that was heard quite often was as follows: "At that land, we will not be able to find any game, any plant food, and any firewood. If we move there, we will look for our life very hard, but in vain." This discourse is not merely a play upon words, but definitely expresses the anxiety of the people about life at a strange land.

In accordance with the people's insistence that they cannot leave their own water, the primary factor that hindered the enforcement of the relocation program might have been the difficulty of striking good drinking water. In 1992, a secretary of the Office of the President leaked an informal notice to me that the relocation program had been "frozen." This decision, reflecting the government's hesitation, was probably caused by the strong criticisms of the Botswana policy voiced in many Western media. Thus, the sudden change of the situation starting from 1996 was a great surprise to me, all the more because I had felt at ease, believing that the program would be "frozen" forever.

In August 1996, when I visited Xade after one and a half years of absence, I found that many people were inclined to accept the government's proposals. Several incentives for them to change their minds could be identified: a large compensation for their huts that would be deserted, the promise of the government to distribute livestock, especially cattle, at the new settlement, and the promise to employ many people at quite high wages for laying the water pipes underground. In sum, the G/wi–G//ana people seemed to yield to material temptation. However, analyzing the discourses I collected at Kx'oensakene in July 1998, about one year after the relocation, I found the above formulation to be too simple.

Informal interviews were carried out with three old men, /Koa≠kebe (KO), !Kao!kae (KK), and /Xoi (XO), as well as with two adult men, Shooxo (SH; KK's son) and Ousa (OS), all of whom were G/wi. I shall rearrange the sentences abstracted from their discourse according to several different topics.

The Interpretation of the Modern History by the G/wi

(XO1) <<We met Silberbauer at a pan. We were distressed by the sun. Silberbauer said, "How are you doing?" We said, "We are distressed by the sun." He said, "If a man sprinkles his body with sand, then the body becomes cool, doesn't it?" We said, "*Aeh*, we wash ourselves with sand. It makes a man's body cool." Then, returning and going back, we found him owning a drum of water. We begged water from him. He said, "Oh! This is little. If I give it to you, then after my leaving, you will feel more pain. Keep quiet. I shall go beyond there to meet the government, and then make water for you.">>

(XO2) <<He went back and found the government, began [negotiations] in a distant place, taking the paper for the water and finished many talks. At that time, the

sand was still beautiful, and the words were still beautiful. Finally, the government agreed with him, and then gave us water. The things were going on, going on, and we begged for a living place, and then for a school. And in turn we begged for a clinic, and then for houses. Also for a store. Then we finished. We said, "Yes, thus it's beautiful." And sitting, we made our things. Then, when we made the skins, we sold them to the 'Botswana Craft.'>>[9]

The discourse (XO1), which vividly depicts the first encounter of the G/wi with George Silberbauer, is very similar to the G//ana man's reference to the "water" cited above. The most important point of the discourse (XO2) is, that at the beginning of the RADP, the establishment of infrastructure was experienced as a happy event, at least by this informant. Furthermore, these changes are not interpreted as a forceful intervention from the outside, but as the fruits brought about by the spontaneous efforts of the people to 'beg' things from the government.

How Is the Life at a New Land?

As soon as I arrived at Kx'oensakene, I asked my assistant, "How is life in Kx'oensakene?," and he answered, "In Kx'oensakene, there are no lives (kx'oen-zi: plural form)." This answer, just substantiating the anxiety expressed in the 'play upon words' that was cited above, is not an exaggeration.

(OU1) <<The government told us that we would come to the [land of] 'rich year' and that we would eat, but we fail to find such things. Look! After migrating, we were given the death itself here. So we are astonished. We are not happy. In other words, we are always dead. Food—those things which we used to eat on our sand, such as /kaa, //qane, and kx'om—we cannot find such food. Look! There are no ≠nan≠ke and !om/e. We cannot find what we used to eat on our sand. We have come here; we were taken to the [land of] death. All the food that was [available] at our land is absent here. There is no game for snares. Steenbok skins—we lived that way, rubbing steenbok skins. There are none of them here. Foods such as /kaa, !om/e, //qane, ≠nan≠ke, qan, and //nan—all of them are absent.>>

(XO3) <<There are no such foods as we could find there. Our parents chewed /kaa. And then, they ate !om/e, //qane, kx'om, ≠nan≠ke, con, and koale. However, we have been forced to migrate. We don't like it. Our hearts still ache. We are not happy. We are still thinking of our sand, and our hearts weep.>>

These discourses are definitely patterned by a common perception of the new environment shared among the people. Most of the species of plant food which

were enumerated are included by the category of "major food" of the G/wi and
G//ana (Tanaka 1980:56).[10] The scarcity of these food resources around the new
settlement further enhances the dependence on governmental food rations.

How Did the Government Persuade the People to Migrate?

(KO1) <<[The government said,] "No, you cannot find your life here, and you cannot become rich. If the people go there, then they will be made rich. There, they
will be given cattle, goats, and donkeys. If you are here, you are in the '*Zebra Game.*'
Therefore, so far as you are in the land of *kx'ooxo* [eat-thing, namely animal], you
cannot become rich by receiving cattle." Those who had sucked the milk of cows
and found it delicious agreed with the government. "We will go to drink the milk
of cows. We will agree with those stories. Therefore we will migrate. That milk
will make a man fat." They migrated. The government also said, "If there are
people who migrate, I will migrate with them. I will go to let them live. I will not let
those live who are sitting and remaining in that old way. They are opposed to me.
Therefore, their life is little. They will be supplied only with porridge [maize flour],
and drinking water. They will be given neither cattle nor money. Their school will
not be enlarged. Their school will fall down." Thus, the people sadly gave up. "Let
us migrate. Because other people have migrated ahead. [If we migrate,] we will become human.">>

(XO4) <<We heard. They said, "You are living in the *Game.*" We could not understand. We thought, "Ah? Eh? *Game?* Then, where are our things?" "This our sand?
Has it now become *Game?*" Since old days, we had encountered the lion, and lived in
the same land. We [the people and the lion] were created together. And encounter-
ing each other, and foraging. We cannot fear it. Even though the lion eats our things,
we cannot stand up to escape to a different land. Who can do such a thing?>>

(XO5) <<[The government said,] "I will not help those who remain here, and en-
close them. Because they are within the *Game.* They will starve to death." We were
astonished. "If you make a fence around the *kx'ooxo* [big game], the *kx'ooxo* will be
enclosed. Then, we are human, but will we be enclosed?" "We will migrate, since
all that we have to eat has been eaten up by the lions. If we make it new, we will see
good things.">>

Firstly, an interesting feature is to be noticed on the rhetorical level. That is, the
policy of the government is always represented by direct speech, which may actually have been delivered by some officer in a public meeting. This feature may
reflect the way in which the G/wi perceive any kind of institutionalized organiza-

tion, namely as a personified agent rather than an abstract entity. More trivial but not less striking is the fact that the people confuse the name of the CKGR with another curious name, Zebra Game. The reason for this confusion is unknown.

Secondly, these discourses suggest that it is too hasty to conclude that the people spontaneously agreed with the program. The most essential factor to be noticed is the heterogeneity among the G/wi–G//ana themselves. This heterogeneity was produced at the commencement of the RADP, when hundreds of people migrated into the Xade settlement not only from other areas in the CKGR, but also from farms and towns outside the reserve. As most of them had long ago deserted the hunting-gathering way of life, it might have been an attractive option for them to accept the proposal of the government to offer cattle. It was not until a part of the Xade population had migrated to the new settlement that it became far easier for the government to press the remaining people to move. In other words, the government succeeded in splitting the residents into two parties with different values and intentions.

Lions frequently killed people's livestock at the Xade settlement. When they complained, the government cleverly made use of this argument, saying that the problem was to be ascribed to the very fact that they were living in the game reserve ("Zebra Game") where the hunting of lions had been strictly prohibited. Discourse (XO4) plainly expressed the intention to resist such tactics, taking recourse to the values intrinsic to the way of life in the bush. However, the same narrator soon withdrew in the succeeding discourse (XO5).

The Logic of Objection against the Government

(KK1) I did not like Kx'oensakene. Therefore, I rejected. They cheated me. When the "pencil" [an officer who recorded the huts] came, I was lying. She wrote my name. I rejected it clearly. I said to that woman, "Look! Instead of doing such a [stupid] thing, take me to Tsetseng, my land." She said, "Do you want to migrate to Tsetseng?" I said, "Yes, if I migrate to Tsetseng, and once I die there, my kinsmen will bury me."

(XO6) *Aeh,* we (*m. pl.*) refused. And said, "Why can we do so? Although the government tells us that we should stand up and leave the land where our parents lived and consumed." Probably the new land where we are going to will not be suitable for us.

(KO2) Previously, I supported [/*kii*] the Donkuraxa [jack; the emblem of the BDP]. As I was bothered by the matter of migration, I threw away the Donkuraxa. Now I'm supporting [/*kiyaaha*; the progressive form of /*kii*] the *faifutii piipul* [First People]. *Eheh'i,* it is the 'past man.' I say to Botswana, "Did only you own the *kx'ooxo* [eat-thing; animal] of the land? Look! You owned the cattle, and then, do you in turn also own the *kx'ooxo*? Look! Because they are those which god-spirits [//*gama-xari; mf. pl.*] created long ago. Who gave birth to the Kūa? Isn't the Kūa a child of god? Is only the Tswana a child of god? Did the Satan give birth to the Kūa himself? Do you, the Tswana, yourselves call the name of the Kūa's parent?" In such a way, I ask him. But he does not answer.

(KO3) [In this discourse the names of tribes and ethnic groups are enumerated. Although, in English grammar, a group of people should be denoted by the pronoun of plural form, the following translation follows the original G/wi style of expression, in which each group is personified and referred to by the masculine singular pronoun.] Give him the land of the Kūa. *Eheh'i.* That is, the Botswana is Mukuwena [the name of a Tswana tribe]. Motswana [the Tswana-speaking people]. He lives in Molepolole [the name of a city]. His land is Molepolole. We Kūa comprise the G/wi-men, G//ana-men, !Xoo-men, and *qabe*-men [Nharo]. Similarly, the Botswana comprises Mukuwena. He owns Molepolole. Motswana, Motswana comprises Ngwaketse. His land is Kanye [the name of a town]. [several sentences omitted; enumerating five tribes of the Tswana] This is the way in which the Botswana has been. He each has the land. Where is the Kūa's? There is no Kūa's [land]. But he says, "The Kūa is Motswana." *Eheh'i,* this is where the difficulty lies. *Eheh'i,* that is, the Kūa does not agree with the Tswana. This is, he lacks land.

(OU2) I was paid a little money for the migration. But, my things—all my huts are remaining there. The land is remaining. But I was not given money. My hut, my enclosure, my field, and my store hut—all those things are remaining. But I was given only 3,000 pula.

Even among the G/wi people who wanted to remain at Xade, the strategies for resisting the government policy were variable. The government itself sometimes suggested multiple options for places to where the people were to move. Thus, !Kao!kae and his family tried to counter the government's attempt by claiming that they would migrate to their home land (KK1). However, the most confident strategy was adopted by /Koa≠kebe (KO), a former member of the Council, who became a sympathizer of the party 'First People of Kalahari.' It is evident that the discourses (KO2–3) were strongly influenced by the ideas of this organization for the self-empowerment of the Basarwa (Bushmen) in Botswana. We have to suspect that these ideas are not necessarily rooted in the indigenous thought of the G/wi–G//ana, but rather affected by the Western ideology of monotheism. Moreover, /Koa≠kebe's discourse itself paradoxically reveals that the 'right of land tenure' may be quite a new idea for the people themselves. In fact, in the discourse (OU2),

Ousa does not seem to know that the kind of fertile land they were forced to leave cannot be compensated for by any large amount of money. Even if this is true, it is to be emphasized that at least some of the people, like /Koa≠kebe, can quite accurately and rapidly internalize this idea so as to use it as their own weapon.

How Was the Money Exhausted?

(KO4) I took money. I took 11,000 pula. *Aeh,* the things of the Tswana are expensive. These things let it be exhausted; the bedclothes. I bought things, and I bought a male horse. I lent 500 pula to Campasi. I said, "Pay it with goats," but he has not yet paid it back. I lent Gyurai 500 pula. Therefore, I said, "You should pay a horse, because you are so incapable that you cannot find any goats." That man borrowed money. He has not yet paid it back.

(KK2) My son knows the money. He can count the numbers. Therefore, taking that money, I came home. Then a blanket was torn. Then I bought a blanket. Here it is now. I bought a shovel. And in turn I bought two female horses. If you say horse, it is that kind of thing. They make fun of me. I merely threw away my money. Now it has run out.

(SH1) Daddy had put 1,000 pula in the post office. *Aih,* we (*m. dl.*) went to take 600 pula. Then, we went and went to take 400 pula. Then, when we went, they said, "Your money is finished. And only 20 pula remain." *Eheh'i,* we could not understand, "What happened to our money?"

(KO5) Even if I go back to Xade, why could the government arrest me? Do you say because I took the government's money? His money itself was what he defrauded me of. He usually cheats you. In Japan he cheats you. Going and going [to Japan] and cheating you, he says, "Because the Kūa people are in distress there, I have come to beg money from the big [Japanese] government. He cut the money in pieces, one of which he gave me. He took it, and came to give me a particle of what he had filched. It's my money. Not his. How can he arrest me?

These might be very familiar stories for many hunter-gatherers just before the twenty-first century, who become inescapably involved in the cash economy and commoditization. With few exceptions, most of these stories do not end so pleasantly. If they obtain a lot of money, they mostly cannot save it for the future. Much is used up for buying alcoholic drinks, while some amounts flow into intricate networks of borrowing and lending. However, in the context of relocation, one striking, or rather incomprehensible fact underlies these ordinary stories. That is, even those who were reluctant to migrate, finally received the compensation. Moreover, when they complained that the new settlement was a 'land of death,' they often expressed their wish to go back to Xade. Here, to my surprise, they seemed to perceive no inconsistency of their previous choice with their present complaint or wish.

I was sometimes irritated by the very naive stance the G/wi adopted in the negotiations with the government, because, according to my common sense, it is the ABC of any political struggle not to receive money or any other object of material value offered by the opponent party. The discourse (KO5) was the response /Koa≠kebe gave to my question, which was based on this irritation. Although his logic seems to be quite intricate, it is supported by his knowledge of the world system. He knew that much of the money spent for the development of the 'Basarwa' came from European countries. Although Japan did not supply Botswana with such aid, he confused Japan with these European countries. Thus, his logic is as follows; (1) Japan (or other developed countries) gave Botswana the money in order to help the Kūa. (2) Therefore, that money originally belongs to the Kūa. (3) Botswana gave the Kūa only a small particle of that money. (4) Therefore, the Kūa are not obliged to follow Botswana, even though they received money from 'him.'

However, it might be misleading to try to read consistent logic from the actual practice of the people. When I frankly expressed the above irritation to my assistant, saying, "How incapable the G/wi people are! After consuming the money given by the government, they are beginning to talk about going back to Xade!" he answered, "But, it is good to get money, every time when it is available." Such a way of thinking and acting is often characterized as 'opportunism.' In the final section, I shall develop the point that the opportunistic attitude is an essential feature of the G/wi negotiations with the agents from outside institutions.

DISCUSSION

In this paper, I have described various aspects of the G/wi–G//ana interactions with the outside, using three different kinds of materials: the naming conventions and the narratives of life history, everyday conversations, and the discourses drawn from informal interviews, which were made at three chronological stages: before the sedentarism, during the settlement life at Xade, and after the relocation.

In order to elucidate the essential characteristics of the relationship between the hunter-gatherers and the outside in the context of the Central Kalahari, I would like to use terms such as *realism, optimism,* and *opportunism* as clues, which have already been used rather loosely in the previous literature. It is necessary to quote Tanaka's characterization again: "The San are basically realistic and rational, having no systematic beliefs about any supernatural powers and no interest in matters not related to their daily lives" (Tanaka 1980:110). "They neither dwell long on past events nor worry about what the next day will bring. They are optimists living only for the present" (Tanaka 1980:94).

It might be easy to criticize this characterization as to some degree biased, as Tanaka's ecological methodology does not pay much attention to "supernatural powers." However, when we try to formulate the ideological aspect of the G/wi–G//ana contact with the Bantu culture, the scheme of practice that can be designated as 'optimistic realism' is of much importance. Many evidences from the naming conventions and the life history suggested that the G/wi–G//ana had at least occasional interactions with the Bakgalagadi, in which they tended to assume a subordinate position. The fact that a number of G//ana people, as well as a few of the G/wi, have mixed blood with the Bakgalagadi shows that some of the relationships between these two ethnic groups have long historic roots. In the light of this history, it is surprising that the G/wi–G//ana maintained quite a low susceptibility to the Bantu ideology, especially sorcery and witchcraft, even though a few people of 'liminal' position have shown a strong disposition to these magical practices.[11] In other words, the peculiar G/wi man Ciama could profit from employing this symbolic resource merely because that resource had remained quite scarce.

It is not known to what degree the G/wi and G//ana themselves noticed the harmful effect of sorcery and witchcraft to their deeply egalitarian form of life. Actually, I am rather skeptical of the validity of some kind of functionalism that would explain that the people avoid X because X is harmful to their society. Instead, the notion to which I would like to return is rather the simple dichotomy of the transparency or opaqueness of the intentional goal of the other's act. Here, I am not interested in the philosophical question as to whether the intentional goal of one's act is always transparent to oneself. However, one can always perceive the other's act as one with either a transparent intention or an opaque one. In principle, any strange practice of the outsider, say ritual, is perceived as opaque, until the meaning behind it is internalized by the subject.

Thus, we can formulate the scheme of practice designated as 'optimistic realism' in the context of interaction with the outsider as follows: The outsider's opaque act can be made use of as a valuable resource, if it brings about visible advantages for one's own proximate goals. This formulation entails that any conjecture about the other's intention, desire, or motivation behind the act has to be cut off at a very low threshold. This point is also resonant with Koji Kitamura's claim that in various types of everyday interactions the G/wi–G//ana always put special emphasis on the 'autonomy' of the other party (Kitamura 1990). It also coincides with my impression in the field that their explanations of the reason for other people's acts are usually very superficial. This superficiality extends even to the explanation of one's own acts; for example, "Why did you accept the money from the government?" "Because it is nice to get money."

Paying attention to the final point above, we can shift the focus of our argument to the 'opportunism.' A number of conversational occasions were described in which the "membership categorization device" was activated to distinguish the G/wi–G//ana from the Bakgalagadi, Tswana, and the Europeans. According to the above formulation, various behavioral indices of outsiders were referred to in order to emphasize the opaqueness of their acts. If people are faced with this opaqueness in a context in which their direct interests clash with those of the 'outside' party, it becomes a target of severe criticism.

However, a careful distinction must be drawn between the bitterness of the back-biting against the outsider and the actual manner of face-to-face interaction with the latter. This distinction is quite subtly maintained in everyday interactions, even among the G/wi–G//ana themselves. In many occasions, I wondered at how quickly a man, having been severely criticizing some absent person, changed his attitude in the presence of the latter, and how smilingly he could talk with this person without mentioning any syllable of the criticism of just a few minutes before.

Thus, such a two-faced attitude toward the other is not specific to interactions with the outsider. However, this attitude is of critical advantage, especially when the outsider is a source of prospective interest within a proximate range. To expose plain hostility or antipathy toward the opaqueness of outsiders' acts may be a maladaptive strategy in a social environment in which occasional encounters are open to the possibility of reciprocal interchange. I do not intend to depict the G/wi–G//ana as always calculating their interest. The two-faced attitude may be interwoven with another characteristic of behavior, namely the reluctance to offer any "significant opposition" to a particular proposal by another party (Silberbauer 1982; Sugawara 1998b). These micropolitical strategies constitute an important aspect of the unique form of life, roughly designated as 'egalitarianism.'

As was described in **ga**'s story in Conversation 7, in some situations one might step beyond the usual self-restraint and accuse the other party. Such plain accusations are possible by immediately responding to each other's transparent intentions (Sugawara 1996). This kind of interaction is usually regarded as evoking a so-called 'joking relationship.' In fact, it was said that Poro appreciated **ga** and her husband very much, as he was an excellent bow-and-arrow hunter and therefore earned the highest wage Poro paid. Another point is the fact, that even if a conflict occurs between the G/wi–G//ana and an outsider, they are very reluctant to prolong the tension, as was suggested by the course of events which was observed after Conversation 2—the conflicts with Campasi.

The above observations suggest that the G/wi–G//ana usually do not so much act according to some consistent principle, but that they rather flexibly accommodate themselves to a given social situation. Thus we can formulate the scheme of practice designated as 'opportunism' as follows:

Generally, your choice of how to act toward a partner in a present situation, and also the outcome of this interaction, need not affect the choice in forthcoming interactions with the same party. Particularly, in the context of interactions with an outsider, you can seek your interest within the most proximate range, because you don't know whether this relationship will be long-lasting. Here, you may act according to optimistic realism. Moreover, if you have recurrent interactions with the same party, the choice in the preceding interaction and its outcome need not affect the choice in the succeeding one.

I have been often irritated by the arrogant behavior, which is designated as ≠gaa≠ga-si in G/wi language, in which some Bakgalagadi men treat my G/wi friends derogatorily. This derogatory attitude has been prevalent on the Bakgalagadi side throughout the past contact between the two ethnic groups, and was based on their superior economic status. The G/wi–G//ana coped with this situation, recurring to their practice schemes of 'optimistic realism' and 'opportunism.' The relationship between both parties was so asymmetrical, that the opportunistic subordination of the G/wi–G//ana to the Bakgalagadi became practically institutionalized.

It can be supposed that this subordination not only brought about some economic profit but also might have been accompanied by some curiosity, for example toward magic, witchcraft, and even sorcery. At the early stage of the RADP, the introduction of new institutions as well as the establishment of infrastructure was experienced as rewarding (see XO2). The practice of the G/wi–G//ana of coping with the opaqueness of the extrinsic institution is most typically embodied in the fact that they applied the word /kii (approximately translated as "trance dance") to 'voting for' or 'supporting' a political party (see Conversation 4 and KO2). This point enables them to subtly accommodate themselves to a newly given social environment.

However, behind the opaqueness of the novel institutions, there lies the principle of a 'modern system,' which is far more consistent and perpetual than the derogatory attitude of the Bakgalagadi toward the G/wi–G//ana. Personifying the government or equating it with its agents exemplifies the persistent effort of the G/wi–G//ana to establish the conditions of a face-to-face interaction with an outsider with an opaque intention. At this point, the G/wi–G//ana strategy of opportunistic subordination is bound to fail, partly because the intentions of the State are sometimes not even transparent to its own agents. Many years ago, Pierre Clastres pathetically admired the South American Indian societies, claiming that they accomplished the negation of power within their own society (Clastres 1974). I believe that the G/wi and G//ana's attitude to life shows another way to negate power relationships.[12] However, in face of the overwhelming power of the State, their persistent effort to negate power within their own society makes them too powerless to organize a systematic resistance against the government policy.

NOTES

1. In a recent paper, I have reviewed in detail most of the articles written by the members of this team (Sugawara 1998a).

2. A confusing character of Silberbauer's descriptions of the G/wi nouns is that they mostly include the suffix that indicates gender, number, and case. For the word ≠*ibina*, '-*na*' is a suffix of objective case, plural form, and common gender.

3. In the following ethnographic descriptions, personal names are fictitious.

4. The transcription of the narrative of the informant is put in double angle brackets << >>, within which direct quotations are enclosed in double quotation marks.

5. Those letters, such as *"Aeh," "Eheh'i," "Nh,"* and *"Aih,"* denote interjections that express agreement or confirmation.

6. The prevalence of persistent extramarital sexual relationships called *zaaku* is the most unusual feature of the G/wi-G//ana sexuality. Tanaka (1989) translated the *zaaku* relationship as "love-relationship" and argued that its significance lay in the uniting of two or more married families through a sexual relationship. I also reconstructed a number of episodes of *zaaku* from the analysis of topics in everyday conversation (Sugawara 1991).

7. The text of the conversation is not a full transcription, but a summarized and simplified version of it. Transcript notations are as follows:

[ ]: supplement translation or explanation by the author; *(m., f., mf.)*: gender of pronoun or noun; male, female, and common respectively; *(inc., exc.)*: inclusive and exclusive form of the first person pronoun respectively; *(dl., pl.)*: number of pronoun or noun, dual and plural forms respectively; for example *(mf. dl.)* indicates a pair of male and female; { }: simultaneous discourse.

8. Abbreviated names of females and males are represented by two small letters and two capital letters respectively.

9. Botswana Craft is a nonprofit enterprise that provides the people with the opportunity to earn cash income through the sale of their folk crafts. In 1983 this was reorganized into 'Ghanzi Craft' (Tanaka 1991).

10. The scientific names are as follows: /kaa (*Coccinia rehmannii*), //qane (*Grewia retinervis*), kx'om (*Grewia flava*), ≠nan≠ke (*Bauhinia petersiana*), !om/e (*Cucumis kalahariensis*), qan (*Acanthosicyos naudiniana*), //nan (*Citrullus lanatus*), con (*Ledebouria* sp.), and koale (*Ledebouria apertiflora*) (Tanaka 1980).

11. I borrow the distinction between 'susceptibility' and 'disposition' from the "epidemiology of representation" proposed by Dan Sperber (Sperber 1996:66–70).

12. My recent volume written in Japanese aimed at demonstrating that the core of the G/wi-G//ana's "sense of interaction" is putting much emphasis on the equality between the participants (Sugawara 1998c).

five

Independence, Resistance,
Accommodation, Persistence

Hunter-Gatherers and Agropastoralists in the
Ghanzi Veld, Early 1800s to Mid-1900s

Mathias Guenther

The focus of this historical examination of hunter-gatherer social flexibility and adaptability is on the Bushmen of the northwestern region of the Ghanzi District, in particular the two principal linguistic groups, the Nharo (Naro) and ≠Au/ /eisi of the "Central" and "Northern" linguistic divisions respectively. Geographically the region is known as the Ghanzi veld (or Chanse veld, as it appears on some early maps), a relatively well-watered stretch of the Kalahari, running from around Rietfontein and Kalkfontein, at the Namibia-Botswana border, to around Kobe and Kuki, the district border between Ghanzi and Ngamiland. Its approximately 36,000 square kilometers include the well-watered Ghanzi limestone ridge, the region's topographical spine that includes over 50 pans and water holes, close to half of them containing springs that hold water all year round (Passarge 1904:map 1). The latter region corresponds roughly to the farming block in today's Ghanzi District (see Fig. 5.1). The historical period covered, the nineteenth and early twentieth centuries, is the time period for which some information is available, allowing for a tentative reconstruction of the economic, social, and political makeup of the Ghanzi Bushmen and of their political and structural responses to the various settler groups who

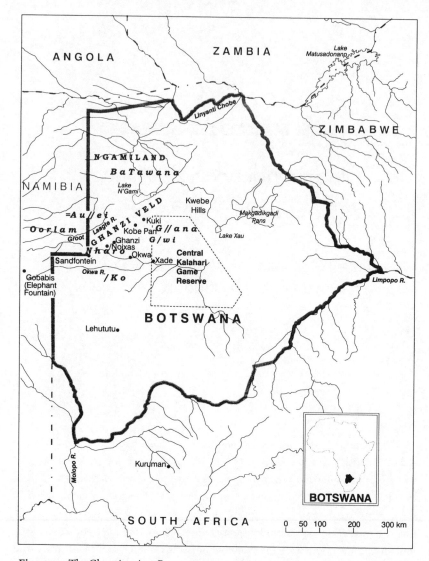

Figure 5.1. The Ghanzi region, Botswana.

began to make inroads, from all directions, on this relatively hospitable stretch of the Kalahari veld by the early nineteenth century. Surveying the responses of these two Bushman groups to these agropastoral outsiders over time will reveal a range of interaction patterns on the part of this African hunter-gatherer society, attesting both to a high degree of flexibility, resilience, and adaptability of such societies (Kent 1996) and to their capacity for retaining political independence and cultural autonomy despite considerable outside pressure.

An account of Bushman history and political organization in such terms would situate this paper within the revisionist "Kalahari Debate" (which, as evidenced by its chief proponent Edwin Wilmsen's most recent book [1997], is as alive as ever). As one of the key arguments in the debate is the reliability of the evidence (as well as the scholarly integrity in its employment), I turn to this matter in the latter half of my paper, which will assess the ethnohistorical evidence, both oral and written.

ETHNOGRAPHIC PRESENT AND RECENT PAST

The modes of subsistence and social organization forms of the Nharo and ≠Au//eisi of the Ghanzi veld fall in line with the "foraging band" pattern described by anthropologists among other contemporary Kalahari Bushmen. Men hunt and women gather, with overlap in this sex-based division of labor, reflecting gender equality or, more broadly, social equality in general. Social groupings are loosely organized, territorially and socially open and fluid in composition, oscillating seasonally between dispersed, small, band or sub-band units and aggregated, large band, or multiband units. This Bushman-wide pattern of social oscillation has a tendency, among the Nharo, toward extended aggregation (Barnard 1992a:223–236), probably because of the relative abundance of year-round surface water along the water-rich Ghanzi limestone ridge (Wilmsen 1997:111, 114, 200). The subsistence economy is of the non-accumulative "immediate-return" type; food, especially meat, is shared, as are non-food items, along somewhat formalized lines and wide networks of exchange partners. Leadership and ritual roles are loosely defined. The latter role is performed by the trance dancer, whose curing dance, performed with the vital assistance of the women, is a ritually and symbolically elaborate rite of intensification.

That, in rough outline, is how late-nineteenth (Schinz 1891a:388–399) and early-twentieth-century observers (Passarge 1907:16–75 / Wilmsen 1997:137–175; Kaufmann 1910; Bleek 1928b) described the Ghanzi Bushmen (with a number of significant deviations from this pattern, to be noted below). It is also how contemporary anthropologist in the 1960s and 1970s (Steyn 1971; Guenther 1986c; Barnard 1992a:135–155) described the "traditional" Nharo of the Ghanzi District, that is, those not attached to cattle ranchers and drawn into their economy and society. It was a pattern also that could be distilled from the farm Nharo and ≠Au//eisi, in part, on the basis of reconstruction from memory culture, in part, on the basis of observation of those individuals and families who, because of unemployment or underemployment, drifted away from the farms and resumed, more or less extensively, foraging lifeways.

In the Ghanzi veld, which is the region within which the settler groups established most of their ranches, virtually all of the Bushmen have been drawn into the cattle economy and society of the largely white farmers. These were initially primarily Afrikaners (or Boers) who had established their sprawling ranches in this Kalahari stretch around 1900, on land secured by them through treaties British colonial agents had negotiated with the Tawana paramount chief (who, as will be seen below, laid claim to the territory). For the first two or three generations of Boer-Bushman interaction, until the 1960s, the Bushmen were an underemployed, exploited labor force for the largely Afrikaner (Boer) ranchers. The latter extended toward the Bushman laborers and domestics in their employ, as well as their dependents, the kind of paternalism characteristic for the frontier Boer, that is, a blend of racialist superiority and harshness and qualified benevolence and curtailed largesse. Sometimes that relationship would last for two or three generations, with the same Bushman family attached to the same Boer employer, and generations of Boer children looked after by generations of Bushman nannies, creating a pattern of hereditary servitude (Russell and Russell 1979; Guenther 1986c:42–46, 1996). Cash wages were low and were supplemented with food rations, the occasional slaughtered beast (or one found dead in the kraal or veld), cast-off clothing, medical treatment and, in the case of some farmers, the right to plant maize and graze a few goats, or even calves or cows. The latter might be provided to the laborer by the farmer in order to promote greater vigilance in his Bushman herder.

This sort of arrangement is similar to the cattle-loan system of the Tswana called *mafisa*, whereby a man will leave his cattle to be looked after by another person, in return for the rights to take milk, some of the calves born in the course of the arrangement, to eat the meat of beasts that had died naturally, and to use the animals for ploughing (Passarge 1907:121/Wilmsen 1997:205; also see Wilmsen 1997:255–256; Morton 1994:215; Wilmsen 1989:99).[1] Several hundred Ghanzi Bushmen, those living within the economic and social orbit of black herders, in the southwestern and northeastern regions of the Ghanzi veld, were drawn into this socioeconomic pattern (Silberbauer 1965:127–131; Silberbauer and Kuper 1966; Guenther 1986c:178–181).

The Ghanzi farm Bushmen continued then (as they continue still today)[2] to draw on the veld for food, especially for plants. These the women, who were less tied to the farms because only few of them were employed, gathered on sporadic, frequently extended, gathering outings. Men set snares around the farms, bringing in modest amounts of small game (while boys, their slingshots ever at the ready, went after birds, for tasty meat-snacks). In addition to retaining these foraging subsistence patterns throughout these three to four generations of attachment to Boer farmers, the farm Bushmen also retained such key elements of their traditional way of life as patterns of social and spatial fluidity and mobility, the sharing ethos, marriage, kinship, and child-rearing patterns, female initiation rites and, in particular, the trance dance (Guenther 1986c:286–295). Thus, despite economic dependence and a more sedentary life, in villages at the white farmers' residences or at his cattle camps, or as "serfs" to black masters (Silberbauer and Kuper 1966:179), much of traditional Bushman culture persisted.

It was only well into the second half of the twentieth century that these social and cultural patterns became increasingly eroded. The reason was a combination of ever-increasing economic dependence of more and more farm Bushmen on fewer and fewer farm jobs. Their decline was due to the increasing mechanization of ranching operations, rendering Bushman labor obsolete, notwithstanding the fact that the actual number of farms the government made available to white (as well as "coloured" and black) ranchers increased progressively. The placement of children in a national school system, the spread of, and desire for Western consumer goods, work abroad, the increasing, and hegemonic spread of the agenda of the state and of the Western market economy, have had the expected undermining effects on the cultural integrity of the Ghanzi Bushmen, as they would of any other indigenous culture. In combination, the aforementioned post-foraging Bushmen of contemporary Ghanzi, and of the country and region as a whole, can now be said to have undergone a social and cultural transformation. The Bushmen now model their society, their life courses, careers and expectations, their ideas and values on those of the mainstream, modern society and nation of which they are an integral component.

NINETEENTH CENTURY

The nineteenth century, like the twentieth, was a century of turmoil and change for the Bushmen of the Ghanzi veld. Their stretch of Kalahari land provided rich grazing for teeming herds of game, the abundance of which and astonished early travelers through the region (Andersson 1856:383, 385, 420; Baines 1864:153, 155, 383, 394; Chapman 1971, vol. 1:27, vol. 2:182). Rhinoceroses and elephants were especially abundant. The riches of game are what attracted agropastoralists to the region, especially elephant, a species that, in the second half of the century, also drew increasing numbers of white hunters and traders into the region. Toward the end of the century two of the Bantu-speaking groups just outside the Ghanzi territory, the Tawana and the Barolong, also established sporadic cattle camps in the area, around some of the water holes along the Ghanzi ridge (Tawana) and along the Okwa River bed in the south (Barolong) (Guenther 1986c:37; Passarge 1907:8/Wilmsen 1997:133; also see Wilmsen 1997:112). The incursions of these outsiders became more and more determined and far-ranging throughout the century, especially those of the agropastoral settlers, who were establishing state societies to the north and west of the Ghanzi veld and declared that veld as their hunting preserve, in which they hunted, and overhunted, with wild abandon (Baines 1864:112; Passarge 1907:10, 114, 119/Wilmsen 1997:134, 199, 203; Lau 1987:45).[3] Its Bushman inhabitants they declared, ever more resolutely, as their subjects, from whom they exacted tribute and labor wherever they could. In this they followed a process and pattern of subjugation they had brought to bear on the local Bushman (and certain non-Bushman) populations in their respective newly settled country, Ngamiland in the Okavango Delta (Passarge 1907:120–124/Wilmsen 1997:204–207, 255–256) and the Omaheke in Namibia (Lau 1987:66–68). How did the Bushman hunter-gatherers of the Ghanzi veld fare throughout these times of trouble? How much resistance did the people offer in their encounters with these intruders? How was that resistance manifested and sustained? And what made it cease? To what extent did capitulation (i.e., enserfment) erode the integrity of the foraging mode of existence?[4]

Some of the ethnohistorical evidence suggests that the structural and temporal developments on Ghanzi Bushman society during the first half of the nineteenth century differed markedly from those of the second half. It appears that throughout the first half, the Nharo and ≠Au//eisi hunter-gatherers were organized in social formations that were larger and more complex politically than the foraging bands described above (Passarge 1907:81/Wilmsen 1997:178). Hunting was the more significant component of the foraging economy. Antelope and big-game species were hunted in large numbers and on hunting territories to which access was controlled. Hunts were often high-yield as they utilized deep, double-chambered game pits, 4 m long and 4 m deep—some of them placed within dry riverbeds (Andersson 1856:374–376). Sometimes the pits were placed at the end of a converging row of palisades that stretched for kilometers. Here the hunt might be conducted by groups of up to 300 Bushmen; this activity, and the communal labor of digging the "countless" pits and erecting the palisades, required the organization of a considerable labor effort (Passarge 1907:80, 117/Wilmsen 1907:178, 201). The aggregation phase of the seasonal cycle was extended—possibly in view of year-round availability of water along certain stretches of the Ghanzi limestone ridge—and social groupings were probably larger and more nucleated than among other Kalahari Bushmen.

It appears that leadership was well defined and differentiated amongst the Ghanzi veld Bushmen of the early to mid-nineteenth century. According to Passarge, in addition to "family heads" (*Familienoberhaupt*) and "chiefs" (*Häuptling*) of individual and several bands, respectively, there was also a "paramount chief" (*Oberhäuptling*) who ruled over all of the bands of a large stretch of land, that also included bands from different Bushman "tribes" (1907:114–117/Wilmsen 1997:201–202).[5] The reasons for this relatively high degree of political status differentiation were in part economic, in part political. The coordination and supervision of the labor that went into some of the communal hunting endeavors required, says Passarge, the force of an "iron will" (1907:80, 117/Wilmsen 1907:178, 201). Game animals provided not only food but also trade commodities and may have provided the basis for accumulation, wealth, control, and power (although the early records provide no direct indication that such was actually the case).

The main impetus behind the organizational elaboration of leadership and politics was likely the state of hostility between the two Ghanzi Bushman groups, which appears to have been keen in the early part of the nineteenth century. Oral historical evidence suggests that the ≠Au//eisi—whom the Nharo to this day tend to look at warily and consider to be aggressive and given to sorcery—had begun to move into the northwestern stretches of the Ghanzi veld, from their home area in Namibia to the west and northwest (between Rietfontein and "Elephant Fontein," or Gobabis). The fact that many of the place names in the territories inhabited by !Kung-speaking ≠Au//eisi and Ju/'hoansi apparently are Nharo words further suggest the latter's displacement by the former (Passarge 1907:30/Wilmsen 1997:146–147). The result was "intertribal" conflict between the two groups, with the ≠Au//eisi as the dominant party.

This position peaked under the rule of the ≠Au//ei chief ≠Dukuri, whose reign an old Nharo Bushman, Passarge's Dutch-speaking servant //Kochep, describes in detail (Passarge 1907:114–115). What he offered Passarge was a personal, eyewitness account of something he himself experienced, as "a youth," placing the described events somewhere into the 1840s. He describes ≠Dukuri as a "mighty chief," ruthless and far-reaching in his reign, over many Bushman bands, from whom he exacted payments of tribute. As "paramount war chief" (*oberster Kriegsherr*), he owned an "arsenal" of spears and other weapons that were stored in several huts and that equipped his followers. The latter would, at his single summons, assemble whenever ≠Dukuri mounted raids against recalcitrant families, sometimes exterminating entire bands. "All men are armed and warriors," noted Kaufmann (1910:138), in his account of the ≠Au//eisi around Rietfontein, whom he describes even then—the early twentieth century—as being exceptionally warlike and as given to raiding and blood vengeance. Another one of ≠Dukuri's political roles was that of "supreme judge," adjudicating over family feuds. As a "paramount chief," ≠Dukuri's office was hereditary; other band headmen were his councilors and vassals (Passarge 1910:114); this system of "closed political organization" and "well-organized state formation" Passarge likened to a feudal system (Kaufmann 1910:114, 116).

The political system of the Ghanzi Bushmen of the past rested on a secure economic base of big-game hunting, of a then superabundant supply of game. Hunting, Passarge notes, provided the economic base for large populations that could reproduce themselves prodigiously; the hunt "was the basis for all social and economic conditions, all rights and laws, the entire political organization" (1907:81, 119/Wilmsen 1997:178, 203). The purpose of hunting was both subsistence and trade. Animal skins, ivory, ostrich feathers, and eggshell beads—the most sought-after trade item—were the commodities traded with the Tawana in the northeast and the !Kung in the northwest, in return for iron goods, wooden implements, and cereal. Trade was conducted from band to band, through far-flung networks of exchange involving numerous Bushman and Bantu-speaking tribes, rather than along trade routes, by means of markets or trade caravans (Passarge 1907:118, 202–203; see also

Wilmsen 1997:298–299). However, Passarge surmises that the last were occasionally mounted by the sedentary Tawana into Bushman territory, in a fashion that may have been similar to the copper-trading Bantu-speaking Ovambo in the Otawi region in northern Namibia, who embarked on these trade expedition only with the explicit permission of the Bushmen living in the region (Passarge 1907:118–119, 203).

According to Passarge's informant, ≠Dukuri also waged war against neighboring tribes, so effectively that "the Batuana dare[d] not enter in their [the Bushmen's] territory." It was only some of the Bushmen bands at the northern fringes of the Ghanzi region who fell under the Tawana sway. Yet even there some Bushman groups, such as the Tsao (Tsau), were so effective at resistance that the Tawana chief Moremi had to resort to acts of treachery, such as ambushing an unarmed troop of Tsao on their way to parley with the Tawana and shooting them down (Passarge 1907:120/Wilmsen 1997:204). As for the Oorlam, they only entered Ghanzi for raiding skirmishes; indeed, the Bushmen of the Ghanzi veld were "totally independent" (Passarge 1907:115/Wilmsen 1997:200). The Bantu-speaking Herero, too, who made incursions into the Ghanzi veld from the northwest, were kept at bay, as evidenced by Baines and Chapman's accounts of their journey into ≠Au//ei country in 1861, at which the explorer-hunters' Herero crew were treated with intense hostility by the ≠Au//eisi (and vice versa), culminating in an imminent attack on some of the Herero by a Bushman band, which the travelers were only barely able to curtail (Baines 1864:334–335).[6] Turning to the southern stretches of the Ghanzi veld, the occasional Griqua hunting and trading party venturing north through the Kalahari—the "Great Southern Zahara"—treaded warily, in view of the fierceness of the Bushmen living in the Ghanzi region (Campbell 1822:116; McCabe 1855:417–418, 422).[7]

The two agropastoral states exerting the greatest hegemonic pressure on the Ghanzi veld and its people, the Tawana around Lake Ngami to the north and the Oorlam "Hottentots" of Gobabis (known also as Kai/khauan or Amraalse ("Amraal's people") around Gobabis to the west, arrived at their respective locations at the turn of the century and in the 1840s respectively (Tlou 1972:147; 1976:52; Köhler 1959:16). Each claimed possession of the Ghanzi veld; however, the political organization and power of the Bushmen prevented them from realizing that claim. The Tawana, a relatively weak and loosely centralized and consolidated state of at most 1,000 people (Schinz 1891a:382; Wilmsen 1997:84–85, 273), were also busy consolidating their hold over Ngamiland, against enemies from the south and east, the Kololo and Ndebele raiders (Nettleton 1934:345–347; Tlou 1976:52). Thus, they did not venture all that much into the Ghanzi veld, beyond the occasional hunting excursion and punitive raid into the northeastern periphery of the region, or, as noted above, on peaceful trading expeditions. For the Oorlam these hunting expeditions and raids were more extensive (Lau 1987:45–46). However, until well into the second half of the century, neither group was able to undermine the political independence of the Ghanzi Bushmen, or their cultural integrity as a "hunting people par excellence" (Passarge 1907:110/Wilmsen 1997:196).

Starting around the 1870s, the incursions by these two states became more frequent and more determined, especially those by the Tawana. In 1879, they even resulted in a "war"—more properly, a skirmish—between the two somewhere in the middle of the contested land stretch (Vedder 1930:537; Stals 1991:359–360, 371), with the redoubtable Hendrik van Zyl, the region's first white settler, in the midst of all the action. Other white traders and hunters, with wagons loaded with guns or ivory, passed through Ghanzi, en route to Lake Ngami or Gobabis and beyond, stopping only long enough to hunt whatever elephant or other big game creature came their way. There is no mention of ≠Dukuri or anyone like him in the journals and books of the early travelers Andersson, Baines, and Chapman who traveled near or through the region in the 1850s and 1860s. Passarge notes that ≠Dukuri had died by that time and had been followed by his son, who, devoid of the chiefly might of his father, had offered little resistance to the Tawana. He and his family had been captured and taken to Lake Ngami (Passarge 1907:120/Wilmsen 1997:204). It thus appears that the Bushman empire died with ≠Dukuri.

The radical decline in game and the resultant condition of severe hunger[8] likely led to the decline also of the human population of the region (Passarge 1907:10/Wilmsen 1997:134). The smallpox epidemic that ravaged Namibia during the 1860s (Vedder 1934:417–418; Lau 1987:123–125) reached Gobabis and Rietfontein in 1863, where Chapman, in June of that year, reported meeting Bushmen who had recently survived the disease, "their sores not yet healed" (1971, 1:298; also see 1868, 2:298). He makes no mention of smallpox east of Rietfontein and it thus appears that the smallpox epidemic never reached the central and eastern stretches of the Ghanzi veld. Another health problem was infectious malaria, which was capable of wiping out entire bands (Kaufmann 1910:136; Bleek 1928b:40; also see Lau 1987:123). These conditions of existential stress likely further weakened the Ghanzi Bushmen's resistance to settler incursions.

In combination, the decline of game and of human populations may also have brought about the shift in the economic and social organization of the Bushmen of the Ghanzi veld from big-game hunting to foraging (Passarge 1907:57, 81/Wilmsen 1997:163, 178), and from an organizational pattern reminiscent of a tightly structured patrilocal band (à la Steward), to a loosely egalitarian foraging band (à la Lee [1976]). As reflected from early ethnographic accounts, these late-nineteenth-century Nharo and ≠Au//ei foraging bands, despite their structural simplicity and looseness, evidently still contained certain economic and structural remnants from the earlier period of big-game hunting, political complexity, and centralization. Schinz (1891a:388) reports the Nharo (whom he calls //Ai) at /Noixas in western Ghanzi as until recently having used game pits to hunt such game animals as elephant, giraffe, and hippopotamus (the last a somewhat dubious species this far west of the Oka-vango). He also mentions the Nharo's strong reluctance to cross the territorial boundaries of neighboring bands, especially those of the ≠Au//eisi, toward whom they keep their wary distance (Schinz 1891a:389; also see Kaufmann 1910:156). About four decades later Dorothea Bleek (1928a:4, 17) conducted fieldwork among the Nharo at Sandfontein at the Namibia-Botswana border. Like Schinz before, she learned of Nharo bands fighting with other bands over territorial infractions and of hostilities between the Nharo and the ≠Au//eisi (Bleek 1928b:4, 17; also see Passarge 1907:52, 63/Wilmsen 1997:159, 167). The German colonial Lieutenant Kaufmann (1910:155), writing in 1908 about the Auen (≠Au//eisi) around the border post of Rietfontein where he was stationed, applies the term *Todfeindschaft* (mortal enmity) to the relationship between the Auen and the Nharo. Lebzelter, writing about the same period, describes the relationship between the two Bushman groups as one of servitude, with the ≠Au//eisi in the superordinate position and the Nharo their ser-vants.[9] Bleek was told that the former group's chief had held overlordship over one section of the Nharo (Bleek 1928b:4, 17, 36). Bleek received this bit of recent historical information from an old man by the name of /Kururib, who claimed that the ≠Au//ei chief of his account had been his father. This raises the tempting question if Bleek might, perhaps, have talked to ≠Dukuri's son.

As regards the interaction of the Nharo and ≠Au//eisi with their agropastoral neighbors and enemies during the this later phase of the nineteenth century, it ap-pears that the Bushman groups living in the central, eastern, and southern stretches of the Ghanzi veld were, as before, little affected. The Ghanzi Bushmen may have witnessed, and have had brushes with, the occasional raiding or hunting party, or white, "coloured," or black traders and ox wagon caravans passing through their ter-ritories. Apart from bringing in trade goods and extending the Ghanzi people's trade networks, these contacts appear to have had little impact on the social organization of the interior Ghanzi Bushmen (Passarge 1907:18/Wilmsen 1997:1339). It continued to be the people living at the northern and western flanks of the region, around Sandfontein, Rietfontein, Oliphant Kloof in the west and Kuki and Kubi in the north, who were most affected. They suffered frequent attacks from the Oorlam and especially the Tawana.

At this time the Tawana, with more determination than before, attempted to se-cure their hold over their rich hunting and potential new grazing lands at their southern frontiers and to subjugate its troublesome hunter-gatherer inhabitants. The mode of subjugation was to press them into the agropastoralists' service, as tribute- and labor-rendering serfs, servants, or slaves.[10]

The pattern of dependency between the Ghanzi Bushmen and their nineteenth-century masters was a harsh version of the twentieth-century paternalistic heredi-tary service pattern between the Bushman farm laborers and serfs and their Boer and black masters, respectively, that was described above. As noted by the historian Brigitte Lau, the domination pattern of the Oorlam extended "over the barrel of a gun" over their 1,000-odd Bushman—as well as Bergdama and Herero—dependents, built "on very old structures . . . of feudal and other non-capitalist forms of domination." The information on the nature of that dependency relationship is more comprehensive and more specific for the Tawana (and the Tswana people in general, of whom the Tawana are a part).[11] The Bushmen, as other Tswana subject people, were incorporated into the *bothlanka* serfdom pattern (Morton 1994:215). Prior to its reformation and relaxation in the late nineteenth and early twentieth century, as a result of pressures on the Tswana chiefs from the colonial government (Hitchcock 1996:20), being a *bothla*-serf was at times very hard on the Bushmen. Apart from paying tribute, in the form of ivory, venison, and ostrich feathers, the precolonial *bothla* also had to render labor service, especially as cattle herders and farm workers. Other than milk, the Bushman cattle herders were paid no remuneration; the aforementioned element of *mafisa* was introduced only later, as part of the reforms. The Tswana, especially the Tawana in Ngamiland, as key players in the nineteenth-century ivory trade, exacted another labor service from the Bushman serfs, elephant—and other big game—hunting. Bushman families were "owned" by their Tswana masters and bequeathed as property to their sons. Although no master had the right to sell or buy any serf, at times Bush-children were sold as slaves to colonists in Cape Province to the south.

The treatment received by the Bushmen from their agropastoral masters was very harsh, as evidenced from contemporary oral history and archival and published writings. Brutal punishment—whippings, maimings, or even summary execution—sometimes awaited Bushman serfs who withheld tribute or who were amiss at the tracking and hunting labors they performed for their masters, or who tired at the toilsome task of carrying ivory and meat (Morton 1994:224–226). Both oral and archival sources speak of punitive raids against Bushman individuals or bands, especially those suspected of stock theft or of engaging in "black market" trade with whites. Punishment was also directed against employed herders who had lost cattle under their care, and torture and execution was the fate of captured Bushmen (Morton 1994:232–234). Their women and children were carried away into servitude or slavery—the latter "being the only use they make of the country," as noted in an early archival report on the region (Botswana National Archives HC144). Acts of revenge by the Bushmen were met with brutal reprisals, triggering "a chain of murder and mayhem" (Passarge 1907:122–123/Wilmsen 1997:206, also see p. 265).

Later visitors to the Ghanzi Bushmen sometimes commented on the passive, timid demeanor of the people, in marked contrast to reports two generations earlier, for example by Baines and Chapman. Dorothea Bleek, who visited the Nharo of western Ghanzi in 1921, mentions people talking about Nharo women and men having been slaves and servants to the Nama, who spent months at a time hunting in Nharo territories (Bleek 1928b:25). She was struck by the deferential deportment of the Nharo toward the Nama and Tswana, "letting themselves be tyrannized without resistance" (1928b:24). In fact, according to Captain Fuller, the colonial agent who negotiated the land treaty with the Tawana that ceded their right to the Ghanzi region to Boer settlers, one reason the Bushmen of the Ghanzi veld so readily accepted the Boer farmers at the turn of the century was the expectation that they would offer them protection against Tawana raids and servitude (Botswana National Archives HC.144).

For all its intensity, this period of oppression and enserfment was, however, relatively short-lived in the Ghanzi region, affecting primarily only those groups living in the western and northern stretches of the District. With the death by smallpox of the Oorlam chief Amraal, along with most adult members of his family in 1863, the power of this state began to decline, as well as lapse into anarchy (Baines 1864:80, 325; Vedder 1934:522–525). The *Pax Britannica* and *Pax Germanica*, which became established with colonial rule during the last two decades of the century, further curtailed the power of the states flanking the Ghanzi veld and prevented the full realization and spread of their hegemony over the Bushman inhabitants of this region. Thus, in the final analysis, their experience of subjugation and dependence at the hands of the two major agropastoral state societies to have made incursions unto the Ghanzi veld during the nineteenth century did not undermine the political independence and cultural autonomy of most of the region's Bushman inhabitants to any great extent. The curtailment of political independence and cultural autonomy was very much less for the Ghanzi Bushmen than it had been for Bushmen in other areas of southern Africa, such as the some of the Khoe Bushmen of eastern Botswana or some of the agropastoral groups of northern Namibia and southern Angola.

In sum, we see that the Ghanzi Bushmen during the first three-quarters of the nineteenth century were quite different in their political and economic makeup from those of the last quarter. The first are seen to be politically complex, organized, centralized, militarized, and able to assert their independence over agropastoral settler groups pressing onto their territories from all directions. The second are seen to be politically loose and labile, as well as, in some instances, dependent, tied in a tributary and labor-rendering relationship to Bantu-speaking and Nama pastoral state societies. These latter Ghanzi Bushmen, economically, were in the process also of obtaining stock animals, engaging in incipient pastoralism alongside hunting and gathering. Because of the marginal nature of the pastoral activities of the Ghanzi Bushmen, which supplemented rather than supplanted the hunting and gathering subsistence and production mode, and the short duration, historically, of their dependency relationship, it is doubtful that pastoralism had much of an effect on the economic and social organization of these inveterate hunting-gathering peoples. Most of the Ghanzi Bushmen throughout the nineteenth century retained their foraging economy, which, in the first half appears, among some groups, to have had a strong emphasis on hunting, so that the political prominence of the warlike men was reinforced economically by "man the hunter." In the latter half of the century, partly because of the decline of Bushman political power and organization, and of the Bushman population and their game resources, foraging, rather than big game hunting, had become the subsistence mode. Further reducing the subsistence importance of the hunt at that time was the fact that hunting was for some of the Ghanzi Bushmen primarily a tributary labor task, rather than a subsistence activity.

Foraging, and the social organizational pattern that goes along with it, continued through the twentieth century, with the dependency relationship transferred from black (and yellow) masters to white ones. Because of the presence of the latter squarely within the Ghanzi veld, within which the white ranchers' farms came to be located, more Bushman individuals and families than ever before were drawn into a relationship of dependency on a paternalistic *baas*-employer. Yet, as had been the case throughout the century preceding, here, several generations of farm Bushmen of the twentieth century retained a number of key elements of their traditional way of life and culture, despite their quite close attachment to the Boer farmers.

It was only during the last two or three decades of the twentieth century that these social and cultural patterns became increasingly eroded, when the new generation of Bushmen turned their efforts toward remedying their condition of poverty and position of social and political discrimination and marginalization. They did this by articulating and operationalizing their goals and aspirations at the community, national, and regional levels, in a modern language and manner—of community development, mobilization, and activism, regional networking, identity politics (Hitchcock 1996)—that commands a response from the state. Like other foraging peoples in other parts of the world, the Bushmen of Ghanzi, Botswana, and southern Africa have become post-foragers. The foraging lifeway, which they had followed in some form or other throughout these last two centuries, in the face of ever more persistent and pervasive settler contacts, and, one would assume, for uncounted centuries before that, is now in the process of dissolution and absorption into the Bushmen's own version of modernity. It will be most interesting to observe what impact the foraging social and ideological pattern may exert on that process of change and transformation.

THE "BUSHMAN REICH" IN GHANZI: FACT OR FICTION?

Let us turn back to the nineteenth century once again, this time with a number of specific methodological questions. How much can we know about the Bushmen at that time? By what sources? How reliable are these sources? What further source material could be tapped? The further back we go, the more urgent these questions become. Thus, in the context of the historical time span covered in this paper, the period of ≠Au//eisi political mobilization, organization, centralization, and suzerainty is what is most in need of critical examination. Apart from the distance and dimness in time of this phase in Ghanzi Bushman history, another reason for being critical about the available information is because what it reports, about economic, social, and political patterns, is quite unusual and unexpected for a foraging people such as the Kalahari Bushmen.

Written Sources: Another reason for caution is because there are certain doubts on the reliability of the writer describing and proposing it. These doubts were first raised by Gustav Fritsch, a contemporary of Passarge's and his senior by several decades, who had himself published anthropological accounts on the Bushmen, amongst whom he had worked in the 1860s in the southern Kalahari. In a lively debate[12] Fritsch accused Passarge of having created a "distorted picture" (*Zerrbild*) of the early nineteenth-century Ghanzi Bushmen. The lifeways of these *Ureinwohner* ("original inhabitants") of an arid land, Fritsch contends, "entirely preclude a rigid state organization," allowing only for "nominal forms of leadership" (Fritsch 1906:72). "The mighty *Buschmannreich* belongs into the domain of the fable," he noted (Fritsch 1906:73; also see Schott 1955:134, for a similar assessment), for if it were to have been fact, why did none of the early travelers (Andersson, Baines, Chapman, Livingstone) make any mention whatsoever of it? (To which Passarge replied, quite rightly, that the first three traveled through the area after ≠Dukuri's reign while the last, David Livingstone, the "discoverer" of Lake Ngami in 1851, had never been in the Ghanzi veld.) As one of his points of criticism, Fritsch cast doubt on the reliability of Passarge's information, specifically his chief informant. This was a Dutch-speaking old Nharo man, who was searching his memory for information about the days of his childhood and, so Fritsch suggested somewhat gratuitously, told Passarge a pack of lies (Fritsch 1906:72).

Whether or not such was the case—Passarge decidedly dismissed this charge, attesting to the reliability of "my good old //Kochep," whose statements Passarge constantly checked and double-checked (Passarge 1906:412)—it is true that Passarge did have only one informant providing this information. Moreover, as a geographer he was not trained for ethnographic fieldwork. He based much of his information on hearsay from white traders—in particular the ubiquitous trader Müller who appears to have been Passarge's chief source—or on local Batswana. At times Passarge was careful about such information, however, and expressed doubts and caveats about it, for instance, about the interpretation of Bushman tattoos as "tribal markings" provided to him by his Barolong informant Peter Sesebicho (Passarge 1907:26–27/Wilmsen 1997:144). Much of his information was anecdotal and ad hoc and the lengthy ethnographic sketch of the contemporary hunting-gathering Nharo, which does contain some good firsthand observations, is presented in the format of an essentialist, composite narrative that takes the reader along on a fictive journey undertaken by a fictive band, describing the plight and perils experienced along the way. While it appears that Passarge did have some command of Setswana, he likely did not speak any Bushman language (even though appended to his monograph are Nharo and ≠Au//ei word lists and Nharo sentences). Of the three years he spent in the Ngami-Ghanzi-Dobe regions, as chief surveyor of the British West Charterland Company, only about four months were spent in the Ghanzi veld, on three expeditions to the region.

It would seem that for Passarge, as for many another Khoisan scholar before and after him,[13] the Bushmen were a screen onto which he projected his personal *Weltanschauung*. This was evidently well defined in his mind and its contents shaped his scholarly work. The German geographer and Passarge biographer Gerhard Sandner refers to Passarge as "one of the most active political geographers of Germany between 1896–1935" (1989:348). Politically committed, verbally aggressive (and occasionally sued), colonialist and imperialist, Social Darwinist, and later in his life, also National Socialist, Passarge had a penchant for melding ideology and scholarship. Sandner characterizes Passarge's work as an instance of *Zweckswissenschaft*— "purposeful science related to political goals" (1989:342)—and of stating personal opinion on matters close to his heart (such as anti-Semitism), in the guise of a scientific utterance (1989:347–48; also see Fischer 1990:54; Fahlbusch et al. 1989:355).

In his early career Passarge applied, unsuccessfully, for a job in the German colonial service (Wilmsen 1997:16) and a number of his Kalahari and Ngamiland chapters are written from the perspective not just of science but of the colonialist enterprise. That is, the land and people surveyed by the geographer-anthropologist are assessed in terms of their potential suitability for exploitation and settlement by European colonists. In Passarge's considered opinion, neither the Kalahari nor the Okavango are all that significant for European interest. And as for the Bushmen, a "race bred . . .exclusively for the hunt" (Passarge 1907:128), they are quite unsuitable for farm labor on European ranches. Nomadism is bred in the Bushman's bone, its imprint on the collective mind of the Bushman "has to lead to inconstancy, unreliability, restlessness and love of freedom," all character traits incompatible with the regimen of farm labor.[14] These traits mark the Bushman's character as akin to that of "most carnivorous animals which, as they, lead restless hunters' lives" (Passarge 1907:128). Is there any other choice for the "man of culture" (*Kulturmensch*, i.e., the European colonist), asks Passarge rhetorically, but to place the Bushmen of present times into jail and prison—or, as such cannot be found in remote frontier regions, to shoot them (1907:124)?

When he turns to the "the Bushmen of the earlier times," Passarge's estimation of the character of the people becomes markedly different. He finds, back then, in the Bushmen's Golden Age, a people very much in accord with his imperialist romanticism. Its ingredients—the drive for *Lebensraum,* territoriality, *Herrenmensch* aggressiveness and power, warlords and warriors, routs and raid—all were elements of *Buschmannreich* as he perceived and describes it in *Die Buschmänner.* Today, they are gone, and gone with them is the Bushman's "cultural fitness." In line with his Social Darwinist appraisal of pacifism as a pathological, degenerative process of domestication (Sandner 1989:347; Fahlbusch et al. 1989:355), Passarge attributed the "cultural unfitness" (*Kulturunfähigkeit*) of the contemporary foraging Bushmen directly to their "charitableness" (*Mildtätigkeit*) and "communal spirit" (*Gemeinsinn*):

> Charitableness and communal spirit are praiseworthy qualities. However, if they are taken so far that no one becomes prosperous, because everything, to the last particle, is shared with others, then this virtue becomes a fault, as a culture is only thinkable with healthy egotism and the striving to get ahead and to care for one's family. Indeed, one has to hold this exaggerated virtue to be a significant cause of the Bushman's cultural unfitness. (Passarge 1907:125, my translation)

Passarge's ideas on colonialist policies, which he offers at the conclusion of his general essay on the cultural ecology of Kalahari peoples (Passarge 1905:87–88 / Wilmsen 1997:93–94), further reflect this imperialist, "might-is-right" ideology. Contrasting the German and Portuguese with English colonization policies, he expresses strong doubts on the latter, specifically its policy of indirect rule. "This cannot last in the long run," Passarge ominously opines, "the longer the peace lasts, the harder the war will be" (1905:87, 93). Continuing his dark ruminations, he predicts that the Bushmen and Khoekhoe, under English colonial rule, will all perish in the near future, while the Bantu-speaking peoples will increase enormously in numbers and blend into a number of homogeneous, united groups. They will soon constitute the "black threat" for white settlers, who might well be swept away, the same way the storm tide in Haiti swept away the French.

In the context of his exchange with Fritsch, who challenged Passarge about the likelihood of the fabled *Buschmannreich*'s existence, Passarge can be seen to back down somewhat on his position on this matter. Contrary to what he had stated in his monograph, in the rejoinder article to Fritsch he stressed that tight political organization was found only within individual (and small) Bushman tribes, rather than over them all. Even chief ≠Dukuri, Passarge now contends, ruled only "in a small part of Ghanzi" (Passarge 1906:412). In fact, even in *Die Buschmänner* Passarge seemed conflicting on the extent of political consolidation and power of these early Bushman "feudal" societies. Even though he presented them as "well organized state systems," he nevertheless also expressed surprise at coming across so large, complex, and tightly structured a political system amongst the Bushmen, given this people's *ungebundenen Sinn* ("unbounded spirit"), and their penchant for wide dispersal, both of which would militate against "a strict regimen" (Passarge 1906:116/Wilmsen 1997:201). Moreover, rather than a tightly organized, centralized, state-like political system among the Ghanzi Bushmen—as well as other groups further northeast, in the country of the Ju/'hoansi—being an institutionalized social formation, Passarge (1906) attributed its appearance to the strong personality of an individual "paramount chief."

So, in view of these problems, and Passarge's own amendments and ambiguities, what should we make of Passarge's Reich of Bushman big-game hunters? As I described elsewhere (Guenther 1997:132–134), other written records, as well as oral history accounts from contemporary farm Nharo, bear out the sort of development Passarge points to in his revised, toned-down version of the political organization of the Ghanzi Bushmen of the early and middle nineteenth century. As regards the economic component of the geographer's reconstruction of the lifeways of the Bushmen of early times—their big-game hunting—Passarge appears to be on safer evidential ground. The early historical writers consistently remark on the abundance of game, on game pits (into one of which Andersson fell, horse and all!). Oral historical reports I obtained from old people in the Ghanzi district confirm both of these points (including dramatic accounts of the dangers facing the hunter if a lion had fallen into the game pit).

As regards leadership patterns in the Ghanzi veld of early times, there is evidence of at least two Bushman "chiefs," who, in the course of their own lifetime, and through their own ambition, charisma, and strength of personality, displayed leadership ability, cunning, ruthlessness, and bravery. In the one case, the Gobabis Nama renegade by the name of Gert, this amounted to a position of considerable power. Gert, mounted and armed with a firearm, was able to assemble about a hundred Bushmen around himself and "assume the rights and privileges of a chief over the Basarwa, exercising a despotic and arbitrary sway over them," as reported testily by Chapman (1971, II:172, 1868:312–313), who had once employed Gert as a guide on his 1861–62 expedition from Walvis Bay to Lake Ngami (Guenther 1993/94). It had been from his expedition that Gert had absconded, during the Ghanzi leg of the journey, with all of the expedition's horses and with a gun stolen from Chapman.

Oral Sources: The other case is drawn from the record of oral history, which I collected among the Ghanzi farm Bushmen in the course of my fieldwork. The narrative in question is a family memoir I collected from an old man, born around 1907, who told the following story about a Tawana raid, which happened when his mother was a small girl. This would place the event described at sometime during the 1880s.

This happened before there were any Europeans in Ghanzi, except for some, very few. In those days there was an old Nharo man; his name was Tsabu. He was the chief of the Nharo. He had two sisters at ≠Xoi tsa farm, an older one and a young one. [The latter was the narrator's mother.] When he stayed at that place, visiting his two sisters, the Tswana came from Ngamiland. They had heard that he was at ≠Xi ta and they came to kill him, along with other people, and to take their people to Ngamiland. And they came, especially, to kill him. When they came Tsabu defeated them and he killed them and the rest of the Tswana men ran away, back to Ngamiland. More Tswana came and they came and killed him. The reason was that after the first battle had ended Tsabu spoke with his people to tell them to get away but the people refused. So he told them that he, too, would stay; "I won't move, I'll just stay at this farm." This is why the Tswana found him there, when they came back the second time. When they came they made a kraal and put it around them and put all the children inside. They caught the chief and two men and tied them to a tree. They spent a day asking him questions and then tried to take him to Ngamiland to make him a servant. He refused. They talked to him till five o'clock and then shot him dead, and also those other two men. And the people ran away. Tsabu's two sisters were there; the oldest and a younger one. And those two girls scattered. And there was then no longer any chief. (Field Notes, D'Kar, 29 Oct. 1969)

This is one of a handful of oral history accounts I collected in my work on the oral traditions of the Ghanzi Nharo (Guenther 1989). The stories I collected were about black raiders (mostly Tawana "from the north or east," or Herero) and the atrocities they perpetrated among the Bushmen they attacked. They also dwelled on the people's resistance, especially their chief's (//*exa*, the Nharo term also for headman). It was offered either in the spirit of bravery, defiance, or forbearance, or with guile (sometimes through the adroit and cunning actions of a child). The foolishness of the Bushmen may be another theme, especially their unwillingness or inability to heed warnings and take evasive action.

How much of an insight do these tales provide into the history of the Bushmen of the Ghanzi veld, and how well do they corroborate archival and published sources? What they do corroborate is the existence of local leaders and of the ever-present threat of black raiders, as well as of their depredations and their kidnappings of people into servitude. Their victims, the raided Bushmen, are seen to use their wits, to outsmart the raiders, to warn one another with birdcalls or to use magic against them (Schmidt 1989, 2:384, 387–390). However, these tales tend to be quite stereotyped; that is, the same basic tale will be told by different narrators, with the substitution of specific names for the principals and the places. This suggests that the historical contents have been generalized and that the memory of specific details has faded, thus reducing their value as historical documents. This process of "de-historicizing" historical narratives is perhaps none too surprising, given the absence in Bushman society and culture—as in foraging societies and cultures generally—of descent systems and genealogical reckoning and the low development, as a result, of an appreciation of the depth and passage of time.

As noted elsewhere (Guenther 1989:152, 1997:125, 134), it would seem that one of the least developed genres of Bushman oral tradition are, in fact, historical narratives. In my collection of Nharo folklore I collected only about half a dozen narratives about the people's contact, in historical times, with blacks. One of these was cited above; another (of which I collected three versions, featuring either Tawana or Herero) describes an attack by black raiders that is foiled through the resourceful actions of a small boy, who warns his family in time. This tale appears in a number of versions in the corpus of other Bushman and Khoekhoe groups (Schmidt 1989, 2:387–388). It is the most prevalent historical narrative and almost the only one. In her comprehensive, double-volume catalogue of Khoisan oral literature (1989) that contains over two thousand tales (and versions thereof), Sigrid Schmidt (1989, 2:387–390) lists only eight tales (and five versions) that describe hostile encounters with raiders, who are either Nama, Korana, or one or another Bantu-speaking group. In addition, she lists some tales about the generally peaceful encounters of Khoekhoe groups with Europeans (1989:391–393). The huge /Xam corpus, collected by Wilhelm Bleek and Lucy Lloyd during the 1870s and 1880s, seems to contain only four such narratives (all of them featuring Korana as the raiders).

What the Bushmen appear to prefer to tales of the recent historical past are tales about the "old people"—and the early animals, some of them ontologically blended with humans—set within the old and timeless mythological past. "It is the animal world," observed Dorothea Bleek in her summary of /Xam mythology, " not the human hero, that looms large in the sight of the Bushmen." Other than fairly recent personal or family accounts, or place legends, going back two or three generations, to the times of the ox wagons and the first generation of Ghanzi Boers, as well as specific, salient Boer farmers,[15] the set narrative repertoire of the Ghanzi Bushmen contains few tales about the less recent history, set in the nineteenth century or before. This is not to say that such narrative materials cannot be elicited from specific informants. An example of oral accounts from the nineteenth century is Richard Lee's recent work among the Botswana Ju/'hoansi (1997, also see this volume), in part carried out in collaboration with the archaeologist Andy Smith, with Ju/'hoansi informants providing interpretive commentary on the excavated objects (Smith and Lee 1997). Another example is the set of detailed narratives Oswin Köhler (1989a) obtained from the Kxoe of northeastern Namibia from the 1950s through to the 1980s, on their interaction patterns with such Bantu-speaking neighbors as the Mbukushu, Mbwela, Mbari, Lozi, Tawana, and Herero.

Given the apparently low representation of such narratives in the culture's standard oral repertoire and the preference, instead, for *hua*—for tales, among the Nharo, about the "old people" set in pre- or nonhistorical, mythological times—we also find a penchant for "mythologizing" historical happenings, and for melding these with figures and events from the world of myth. Thus, the pioneer Boer *baas* is seen pitted against the Bushman mythological trickster Jakkals (Jackal); indeed, the former figure may be conflated with the lion, the *baas*'s cognate, as the lion of Bushman stories is like the Boer—strong, irascible, but stupid, and thus the trickster's eminently dupable antagonist (Guenther 1989:115, 122–139). In the version of the widely told tale of the black raiders and the resourceful Bushman boy mentioned above collected among the Hei//om by E. W. Thomas (1950:51–52), the black raiders appear in the story as black ants; transfiguring and transporting this relatively recent historical event straight into the sphere of myth. In a Dama tale the raiders, who are the Dama, transform themselves into crows and raid their Nama adversaries in this guise, while the /Xam told a story in which a Korana raiding party was destroyed with its own weapons by a bat-eared fox, which was then a man (Schmidt 1989:384, 390).

The border between myth and history thus appears to be quite fluid in Bushman oral tradition, increasing the need for vigilance on the part of any researcher wishing to mine Bushman folklore for historical information. The ethnohistorian working in this capacity with Bushman material has to be especially mindful of the pitfalls that lie in the path of such an exercise. Apart from the ever-ready penchant for a historical account to cross over into the realm of legend or myth, there are orality-related methodological problems that can be expected to be all the more acute among the Bushmen, an exceptionally oral culture whose members use "talking" or metaphorical turns of phrase not only in the context of storytelling but in the course of everyday social life and communication (Marshall 1961; Biesele 1993, especially pp. 51–67). These are such problems of oral transmission and performance as mixing up materials from different times and places, transposing "cannibalized" segments from one account to another, resorting to stock characters, plot twists or narrative phrases, employing performance-driven innovations to increase the story's appeal to the audience, or textual or textural innovations as mnemonic devices (Vansina 1985). To corroborate this shaky ethnohistorical record, archaeological work along the lines of Karim Sadr's work at Thamaga in southeastern Botswana (this volume) should be undertaken in the Ghanzi region,[16] at some of the key wells along the Ghanzi ridge or riverbeds such as the Okwa and Groot Laagte in the south and north of the Ghanzi veld.

CONCLUSION

The ethnohistorical evidence on the history of this remote region of the Kalahari is thus anything but conclusive. Yet, notwithstanding all the gaps and question marks, there is nevertheless enough evidence in the Ghanzi veld to suggest that the Bushman hunter-gatherers of that part of southern Africa were capable, for two or three generations, of maintaining their political independence and cultural autonomy, in the face of marauding, state-organized black and yellow settlers. What enabled them to do this was a relatively complex political system which, while hardly a feudalist empire, was nevertheless a good deal more structured and centralized than what is found today among the Ghanzi Bushmen (as well as other Kalahari groups). The Ghanzi people kept their stance of independence and autonomy also when face to face with white traders and hunters who passed through their lands, and who kept a wary eye on the tall, well-fed and well-armed Bushmen, who, by the dozens or hundreds, approached their wagons with an "air of manly independence" (Baines 1864:144).

In the latter half of the nineteenth and the first three-quarters of the twentieth century this independence and autonomy were threatened and undermined, yet never fully eroded. The foraging mode of subsistence, production, social organization, and ideology underwent change throughout these two centuries, from hunting-gathering to gathering-hunting, from foraging-farming, to farming-foraging, from labor for cattle to labor for cash. The context of these socioeconomic patterns was either independence or dependence, resistance or accommodation. Throughout these various structural and historical phases the foraging mode persisted, attesting to its considerable resilience and adaptability.

NOTES

1. For an account of a similar scheme of cattle management among the Oorlam / Nama of Gobabis see Lau 1987:65–68.

2. A household survey of D'Kar village in the Ghanzi District, which I conducted in 1997, revealed that 72 of the 88 Basarwa households surveyed, that is 81.8 percent, used wild plants as part of their subsistence provisions. Twenty-one households (23.9 percent) used such foods quite regularly, especially in late summer and early winter when the desirable species (*khutsus* and *morammas*) are in season.

3. The Wilmsen citation alongside citations from Passarge's 1907 monograph on the Bushmen of the Kalahari (most of them the Nharo), refers to Wilmsen's recent translation (1997) of this work (along with other Passarge papers). The reason for also providing the original citation is that Wilmsen's translation is riddled with inaccuracies and the reader wishing to refer to the cited passage would thus be advised to consult the original German text.

4. I have answered these questions and described the events around them more fully elsewhere (Guenther 1993/94, 1997, 1999:ch. 2). The account here presented is a shortened summary.

5. Passarge does not use these terms clearly or consistently, especially the terms "chief"

(*Häuptling*) and "paramount chief" (*Oberhäuptling*) which occasionally seem to be synonymous. This may explain the inaccuracies in Wilmsen's translation of this section of Passarge's *Die Buschmänner der Kalahari*, which either obscures or conflates Passarge's leadership status distinctions.

6. About three decades later Passarge also had occasion to witness the Ghanzi Bushmen's (probably ≠Au//eisi's) intense hostility toward the Herero, at the German garrison of Rietfontein, at the South West African border. About a hundred Herero, who were trying to enter the Ghanzi veld into Bechuanaland, were held up by the three-man garrison. A few Herero were shot and the rest surrounded the fort. The Bushmen supplied the beleaguered soldiers with ostrich eggs and water, "out of hatred for their deadly enemy" (Wilmsen 1997:113).

7. The Bakgalagadi and Barolong, two other Bantu-speaking peoples now found in the southwestern regions of the District, only arrived in the 1890s, about the same time the Boer settlers took over the ranches granted to them by the British colonial government, after treaties with the Tawana that ceded the land to the white settlers (Gillett 1969; Guenther 1997:129–131). The latter curbed the subsequent expansion, in the twentieth century, of the black herders from the south (Russell and Russell 1979:12, 33; Childers 1976:10).

8. Passarge attributes the decline of the Ghanzi region's Bushman population primarily to hunger—"ruin by hunger would seem to be the principal reason for the dying out of this ancient race" (Passarge 1907:10)—caused by both the decline of game and of wild plants, specifically *tsama* melons. Passarge points to the interconnection of these two deleterious developments noting that with the decline of antelope species, which eat *tsama*s and excrete their seeds and broadcast them in their migratory movements, both the volume and the spread of *tsama* has become drastically reduced (Passarge 1905:74–75/Wilmsen 1997:81, 94–95).

9. Citing Seiner, Lebzelter suggest that the tribal designation for the subordinate group may be derived from the ≠Au//ei term *naru*, meaning "subordinate" or "slave" (Lebzelter 1934a:68).

10. Which of the three patterns characterized the dependency relationship between the Bushmen and Tswana was to become a topic of official investigation in the 1920s to 1930s (Barnard 1992a:119–120; Hitchcock 1996:20–22).

11. See Passarge (1907:122–123/Wilmsen 1997:206–207, also see pp. 255–256, 266–267); Hermans (1977); Morton (1994); Hitchcock (1996:18–21); Silberbauer and Kuper (1966); Wilmsen (1989:99, 133, 138, 284–286); Gadibolae (1985); also see Solway and Lee (1990).

12. Wilmsen (1997:14–16, 37) and Wilmsen and Denbow (1990:489–490) dub this exchange the first round of the Great Kalahari Debate, as it was in part over the same question, whether to regard the Bushmen as aboriginal and culturally autonomous or marginal and politically dependent. It was conducted on the pages of the 1906 volume of the *Zeitschrift für Ethnologie*. Wilmsen sees Passarge and Fritsch as upholding the revisionist and isolationist banners, respectively, and suggests that had Lee & Co. only read Passarge, "the opportunity could have arisen of forestalling the subsequent dreary, sterile, and distracting debate regarding that ethnographic category" (Wilmsen 1997:15). See Gordon (1990:509), Guenther (1990:509–510, 1999), and Lee and Guenther (1993:212–216) for critiques of Wilmsen on that point.

13. See Mielke (1988), Gilman (1985), Konner and Shotsak (1986), Wilmsen (1989:24–32), Lee (1992a), Skotnes (1996), and Gordon (1992).

14. In her recent study of farm Bushmen amongst the Boer and German ranchers of the Omaheke District in Namibia, Reneé Sylvain came across much the same notion amongst the white farmers about the Bushmen's capacity for farm work (1998:339–340).

15. Sigrid Schmidt recently (1998) published a collection of personal accounts, by contemporary urban- and rural-based Nama and Dama from Namibia, drawn from the narrators' own life experiences or from that of their parents or grandparents. The collection is rich in information and provides a grass-roots perspective on the everyday lives of ordinary people during recent historical times.

16. I have learned from Karim Sadr (personal communication) that Nick Walker has excavated a site on the Ghanzi ridge. The analysis is in progress at the time of this writing.

six

Dangerous Interactions

The Repercussions of Western Culture,
Missionaries, and Disease in Southern Africa

Susan Kent

E thnohistorical sources and archaeological reports document the presence of hunter-gatherers throughout southern Africa until the late nineteenth and early twentieth centuries. Later, autonomous hunter-gatherers were more restricted in their range, until the only ones left at the middle to end of the twentieth century were those occupying the Kalahari Desert in Botswana and Namibia (Fig. 6.1). When interacting with Bantu-speakers, hunter-gatherers maintained their autonomy for almost 2,000 years (see Chapters 2 and 3, this volume). However, once hunter-gatherers began relations with Westerners, their autonomy was quickly endangered in those areas where they were in competition for resources and in continuous contact with Europeans. Why were hunter-gatherers able to maintain their autonomy for 1,500 or more years of interaction with Bantu-speaking agropastoralists, but in most places, lost it after only 300–400 years of interactions with Westerners? I suggest that the inherent dissimilarities between the Western and the Bantu cultures led to fundamentally different intercultural interactions. I also suggest that the incursion of the Western nation-state in southern Africa changed the precontact relationship between foragers and nonforagers in most, but not all,

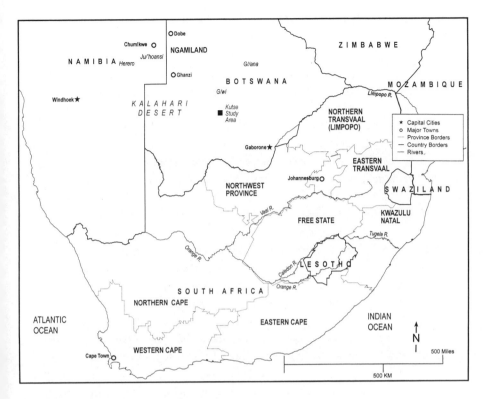

Figure 6.1. Map of southern Africa.

regions. If most hunter-gatherers lost their autonomy 100 or more years ago in southern Africa, how did the Kalahari hunter-gatherers persist? I show that the nature of the interactions with both Bantu-speakers and Westerners were dramatically different with the Kalahari foragers, for reasons that have to do with a range of factors, from environmental to social and political, as well as settlement density and mobility. If the Kalahari hunter-gatherers were able to survive for hundreds of years after Westerners first colonized southern Africa, why is it that now, at the end of the twentieth century and beginning of the twenty-first century, these foragers have lost their autonomy? I suggest below that the Western nation-state did not impact Kalahari peoples until recently. The emergence of the Botswana nation-state, along with the adoption of Christianity and new technology, has eroded the Kalahari hunter-gatherers' autonomy at the end of the twentieth century (also see Guenther, Chapter 5).

This chapter does not refer to different individuals, but to different cultures. Certainly individual interactions varied from one another and were not necessarily always representative of the European or Bantu views of the "other." It is incorrect to blame any group(s) for events in the past, although events can be regretted and, hopefully, prevented. Intergroup relations are neither arbitrary nor separate from the general configuration of a society's culture. They are based on the different ethos of Bantu culture and Western culture. Therefore, the interactions and changes wrought by the Europeans were, I propose, not analogous to the changes resulting from the precolonial Bantu-speaking agropastoralist and hunter-gatherer relations. I posit four cultural reasons that created significant differences between Westerners' and agropastoralists' interactions with hunter-gatherers: (1) advanced technology, (2) racism/ethnocentrism, (3) the influence of missionaries, and (4) an intolerance of cultural diversity. These are in addition to one noncultural reason—European-introduced diseases.

PRECOLONIAL HUNTER-GATHERER AND HERDER INTERACTIONS

Many archaeologists agree that during the Early Iron Age, trade and amicable relations characterized the interactions between Bantu-speaking agropastoralists, Khoi herders, and hunter-gatherers (Cable 1984; Sadr, Chapter 2, this volume; Kent, Chapter 3, this volume, Wadley 1996; and others). Intergroup relations became more complex and, I suggest, more variable, throughout southern Africa during the Late Iron Age. In a very few areas, but not all, agropastoralists did force local hunter-gatherers to abandon their original territories, assimilate, or become impoverished serfs (e.g., Hall and Smith 1998). However, I suggest in Chapter 3 that these areas were the exception and not the norm. The archaeological data from other parts of southern Africa indicate that such unequal interactions were *not* isomorphic (Chapters 2 and 3). In other words, although assimilation due to contact with the Bantu-speaking pastoralists may have occurred in a few areas, it does not invalidate the general trend, which was that hunter-gatherers and pastoralists remained autonomous until the arrival of the Europeans. For example, Smith, Sadr, Gribble, and Yates (1996:89) conclude that "hunting societies which were aboriginal at the Cape, continued an existence separate from later herding economies until well after European settlement." Mazel (1981:89) wrote that Iron Age peoples in the southern Natal probably were not a threat to hunter-gatherers' lifestyles. He then concluded that autonomous hunter-gatherer culture may have persisted undisturbed until the arrival of the Europeans (Mazel 1981). Mitchell, Parkington, and Yates (1994:51) surmise that in the Caledon River area, South Africa, and Lesotho, during the Late Stone Age, "a pronounced cultural boundary may be indicated by the absence of Smithfield ceramics to the east of the Caledon River. This may reflect a long-standing and relatively unstressed interaction between hunter-gatherers and farmers in areas beyond the limits of Iron Age settlement."

Numerous missionaries and explorers described the presence of autonomous hunter-gatherers throughout southern Africa from the 1600s to early 1900s (e.g., Ellenberger 1912; Dunn 1873, 1931; Neville 1996; Rudner 1979; among many others).

Even "when the first PEMS [Paris Evangelical Missionary Society] missionaries arrived in [Lesotho in] the 1830s, San [hunter-gatherer] languages were widely used in the southern highveld, indicating a rather widespread presence of San communities. . . . These points indicate clearly that Sotho dominance was uneven and in some places very recent and that many independent San communities still existed" (Gills 1992:38). Explorers traveling north of Cape Town in 1660 and 1685 likewise noted the presence of hunter-gatherers (Parkington 1984:156–157; Thom 1958; Serton, Raven-Hart, and de Kock 1971). For instance, Manhire (1987:126–127) argues that, after an initial adjustment to the influx of Bantu-speakers in the Cape Province, South Africa, the foragers maintained their autonomy for at least 1,500 years until Western colonialization, when both societies suffered. The same pattern of native intergroup autonomy was characteristic elsewhere in southern Africa. A third indigenous group also occupying southern Africa was the Khoi herders who apparently were able to coexist with their hunter-gatherer and Bantu neighbors, but who were most vulnerable to the destructive relations with Westerners. The archaeological data show that it was the arrival of Europeans, not the Bantu, that ushered in the demise of many hunter-gatherer (and Khoi) societies in southern Africa (Kent, Chapter 3, this volume).

In the 1920s, hunter-gatherers were still observed in Lesotho, but by then they were mostly a demoralized, destitute group (How 1970). Hunter-gatherer cultures, if not actual populations, in other parts of South Africa had been extinct for centuries. In contrast, in areas where Europeans did not colonize, such as much of the Kalahari Desert in Botswana and Namibia, hunter-gatherers were able to exist until the middle to the end of the twentieth century. Szalay (1995:30–31) concludes that during the 1860s, there were areas south of the Orange River, South Africa, where hunter-gatherers were still autonomous, and they were observed even later in Lesotho (Ellenberger 1912). Studies in Botswana show that hunter-gatherers were present during the mid to late 1960s (the Ju/'hoansi, formerly known as !Kung; Marshall 1976, 1999; Lee 1979) to 1997 (e.g., Kutse Basarwa, Kent 1993, 1995, 1996b).

Agropastoralists' relations with hunter-gatherers allowed for cultural autonomy throughout much of southern Africa. European colonization differed significantly from that of the Bantu, resulting in different consequences for hunter-gatherers. While the majority of reasons for these differences are cultural, one important reason is biological. The biological consequence was an *unintentional* result of the Europeans' presence.

NOT ALL INTERACTIONS ARE CREATED EQUAL— THE INFLUENCE OF BIOLOGY

The influx of Europeans in southern Africa at the beginning of the seventeenth century introduced new diseases that were contracted by the native peoples in southern Africa (Elphick 1977; Wilson 1969). While native African mortality rates were not often recorded by colonizers, there are documents that indirectly indicate the number of people affected. For example, during the Anglo-Boer war, European "civilians in the Cape or Natal died of typhoid fever at a little more than twice the rate than was current in England and Wales, while the Cape Coloured population, consisting of Khoi (Khoikhoi, Khoekhoe, Khoe) and hunter-gatherers, died at a rate 77 percent higher than the whites" (Curtin 1998:208). In the African "refugee" camps occupied by Khoi, hunter-gatherers, and Bantu, 60 percent of the mortality was from pneumonia, and 17 percent from gastrointestinal infections (Curtin 1998:215).

Smallpox was unintentionally introduced by the Europeans and several epidemics were recorded in the eighteenth and nineteenth centuries. According to Slome (1929), a historical burial ground contained the skeletal remains of 50 hunter-gatherers who had died during an 1860s smallpox epidemic. Smallpox and other European-introduced diseases were reported in the Western Cape of South Africa from 1713 to 1724 (Penn 1987:470–471; Elphick 1977). Between 1721 and 1724, smallpox raged through the Namaqua people, who by then had few cattle or sheep due to depredations of rustlers of various cultures, including hunter-gatherers and Europeans (Penn 1987:472). The impact of each smallpox epidemic is difficult to assess (Smith 1989:26). However, surviving three or more separate epidemics within a generation, while watching their loved ones die, created more demographic, social, economic, and political havoc for the native peoples than any single epidemic did by itself. An eyewitness in the early eighteenth century wrote "the Hottentots died in the hundreds. They lay everywhere on the roads. . . . Cursing at the Dutchmen, who they said had bewitched them, they fled inland [further spreading the disease]" (Valentyn quoted in Elphick 1977:232). The devastation caused by multiple smallpox epidemics and other exotic diseases brought by Europeans must have further demoralized native peoples who, at the same time, had their livestock and land taken away, and their wild animal and plant resources decimated. Significantly, smallpox "viruses continued to circulate among southern African peoples for a century, causing disruption whose scale and historical significance may never be fully known. Not only did it kill the majority of the population, but it also eliminated those vestiges of traditional Khoikhoi [Khoi] social structures" (Elphick 1977:233). I suggest that not only were Khoi afflicted on such a large scale, but that a high proportion of the Cape hunter-gatherers also succumbed to the epidemics.

To perpetuate an epidemic, it is necessary to have a large enough aggregated and sedentary population to continue the cycles of disease. Not all hunter-gatherers were dispersed and mobile. Some southern African foragers probably occupied more sedentary, aggregated camps in well-watered regions, contra the erroneous assumption that all hunter-gatherers throughout time and space resembled the contemporary Ju/'hoansi (!Kung) of the Kalahari. There were also sedentary hunter-gatherers at mission stations, or in servitude to Westerners, who were vulnerable to these diseases because of their poverty and stationary settlements. Although a sedentary, aggregated population is needed to perpetuate an epidemic, one only needs to be in contact with someone who is ill or a carrier of the pathogen to die from the disease. The missionaries, colonialists, Khoi, and Bantu maintained the cycle of diseases, infecting hunter-gatherers who visited or interacted with them long enough to acquire the disease. The 1950s Kalahari smallpox epidemic occurred, not surprisingly, at Ghanzi where there were less nomadic Basarwa field workers employed by European farmers (Guenther, personal communication). In this case, Nharo Basarwa were able to infect others with whom they came into contact.

The effects of the infections were not uniform throughout South Africa, much less through the rest of southern Africa. In fact, the first smallpox epidemic recorded for the Botswana Kalahari was as late as the 1950s (Silberbauer 1981). Smallpox did not spread with the devastating effects of most epidemic diseases because the Kalahari Basarwa at that time were seminomadic and lived in small groups. The same was true for another highly infectious disease—AIDS. Botswana had the highest rate of new cases of HIV-positive individuals of any country in the world at the end of the twentieth century, and yet AIDS had not yet spread to the interior of the Kalahari, although how long this will be true is not known.

Rather than physical extinction, the most consequential and permanent outcome from the European-introduced epidemics, in my opinion, was the breakdown of native societies (also see Szalay 1995). Smith (1989) and Szalay (1995) propose that the native demographic decline was not as steep as some historians suggest. There are many descendants from former Khoisan hunter-gatherers and Khoi herders living today in the Cape Province (lumped together and classified as "coloured" by the white government during apartheid; Szalay 1995:119–121). Even if the epidemics were not pivotal in physically eradicating hunter-gatherers and Khoi herders, the devastation from continuous cycles of disease assisted in the loss of their culture during a particularly stressful time in history. In other words, the native people lost something almost more valuable than their lives—they lost their culture and identity.

I propose that prior to Western contact there was more variability among hunter-gatherer societies in southern Africa than is recognized historically or today. Differences in culture, mobility, and settlement patterns were important in determining the history of hunter-gatherers' initial contact with agropastoralists and later with European colonists. It is fallacious to use a single group of specific foragers, the Ju/'hoansi (!Kung), as representative of all hunter-gatherers through time because cultural, mobility, and settlement-pattern differences existed among the different forager societies. For example, Cape and other hunter-gatherers were recorded living in sedentary communities. One of many consequences was that they were more likely to suffer from smallpox, typhoid, dysentery, and phthisis than the more dispersed and mobile hunter-gatherers. Schapera (1930:214) noted that among hunter-gatherers in the early 1900s, where "contact with other peoples is frequent, syphilis is often found, as well as measles, influenza, whooping-cough, scarlet fever, and other European diseases." Schapera also recorded that

> European clothing and dwellings have a bad effect upon the Bushmen. They are particu-
> larly susceptible to pulmonary affections when removed from their natural surround-
> ings, and a considerable number of those who have suffered from bronchitis, pneumonia,
> etc., subsequently succumb to tuberculosis. When imprisoned, as many of them are in
> South-West Africa [today, Namibia] for cattle stealing or breaking the game laws, they
> rapidly decline in strength and die in great numbers, however kindly treated by the
> authorities. (1930:214)

Mobile hunter-gatherers were much less vulnerable to foreign epidemics than those who lived near Westerners or pastoralist communities. While nomadic, they often lived in dispersed camps in numbers too small to maintain an epidemic, which thrives best in larger sedentary communities. Gordon observed that "smallpox killed many in 1713 [in the Cape], but that the disease had not penetrated deeply into the interior" (Smith and Pheiffer 1994:33). Elsewhere, the highly mobile foragers oc-cupying the Kalahari Desert had little contact with infected persons. Even when they did, their way of life was not conducive to the spread of infectious diseases. As noted, smallpox apparently did not penetrate the Kalahari until the 1950s, when Sil-berbauer (1981) and others recorded the first epidemic. Even in 1969, physicians characterized the mobile Kalahari Ju/'hoansi (!Kung) as "remarkably healthy" (Truswell and Hanson 1976).

THE INFLUENCE OF CULTURE ON INTERCULTURAL INTERACTIONS

As noted earlier, I suggest that there are four specific features of Western culture that affected intergroup interactions with hunter-gatherers (advanced technology, racism and ethnocentrism, influence of Christian missionaries, and intolerance for cultural diversity). The culture of the Bantu-speakers or the Khoi was quite dissimi-lar from the Westerners' and this resulted in qualitatively different interactions with resident hunter-gatherers. In other words, intercultural interactions vary ap-preciably among societies. None of the afore-cited cultural reasons by itself would have resulted in the vast changes of native groups over the past 300–400 years in southern Africa. Taken together, however, they explain the spread of Western cul-ture and its impact on the people encountered.

1. Advanced Technology

Prior to European contact, Bantu-speaking pastoralists basically had weapons equivalent to those of the hunter-gatherers (primarily bows, arrows, and spears). Neither group had transportation or communication superiority over the other. Guns and horses were not available to either pastoralists or hunter-gatherers prior to their introduction by Europeans. Both military and administrative weaknesses also aided in diminishing the Bantu-speakers' power to make excessive demands of the hunter-gatherers (Adas 1992:90).

Guns were primarily limited to Europeans and their allies until the 1880s (Westbury and Sampson 1993), giving them unprecedented strategic power against any groups that resisted exploitation or expansion. Ellenberger (1912) noted that many groups were relatively helpless against those that had acquired guns and horses from the Europeans. "The superiority of their weapons, and mobility [with horses], enabled the Korannas to go raiding in parties of only eight or ten men, and the Basuto [of Lesotho] were seldom able to protect their property from foes who appeared suddenly, as it were, from nowhere, slew their herds from a distance, and were gone with the booty before a force to resist them could be assembled" (1912:213–214). In addition, Ellenberger reported that "Besides cattle, the Korannas captured numbers of women and children, whom they sold as slaves to the [white] farmers for cattle, guns, and ammunition" (Ellenberger 1912:214). Hunter-gatherers and pastoralists were not passive during this period. Although the native peoples did counterattack to protect themselves and their lifestyle, their technology was no match for the imported Western technology.

From the above example, one can see the connection between weaponry, or technology, and the slave trade. The antiquity of an intercultural slave trade in southern Africa has long been contested, with the majority of scholars assuming that the Batswana, Zulu, and other sociopolitically complex Bantu groups enslaved the Bantu Bakgalagadi, Khoi herders, and hunter-gatherers. I suggest that any slave trade that may have existed prior to the Western colonization was small to nonexistent. One reason is that the Boers had larger fields and herds, and thus a need for slaves that the native groups did not have. Slaves were at first imported from West Africa to colonial South Africa. However, it did not take long for the colonists to realize that it would be much easier and cheaper to force the local people into slavery. The Boers demanded that their government sanction their actions to force all "Bushmen captured by commandos or by private individuals . . . be retained in perpetual slavery . . . they and their children after them" (Le May 1995:36).

The domination of local peoples was necessary to meet the demand for numerous laborers to work on the large European farms or with their large herds. For example, toward the end of the 1700s, the Dutch East India Company assisted settlers by offering a premium, payable in cash, for each hunter-gatherer taken alive by commandos for the expressed purpose of encouraging the capture of slaves (Newton-King 1999:120). I doubt that a similar situation occurred when the Bantu-speakers migrated into southern Africa circa 2,000 years ago. Thus, not only did European weaponry directly harm native populations, but it also contributed to their cultural destruction by encouraging a slave trade that was probably not present, or certainly not as large, prior to colonization.

The human cost to the native people as a consequence of European guns and horses over arrows or spears was catastrophic in parts of South Africa. In 1774 it took only 27 Dutch settlers and 38 Khoi to kill 142 hunter-gatherers and capture 89, while losing just one of their own (Penn 1996:85). Three months later, 31 Europeans and a little over 31 Khoi killed 96 hunter-gatherers and captured 21, without suffering any casualties themselves (Penn 1996:86). During Opperman's expedition, one battle resulted in more than 700 people being either killed or captured to be forced into slavery (Newton-King 1999:75). By 1798 over 18,635 men, children, and women in just one district were war captives forced into slavery by the white settlers (Newton-King 1999:118). A group of Europeans and Khoi killed 265 hunter-gatherers and captured another 129, also without suffering any casualties themselves (Penn 1996:86). At the end of the 1700s, Barrow claimed that while the Khoi were harmless, honest, and faithful, their culture was destroyed by Dutch abuse and while the hunter-gatherers were like children, they were mowed down by Boer bullets as they tried to defend themselves with bows and arrows (Barrow 1801–1804). Comaroff and Comaroff (1991:96) wrote that Barrow's observations "were grounded in the very real fact of genocide; there is plenty of collateral evidence to prove that a war of extermination had been waged along the frontier against the Khoisan [both hunter-gatherers and Khoi pastoralists]." If the Bantu had had the same ideas of genocide, there would not have been any hunter-gatherers present when the first Europeans arrived in South Africa.

Sophisticated technology, the means for administrative communication within and outside southern Africa, and the use of horses may not have been sufficient to cause societies to submit to the spread of Western culture, but they added to the difficulty of resistance. This was not the case for the Kalahari Desert, where Europeans' communication difficulties in this region, together with the fact that horses were not able to penetrate the Kalahari due to its aridity prior to the drilling of boreholes (or wells), allowed hunter-gatherers the ability to maintain an autonomous lifestyle until the last few years of the twentieth century.

2. Racism and Ethnocentrism

Although most people in all societies are ethnocentric to some degree, historically Westerners perceived all non-Western cultures and peoples as inherently inferior.

This conception of "others" places non-Westerners in a similar category as non-human animals that can be used or slaughtered by Europeans. For instance, Livingstone described numerous "bloody massacres" that were inflicted on local people by Europeans who had little remorse for their actions (1857:38 and elsewhere). It was thought by some colonists that the natives' inherent inferiority justified the eradication of local cultures for the Westerners' benefit. Some rationalized that the concept of "divine right" justified their stealing Bantu and Khoi livestock, as well as land used by hunter-gatherers and other native groups. Historians have suggested that some missionaries, such as Moffat, instigated wars specifically to enable Westerners to acquire the slaves so important to the colonists (Comaroff and Comaroff 1997:182). Bantu speakers, in contrast, did not view all other societies as nonhuman. Dominant Batswana used low-status Bantu Bakgalagadi for forced labor as serfs, and occasionally hunter-gatherers, but on a relatively small scale and with many more freedoms than were permitted to the Westerners' slaves.

Racism and Slavery / Serfdom

While some colonialists still believed that native Africans had low intelligence and social abilities (Morton 1987:2), many thought the natives were capable of fulfilling the slave duties imposed by the Europeans. The colonial administrators throughout Africa most admired assimilated Africans who spoke English, wore Western clothing, believed in Christianity, and accepted the colonial rule (Morton 1987). As a result, Boers stole very young children from the various local groups, so that the children would soon forget their parents, culture, and language and be less resistant to their slavery (Livingstone 1857:36–37; Penn 1996). The kidnapping of these children and women was considered to be a bonus when stealing Bantu or Khoi cattle. Livingstone (1857:37), who abhorred this practice, wrote that, "seldom [could individual Boers] resist the two-fold plea of a well-told story of an intended uprising of the . . . [local tribe], and the prospect of handsome pay in the division of captured cattle besides" (Livingstone 1857:37). Men often were shot because Boers perceived them as not having any economic value, while women and children were captured for slave labor (Penn 1996:89). The killing was sometimes rationalized as being in the best interests of the people. Nicolaas van der Merwe, for instance, thought he killed out of mercy. He wrote that he had "order[ed] wounded San women and children be shot in order that their death might not be still crueller" (Penn 1996:89).

Even if Late Iron Age Bantu-speakers did not see the indigenous hunter-gatherers as equals, or perhaps as anything more than a source of labor or goods (see Schapera 1953), we have little evidence that the agropastoralists attempted to enslave large numbers of them, assimilate them, or decimate them and their culture, prior to the incursion of Westerners (see Kent, Chapter 3). Some Batswana Bantu-speakers during the 1800s derogatorily referred to hunter-gatherers as "Masarwa." The prefix "Ma" is used to designate animals (humans are called "Ba" as in "Basarwa"). Although not referring to hunter-gatherers, Mautle (1986:25) wrote that the exploited Bakgalagadi agropastoralist Bantu-speakers were occasionally considered to be non-human animals by the dominant Batswana society. This indicates that the Batswana did sometimes refer to the people they dominated as animals. Still, such prejudiced thinking does not mean that the dominant Batswana also practiced genocide, large-scale slavery, or massive forced assimilation.

Some anthropologists' beliefs about the enslavement of native southern Africans may be based on cultural misperceptions. The payment of tribute, for example, does not automatically imply serfdom, as some researchers think (e.g., Wilmsen 1989). Europeans pay tribute or taxes to their government, which does not necessarily imply that Europeans are slaves or serfs. Batswana themselves and Bakgalagadi regularly had to pay tribute to their Batswana chief. Schapera (1941:121) reported that "All members of the [Batswana] tribe . . . paid tribute in various forms to their chief. Each [Batswana] village or group of wards cultivated a special field for him, every woman sent him a basketful of corn after reaping, . . . and successful [Batswana] hunters gave him specified portions of their gain." Furthermore, the chief could call upon his subjects at any time for unpaid, compulsory labor, including hunting, building his huts, or clearing his fields (Schapera 1941:120). The entire Batswana chiefdom did not consist of Bantu slaves or serfs of their chief, despite performing this involuntary labor. Tribute, also was extracted from a chief's own Batswana subjects, who were otherwise basically free. None of these demands meant that the subjects were enslaved and the same was true for the few hunter-gatherers living near Bantu settlements who had to pay tribute.

While paying tribute in and of itself does not imply slavery/serfdom any more than does paying income tax, this is less true for the Bakgalagadi Bantu speakers who were mentioned in ethnohistorical sources as serfs of the Batswana much more commonly than hunter-gatherers. In fact, the Bakgalagadi are invariably cited as having had to pay tribute, often in the form of wild animal hides, meat, and other wild products available in the Kalahari region (Mautle 1986; Willoughby 1912). In contrast, hunter-gatherers are cited much less frequently as serfs than the Bakgalagadi and often not at all when discussing serfdom in Botswana (e.g., Willoughby 1912).

The substantially increased need for cash, hides, and other products caused by the desire for European goods is rarely noted when discussing tribute after Western contact. Money became indispensable to the agropastoralists, not only to acquire European clothing, food, tools, blankets, ploughs, and other commodities, but also to be able to pay school fees, church dues, and colonial taxes (Schapera 1941:124–125). Stimulated by the presence of foreign goods and the need to pay administrative taxes imposed by the colonists, chiefs had new incentives to acquire money and objects that could be turned into cash. Before Western colonization, groups were self-sufficient and did not rely on other Bantu-speakers or on hunter-gatherers for any special commodities, although raiding weaker neighbors was a favorite way to add to the cattle they already owned (Schapera 1941:122). Therefore, what agropastoralists coveted most, cattle, was something not available from hunter-gatherers. Fellow semisedentary to sedentary Bantu-speakers, I suggest, would have been easier to extract tribute from than nomadic hunter-gatherers who did not stay in one place and did not own more than they could carry. Moreover, Bantu-speakers would have been more resigned to paying tribute than hunter-gatherers because it was a part of their hierarchical culture. Before colonization, dominant agropastoralist groups, such as the Batswana, did not, I suggest, demand much from the hunter-gatherers because hides and game were provided by their Bantu-speaking subjects or by culturally different Bantu-speakers whom the Batswana ruled, such as the Bakgalagadi in Botswana (Schapera 1941).

The attitudes of the agropastoralists toward the hunter-gatherers were not very different from other stratified chiefdom-level societies with rigid hierarchies. However, I propose that it was only after the rise of, for example, the Botswana nation-state and the adoption of Christianity and other aspects of Western culture that Bantu-speakers' interactions with hunter-gatherers mirrored those of Western society. The evidence supporting this stance is the fact that in the modern countries of South Africa and Botswana there were still culturally distinct and autonomous hunter-gatherers after more than several thousand years of contact with Bantu-speakers and Khoi herders, but there were few to none left during the last few years of the twentieth century after only three centuries or less of interaction with colonialists.

Some ethnographers counter my perspective of prehistoric agropastoralist and hunter-gatherer interactions by referring to European explorers' recordings of hunter-gatherer serfs/slaves of the Bantu. They fail to recognize that not all Bantu-speaking societies kept serfs. In Botswana, serfdom existed primarily between a few of the Batswana groups and the Bakgalagadi Bantu-speakers (see Solway 1994; Kent 1998). In Botswana alone, Schapera (1970:86) recorded that only two of the four western Batswana chiefdoms kept serfs (the eastern Batswana did not have serfs; note that their concept of serf is not the same as that in medieval Europe, where serfs had less freedom; see Chapter 4, this volume). Those Batswana groups who kept serfs obtained them from three or four culturally distinct societies, one of which included the Basarwa (e.g., the other serfs included the Bakgalagadi, Bambuskushu, Bayeei, and others; Schapera 1970:86, 88). Most Bantu-speakers could not afford serfs. Owners were usually the elite of the Bantu society who also used poor relatives to perform necessary menial tasks. Although not all informants agreed, most stated that the use of serfs was instituted among the Batswana from 1830 to 1847 and among the Bangwato from around 1817 to 1828 (Schapera 1970:80), that is, after European contact. To assume without evidence that the same oc-curred prior to European contact is to ignore the complexity of historical intercul-tural interactions. The western Batswana are thought to have moved from South Africa relatively recently into what is today Botswana—in the 1700s when they first encountered the groups that were later used as serfs (Schapera 1970:3). According to Willoughby (1912:40), when the Batswana migrated into Botswana, they en-countered a region that was sparsely populated by Bakgalagadi. These Bantu-speaking Bakgalagadi lived mostly in small communities on the margins of the Kalahari (prior to the introduction of boreholes). Simply due to proximity, some Bakgalagadi were quickly and easily forced into serfdom by the Batswana (Wil-loughby 1912:40). This again shows the confusion of scholars who claim that most or all Basarwa (Bushmen or San) were enslaved, while ignoring the more common slavery of the local Bantu-speakers.

Those few hunter-gatherers living in or near the Bakgalagadi communities may have been forced into serfdom, just as the Bakgalagadi were, although Willoughby (1912) did not note the enslavement of hunter-gatherers. I suggest that those Basarwa living next to Bakgalagadi communities who did not want to be serfs simply moved further into the Kalahari. Those who were unable or unwilling to move away from the Batswana were probably a small percentage of the hunter-gatherer population.

Citations regarding the presence of Bakgalagadi Bantu-speakers and hunter-gatherer serfs living on the fringe of the Kalahari are from the 1800s or later when both groups had altered their traditional mode of interactions due to the chaos cre-ated by colonization further south (Mautle 1986). Between 1800 and 1830, con-sumer products from Europeans living in the Cape of South Africa, were available to Batswana Bantu-speakers in Botswana for a price that was usually payable in wild hides, ivory, ostrich feathers, and other products from the Kalahari (Mautle 1986:21). Mautle attributed the further exploitation of the Bakgalagadi to this cir-cumstance (1986:21). After colonization, the Bakgalagadi were a conquered Bantu-speaking group whose land had been taken over by the Batswana, but they were not enslaved. Intermarriage between Bakgalagadi and Batswana prior to the 1800s was not uncommon, and the main obligation to the Batswana was the payment of tribute. All this changed when the Batswana were able to obtain European trade items, which increased the Bantu-speakers' demands of the Bakgalagadi who now had to provide labor, trade goods from the desert (e.g., wild animal products), and domesticated animals (Mautle 1986:21).

As the need for slaves increased because of the European trade goods, children were taken from the Bakgalagadi to work for the Batswana or to trade to Europeans (Mautle 1986). Hunter-gatherer children were similarly taken, although I propose that they would have been more difficult to locate because of their parents' mobility and distance from the Batswana compared to the Bakgalagadi. Schapera (1970) and Mautle (1986) both confirm that the enslavement of mostly Bakgalagadi, and to a much less extent hunter-gatherers, occurred late in the 1800s. Before European disruptions further south, serfdom was rare in most of southern Africa, and its rise was, I suggest, directly related to the presence of Westerners and their trade goods. This created a need for larger surpluses of Kalahari items that was not present prior to the Europeans' arrival.

The colonists' displacement of agropastoralists in the Cape and elsewhere impinged on people living in the north, even as far away as Botswana, as one group had to relocate to another group's territory. The indigenous Bantu-speakers and hunter-gatherers reacted hostilely to the invasion, changing the nature of pre–European contact interactions. Even so, those forced out of their traditional territories were not necessarily enslaved, as demonstrated by the Batswana who were displaced from the Transvaal, South Africa, and moved to what now is Botswana, becoming the dominant group in that country. In other words, there is no conclusive evidence demonstrating a long-standing or prehistoric use of hunter-gatherers as serfs in Botswana, and, I suggest, probably elsewhere in southern Africa. Westerners' relations with natives definitely cannot be used as a model of pre–European contact interactions between agropastoralists and hunter-gatherers throughout prehistoric southern Africa. Even Schapera's (e.g., 1938, 1956) accounts of warfare, conquest, and subjugation of hunter-gatherers and other Bantu-speaking groups occupying newly seized land by the Batswana are all from the postcontact era. Furthermore, as I present in Chapter 3 (this volume), and Sadr in Chapter 2, the archaeology does not conclusively indicate prehistoric enslavement of the hunter-gatherers by the agropastoralists. Instead, I suggest that the archaeological record mostly indicates autonomy or mutualistic intercultural relationships until the arrival of the Europeans.

At the same time, the lack of enslavement by no means implies that the agropastoralists had a philosophy of cultural relativism. Ethnohistoric sources describe cruel treatment among and between native peoples, although it is difficult to discern which events were the result of the pressure on resources, land, and people from the immigration of Europeans to southern Africa, and which events were part of prehistoric indigenous relations. Ironically, the groups that probably had the most hostile interactions with the Bantu-speakers are the Khoi herders. The Khoi subsistence and economy overlapped with those of the Bantu-speakers. As a result, the Khoi were more likely to have been in competition over resources with immigrating Bantu agropastoralists than were the hunter-gatherers.

Hunter-gatherers exploited the land differently than either the Khoi or the Bantu-speakers. When the Batswana, for example, fought with other societies, they usually did so for the cattle (Willoughby 1912), a commodity the hunter-gatherers did not possess. Schapera's (1930:351–356) section on Khoisan warfare in his study of the

Khoisan peoples primarily describes wars between Bantu-speakers and Khoi and not with hunter-gatherers. Yet, the Khoi are acknowledged by most researchers as having retained their cultural identity and autonomy even while in contact with Bantu-speakers for 2,000 years, until Western colonization. For some reason, anthropologists cannot believe that hunter-gatherers could coexist for 2,000 years with the agropastoralists, but Khoi could. They do not take into account that once Westerners arrived with their technology, missionaries, and diseases, intercultural relations changed dramatically. As noted by Sugawara in Chapter 4 (this volume), once confronted with the pressures wrought by colonization, G/wi and G//ana hunter-gatherers may have had a difficult time resisting the more dominant Bantu-speaking groups who were able to inhabit the Kalahari at the borehole where he worked (Xade) at the end of the twentieth century (but also see Chapter 3, this volume).

Racism and Religion

Ethnocentrism was present and continues today among the Bantu-speakers whose ancestors preceded the Europeans. However, the difference between these groups was that the precontact Bantu-speakers did not have a religion that perceived all nonbelievers as heathens who would be punished by God unless they were "saved" by adopting Christianity. Traditional Batswana (Bantu-speakers) religion was primarily concerned with a family's relatively recent ancestors and the village chief—not those of unrelated families or unrelated societies (Schapera 1953:59–60). Spirits could punish the living by causing illness and misfortune, but their control and influence were exerted on living descendants rather than on non–Bantu-speakers, such as neighboring hunter-gatherers (Schapera 1953:59). Although Bantu-speakers who did have dependent hunter-gatherers during the nineteenth century tried to control or manipulate them, the hunter-gatherers were not forced to assimilate into Bantu society nor abandon their own culture. For example, Nharo hunter-gatherers worked for agropastoralists while maintaining their separate cultural identity (Guenther, Chapter 5, also 1986, 1996).

The inherent differences between the Bantu-speakers' and the Europeans' religions resulted in different attitudes and behaviors that cannot be ignored by anthropologists. Based on Western religion and philosophy, Europeans did not see hunter-gatherers or agricultural pastoralists as truly human. Therefore, Christians' perception of killing native people during war was different from the Bantu-speakers' views.

Most Bantu-speaking groups had numerous taboos when engaging in warfare (Willoughby 1912:172). After killing a fellow human, a Bantu-speaker had to undergo purification ceremonies that were not necessary when the same person killed either a wild or domesticated animal. An entire regiment of warriors had to be cleansed after warfare, but the individual who actually killed someone during battle had to perform further special rites to purge his uncleanness (Willoughby 1912:175). Those purification rites included washing with medicated water, eating meat with medicine, and being hit with a stick and struck with an inflated colon from a sacrificial cow slaughtered for this event (Willoughby 1912:211). Even if the killing was justified as self-defense, warriors had to undergo these rites before being able to function normally in the society. Because of their religion, killing people had a greater impact on Bantu speakers than on colonizing Christians. One reason, I suggest, is because the Bantu speakers believed that all humans had souls that became ghosts who could cause illness and misfortune, whereas nonhuman animals, whether domesticated or wild, did not (i.e., it was not for the appreciation of cultural diversity that the immigrating Bantu-speakers did not annihilate the indigenous peoples of southern Africa prior to European contact, but because of religious beliefs).

Christians regard humans as singular beings because they are thought to mirror God (Guenther 1999:225). This belief facilitated ideas of the superiority of Westerners and inferiority of anyone who did not look like a European (i.e., that person was not in the Western image of God and therefore was less than human). By defining enemies as lesser beings, often nonhuman animals, Christians did not have to grapple with the ethics of killing a fellow human, whatever the situation. Thus, there was a fundamental difference in the consequence of taking a human life between Bantu-speakers and Westerners. I suggest, but cannot prove, that the differences in the repercussions of killing humans between the two societies may have allowed a large number of Westerners to more easily transcend their morals and kill people whom they did not consider fully human. Regardless of the validity of this proposition, we can state that there were fewer religious restrictions and consequences for Europeans who killed non-Westerners than for Bantu-speakers. It is possible that these perceived differences resulted in the Westerners' implicit acceptance of the slaying of hunter-gatherers and other native peoples, since most settlers were not punished in any way for killing Africans but often were punished for killing fellow Europeans. In my opinion, the Bantu-speakers did not have a religion that permitted the indiscriminate killing of hunter-gatherers before the havoc brought by Western colonization.

Racism and Colonialism

Foucault (1980, 1983) states that Europeans' entire notion of power is unique to Western and other highly nonegalitarian, sociopolitically complex societies. This concept of power is a result of the rise of Christianity in the sixteenth century, and particularly in the eighteenth century, when nation-states emerged (Foucault 1980, 1983). I posit that Western religion and technology, political imperialism, and hierarchical social relations, combined with Western ethnocentrism and racism, helped Europeans colonize and dominate chiefdoms and less socially/politically complex societies. Because colonialization and the impact of Europeans on southern African societies was a cultural phenomenon, a similar type of interaction with similar results to the native peoples occurred not only in Africa, but all over the globe.

Historians of colonialism discuss the nature of Western society in promoting the exploitation and domination of Africa. For example, Stuart (1995:116–117) wrote that missionaries' often-unflattering views of native Africans were not necessarily the result of culture conflict or the settlers' prejudices. Instead, the views were a product of an ideology that had, he suggested, its "roots, branches, and leaves" in Western culture (Stuart 1995). Colonialism and the need to develop non-Western societies "provided an ideology of progress and scientific measurement in which the state became an enlightened representative of progressive forces and morally responsible for their propagation" (Ludden 1992:252). Perhaps most importantly, as noted by Ludden, was that when "capitalist states acquired new territory, they exerted power in the name of progress. Underproductive resources had to be developed. Past systems of resource control had to be denigrated, dismantled, and replaced by rational policy and social order designed by enlightened rules to benefit people victimized by their past."

The colonial ideology and goals were often validated by Christianity. For example, the decimating of wild animals in southern Africa was legitimized by the Church, resulting in the destruction of an important food resource on which local people depended. In addition, European religion promoted the belief that all animals (including non-Western humans) and all plants were put on earth to be exploited by Europeans. Because the Christian religion perceives humans as superior to all other animals, it unintentionally justified the massive slaughter of game and the degradation of their habitats. As noted by Newton-King, "whether the purpose of the [colonists'] hunt was domestic, manufacture [of hides] or commercial profit, European hunters were distinguished from their indigenous counterparts by the sheer scale of the destruction" (1999:101). The difference was that the colonists indiscriminately killed massive numbers of wildlife and degraded the land. Europeans' hunting trips often resulted in the killing of massive numbers of wild animals, exceeding their ability to use all the meat (Newton-King 1999). By the end of the 1770s, elephants were already extinct in parts of the colony (Newton-King 1999:102). The local people recognized the environmental destruction occurring and some even complained to van der Merwe that Europeans were taking all of the places where the eland and other game grazed (Newton-King 1999:90), making the land unable to sustain the native people and forcing them into serf or slave labor for the colonists.

I submit that this belief in game and plant resources being provided by God for human exploitation justified the destruction of the environment. Religion also legitimized slavery, the appropriation of land, killing, and other events, such as culture-cide, that occurred when the Europeans entered southern Africa. Livingstone (1857:36) wrote, "Nor have the Boers any wish to conceal the meanness of thus employing unpaid labor [i.e., slavery]; on the contrary, every one of them . . . lauded his own humanity and justice in making such an equitable regulation. 'We make the people work for us, in consideration of allowing them to live in *our* country'" (Livingstone 1857:36; emphasis added). When the Boers invaded what is today Botswana, they "claimed that all the Natives in the country north of the Vaal River were their subjects, and consequently liable to labour taxation" (Schapera 1942:10). Native men and women not only worked on the Boers' farms, but some men fought with the Boers against other local groups (Schapera 1942). Livingstone writes that the Boers called themselves "Christians," and all others "black property" or "creatures" (1857:37).

Not all Westerners saw the local people this way—which created a tension among colonists. The military often considered natives as inhuman vermin to be exploited, if not also exterminated, but not all Westerners, including most missionaries, agreed. The differences result partly from the dissimilar reasons for being in southern Africa and partly from the disparate goals of the two factions. The incongruity between the European groups was visible in their different interactions with the native peoples. Missionaries such as Ellenberger (1912), while he abhorred the treatment of the indigenous peoples by the colonists and military, tried to assimilate them.

Ethnography and ethnohistory do not suggest that the Bantu-speakers considered all animals, plants, and other humans to be put on earth for their exploitation. Nor am I aware of traditional Bantu-speakers' religions that professed it was in the best interest of everyone to destroy the culture of all groups that differed from their own. Bantu agropastoralists associated morality with ancestor worship (Willoughby 1912:259), and did not feel obligated to force other cultures to adopt their morals, ethics, ideology, clothing, or behavior. I suggest Bantu-speakers had less of a cultural reason than Europeans to want to change the hunter-gatherers' moral, social, and political existence. The same is not true today because the Bantu-speakers have embraced Christianity and Western nation-state ideals. Consequently, the Bantu-speakers' precolonial intrusion into southern Africa was not analogous to the Western intrusion, nor to the current treatment of Kalahari hunter-gatherers by the Bantu Botswana government.

3. Influence of Christian Missionaries

Either covertly or overtly, the European missionaries' motives were to change the local peoples' religion, in addition to all other aspects of their culture. Rather than simply ignoring the native religions, as probably occurred prehistorically with Bantu and Khoi intercultural interactions, Westerners actively sought to convert native peoples to Christianity, which was thought by many at that time to be a noble and moral practice. "By the 1830s–1840s, a mission was established in Lesotho where missionaries introduced, among other things, new crops, animal breeds, and building techniques from other parts of the [Western] world" (Gill 1992:7). Among the local people, a split occurred between the traditional Basotho Bantu-speakers who opposed many of the changes introduced by the missionaries and those individuals who embraced conversion (Gill 1992:7). By 1848, tensions ensued between the missionaries and many of the agropastoralists concerning marriage, polygamy, initiation, and burial practices imposed by the missionaries (Gill 1992).

According to the European colonists, including missionaries, "Sin in Africa was not only to be found in the human heart, but was inscribed in the social fabric of African culture" (Stuart 1995:120). Mission stations were established where hunter-gatherers "were offered a comprehensive 'civilizing programme' which included, in addition to agriculture and livestock-breeding, the building of houses and dams, and the laying-out of streets, sewing for girls, and school education centering on literacy" (Szalay 1995:46). During the seventeenth and eighteenth centuries, hunter-gatherers were compelled by Europeans to practice pastoralism. While there were individual exceptions, in general, the success of a mission was determined by how many people were "civilized"—that is, Westernized, which was equated with being "Christianized" (Andersson 1856:27). Many Europeans perceived native peoples as "savages" who were in direct contrast to "civilized" Westerners. "This process involved the projection of images rather than the description of realities" because the "difference of the 'savage' was a mechanism for European self realization" (Stuart 1995:116).

Several illustrations of the attempts by missionaries to force the local people to assimilate were reported by various explorers. In 1856 for example, the explorer-historian Andersson wrote that missionaries were laudably and strenuously trying to convert the Damaras pastoralists to Christianity. To become Christian, adherents had to abide by Western culture's standards of morality, gender, politics, and all other facets of culture (Andersson 1856). In other words, in order to be Christian, native peoples had to forsake their own culture and adopt the European one. The anthropologist Schapera (1953:48) reported that newly Christian Batswana Bantu-speakers had to "conform to the social and moral ideals preached by the Church, dress in a 're-spectable' manner, and abstain from certain tribal customs regarded as incompatible with true Christianity" (e.g., polygamy and circumcision). Moreover, "Christianity has brought much more to the Tswana than merely a new set of religious beliefs. The missionaries built churches, introduced the vocations of preacher and catechist, established local Church councils, instituted new ceremonies (e.g., baptism, confirmation, and communion)" (Schapera 1953:58). Introducing new forms of marriage, death, and religious rituals through their hymns, Christianity provided a new and very popular form of music (Schapera 1953:58). Basically, "Missionaries sought to impose a new system of morality conforming to Christian ideals, and to this end introduced sanctions of various kinds governing the lives of their members" (Schapera 1953:58).

That these particular citations mention Khoi or Bantu speakers instead of hunter-gatherers does not mean hunter-gatherers were immune from such pressures. It just indicates that hunter-gatherers were not targeted as a group to convert and assimilate as were the Khoi and Bantu-speakers. This is one of many reasons hunter-gatherers persisted and some remained autonomous for 300 to 400 years longer than did the Khoi. Guenther (1999:224) characterizes missionaries' attempts to convert hunter-gatherers in the Cape as "halfhearted" and ineffective because many missionaries were "dubious about the whole enterprise from the negative estimation in which they held the Bushmen and their capacity for Western religion and civilization." Those hunter-gatherers living near mission stations, who were, according to Szalay (1995), by then mistakenly called "Hottentots," were strongly encouraged to convert. Those who did not convert willingly were often forced, through the appropriation of their land and animals by settlers, to conform to Western culture through the adoption of Christianity. At the same time, hunter-gatherers occupying regions without missions were not pressured. This variability in the frequency of contact and the resultant consequences of interactions with colonialists formed the diverse patterns of cultural autonomy/subjugation recorded by ethnographers among twentieth-century southern African hunter-gatherers.

For many years missionaries were responsible for the Western education, health care, social activities, and other nonreligious facets of the native peoples' lives. Schapera (1953:58) wrote "The missionary himself has become not only the tribal priest, but also the guide and adviser of the people in many spheres of life remote from religion." Some natives adopted Christianity and became missionaries themselves. Their goal, like those of the European missionaries, was to "press . . . universal or European-style ideas on the Batswana" (Parsons 1985:26). The continuous moral and financial support of missionaries from distant European countries allowed individuals to build and maintain missions for several decades or longer than would otherwise have been possible.

Missionaries were powerful cultural brokers, many of whom sought the spread of Western culture for what they thought was the good of the natives. Although speaking of the Spanish colonization, Rafael's (1995:67) comments are germane here because European colonialization in both cases and at both periods was still based on Western ideology. "Missionaries sought to capture not only native bodies but, more important, native minds and souls." Missionaries were individuals implementing projects conceived by Europeans unfamiliar with the specifics of South Africa. Missionaries themselves varied in how they interpreted their position, instituting and enforcing policies determined largely by their employers in Europe (Schapera 1970:233). So, while individuals enacted the policies in southern Africa, the conception of the policies come from Europe and was based on European culture. No equivalent evangelical group in the Bantu-speaking pastoralist culture was so concerned with the assimilation of hunter-gatherers or other societies, explaining the cultural diversity found in Africa when Westerners first arrived.

Not all missionaries were concerned with transforming native cultures to that of their own. Some missionaries were more interested in the welfare of the hunter-gatherers and other local people. Livingstone and Ellenberger are examples of admirers of native cultures. Even so, the basic goal of most missions, and the people in Europe who were supporting them, was to effect culture change. Native culture-cide the world over was associated with European colonization and Western religious beliefs. Individual missionaries did not have the power or resources to destroy entire societies in southern Africa or elsewhere, but the enterprise of missionization and the theology of Christianity did.

Because of the differences in the religions and overall culture of the Bantu-speakers and the Europeans, I posit that it is erroneous to assume that an analogous relationship existed between the Bantu-speakers and hunter-gatherers before and after the arrival of Westerners. As far as can be known, and based on ethnographic and ethnohistoric sources, there was nothing similar to missionaries in the Bantu-speakers' religions. These religions emphasized individual family ancestor worship and not the conversion of others to their culture.

There were relatively large areas of southern Africa where missionaries and other Europeans did not invade. The Kalahari Desert that stretched over much of Botswana and eastern Namibia was also occupied by only a few Bantu-speakers. The majority of Bantu-speakers lived on the margins of the Kalahari because of the region's poor agricultural potential and unpredictable herding pasture before the advent of modern boreholes (or wells). These factors also discouraged European settlement. The Kalahari provides a good example of the diversity in relations in southern Africa. According to Stein (1998:220, 246–245), the further away from a core area occupied by a dominant group, the more likely interregional or intergroup contact will be characterized by an essential equivalence in power relations, rather than the hegemonic control of the colonizers. Because the Kalahari hunter-gatherers were located far from the European colonizers' core, they were able to practice their pre-contact culture as they had before the appearance of Westerners in southern Africa.

4. Intolerance for Cultural Diversity

Europeans' rigid intolerance for cross-cultural differences and an unquestioned belief in Western superiority resulted from a "fear of the Other, pre-occupation with white prestige [and] . . . white supremacy" (Stoler 1992:322). The result was the common requirement that any person who wanted to interact with Westerners had to think and act like them. At times, this type of thinking meant that South African colonists and missionaries demanded policies that were impractical, including one specifying that all native South Africans had to farm and herd cattle, regardless of the available resources. European missionaries sometimes complained that the pastoralists abandoned the mission stations claiming to not have sufficient grass for their cattle (Stuart 1995:123). They thought the real reason native Africans deserted was their lack of belief in Christianity or a general disinterest in improving their lives (i.e., adopting Western culture). In reality, some mission stations did *not* have sufficient grass to support large numbers of cattle, so the native peoples had to move for survival (Stuart 1995).

Educated descendants of converted Bantu-speakers claimed the early missionaries were ethnocentric (Setiloane 1976). "Any cultural differences to them [missionaries] would have been more evidence of how 'depraved' and 'uncivilized' 'the lower races' [Bantu-speaking peoples] were" (Setiloane 1976:89). Stuart (1995:122) observed that for native southern Africans to be saved by the Europeans, it was not enough for the natives to adopt the culture of "civilized" Western society, they had to literally assimilate and become British. Not surprisingly, such thinking led to an impossible situation: "Of critical importance, was the missionaries' belief that civilized life was premised on the practice of settled agriculture. Hunter-gatherers and nomadic pastoralists, such as the so called 'Hottentots' and 'Bushmen' as well as a number of various other people on the fringes of the colony were thus inherently savage" (Stuart 1995:123).

Penn (1996:89) described the European viewpoint as being particularly ethnocentric in part because hunter-gatherers

were as far removed from the European norm as any people the Dutch had ever encountered . . . imbued with a sense of their own superiority under God's guidance, it was hardly surprising that the colonists should imagine the San [Basarwa, Bushmen] to be completely 'other' than themselves . . . contempt, hatred and the almost unrestrained license to violence provided by the context of a legitimate war on the furthest frontiers of European expansion, ensured that the war against the San would be marked by genocidal atrocities. (Penn 1996:89)

Certainly, hunter-gatherers did not passively accept this violence. Until the late 1700s, they were able to successfully wage a guerrilla war against the Dutch. Their problems were exasperated by inferior weapons, a lack of animal transportation, small groups, and the absence of a complex, hierarchical political or social organization similar to that of the Zulu and other Bantu-speaking groups. Sociopolitical complexity allowed some of the Bantu-speaking groups to avoid the culture-cide and genocide experienced by the hunter-gatherers and Khoi herders in the Cape of South Africa.

The Western intolerance for diversity, in and of itself, would not have been sufficient for the destruction of cultures, peoples, and wild animals in southern Africa and elsewhere. However, in combination with their superior technology, their culture, including religion and general ideology, and the introduction of European diseases, interactions between Westerners and hunter-gatherers were qualitatively different than the interactions between Bantu or Khoi and hunter-gatherers.

THE IDEOLOGY OF COLONIALISM

When European colonialists instigated change, it was usually in the name of "progress" or "development." These terms are still used today. In the past, as in the present, unproductive resources must still be developed and previous methods of controlling resources need to be replaced by "rational policies" so that the "enlightened" can rescue those who have been victimized by their past (Ludden 1995:252). In other words, both colonization in the past, and nationalism today, operate with similar principles: "(1) ruling powers that claim progress as a goal, (2) a "people" whose condition must be improved, (3) an ideology of science that controls principles and techniques to effect and measure progress, and (4) self-declared leaders who would use state power for development" (Ludden 1995:252). In ideology, Western science objectifies otherwise abstract concepts, such as the economy and living conditions, in order to make them real objects that can be manipulated for growth and improvement (Ludden 1995). This ideology, according to Ludden (1995), glorified Westernization and its benefits to other cultures.

Until recently, missionaries avoided much of the Kalahari Desert. During the past century, a mission was established among the Nharo Basarwa where Afrikaners (Boers) and British had farms in the Ghanzi region, Botswana. The other non–hunter-gatherers at Ghanzi and northwestern Botswana also have a very shallow history. The Boers arrived around 1898, the Batswana a little earlier in the 1800s, the Oorlam Bantu-speakers in the early 1840s, and the Bakgalagadi, Barolong, and Herero Bantu-speakers all settled in the area at the end of the 1800s (Guenther, Chapter 5, 1996). However, the impact of these non–hunter-gatherers was not as great as it had been in South Africa, partly because of the Nharo's mobility, which made it possible for the hunter-gatherers to come and go as they pleased (Guenther, Chapter 5, this volume; Barnard and Widlok 1996; Guenther 1996). In other words, there were parts of the Kalahari where Bantu-speakers and Europeans did not settle and the issue of clashing cultures did not impact the hunter-gatherers living there. Therefore, autonomous hunter-gatherers were able to survive the onslaught of

Western colonization through the mid-nineteenth century in Lesotho and the eastern Free State, South Africa, and to the end of the twentieth century in parts of the Kalahari.

Since the Bantu Batswana nation-state of Botswana emerged (1966) and became established (1980s–2000), the Kalahari hunter-gatherers have been forced by the government to give up their foraging way of life and autonomy, as the Western nation-states forced hunter-gatherers to do outside the Kalahari centuries before. At the Kalahari resettlement government communities, hunter-gatherers are pressured to forsake their culture for a sedentary agropastoralist culture. Bantu missionaries at these settlements attempt to further assimilate the Basarwa, as did Westerners in the past. As part of the resettlement package, the Botswana government drilled a borehole, gave each head of the household a choice of goats or cattle, money to participate in the Botswana cash economy, and seeds to plant. Children are required to attend a Bantu-run school where they are taught the Bantu language and history. People are encouraged to take advantage of Western health-care provided at a community clinic and to join in the community discussions at the Bantu-style *kotla* where the government-appointed Bantu chief presides. Hunting is now illegal and collecting wild plants unfeasible due to the large number of cattle and other livestock that have destroyed the habitat. Thus, it can be seen that much of what happened outside the Kalahari historically occurred in response to the Western nation-state as much of the forced assimilation occurring today is a response to the Botswana nation-state (also see Sugawara, Chapter 4). Whether the nation-state is composed of Europeans or Bantu seems to have little effect on the overall policy of imposed culture change and loss of autonomy.

It is important to emphasize that not all Europeans agreed with colonial policies, anymore than all modern Bantu agree with their government's resettlement scheme designed to assimilate hunter-gatherers into the agropastoralist dominant society. There were Europeans whose sympathies were primarily with the local societies (e.g., particularly the early anthropologists, Bleek 1928, 1932, and elsewhere; and missionaries such as Lebzelter 1934:4; Livingstone 1857; and others). Likewise, not all Bantu-speakers were cultural relativists or less ethnocentric than other stratified chiefdom-level societies. The events that occurred in southern Africa resulted from the ideology and behaviors produced by Western or Bantu culture and are not the result of individual interactions.

Most anthropological models of interaction emphasize inequality in power, economics, and cultural prestige. These models are appropriate for some cultures, particularly those of modern nation-states, that tend to emphasize inequality, which influences the nature of their interactions with groups who do not share the same culture. Such Western "models are suited to understanding a relatively narrow range of contact situations, primarily those pertaining in the modern world"

(Schortman and Urban 1998:104, 105). They involve Western or similar highly complex state-level societies, while at the same time offering little room for creative resistance or a two-way exchange of ideas and behaviors (Schortman and Urban 1998:104, 105; Stein 1998).

I suggest that the world systems (or political economy) view of culture contact is not appropriate for the types of interaction that occurred during the 1,000 or more years of Bantu-speakers' presence in southern Africa. There are common concepts and assumptions that shape the political economy perspective that are inappropriate for the interrelationships between local groups before European contact. These concepts include the predestined exploitation of indigenous peoples, the inevitable destruction of local cultures, survivors' assimilating or maintaining an impoverished form of their previous culture, and an overemphasis on political and economic variables in intersocietal transactions (Schortman and Urban 1998:106). The concepts predetermine the type of interaction between Europeans and hunter-gatherers, making them qualitatively different from those between the Bantu and hunter-gatherers. Consequently, contact with Europeans and Bantus had different effects on hunting-gathering sovereignty in southern Africa.

As a product of Western culture at that time period, European colonists did not think of themselves or their actions as immoral or wrong. Foucault's (1983:208) study reveals that power has been used to create a perception of the "other" as inhuman or what he terms "subjects." Once conceived of as such, hunter-gatherers could be rationalized as nonhuman or objects/slaves. This perception alleviated Europeans' questioning, moral dilemmas, and/or guilt for destroying autonomous societies (the same dehumanization and alleviation of guilt occurred in the nineteenth century with Native American and with African American slaves). Foucault (1983:213–214), in fact, goes to great length to demonstrate that European power, as conceived by many scholars, is a product of the development of the state, which originated in its modern form beginning in the sixteenth century and was accentuated in the eighteenth century with the spread of Christianity and the development of modern states (Foucault 1983:214). I suggest that any religion associated with a state-level society has similar consequences, be it Hinduism, Confucianism, or Islam. The end result is the presence of power as an integral force or influence throughout the culture, whether it is Western, Asian, or Arabic. None of these characteristics of religion or state are relevant to the immigrating Bantu-speakers who represented paramount chiefdoms during the Late Iron Age. It is, I believe, a mistake to think otherwise.[1]

Conversion to Christianity was thought to be in everyone's best interests, as it offered salvation of the native peoples and concretized the domination of Western culture. As Stuart notes, "The unequal power relations between Africans and missionaries, and between Africans and the social, political, and economic order which missionaries represented, were however a profoundly significant reality. The connections between savagery and sin left no doubt about the 'guilt' of being African. Once the sinner became convinced of sin it was a short step to becoming a servant" (Stuart 1995:129). The Dutch conceived of the world and their place in it completely differently from the hunter-gatherers or the Bantu-speakers. According to Penn (1996:91), "the focused drive of the Europeans, with a cluster of concepts based upon Christian certainties, a linear sense of historical progress and a notion of power derived from material gain, proved to be of greater utility, in the long struggle for survival on the Cape frontier" than the inherent cultural beliefs of the hunter-gatherers or of the pastoralists who preceded the Europeans. Western notions of sin and redemption, development and progress were not integral parts of most precolonial Bantu-speakers' cultures.

As colonizers took over land for themselves or destroyed formerly productive land, the local peoples had few choices but to migrate to mission stations or small communities to seek employment. Large numbers of people, regardless of cultural affinity, were made dependent on Europeans for food, clothing, and other necessities. The practice of avoidance as a means to escape the demands of a politically dominant group became obsolete. This, in turn, forced native groups to directly confront colonizers with their less efficient weapons and war strategies. Most vulnerable were the dispersed, loosely organized societies (Sugawara, Chapter 4, this volume). As a result, the hunter-gatherers and the Khoi herders were the first to be culturally destroyed in those areas inhabited by Europeans. However, some southern African societies, such as the Zulus, were culturally better able to resist Western expansion. Their complex sociopolitical organization was hierarchical and well organized with an authoritarian kingship. This allowed Westerners to negotiate with one person in a way that was familiar to them. The Zulu also maintained a standing army of warriors who were taught how to fight, which allowed the Zulu to maintain a coherent culture in the face of European expansion far longer than the less highly organized and less complex societies. Hunter-gatherer and Khoi "acculturation in the Cape was more far-reaching. Their culture and identity were completely obliterated. This was a result of factors such as population size and density, social structure, and colonial attitudes" (Szalay 1995:119).

Because territoriality is culturally constructed, it has different connotations in dissimilar societies. According to Barnard (1992a:145), "When herders move into hunter-gatherer territories there is no necessary conflict [because they exploit different ecological niches], though there would be if other Bushmen were to move in and take over." In the Kalahari, "The Nharo have lived in a reasonably symbiotic relationship . . . [as have] !Kung with Tswana and Herero pastoralists. . . . [The] incursion of non–hunter-gatherer populations has not led to explicit defense of territorial boundaries or to widespread displacement of hunter-gatherers" (Barnard

1992a:145). The implication, then, is that the movement of Bantu-speaking agropastoralists into southern Africa did not necessarily disrupt hunter-gatherer culture and
land. Individuals may have hired or kept some hunter-gatherers to help in herding
and other jobs, but this cannot be generalized to a loss of all hunter-gatherers' autonomy. The same can be said about individual Europeans who occasionally hired
hunter-gatherers for odd jobs without necessarily interfering with their way of life,
as in the case of ≠Aã Nharo inhabiting the Ghanzi region of the Kalahari Desert,
Botswana (Guenther, Chapter 5; Barnard and Widlok 1996).

DISCUSSION

The unrest caused by colonization forced many groups, including Bantu-speakers
and Khoi, to move into areas formerly inhabited primarily by hunter-gatherers. For
example, by 1800, the area north of the Orange River was quickly overpopulated
with agropastoralists (Szalay 1995). As a result, Cape hunter-gatherers could not escape the Boer colony by fleeing elsewhere (Penn 1996). Even if the hunter-gatherers
could penetrate into regions that they had not inhabited before, they still had nowhere to go because the lands were already densely occupied by other groups. For
example, the Kalahari Desert was already inhabited by hunter-gatherers who had
lived there long before Westerners or Bantu-speakers entered the region. Even if
the Cape hunter-gatherers attempted to migrate to the interior further north to
avoid enslavement, the adaptation to environmental and social conditions so different from the Cape would have been a most difficult adjustment (Szalay 1995:111–
112). Once in the labor force, Cape and other hunter-gatherers were reclassified as
"Hottentots" and later as "Colors" (Szalay 1995:108–111). The predecessors of modern Kalahari foragers, however, were not subjected to the same forces of assimilation, before or after the European intrusion.

   Although some of the Bantu-speaking groups did keep slaves, as is common in
chiefdom-level societies, I propose slaves were not treated nor viewed as Euroamericans' slaves were. The *Webster's New World Dictionary and Thesaurus* defines
slaves as human beings who are owned as property by, and are absolutely subject
to the will of, another(s); bond-servants divested of all freedom and personal
rights. It is unfortunate that Silberbauer and Kuper (1966) and other researchers
and explorers used the term *serf* or *slave* to characterize Bakgalagadi and Nharo
hunter-gatherer relations. Their article makes it quite clear that their usage of the
term *serf* or *slave* is not standard. Although there is no doubt that Bantu-speakers
looked down on the hunter-gatherers, sometimes even calling them their "serfs,"
the hunter-gatherers were free to come and go as they liked (Silberbauer and
Kuper 1966:176). The hunter-gatherers decided, without penalty, retribution, and/
or coercion, if they felt like working or not (Silberbauer and Kuper 1966). The

Nharo occupied their own camps or communities several miles away from the Bakgalagadi settlement. "They lived their own lives, and the master-serf relationship [which is not at all what one usually defines as serfdom] is only activated during bad times, when the Bushmen urgently need help from their masters or during the relatively rare periods when their masters require extra labour for harvest or for moving cattle" (Silberbauer and Kuper 1966:174). Of particular importance is Silberbauer and Kuper's (1966:179) conclusion that even as late as 1966, this relationship had not destroyed the hunter-gatherers' culture. They still had their own language and cultural identity: "band organizations and kinship structure seem to have remained intact" (also see Guenther 1996; Barnard 1992). This obviously is a significant departure from the definition of either slave or serf that most researchers use when they employ the terms today.

Not all, or even most, of the people who were called slaves or serfs in the literature were hunter-gatherers. In fact, the majority were the less dominant Bantu-speaking groups, particularly rural Bakgalagadi (as noted by Mautle 1986; Solway 1994). Furthermore, rural Bakgalagadi were forced to contribute wild hides, meat, and other goods to the Batswana chiefs as tribute. The hunter-gatherers were much too mobile and unpredictable to be forced into servitude, I suggest (Kent 1998b).

I maintain that hunter-gatherers were not more passive than the pastoralists and other native peoples occupying Africa, either before or after Western colonization. They maintained strategies to deal with nonforaging populations, including trade, relocation when necessary, and mobility. Barnard wrote that "Schapera's general assessment of the relations between Bushmen and other people . . . was that contact between blacks and Bushmen, particularly in the Eastern Khoi Bushman area, had 'on the whole been less disastrous' than contact between whites and Bushmen elsewhere" (1992b:1120).

Importantly, there is no solid evidence suggesting that the murder and intimidation of hunter-gatherers by Bantu-speakers was present prior to the arrival of Boers who introduced guns and horses. Bantu-speakers were forced out of their territories by Westerners, or by other agropastoralists disturbed by the colonists, and had to move to different regions. For example, the Batswana were forced out of South Africa into Botswana and the Basotho were forced from South Africa to what is today Lesotho. This, then, disrupted all the native peoples, hunter-gatherers, Khoi, and other agropastoralists, living in the areas they settled. The resulting turmoil created numerous problems that were not experienced on such a large scale prior to Western colonization. Gordon (1992:28–29), for instance, noted that in the northwestern Kalahari (present-day Namibia), Nama (Khoi), Oerlam, or Herero Bantu agropastoralists did not infringe on hunter-gatherer territories until after the arrival of Europeans in southern Africa and the adoption of firearms. With their superior weapons, Namibian colonialists took over the best Herero pasture, which forced the Bantu-speakers to move their cattle into regions previously occupied by hunter-gatherers (Gordon 1984). Prior to this, Herero stayed in their area outside hunter-gatherers' territories and peacefully traded with the foragers. The killing, therefore, was the result of the Western invasion. Previously, these groups lived on the periphery of hunter-gatherer land. Interaction occurred, but it was not necessarily adversarial.

The very fact that the Bantu and Westerners represent different cultures, and that intergroup interactions are cultural exchanges (economic, social, etc.), implies that the context and repercussions of their interactions with hunter-gatherers are likely *not* similar in nature or scope. In addition, as groups tried to move away from European colonization, they invariably invaded someone else's land. This is why after 2,000 years of contact with Bantu-speakers, there were still autonomous hunter-gatherers present in southern Africa (as described by the first European explorers), whereas after just 300 to 400 years of contact with Westerners there were no autonomous hunter-gatherers left in South Africa.

In regions such as the Kalahari Desert, Europeans did not colonize and did not proselytize to the same extent as in South Africa. The consequence was that Kalahari hunter-gatherers did not encounter the forced assimilation demanded by Westerners elsewhere in southern Africa. However, history repeated itself when the Bantu Botswana nation-state became established, with the same disastrous results of a loss of cultural autonomy and identity for the Kalahari foragers. The similarity between the repercussions of the Western nation-state and the Bantu nation-state shows that what happened in colonial South Africa was not a consequence of any single people, but of the nation-state system that first become popular and powerful in Europe and then spread more recently to other regions.

Colonization by Westerners irrevocably changed the cultural heterogeneity of southern Africa. Livingstone (1885) and others noted the Boer settlers' constant demand for slaves, which encouraged groups to prey on the different native societies present in southern Africa. As described above, the Khoi and Bantu-speakers were quite willing to capture hunter-gatherers, who were easier to capture than individuals from the more sociopolitically complex and densely populated Bantu or Khoi societies. I suggest that the need for slaves was not as high nor as constant prior to colonization. According to Szalay (1995:13), the colonial "expansion in the Cape had two goals: first, the seizure of the land and, second, the exploitation of the indigenous people as labourers." Whereas the first may have been a goal for the incoming Bantu-speaking pastoralists, the second, I suggest, probably was not. The need for slaves was so acute for the Europeans that they initially imported slaves from elsewhere, before forcing the indigenous peoples into slavery at the end of the eighteenth century (Szalay 1995).

The Westerners' motivations were prompted by the way in which Western culture is organized. As a result, similarities between Westerners' interaction with southern African hunter-gatherers and with Native North American societies are striking. Europeans wanted native slaves in North America as badly as they wanted them in southern Africa. In both cases, they provided culturally different native groups with guns so that one could force another into servitude. "By arming Indian groups on their western frontiers, Virginia and Carolina traders could be assured of a steady supply of slaves" (M. Smith 1987:135). According to M. Smith (1987:135–137), "The desire to capture slaves and the military advantage conferred by firearms thus combined to terrorize the Indians of the study area by the last third of the seventeenth century. This pressure caused vast population movements."

It is no coincidence that the repercussions of colonization were similar in southern Africa and North and South America showing that these consequences were a product of Western culture and not of local conditions that could have occurred prior to European contact. The often-compulsory conversion to Western religion and culture by missionaries, and the ownership of superior weapons, communication, and travel (i.e., horses), resulted in the erosion of native cultures in southern Africa and North America (M. Smith 1987:145). European colonization of southern Africa and of the Americas also occurred with the early onslaught of epidemic diseases, giving the invaders an advantage from the resulting demoralization, disruptions, and depopulation caused by the introduced pathogens.

It is important to understand that my purpose is not to affix blame for what occurred during the Western colonialization of southern Africa. We can regret many events that happened in the past, but that will not change them. Still, historical incidents must be acknowledged and studied, if for no other reason than to ensure that they are never again repeated. Although I do not think that it was ever anyone's intention, the insistence that hunter-gatherers were assimilated and/or dominated by immigrating Bantu-speakers makes the colonialists appear less responsible for the culture-cide and genocide that occurred. That is, if the plight of hunter-gatherers did not result from European occupation, but from Bantu occupation that occurred several thousand years ago, then Westerners need not feel guilty about destroying hunter-gatherers' cultures. Today's twenty-first-century Westerners should not feel guilty about events they had no participation in, control over, or knowledge of, but they should understand the past in order to better understand the present and the future.

CONCLUSIONS

Is it possible to objectively understand the reasons underlying the very dissimilar interactions and consequences between Europeans and hunter-gatherers in contrast to earlier interactions between Bantu-speakers and hunter-gatherers? I think it is. As noted in Chapter 3, the archaeological record does *not* contain evidence of the enslavement of most hunter-gatherer groups before the arrival of Westerners, except perhaps in a very few areas in southern Africa. These occurrences were apparently the exception rather than the rule in agropastoralist and hunter-gatherer relationships.

It is necessary to view history and prehistory within the cultural context present at the time. Some Europeans enjoyed and wanted to preserve the diverse cultures in southern Africa. They were concerned about local populations and were dedicated to helping hunter-gatherers and pastoralists in any way they could. Many other Westerns, however, felt the opposite. History is replete with the actions and atrocities of a dominant society exploiting or exterminating another society. It certainly is not unique to Western culture. That many Europeans, particularly the missionaries, thought they were acting morally and in the best interests of the natives also cannot be overlooked. In this chapter, I am only referring to the cultural level and its influence on intergroup interactions, not the individual level or a single person's relationships with others. While there were, doubtless, individual Westerners who were tolerant of cultural differences, there also were those who were not. From my interpretation of the archaeological record of southern Africa, no prehistoric data definitely demonstrates that culture-cide occurred among the hunter-gatherers, Khoi herders, and others, until after Westerners colonized the region (see Sadr, Chapter 2; Kent, Chapter 3; and Brooks, Chapter 8).

Because specific attributes of Western culture were either not present or were not present to the same degree in southern African Bantu culture, different responses were produced from their interactions with the hunter-gatherers. The dissimilarities were not on the level of individuals, but, instead, on the level of culture. That is, the differences exist on the level of the Western and Bantu-speakers' distinct cultural ideologies. Related to the strongly hierarchical nature of the Western nation-state culture, Europeans' sharply stratified worldview differed from that of most southern African cultures. The more complex Western nation-state encouraged an imperialistic view of natives as inferior or inhuman, peoples whom they had a divine right to exploit, or at least change. The Bantu did not share the same cultural view of hunter-gatherers. As a result, culture-cide and genocide occurred in those areas colonized by Westerners, but did not occur in regions occupied by Bantu prior to the arrival of Europeans. Ironically, when the Bantu adopted the tenets of the nation-state and Christianity, they also demanded cultural homogeneity at the expense of the previous Kalahari cultural diversity and autonomy.

A consequence of Western ethnocentric ideology that encouraged, or at least justified, the destruction of societies different from theirs, was the European initiation of programs of culture-cide and sometimes genocide when they colonized an area. Some of the first Europeans in parts of southern Africa, such as Lesotho, were missionaries whose explicit purpose was to change the culture of local peoples. With superior weapons, foreign epidemic diseases, and the destruction of the environment, Westerners were able to destroy the hunter-gatherers' cultures and decimate their populations over a relatively short period of time. Groups inhabiting areas not of interest to Europeans, such as parts of the Kalahari, did not experience the complete destruction of their way of life, as did the South African and Lesotho foragers.

When the Boers first appropriated the best agricultural/pastoral lands for themselves, Bantu-speaking agropastoralists had nowhere else to go but to areas inhabited by hunter-gatherers. Westerners' use of resources made other groups' use of wild plants or animals virtually impossible. Guns rapidly depleted the local fauna in ways not possible when only arrows and spears were available. Horses made transportation and warfare more effective for those groups that had access to them. Superior Western communication systems were strategically important for conquering and incorporating non-Western societies. Resource competition led to violence at the expense of the hunter-gatherers and herders as well. That is, some pastoralists and hunter-gatherers were forced into killing and stealing as Westerners encroached upon them and their neighbors. Others, such as the Zulu state, could expand and conquer other pastoralists because of the initial turmoil caused by the European technology and contact.

Colonization not only physically affected the native peoples. It exacted an emotional and psychological toll as well. The magnitude of the stress that the indigenous South African people had to endure as a result of European-introduced diseases, in addition to the forced displacement of entire families through slavery, may have inhibited fertility. The fear and helplessness they felt as a result of the introduced epidemics was probably not too dissimilar to that brought by the plague in medieval Europe or the smallpox and measles epidemics during the first 200–300 years of Western contact with the indigenous peoples of the Americas. Though perhaps not as devastating numerically as the introduced epidemic diseases in the Americas, the psychological suffering, combined with the other stressful events occurring at the time, must have been emotionally catastrophic for the native peoples of Africa. This was probably particularly true in the Cape Province of South Africa, where most of the colonists lived, at least during the first 200 years of occupation. Because many hunter-gatherers lived in relatively small camps that were both dispersed and mobile, and because of the epidemiology of infectious diseases that requires large numbers of sedentary, aggregated people to maintain an epidemic, not all hunter-gatherers were equally affected. The impact of these epidemics was variable in areas to the north of the main European settlements and farms in South Africa. Smallpox did not affect the Kalahari foragers until the 1950s when there was more contact with Europeans. The disease did not spread and have the same impact as it did elsewhere because the lifestyle of these Basarwa was not conducive to perpetuating an epidemic.

We have no solid evidence that the Bantu-speaking agropastoralists who migrated into southern Africa around 2,000 years ago had the Western philosophy of intolerance to other cultures. They also did not have vastly superior weapons, horses, and/or diseases against which the hunter-gatherers had little immunity. After the arrival of Westerners, there are documented historical accounts recording the indiscriminate murder of hunter-gatherers by some Bantu-speaking groups. However, I suggest that the slayings, at least partly, if not wholly, were in response to the demand for slaves by European colonists, the disruption in traditional subsistence pursuits, the relocation of local peoples created by the European appropriation of their lands, and the acquisition of guns and horses to which the hunter-gatherers did not have access. While hunter-gatherers living outside the Kalahari were unable to maintain their autonomy through the twentieth century, ethnohistorical sources state definitively that there were autonomous hunter-gatherers in parts of South Africa, Lesotho, Namibia, and Botswana until the 1900s and beyond. Ethnographies from the twentieth century clearly show that there were independent groups of foragers living in the Kalahari and other areas that were not permanently occupied by pastoralists or Westerners until the advent of mechanical boreholes or wells.

The fact that hunter-gatherers were able to maintain their cultural autonomy in most, although not all, of southern Africa for at least 1,500 years while interacting with Bantu-speaking agropastoralists, but were dominated within 300 to 400 years of contact with Westerners, illustrates the difference in the nature of hunter-gatherer's interactions with Bantus and Europeans. It is crucial, although admittedly difficult, to shed our Western-centric views of non-Western interactions in order to understand cross-cultural dynamics. Europeans were not acting immorally according to their culture when they destroyed native societies because Western culture legitimized its behavior through religious ideology, social tenets, and political beliefs. Western missionaries felt a moral obligation to "civilize" and "Christianize" the native peoples of all societies, just as the Bantu missionaries feel today. The prehistoric agropastoralist culture underlying the Bantu-speakers' relationships with hunter-gatherers allowed less aggressive or oppressive interactions than those possible with Westerners. The nature of the Bantu-speakers' cultures permitted greater hunter-gatherer cultural autonomy and identity than Western culture could. Thus, it is and was the culture—not individuals—that exterminate(d) societies.

It is important to understand why Western and agropastoralist relationships with the hunter-gatherers in southern Africa were so different. As anthropologists who are aware of cultural variability, we should question models that assume that non-Western societies interacted with one another exactly the same way as Western society did or does. Once we can learn what causes different types of interactions and why, we can, as a society, eliminate or control those elements that tend to promote deleterious relationships. We cannot change the past, we can only learn from it. I suggest that it is only by being as historically accurate as possible, that it is plausible to use the past in order to create a better future.

ACKNOWLEDGMENTS

I thank Alan Barnard, Mat Guenther, and Frank Marlowe for constructive suggestions. However, not all readers agreed with the conclusions and they therefore should not be held responsible for them or for any mistakes, misunderstandings, or other problems that may still remain in the chapter. I appreciate the important editorial comments made by Leona Ripley, Rebecca White, and Mary McNeeley on a rough draft. Figure 3.1 was drafted by Mary McNeeley. As always, I am indebted to the people of Kutse who so patiently taught me about their way of life and culture in general.

NOTE

1. Foucault states (1983:215) definitely that the post-structuralism portrayal of power is the consequence of the internal structure of modern states, *not necessarily of all societies*. He wrote (1983:215) "the multiplication of the aims and agents of pastoral power focused the development of knowledge of man around two roles: one, globalizing and quantitative, concerning the population; the other, analytical, concerning the individual." Individual power and collective or state power are steeped in the nature of the modern state, for Foucault continues:

And this implies that power of a pastoral type, which over centuries—for more than a millennium—had been linked to a defined religious institution, suddenly spread out into the whole social body; it found support in a multitude of institutions. And, instead of a pastoral power and a political power, more or less linked to each other, more or less rival, there was an individualizing "tactic" which characterized a series of powers: those of the family, medicine, psychiatry, education, and employers. (1983:215)

seven

Solitude or Servitude?

Ju/'hoansi Images of the Colonial Encounter

Richard B. Lee

What is at stake in the so-called Kalahari Debate? It is the question of who the San peoples are historically: foragers or serfs. The "revisionists" argue that the Nyae Nyae and Dobe area Ju/'hoansi have been bound into regional trade networks and dominated by distant power holders for centuries. They were not even hunters in the past but cattle keepers, or servants of cattle people, raising the possibility that the unique Ju/'hoansi cultural features of sharing and egalitarianism come not from their hunting and gathering traditions, but rather from being outcasts, at the bottom of a social hierarchy.

Letting the subaltern speak is ostensibly the prime directive of the postmodern rhetoric driving the revisionist agenda. Curiously, until recently, neither the revisionists nor their interlocutors had bothered to systematically ask the Ju people themselves for their views of their own history. How do the Ju/'hoansi interpret their past and how does that picture square with the evidence from archaeology and history?

Beginning in 1986–87 when the revisionist debate began to heat up I started to ask Botswana Ju elders focused questions about the time they refer to as *n//a k'aishe* or

Table 7.1

Oral History Informants 1986–97

Name	Decade of Birth	Location/Date
1. /Ti!kai-tsau	1910s	!Goshe 1986
2. /Ti!kai n!a	1900s	!Goshe 1986
3. Kumsa N/i	1920s	!Goshe 1986
4. Kumsa-nwhin	1910s	Dobe 1987
5. /Tontah Boo	1930s	Cho/ana 1995
6. N!ae Kommsa	1930s	Cho/ana 1995
7. Dam	1920s	Cho/ana 1997
8. N!ani	1930s	Cho/ana 1997
9. N!ani N!a	1930s	Tsaman 1997
10. /Gau N!a	1920s	Tsaman 1997

"first time" (Lee 1997). The goal was to elicit collective memories of their precolonial past, a time we could date historically to before 1870. Subsequently I returned for two more periods of interviewing, in 1995 and 1997, with informants from the Nyae Nyae and Cho/ana areas of Namibia. Now there are five major areas of Ju/'hoansi settlement represented in the oral history accounts.

There is a growing critical literature on the uses of oral histories and oral narratives generally. Historical memory can be selective and self-serving and the oral history cannot be read as a direct unmediated chronicle of the past. However by adapting methodology from cognate disciplines, anthropologists can evaluate their materials critically and make them more useful as historical documents. Oral histories by themselves are cultural constructions but they gain strength when compared with other sources of data such as archaeology and historiography and with the histories of neighboring ethnic groups such as the Herero, Tswana, and Goba.

BACKGROUND TO THE REVISIONIST DEBATE

Forty years ago the study of nonliterate, non–state-organized societies was the central subject matter of social and cultural anthropology. Few anthropologists doubted that identifiable and (relatively) autonomous cultural groupings existed "out there" beyond the reach of capitalism, and that anthropology had the analytical tools to make sense of them.

In the 1980s and 90s these assumptions have been thrown into question by a powerful argument about anthropological approaches to the world's nonhierarchical societies. Inspired by the work of Eric Wolf (1982), some political economists challenged the view that prior to this century nonstate societies have been autonomous entities at all. They argued that deep historical links of trade and tribute have bound unit societies to larger polities, creating conditions of dependency. Where earlier ethnographers saw bands, tribes, and chiefdoms, revisionists saw only peasants and proletarians enmeshed in the coils of merchant capital, or dominated by regional markets and states.[1] Throughout these discussions the "myth of the primitive isolate" became a prime target.

No one would deny the globalization of economies and the decentering of cultures in the late twentieth century; what is in dispute is the projection of these conditions onto all societies in all periods of history. In the current conjuncture it is highly unfashionable for anthropologists to argue the case for autonomous "others"; yet members of innumerable societies around the world firmly believed in their own autonomy in the recent past and articulated a sense of their own distinctive collective cultural experiences. It is this *disjuncture* between current anthropological discourse and their subjects' articulated histories that provides the rationale for the present paper.

I will address these issues in the context of the San peoples of southern Africa, drawing upon three bodies of evidence on the Nyae Nyae-Dobe area Ju/'hoansi: oral history, archaeology, and ethnohistory. I collected a substantial body of Ju/'hoansi oral histories in Botswana between 1963 and 1969, and augmented these with oral histories collected in Botswana in 1986–87 and from Namibian Ju/'hoansi in 1995 and 1997. As Jan Vansina famously observed (1985) oral histories can serve as historical documents but these must necessarily be of a less reliable nature in the absence of written or other documents capable of providing corroboration. However, during the 1990s Mathias Guenther and I worked through all the available ethnohistoric accounts of the Ju/'hoansi from the period 1870–1920 (Lee and Guenther 1991, 1993).[2] Although sparse, these accounts do provide an opportunity for testing the degree to which the Ju/'hoansi oral accounts can be read as reliable. The two bodies of evidence, taken together, document insider and outsider views of Ju/'hoansi history and provide a basis for evaluating whether the Ju/'hoansi assertions of autonomy and relative freedom of action correspond to colonial constructions of them.[3] Archaeology provides a third body of evidence against which both insider and outsider accounts can be assessed. Andrew Smith and I excavated a Later Stone Age site at Cho/ana in 1995 and 1997 (Smith and Lee 1997).

Throughout this paper the term *Ju/'hoansi* is used to refer to the people known in the literature as the !Kung San; it is their term of self-appellation and it is the term the people of the Nyae Nyae area would like to be known by. The terms *San* and *Bushman* are retained as the generic terms for southern African hunters and gatherers.

AUTONOMY PROBLEMATIZED

Throughout the recent Kalahari debates there has been a remarkable lack of attention to the question of meaning of terms. Just what is meant by "autonomy," "authenticity," "dependency," "independence," "domination," "integration," "incorporation," is rarely made clear. What constitutes autonomy or dependency of local cultures in an era of global systems? And how does the current conjuncture shape our perceptions of these concepts and our views of the past? The dictionary defines autonomy as "the fact or condition of being autonomous; self government; independence." Autonomous refers to "functioning independently without control by others" (Webster 1976:95).

"Autonomy" has a wide range of usages and nuances at the group and individual levels in the human sciences in a variety of fields including anthropology, politics, economics, feminism, and psychotherapy. I will focus on economic autonomy since much of the current debate in hunter-gatherer studies revolves around this issue.

First of all, economic autonomy must not be equated with isolation. I take it as given that all societies are involved in economic exchanges and political relations with their neighbors. The first general point to be made then is that trade and exchange should not simply be equated with domination and loss of autonomy. Exchange is a fundamental part of human life and appears in all cultural settings (Mauss 1954; Levi-Strauss 1949). Many gatherer-hunter peoples have maintained exchange relations with farming and market societies for hundreds of years (India, Southeast Asia, East Africa) while still maintaining a foraging mode of production.[4]

Autonomy as an economic concept refers to ideas of economic self-sufficiency, and self-sufficiency in turn hinges, not on the *existence* of trade—since all societies trade—but whether that trade is indispensable for the society's reproduction and survival. To demonstrate autonomy one must be able to demonstrate self-reproduction. Dependency therefore may be defined as the inability of a society to reproduce itself without the agency of another society.

At any given moment a society may exhibit greater or lesser "autonomy" in its productive relationships, and it should be possible to make assessments of this degree through empirical investigation.

POLITICAL AUTONOMY

Political autonomy raises interesting problems of its own hinging, not on a society's capacity to reproduce itself—it may do that very well—but on the willingness of other (dominating) societies to *let* it remain autonomous. To put it another way political autonomy is about another society's ability and desire to impose its will, and the core society's ability to *resist* that imposition. On this score Dobe could not be said to be politically autonomous in the 1960s to 1990s. However it is the situation in the *1860s to 1890s* that interests us here.

Another dimension is the question of whether political autonomy is imposed or asserted. In the former case the economic autonomy of a subject group may serve the interests of a dominant group. Therefore the subordinates are encouraged to pursue their habitual round of activities at their own pace while providing goods or services—often at equitable terms—to the dominant group. In the latter case the autonomous group asserts its claims to autonomy through its own strength and political will and these claims are not contested by their neighbors. In practice these two forms may be difficult to distinguish, and the interpretation of which form is present will rely heavily on subjective judgments both by the peoples involved and particularly by the observers.[5] Thus the Ituri Forest Mbuti Pygmies observed by Turnbull (1965) appeared to be entirely subservient to their black neighbors while they were in their villages, but quite autonomous when they were on their own in the forest.

Obviously a great deal more could be said on the question of autonomy, especially when bringing in cultural and political, as well as subjective and objective dimensions. When discussions of the presence or absence are spelled out, it becomes apparent that even the simplest historical statements will involve a whole series of mediating judgments concerning economy, polity, voluntarism, and coercion. Prudence is advised when making such judgments. Automatically classifying San societies in the past as dependent, incorporated, or "peasant-like" seems no more legitimate than to classify these same societies as "primitive isolates."

ORAL HISTORIES

During my fieldwork in the Dobe area starting in the 1960s, the Ju/'hoansi shared their water holes with several hundred pastoralists; they were acutely aware that they were living under the gaze and control of the Tawana chiefdom and, beyond it, the British colonial authority. However in speaking of the area's past, Ju/'hoansi informants spoke of their own autonomy in the nineteenth century as a given: they were foragers who lived entirely on their own without agriculture or domesticated animals. Such statements did not arise from some yearning and nostalgia for a bygone era. Many of the people liked the present-day access to cattle and milk better than the days of strict dependence on foraging. Rather the tone of these statements was matter-of-fact, and Ju/'hoansi autonomy in the nineteenth century was corroborated by Tswana-speaking informants of the present ruling stratum.[6]

The existence of many Later Stone Age archaeological sites in the Dobe area with thousands of stone tools supports this view. But left unexplained is the presence on these same sites of small quantities of pottery and iron, indicating Iron Age presence or contact with Iron Age cultures. The Ju/'hoansi themselves explain the presence of these goods in terms of their long-standing trade relations with riverine peoples. On the other hand, Kalahari revisionists have argued that these archaeological traces are proof positive of domination of the Dobe area by Iron Age peoples and the incorporation of the Ju/'hoansi into a regional polity (Wilmsen 1989; Wilmsen and Denbow 1990). Wilmsen has further argued that people labeled Bushmen had raised cattle in centuries past: "in this century . . . an overwhelming majority of peoples so labelled have pursued a substantially pastoral way of life in symbiosis with, employed by, or enserfed to Bantu-speaking cattle owners . . . this is equally true of earlier centuries" (Wilmsen 1989:1). Despite the methodological problems of defining terms such as "enserfed" or "symbiosis" raised above, the revisionist thesis has been influential in anthropology. And in the case of the Dobe area the evidence for precolonial cattle has been hotly contested. Remarkably, in all the voluminous writings on the "Kalahari Debate" (Barnard 1992b), neither side had systematically investigated how the Ju/'hoansi themselves articulate their own history. It was this lacuna that prompted me to undertake an additional series of interviews with Ju/'hoansi elders in 1986–87 and in 1995–97.

AN INTERVIEW WITH KUMSA NWHIN

This text was recorded in March 1987 from Kumsa nwhin, a 70-year-old Dobe man, former tribal policeman and famous healer.[7] Kumsa was recommended by several thoughtful Ju as a knowledgeable and respected source on oral history. I introduced the interview by asking him if we could discuss the period Ju/'hoansi refer to as *kuriha* ("long ago"), or *n//a k"aishe* ("first time"). I began by asking Kumsa if long ago his ancestors had lived with cattle.

"No," he replied. "My father's father saw them for the first time. My father's father's father did not know them. The first non-San to come to the region were Europeans, not Blacks. We worked for them, got money and obtained our first cattle from the Tswana with that money. The whites first came to !Kubi, killed elephants and pulled their teeth [i.e., ivory]. In the old days the Ju/'hoansi also killed elephants with spears for the meat. At least fifteen men were required for a hunt. They dumped the tusks [they didn't have a use for them]."

"The whites came by *dwa-/twe* [lit. giraffe-horse (camels)]. The whites had no cattle, they had horses and camels.[8] 'Janny'[9] came from the south. Another one made a well at !Kangwa. My father said 'Oh, can water come out of there?' They used metal tools but not engines. This well is not used today. They spoke Burusi [Afrikaans]."[10]

Having learned from him about the prior appearance of Europeans I then asked Kumsa, "Which Tswana came first?"

He misunderstood my question and replied "None. The whites were first."

Reframing I asked, "Before the whites came did you know 'Jusajo'" [black people] here?"

Again his response was unequivocal "No. We only knew ourselves. Ju/'hoansi exclusively."

"But when the blacks did come, who was first?"

"The first black was Mutibele, a Tswana, and his older brother, Mokgomphata. They came from the east following the paths made by the whites going in the opposite direction. They were shown the water holes by Ju/'hoansi including my father /Twi. They were shown the killing sites of the elephants, where the bones lay, the sites where whites killed. And they said 'Oh, the whites have already got the *n!ore* [territory] from us.' Then [Mutibele's] father claimed the land and all the Ju/'hoansi on it, but he deceived us."

"How did he deceive you? When the Tswana claims he is master of you all, do you agree?"

"If he was the master, he didn't give us anything, neither clothes nor pots, or even one calf. The Europeans had given the Ju/'hoansi guns. When the Tswana saw this they decided to give guns to other Ju/'hoansi, including N//au!gusi, the father of /Ti!kai-tsau, so that they could hunt eland and giraffe."[12]

Later in the conversation I explored the nature of San-black interactions in the precolonial period. Some years earlier I had asked /Twi, a Ju elder, "What did you Ju/'hoansi cook with in the old days before you had iron trade pots?" and received this memorable deadpan answer: "Everyone knows that you can't live without iron cooking pots so we must have died!"

I asked the same question of Kumsa, who answered in a more serious vein. "When I was young," Kumsa replied "we had no iron pots. We used the clay pots of the Goba.[13] We couldn't make them ourselves."

"Then how do you account for the fact that there are many potsherds on old Ju/'hoansi sites around here?"

"Our fathers' fathers and their fathers' fathers got them from the Gobas. They would trade for them with skins. The Gobas didn't come up here. They stayed where they were [on the rivers] and we went to them. This went on for a very long time [so that is why there are so many potsherds]."

"We [always] got two things from them: iron and pots.[14] If you go to Danega today you will find the right earth. But the Gobas didn't come here. We always went to them."

Several comments are in order. First, Kumsa's insistence that the Europeans came to the Dobe area *before* blacks was a statement that I had recorded from a number of informants in the 1960s but was one that for a long time I had been unwilling to accept. It seemed counterintuitive that whites could have entered the area before blacks, yet this was the position Kumsa and others insisted upon. Others had also made the point that a long-standing trade existed with riverine peoples *in which the Ju/'hoansi did the traveling.*

Both statements are congruent with a model of autonomy. It would be hard to argue that the blacks could dominate the Dobe area without any physical presence, but I suppose it is not impossible. The trading trips made by the Ju to the east and elsewhere would certainly account for the presence of Iron Age materials on the Dobe area sites. In fact Polly Wiessner has argued that the levels of iron and pottery found on Dobe area Late Stone Age (LSA) sites can be accounted for by *hxaro,* a traditional form of delayed exchange still practiced by the Ju/'hoansi, which historically has been a vehicle for long-distance trade (1990a; 1993).

What is left unanswered is whether the trade goods obtained through *hxaro* (or by other means) were essential for Ju/'hoansi reproduction. One suggestive point was Kumsa's intriguing statement that the precolonial Ju hunted elephant but discarded the tusks, because it indicates that the Dobe Ju/'hoansi were hunting elephant for subsistence and were not part of a mercantile *or* a tributary network, since in either case elephant ivory would have been a prime valuable.

Also interesting is Kumsa's rather dismissive view of the Tswana as overlords. For Kumsa the criterion for being a chief [lit. wealth-person] is giving away, in this context, not exercising power per se. The Europeans were chiefs because they gave guns, the Tswana were 'deceivers' because in Kumsa's terms they claimed chiefly status but gave nothing[15] (see below for contemporaneous European views of the encounter).

A !Goshe Commentary on the Early Days of Contact

Kumsa's remarks, about the absence of outsiders before the Europeans and about the arrival of the Europeans prior to the Tswana are corroborated and amplified in another account recorded in July 1986 at the opposite end of the !Kangwa Valley settlements in the village of !Goshe, 36 km east of Dobe.

/Ti!kai-n!a, then age 80, and /Ti!kai-tsau ("tooth"), age 63, were two of the leading men of !Goshe, the easternmost and most economically "progressive" of the Dobe area villages.[16] !Goshe is the jumping-off point for travel to the east, and the village has boarded Tswana cattle in *mafisa* (a loan-cattle arrangement) since the 1910s. It is the village with the most kinship links to Ju/'hoansi in the east and north, areas of historic black settlement. Therefore !Goshe people, by reason of both history and geography, are the most attuned to links to "Iron Age" peoples.

Though younger than /Ti!kai-n!a, /Ti!kai-tsau is more knowledgeable since he is the son of N//au!gusi, mentioned above, a leading figure from the early years of the century in obtaining *mafisa* cattle and guns. The younger man was also a leading spokesperson for the rights of Dobe area Ju/'hoansi in the 1980s. When I had announced my intention of interviewing on Ju history, many Ju recommended /Ti!kai-tsau as a knowledgeable source. The two /Ti!kais were joined by Kumsa, age 60, a relative from N/ausha, 70 km northwest of !Goshe. I introduced the topic by asking them if we could talk about the *n//a k'aishe* ("first time").

"Certain Europeans in Gaborone," I began, "argue that long ago you Ju/'hoansi [that is] your fathers' fathers' fathers' fathers had cattle. Do you agree?"

"No! Not a bit!" was the younger /Ti!kai's emphatic answer. "Long ago our fathers' fathers' fathers' fathers, the only meat *they* had was what they could shoot with arrows. We only got cows from the Tswana."

I persisted. "But when you dig holes deep down beneath where you live you find pieces of pottery. Where did they come from?"

"Oh, those pots were our own work!" replied /Ti!kai. "Our ancestors made them. They would put them on the fire and cook with them. But since we got iron pots from you Europeans we lost the knowledge of pottery making."

Shifting topic, I asked, "What about iron?"

"We got that from the Mbukushu," said /Ti!kai. "But we learned how to work it ourselves. You see !Xoma's father Karambuka,[17] he knows how to work it. You stick it in the fire, heat it up, and hammer it. . . . We did it ourselves. We saw how the Gobas did it and we learned from them."

"Where did you get the iron itself from?"

Their answer surprised me. "The Europeans," said /Ti!kai. "The Tswana and Gobas didn't have it. They also got it from the Europeans."

I had to disagree. "But," I said, "in the oldest abandoned villages of the Gobas, iron is there. Long before the Europeans came."

At this point the older /Ti!kai intervened. "Yes! /Tontah is right. Long ago the Mbukushu had the pieces of iron that they worked."

The younger /Ti!kai turned to the older and asked, incredulously, "Well, where did they get the iron from?"

Matter of factly, the older man replied, "From the earth."

Much discussion followed on this point. The younger men were unconvinced that the Gobas had iron before the Europeans, but old /Ti!kai stuck to his story.

Shifting topic again I asked, "Long long ago, did your fathers' fathers' fathers' fathers practice //hara [farming]?"

There was no disagreement on this point. "No, we didn't. We just ate the food that we collected from the bush."

The older /Ti!kai added, "When I was a boy we had learned about //hara from the Tswanas. They showed us how [to do it]."

The !Goshe interviews corroborate the account of Kumsa above on the absence of cattle and agriculture before the twentieth-century arrival of the Tswana. They add detail on Ju/'hoansi understandings of the history of pottery and iron use. In the first case they spoke of Ju manufacture of pottery whereas other informants spoke of it as only imported. In the second case there was an intriguing difference of opinion. While there was agreement that iron was imported from the Gobas but only in the recent past, some believed that iron was so recent that the Gobas only obtained iron after the arrival of the Europeans, a view that we were to encounter elsewhere.

N!ae and /Kunta at Cho/ana

Directly west across the border from Dobe is the Nyae Nyae area of Namibia, the site of the Marshall family's renowned studies (L. Marshall 1976, 1999; J. Marshall 1957, 1980). Another round of oral history interviews took place in 1995 at Cho/ana, a former Ju/'hoansi water hole now located in Namibia's Kaudom Game Reserve. Though remote today—the most remote of Namibia's national parks—Cho/ana has long been known to historians as a meeting point for Ju/'hoansi from several regions of occupation. Lying midway between the !Kaudom Valley to the north and the Nyae Nyae to the south, as well as between the Okavango swamps to the east and the southwest African highlands to the west, it was a convenient entrepôt for Ju/'hoansi parties engaged in *hxaro* trade to meet.

Despite Cho/ana's role as a node in the network of *hxaro* trade (Lee 1979), no one had excavated there or had been to the site in the company of knowledgeable Ju/'hoansi elders. /Kunta Bo and N!ae Kommsa were the Ju elders from the Nyae Nyae area water hole, /Aotcha, who accompanied us to Cho/ana in May 1995. The name Cho/ana, according to /Kunta, means medicine (*ch'o*) from the *Acacia giraffae* or camelthorn tree (/*ana*).

In tracing the earliest history of the place, /Kunta saw the original owners as Ju/'hoansi, not blacks or any other ethnic group. In the beginning, asserted /Kunta, only Ju/'hoansi lived here; there were no Gobas. Ju people would come from Nyae Nyae and from the north, to do *hxaro* here. It was a water hole that always held water. People from the South (Nyae Nyae) would bring /*do* (ostrich eggshell beads, OESB). People from the North brought /*an* (glass beads). In /Kunta's words "Hxaro brought them together."

A point of emphasis in our interviews was the question of whether the Gobas made trips to the interior to trade or to make their presence felt. /Kunta was emphatic: "No, [they didn't come to us] we went to them. We saw pots on their fires and wanted them, so they gave us some."

"And what did you give them in return?"

"We gave Gobas /*do* [OESB] in exchange for pots."

The interior Ju/'hoansi's proximity to Iron Age peoples on their periphery and the use of iron as a marker of Iron Age overlordship has been a particular point of emphasis for the revisionists. I was anxious to hear /Kunta and N!ae's views of the precolonial use of iron and its source.

"Did your ancestors have *!ga* (iron)?"

"Are you joking? We didn't know *!ga*. If we needed arrows we used *#dwa* ("giraffe") or *n!n* ("eland") bones."

"Who gave Ju/'hoansi the iron?"

"We visited north and east and saw this wonderful stuff for arrows and knives; we asked Gobas for it and got some. It was very valuable; when others saw it their hearts were sad because they didn't have it; they wanted it so badly they would even fight other Ju for it. Parties went north to seek it; Gobas gave it to them in exchange for steenbok/duiker skins and other things."

"Which came first, pottery or iron?"

"Pottery came first, iron later, because when iron came Europeans were near."

"Where did Goba get iron from?"

Without hesitation /Kunta replied, "From the European."

"Are you saying that before Europeans came Gobas had no iron?"

"Yes, they had no iron."

It is interesting that informants see iron coming ultimately from Europeans; they saw the appearance of iron in their areas as so close in time to the appearance of Europeans that iron was associated with Europeans. While it is true that the amount of iron on Dobe-Nyae Nyae LSA sites is miniscule, it is striking that the long history of Iron Age occupation on their periphery, for example at the Tsodilo Hills with radiocarbon dates as early as 500 A.D., doesn't have much resonance with the Ju/'hoansi informants.[18] When they did obtain iron from the Gobas, it was clearly an item of trade and not a marker of overlordship. In any event the very recency of the trade in iron (post-European) challenges the revisionist view of a deep antiquity of Ju/'hoansi subservience.

This ironless interpretation of their history provided one of the most intriguing examples of selective memory and historical myopia by the Ju/'hoansi informants: Although iron was rare precolonially, stone artifacts are plentiful on all LSA sites in the region, yet most Ju stated confidently that their ancestors did not make stone tools! This implied a rather glaring gap in their sense of their ancestors' technical apparatus. And this led to some interesting exchanges with the Cho/ana informants.

N!ani and Dam at Cho/ana

In June-July 1997 Andrew Smith and I returned to Cho/ana for further research. N!ae and /Kunta had been frequent visitors to Cho/ana but not residents there.

Table 7.2

Did Your Ancestors Know Cattle Precolonially?

Name (Year of Interview)	Response
1. /Ti!kai-tsau (1986)	Definitely not
2. /Ti!kai n!a (1986)	Definitely not
3. Kumsa N/i (1986)	Definitely not
4. Kumsa-nwhin (1987)	No, just game animals
5. /Kunta Bo (1995)	No, we lived without stock
6. N!ae Kumsa (1995)	No, we lived without stock
7. Dam (1997)	No cattle, we just had the meat of the wild ones
8. N!ani (1997)	No cattle, we just had the meat of the wild ones
9. N!ani N!a (1997)	No cattle at all
10. /Gau N!a (1997)	No cattle at all

This time we approached elders who were former residents. N!ani and Dam were knowledgeable men in their late sixties, born and raised at Cho/ana and who only left the area when it was gazetted a Game Reserve in 1975. Today they live in the village of //A//oba, 30 km south of the park boundary.

Much of their testimony corroborated that of earlier informants on the absence of blacks or cattle in the interior before the twentieth century (see Table 7.2). In fact in the Cho/ana area they dated the arrival of blacks as a phenomenon of the post–World War II period, a date corroborated by historical records. But in speaking of their ancestors' material culture, N!ani volunteered this interesting perspective:

N!ani said, "We recent people know how to make things, but those old, old people didn't know how to make things. They could make [tools] with bone only. We have iron nowadays."

I asked, "But didn't they make things with stone tools?"

N!ani was emphatic. "No, they didn't make things with stone. Stones for cracking nuts was the only thing they knew."

We had been working on the archaeological site for several days, yielding several thousand LSA worked stone fragments, so I asked N!ani, "but how do you account for all the worked stone on the site currently being dug up?"

"That is only strike-a-light," he replied, referring to the flint chips widely used to make fire in the Kalahari before matches became readily available. The problem was that a single flint chip in a flint-and-steel fire-making kit could last for months and stone tools on the site represented points, scrapers, knives, and the whole range of the LSA tool kit.

I was intrigued by this turn in the conversations so I took up another tack: "You say they worked bone. What did they work bone with?"

N!ani pondered this and replied, "They worked it with iron, iron implements obtained from the Goba."

"And did the Goba have iron long ago?"

N!ani was emphatic on this. "We already told you that the early Goba had no iron. They just got it from Moruti [missionaries] and Porto [Portuguese]."

"But if earlier Gobas had no iron and earlier Ju/'hoansi had no iron, then how could the Ju/'hoansi of old days have lived?"

N!ani saw the logical inconsistency and was candid in his reply. "We were wondering that ourselves. How could they have gotten skins to clothe themselves? But we now know that the Gobas must have had iron even before the Portuguese arrived. After all they had axes and hoes of iron."

Seeing closure, I pushed the point. "So then if the Gobas *did* have iron before the Portos came, then where did they get the iron from?"

But N!ani was not to be deterred. "We know that the early Gobas had no iron, so somehow, they must have gotten the iron from the Portos even before the Portos themselves came!"

The Portuguese iron-origin theory proved to be remarkably persistent. Another 1997 informant, when repeatedly pushed to account for the Gobas' pre-European use of iron, could only say that it came from wrecked vehicles of the Portuguese. In fact only one of the ten elders interviewed (/Ti!kay N!a of !Goshe) was ready to acknowledge that Gobas indeed had iron long before the arrival of the Europeans.

Discussion

In all interviews there was repeated insistence that no Gobas or any other black occupied their area or even visited prior to the late nineteenth century; several spoke of the Gobas' preference for staying on the river and avoiding the dry interior. We know that the Tswana did set up cattle posts in the interior by the turn of the twentieth century (Müller 1912) and a few Herero sojourned there in 1897–98 and in 1904–05 (Passarge 1904; Drechsler 1985). However the first Goba occupation of the interior was not until the 1930s or 1940s and then at the behest of the South African colonial government. The late occupation dates for Cho/ana and other northern points are confirmed both by historical documents and by oral histories collected from a "Goba" oral history informant in Rundu in July 1997 (Alfons Siyehe, personal communication 1997).

All these accounts illuminate the pragmatic and matter-of-fact approach of Dobe and Nyae Nyae area people to questions of history. These, after all, are questions of the most general nature and the accounts agree closely, not only about the autonomy of the area from outside domination but also about the absence of cattle (see Table 7.2) and agriculture in precolonial times (though not of pottery and iron). There are interesting divergences of opinion on whether pottery was imported or locally made, and on whether the Gobas had iron before the Europeans. Taken together these accounts along with others (e.g., Lee 1979:76–78; Marshall 1976:52–58) constitute a fair representation of mid- and late-twentieth-century Ju/'hoansi views of their forbears' nineteenth-century history of autonomy.

One other indication of the Ju sense of their history is the by-and-large positive self-evaluation of the Ju/'hoansi about the past. They saw themselves as actors, not victims, and this contrasts with the negative self-imagery expressed in Hai//om or Nharo views of their present and past (Widlock 1999; Guenther 1986c:13–15; 232–33). The contrast is heightened by the observation of Dorothea Bleek (1928b), corroborated by others, that the Nharo themselves viewed the Ju/'hoansi, their immediate neighbors to the north, with a great deal of respect.

ARCHAEOLOGICAL TIE-INS

Both in 1995 and 1997 the oral history interviews accompanied archaeological excavation, designed to link archaeology with the knowledge that was part of the living tradition of the Ju/'hoansi. Andrew Smith started excavating a rich Later Stone Age archaeological site at Cho/ana, which provided a continual stimulus for oral history as new and interesting materials came to light in the excavations. The Ju informants' comments provided a valuable adjunct to the archaeological work (and vice versa). They identified plant remains, made tentative suggestions regarding fragmentary bone materials, and provided a social context in which the material could be interpreted. For example, the elders described a kind of white glass bead as one of the earliest of the European trade goods obtained through intermediaries to the north. A few days after the interview precisely such a bead was found in a sealed level in association with an LSA industry.

But the most stunning confirmation of the direct late-nineteenth-century encounter between people with advanced stone-working skills and colonialists was a piece of bottle glass (mouth and neck) showing signs of delicate microretouching that the South African LSA is famous for. This gave a further indication of the persistence of LSA stone-working techniques into the colonial contact period.

The oral history's insistence on the absence of cattle and blacks in the interior was confirmed by the complete lack in the archaeological record of the presence of domesticated animals or of non-Ju/'hoansi people in the area prior to the latter part of the nineteenth century. The results obtained demonstrated the efficacy of this kind of collaborative research. The archaeological evidence is set out in more detail in Smith and Lee 1997.

COLONIAL CONSTRUCTIONS OF THE JU/'HOANSI

Turning to the third body of evidence, what light do ethnohistoric documents shed on these Ju accounts of their own past? Do they support or contradict Ju accounts of relative autonomy? Despite the assertions of the "revisionists," the colonial frontier reached the Nyae Nyae-Dobe area no earlier than the 1870s (Barry Morton, personal communication, November 1994), as European ivory hunters and trekkers began to hunt and pass through the area. Firsthand accounts of the Ju/'hoansi interior however are few and far between. For a group supposedly enmeshed in the coils of merchant capital, the Dobe and Nyae Nyae Ju/'hoansi are remarkably unchronicled by nineteenth-century observers. In fact it is this very scarcity of colonial era accounts that has allowed the Nyae Nyae-Dobe area to be treated as a relative *tabula rasa,* allowing latitude for all sorts of implausible scenarios to be projected upon it.

I will briefly touch on three accounts: Schinz's, who passed through the area in 1886, Passarge's reconnaissance in 1897, and Müller's in 1911. These form a representative cross-section of the available accounts. Guenther and I have analyzed a fuller range of the travel literature in detail elsewhere (Lee and Guenther 1993).[19]

Hans Schinz

Soon after the territory of South-West Africa was awarded to Germany at the Conference of Berlin, the botanist Hans Schinz went through the Nyae Nyae area in 1886 to explore the economic potential of the colony's more remote regions. Yet Schinz's testimony offers little or no support for the revisionist view of Nyae Nyae-Dobe area centrality in the trade. Schinz's account (1891b) offers no ethnographic information about the Nyae Nyae-Dobe area proper. In fact there is little information of any kind on the Nyae Nyae-Dobe area. However Schinz did make some observations on the San people he met in the Omaramba Omatako, a dry rivercourse about 200 km west of the Nyae Nyae. It is worth noting that these San were living astride what was considered a "major" trade route, although "major" in this context might mean one ox wagon every three months![20] Schinz wrote

> The area seemed to be very thinly settled. Nevertheless from time to time we did meet scattered Bushmen hordes. . . . The people who visited us at this occasion called themselves the !Kun San, and were evidently from another tribe than those we had met further up the Omaramba. . . . The entire dress of these poor root diggers consists of nothing more than two small furs to cover their private parts and buttocks, and instead of ostrich eggshell beads their arms and legs are adorned with grass ornaments.
>
> The weapons consisted of a hefty throwing stick, [and] a medium-sized bow with arrows made of thin phragmites reed, the poisoned tips of which were made not of iron,

but of carefully worked bone splinters, which in this part of South West Africa was frequently made of eland antelope. (Schinz 1891:357)[21]

The picture conveyed here, fragmentary as it is, can be interpreted in several ways:
the "!Kun San" could be seen as representatives of hunter-gatherers, not particularly
involved in trade (witness the absence of metal arrows) and wary of strangers, or
they could be viewed as impoverished hunters and "root-diggers," reduced to pen-
ury by the demands of mercantile trade or its passing.[22] Whatever the interpretation,
the people described were not Ju/'hoansi from the study area (see also Szalay 1979).

Siegfried Passarge

Passarge, a German geographer, made a transect of the interior in 1897. His detailed account of day-to-day travels (1904), as distinguished from his better-known
ethnography of the Bushmen (1907, 1997), offers few ethnographic details per se,
but does establish that the interior was entirely occupied by Ju/'hoansi, with the
exception of a few small and temporary cattle camps of Herero who had arrived
only the year before to escape the rinderpest epidemic, a disease that decimated
cattle herds throughout southern Africa in the period 1896–99.

In his 1907 monograph (translation 1997), Passarge concentrates largely on the San
of the Ghanzi area some 250 km south of Dobe, with a few passing references to the
more remote Ju/'hoansi of Nyae Nyae. The importance the revisionists have attached to Passarge's "valuable insights" is curious because, far from portraying the
San in the "land filled with flies" as pastoralists and tribute-paying subjects, Passarge
insisted that the "Buschmännreich" of mid-nineteenth-century Ghanzi was an independent polity based entirely on hunting. He wrote, "They were a hunting people par
excellence. All social and political relations, all rights and laws, their entire political organization was based on the hunt" (1907:119). "The honour of the chief was hereditary
in those days and the Bushmen were totally independent. The Batuana did not dare
set foot into their region and the Hottentots only entered it on raids" (1907:115).[23]

It should be added that by the time Passarge went through the Ghanzi area the
"Buschmännreich" had been destroyed and the Bushmen reduced to vassals of
Tswana and European hunter-traders. There is nothing in Passarge however that
indicates that the Ju/'hoansi of the Nyae Nyae-Dobe area had lost their independent
status.

Hauptman Müller

This view is strongly reinforced by our third colonial account. The German officer
Hauptman Müller traveled through the Nyae Nyae area in 1911, and offers some

unusually detailed observations on the situation of the Nyae Nyae-Dobe area
Ju/'hoansi 14 years after Passarge and some 30 years after colonial trade had been
established. In Müller's account (1912) the area remained remote and inaccessible.
As an indication of how remote the area was, his visit was the first in five years
from the German colony to the west.

Most telling is Müller's ethnographic description of the Bushman inhabitants of
this stretch of land he calls "virginal" [*jungfräulich*] (1912:536–41). He depicts their
state as *noch uberuhrt von aller Zivilisation, in alter Ursprunglichkeit* ["still untouched
by all civilization in their old pristine state"], in contrast to the Bushmen further to
the west, near the location of Schinz's people. He reports with amusement how
European objects such as matches and mirrors were unknown to them, as well as
the camels of his troopers, which startled them and caused the women to grab
their children and scatter into the bush (1912:533). However he did find them using
such things as wooden bowls, glass and iron beads, copper rings, and "Ovambo
knives," all obtained through trade with black neighbors.

Of particular interest are Müller's descriptions of the Bushmen themselves. In
his account they were well-nourished and relatively tall, thanks to an ample diet of
meat (hunted with bone-tipped arrows) and a wide variety of wild plants. There is
no mention in Müller's account of any resident cattle or Bantu-speaking overlords,
though Batswana were visiting the area during his stay. For Müller the association
of the Nyae Nyae Bushmen with the Batswana was not primordial; it was of
recent date and was based on trade and assistance rendered at the latter's hunting
expeditions. The Bushmen were rewarded with gifts for their services and the relationship with the hunter/herders is described as equitable and friendly:

"The Bushmen seem, however, to be good friends with the Batswanas. When I
asked a Bushman if it didn't bother him that the Batswanas were killing off so much
game every year he said 'Yes, but we are getting presents!'" (Müller 1912:535).[24]

Müller's is one of the earliest accounts to be based on actual reports of what he
observed, as distinguished from second-hand accounts at a distance. And the above
short quote is among the very first to cite the actual words of a Ju/'hoansi person.

To sum up this section, both German and Ju/'hoansi testimony are consistent and
mutually supportive. The detail presented by Müller and the others attests to five
propositions that accord closely with statements made by the Ju/'hoansi themselves:

1. the relative isolation of the Nyae Nyae-Dobe area from the German colony to the
   west and the low volume of European traffic, 1880–1911,
2. the absence of cattle in precolonial Ju/'hoansi subsistence (Table 7.2),
3. the absence of Bantu overlords or tributary relations,
4. the relatively favorable terms of trade between blacks and San,
5. the relatively good foraging subsistence base and nutritional status of the San.

These lines of evidence argue the case that the views of the Ju/'hoansi about their historical autonomy are not sharply at odds with the ethnohistoric sources.

HUNTER-GATHERER DISCOURSE AND AGRARIAN DISCOURSE

Both the Ju/'hoansi oral histories and the German historical texts are cultural constructions, and yet, how are we to account for the correspondences between these two bodies of evidence? Why do they corroborate one another? To argue that both are careful fabrications still leaves open the question of why they agree so closely. One would have to invoke conspiracy or coincidence: in either case a tough sell. Surely it would be more reasonable to assume that they agree because they are describing the same reality. If Kumsa's, the two /Ti!kais, N!ae and /Kunta's, and N!ani and Dam's collective accounts of the Ju/'hoansi autonomous past gibe so closely with those of eyewitnesses such as Schinz, Passarge, and Müller, then on what grounds rests the view of the historic Ju/'hoansi as enserfed pastoralists? And why has this view gained such currency in anthropological circles?

A more fruitful approach to understanding the recent debates is to attempt to place them in the context of the intellectual currents of the late twentieth century. How does the current conjuncture shape our perceptions of the situation of indigenous "others?"

Obviously by the 1990s, the processes the Dobe Ju/'hoansi had undergone have brought them now to becoming clients, laborers and rural proletarians, subject to and dependent upon local, national, and world economies. Their current predicament is well understood by recourse to theories arising from political economy, dependency theory, or colonial discourse. Current theorizing is much weaker however, in understanding the antecedent conditions. Part of the inability of contemporary theory to encompass hunters and gatherers as historical subjects is the lack of attention to the differences between discourses about hunters and gatherers versus the discourses concerning agrarian societies and the emerging world system.

In agrarian discourse the presence of structures of domination is taken as given; it is the *forms* of domination and the modes of exploitation and surplus extraction that are problematic (Amin 1972; Cliffe 1982; Hindess and Hirst 1975; Shanin 1987; etc.). In the literature on the agrarian societies of the Third World, stratification, class and class struggle, patriarchy, accumulation, and immiseration constitute the basic descriptive and analytical vocabulary.

In hunter-gatherer discourse it is not the forms and modes of domination that are at issue, rather the prior question to be asked is whether domination is *present*. I have been struck by the eagerness of otherwise competent analysts to gloss over, sidestep, or ignore this question.

There is no great mystery about what separates hunter-gatherer from agrarian societies. The former usually live lightly on the land at low densities; they can move and still survive, an escape route not available to sedentary farmers. The latter with high densities and fixed assets can no longer reproduce themselves outside the system, and are rendered far more vulnerable to domination (Lee 1979:ch. 15).

In the recent debate some analysts seem to have taken the world systems/political economy position so literally that every culture is seen as nothing more than the sum total of its external relations. But surely there is more to a culture than its links of trade, tribute, domination, and subordination. There is the internal dynamic of the means by which a social group reproduces itself ecologically, socially, and in terms of its collective consciousness (a point taken up by Sahlins in several recent writings; e.g., 1994).

Not all groups have had the same tumultuous history of war, displacement, and destruction as, for example, the nineteenth-century Bushman "raiders" of the Drakensburg chronicled by John Wright (1971). In each case the externalities have to be carefully specified and not glossed over. But we have to strike a balance between the world systems type of analysis and consideration of the crucial ways in which cultures reproduce themselves. For the latter, the ethnographic method is uniquely qualified to explore. If Khoisan studies are to benefit from the current debate then it is important for ethnography and political economy to talk to each other and to try to find a common language for airing (and hopefully resolving) differences. (Sue Kent has drawn together recent work emphasizing the diversity of African hunter-gatherers; 1996 and chapters in this volume.)

An historically informed ethnography can offer an alternative to the totalizing discourses of world systems theory. The unselfconscious sense of their own nineteenth- and early-twentieth-century autonomy expressed by Ju/'hoansi hunter-gatherers and its corroboration by contemporaneous colonial observers is one example of how these powerful assumptions can be challenged. They bear testimony that in the not very distant past other ways of being were possible.

That said, autonomy should not be taken as an article of faith, nor is it an all-or-nothing proposition. It is, or should be an empirical question, and each society may exhibit a complex array of more or less autonomy at stages in its history. Even in agrarian societies spaces are opened up, however small, for the expression of autonomous thought and behavior. Thus it need not be the exclusive preserve of nonhierarchical or noncolonized societies (cf. Beinart 1987).

With reference to the latter though, a final point: what is desperately needed is to theorize the communal mode of production and its accompanying worldview. Without it there is a theoretical vacuum filled far too facilely by imputing capitalist relations of production, bourgeois subjectivity, or "culture of poverty" frameworks to hunter-gatherer peoples.

ACKNOWLEDGMENTS

A much earlier version of this paper was presented at the July 1994 Conference on Khoisan Studies at Tutzing, Germany organized by Rainer Vossen. Still earlier versions were presented at the symposium "Narratives of Resistance" at the 1991 CASCA Meetings at the University of Western Ontario, coorganized with Tom Patterson and Harriet Rosenberg; at the May 1994 CASCA Meetings in Vancouver, in a session organized by Blanca Muratorio and Julie Cruikshank, at a University of Cape Town May 1995 seminar organized by Andrew Smith and at the 1999 CASCA Meetings in Quebec City in a session organized by Andrew Martindale. In addition to thanking the above, I wish to thank Megan Biesele, Matthias Guenther, and Jackie Solway for allowing me to present ideas originally appearing in coauthored papers; thanks as well to Henry Bredekamp, Alison Brooks, Jan-Bart Gewald, Robert Hitchcock, Susan Kent, Barry Morton, Michael Lambek, Robert Ross, Gerald Sider, Gavin Smith, Polly Wiessner, and John Wright. Responsibility for errors and interpretations remains my own.

NOTES

1. The study of nonclass societies becomes a kind of victimology, a recitation of the travails of these people and injuries of class and capitalism.

2. These sources supplement several years of ethnographic research extending over the period 1963–69, with additional fieldwork in 1973, 1980, 1983, 1986, 1987, 1993, 1995, 1996, 1997, and 1999 (Lee 1979; Lee and Biesele 1994).

3. Or conversely whether the articulated history serves to conceal an on-the-ground history of domination and dependency at the hands of non-San: Africans or Europeans.

4. Even with "hunters in a world of hunters" exchange relations were part of ongoing social life, a central point of theory in social anthropology, and richly documented ethnographically, for example, by Donald Thomson (1949) and archaeologically by a number of studies (e.g., Earle and Ericson 1977).

5. The subjectivity involved in determining whether a given autonomy is asserted or imposed has been a major problem in articulation theory, regarding the question of whether a given "tribal" communal social formation was preserved because its maintenance was "functional" for capitalism, or whether it was preserved because the people wanted it that way (Foster-Carter 1978).

6. All interviews were conducted directly in Ju/'hoansi without the aid of interpreters, to lessen the biases that may be introduced when testimony is filtered through the cultural lens of non-Ju/'hoansi interpreters. Some of these latter—Herero and Tswana—hold definite views on precolonial history, particularly on land issues, that may be sharply at odds with those of the Ju/'hoansi themselves.

7. Parenthetically, Kumsa happens to be the absent father of N!ai of John Marshall's 1980 film "N!ai: The Story of a Kung Woman" and another of my elder informants (see infra).

8. This is curious since the main form of European travel in the interior in the nineteenth century was by ox-wagon. Kumsa may be conflating this early European presence with later trips involving camels by German police patrols (see Müller 1912).

9. Probably Jan Van Zyl, who accompanied his father Hendrik Van Zyl, on a major elephant hunting expedition into the Gaamveld in August 1877 (Tabler 1973:113–115).

10. That they spoke Afrikaans, not English is significant. It corroborates all the historical sources and contradicts Wilmsen who has claimed that the Englishman Robert Lewis was the first white in the Dobe area (Wilmsen 1989:120; Wilmsen and Denbow 1990:519; Lee and Guenther 1993:201–202).

11. A generic Ju term for all non-San and non-Khoe Africans.

12. By the twentieth century trade rivalries pitting European traders against one another and sometimes Europeans against Africans had reached the Dobe area. It was a common practice to outfit African hunters with rifles and ammunition to produce furs and ivory for the merchant-traders. N//au!gusi, the recipient of a gun, figures in the next account as the father of the principal informant, /Ti!kai-tsau.

13. The term 'Goba' here refers to the riverine agriculturalists such as the Bayei who live 100–200 km east of the Dobe area on the western edge of the Okavango Delta.

14. Other informants also mentioned tobacco as a third item of trade in the last century.

15. The guns the Tswana did supply were loaned not given, and the meat produced was theirs not the Ju's.

16. They have been largely settled (voluntarily) in a line village of mud huts on the !Goshe sand ridge overlooking the !Kangwa Valley since at least 1960. Most of the other Dobe villages didn't build semipermanent mud huts until the 1970s.

17. Referring to a very skilful Ju craftsperson, expert in several media especially ironworking and wood carving.

18. The paucity of iron on archaeological sites and the accounts of bone arrows in use in the 1880s up to the 1900s suggest that, to the Ju, the appearance of Europeans and plentiful supplies of iron might have been perceived as coeval. However, small quantities of iron on Dobe and Cho/ana area archaeological sites antedate European colonial presence by up to a millennium.

19. There we discuss the travel accounts of Andersson, Lewis, Eriksson, the Dorsland Trekkers, Franz Müller, Galton, Baines, Chapman, Hahn, Rath, McKiernan, and Van Zyl, as well as Schinz and Passarge. Nothing in the accounts of these key figures contradicts the position articulated by the Ju/'hoansi themselves: that their nineteenth-century ancestors lived on their own in the Nyae Nyae-Dobe area as foragers without cattle.

20. See Lee and Guenther (1993:190–195) for details on trade routes from 1850 to 1880.

21. "Das Gebiet schien sehr dünn bevölkert zu sein, dennoch kamen wir von Zeit zu Zeit mit vereinzelten Buschmannhorden zusammen. . . . Die uns hier besuchenden Leute nannten sich !Kun San und waren offenbar von einem anderen Stamme als jene die wir weiter oben gefunden hatten. . . . Die ganze Bekleidung dieser armen Wurzelgräber besteht aus nur zwei kleinen Fellen zur Bedeckung der Scham und des Gessäses, anstatt des Perlenschmuckes tragen sie Arm- und Beinringe aus Grasgeflecht. Die Bewaffnung bestand aus einem kräftigen Wurfstock, einem mittelgrossen Bogen mit Pfeilen aus Phragmites-

halmen, deren vergiftete Spitzen aber nicht aus Eisen, sondern aus sorgfältig bearbeiten Knochensplittern der in diesem Teile Südwestafrikas häufigen Elanantilopen verfertigt waren." (All English translations by Mathias Guenther.)

Schinz's collection for the Zurich Museum has been curated (Szalay 1979), with good-quality photos of the bone arrowheads mentioned in the text. Much of the collection of bone points looked stylistical identical to bone arrowhead collections made in the Dobe area by Lee and others in the 1960s.

22. Or with a modicum of ingenuity one *could* argue that these !Kung were in fact something else again, astute traders, only *appearing* to be poor and concealing their metal weapons and ostrich eggshell ornaments until the basis for profitable trade could be established.

23. "Sie waren ein Jägervolk par excellence. Auf der Jagd bauten sich alle sozialen und wirtschaftlichen Verhältnisse auf, all Gesetze und Rechte, die ganze politische Organisation" (1907:119).

"Die Würde eines Oberhäuptlings war damals erblich und die Buschmänner völlig unabhängig. Die Batuana wagten sich nicht in ihr Gebiet hinein, die Hottentotten nur auf Raubzügen" (1907:115).

24. "Die Buschleute scheinen aber gut Freund mit den Betschuanen zu sein. Als ich einen Buschmann fragte ob es ihm denn nicht unangenehm sei dass die Betschuanen jährlich so viel Wild abschiessen sagte er: 'Ja, wir bekommen aber Präsent!'"

eight

Cultural Contact in Africa, Past and Present

Multidisciplinary Perspectives on the Status of African Foragers

Alison Brooks

Did independent societies of hunter-gatherers exist in twentieth-century Africa? The papers in the 1998 American Anthropological Association symposium and in this volume speak to many different dimensions of this question, and provide a rich array of situations and perspectives from which to address it. In addition, however, the papers begin to provide answers to what may be a more interesting and relevant question in the twenty-first century. When two cultures meet, and one has a more developed technology, what factors affect whether the technologically advanced culture dominates and subsumes the other, or whether the other continues to assert or even intensify its identity and independence? This query is relevant not only to the more limited issues raised in the revisionist debates over Kalahari history, but also in the clash of ancient and modern cultures that characterizes the world today. This commentary will review the issues raised in the other papers, and suggest additional data, especially from biological, linguistic, and archaeological sources, that bear on these questions.

The nature of ethnicity and of ethnic identity is an underlying theme of this volume. Kent (Chapter 1), like Gellner (1983) and Anderson (1983), argues that the concept of ethnicity, unlike that of tribe, or "people" is tied to the emergence of modern nation-states. Smith (1986), however, like many anthropologists and sociologists, argues that ethnicity is both an ancient concept and an ancient feature of human society—the word *ethnos* is used, for example, by Herodotus to refer to the Medes. Smith defines six essential characteristics of an ethnic group which go beyond a kinship-based community: collective name, common myth of descent, a shared history, distinctive shared culture which may or may not involve a shared language or religion, association with a "homeland" whether or not they presently occupy it, and a sense of solidarity that overrides divisions of class, kin, gender, region, or community. To Smith, a shared and separate economic organization such as the one implicated in the Kalahari debate over the continued existence of San hunter-gatherers is not part of the essence of an ethnic group, nor is an independent political structure. One might use Smith's definition, however, to examine what is involved in the maintenance or dissolution of ethnic identity among the African people classed as "foragers," and/or in their incorporation into a modern nation.

Five of the papers in this volume—Sugawara (Chapter 4), Guenther (Chapter 5), Kent (Chapter 6), Lee (Chapter 7), and Barnard and Taylor (Chapter 9)—focus on the ethnographic and ethnohistorical record of culture contact and change in the Kalahari since the nineteenth century, while three—Sadr (Chapter 2), Kent (Chapter 3), and the present chapter—provide perspectives from archaeology and other sources on the more distant past. Marlowe (Chapter 10) and Köhler and Lewis (Chapter 11) both discuss the parallels and differences between the history and status of hunter-gatherer groups in eastern and Central Africa and those of the Kalahari.

HISTORICAL MOVEMENTS

Most African hunter-gatherers have passed through at least three different types of culture contact, with very different outcomes. The initial phase dating back perhaps 4,000–5,000 years in Central and eastern Africa, but less than 2,000 years in the south, seems to have been the movement of small-scale societies of farmer-pastoralists from the north. In southern Africa, this coincided with the expansion of Bantu language-speakers into the region from at least two different directions, while in Central and eastern Africa, multiple movements into the region are indicated by the presence of all four African language families within a limited region such as that occupied by the Hadzabe. In both eastern and southern Africa, the initial spread of farming close to and south of the equator involved the adoption by the local hunter-gatherers of small stock (sheep and/or goats) and ceramic technology, rather than a large-scale invasion from outside (Reid et. al. 1998; Ambrose 1998; Deacon and Deacon 1999; Bernard Mbae, personal communication). By 1,500 years ago, Bantu languages and their speakers had expanded to southern Africa, and all of these new farmer-pastoralists were using iron as well as ceramic technologies. One imagines that the population density, even at the height of early Iron Age political integration, was low, and that there may have been plenty of room for hunter-gatherers using primarily stone, bone, and other organic technologies to coexist with the new people, especially in places that were less suited to farming or stock-herding due to low rainfall, dense vegetation cover, or tsetse infestation. The archaeological record (Sadr, Chapter 2, and see below) attests to a long period when some hunter-gatherers seem to have coexisted in a separate society and way of life, even on the immediate periphery of farmer-pastoralist settlements. But as shown by all the authors, especially Sugawara (Chapter 4), Lee (Chapter 7), Barnard and Taylor (Chapter 9), and Köhler and Lewis (Chapter 11), these interactions were characterized by differing degrees of independence, clientship, intermarriage, and assimilation. Guenther (Chapter 5) stresses the role of a strong political leader in Bushman resistance to both Oorlam (Nama) and Tawana encroachment at Ghanzi.

The second major influence discussed by all the authors is the direct and indirect effect of European colonization. For Kent (Chapter 6), European settlement of southern Africa resulted in the most drastic loss of culture and cultural autonomy for hunter-gatherers, due primarily to European attitudes about non-Western peoples. Guenther (Chapter 5) shows, however, that at Ghanzi, European settlement in the 1890s actually blocked the further expansion of both Bantu-speaking and Nama pastoral state societies into this region. Lee's Ju/'hoansi informants suggest that Europeans had little direct effect on the northwest Kalahari, and that, until recently, most of the exotic items in the area had been obtained through trade with Bantu-speaking groups on the periphery of this area. Even at Ghanzi, the indirect effect of both European diseases such as smallpox, and European commercial hunting was perhaps more important than actual settlement in changing power relationships between foragers and farmer-pastoralists. Creation of game parks by European powers in Botswana and Congo (D.R. Congo) had little initial effect on the forager inhabitants of these areas, who were allowed in most cases (not, however, in the northern region of Virunga National Park, D.R. Congo) to continue their traditional lifeways. In the postcolonial era, however, development of these parks for tourism and enforced bans on hunting or even on residence within them have drastically impacted the foraging lifeways of hunter-gatherers (Weber et al. 2001; see also Kent, this volume).

The most recent and perhaps most dramatic transformation of the forager groups considered here is the advent of nation-states. For Sugawara (Chapter 4), it is the nation-state and its attempts to settle nomadic peoples within a defined territory that has most affected the independence of the G/wi and G//anakwe. In Botswana, the government made extensive efforts to settle foragers or "remote area dwellers" around boreholes or wells, restrict their subsistence practices, remove them from actual and potential game parks, institute landownership practices consistent with a capitalist state, teach them agricultural practices, and send the children to school. Often, as at Dobe and Kutse, these efforts decreased the independence of foragers, and made them more dependent on their wealthier Bantu-speaking neighbors. Warfare on the border between Namibia and Botswana brought guard posts manned by Bushmen from far away, as well as lucrative employment as army trackers. This too decreased the potential for an independent lifestyle, and increased dependency.

In Tanzania, the initial adoption of socialism slowed such developments until recently. Since the late 1990s in Mang'ola, however, the advent of large-scale privately owned and massively irrigated onion farms (onions being easily transported over rough roads), together with an active Catholic mission, and a private Hadza tourism enterprise run by a non-Hadza have dramatically increased the population of this rural area and decreased the opportunities for a forager lifeway. When I worked in Mang'ola in August 2001, the tourists seemed to outnumber the Hadza, all the available camping sites were occupied by tourist vans, and the total population of all ethnic groups in this small cluster of villages had mushroomed to more than 20,000, according to the missionaries. At present, acting out Hadza lifeways for tourists is more lucrative than actual foraging. In Botswana and Namibia as well, increased tourism and the accommodations made by the nation-state for tourists, including game parks and roads, have restricted the use of former forager lands, and provided an alternate lifestyle involving acting for tourists. And as African populations have increased, there are fewer opportunities available for a forager lifeway outside restricted game areas. In D.R. Congo (ex-Zaire), on the other hand, the failure, even before the present conflict, to create a true state-level society to provide schooling, health care, a transportation infrastructure or other development may have left more space for traditional forager lifestyles to continue. When I worked in the Virunga National Park in 1985–90 and visited the Parc National des Volcans in Rwanda, many Twa Pygmies of this region continued to hunt and gather in the montane forests, working occasionally as game guides for the gorilla tourism organizations.

Little is said in this volume about the expansion of east African trade into the interior in the thirteenth through the fifteenth centuries, or, except in Marlowe's paper, about the effects of the slave trade during the sixteenth to nineteenth centuries in the remote areas still inhabited by hunter-gatherers. The genetic data of all three areas, however (see below) suggest that relatively few farmer-pastoralists of non-Khoisan or non-Pygmy origin fled from the traders or slavers into the remote regions and took up a hunter-gatherer lifeway.

FORAGER INDEPENDENCE: THE GENETIC AND BIOLOGICAL DATA

The hunting and gathering peoples of Africa have become even more iconic in the genetic literature than they once were in the writings of archaeologists. Current articles on the genetics of Y-chromosomes root the evolutionary tree of all humans in either the Ituri or the Kalahari (Cavalli-Sforza et al. 1994; Underhill et al. 2000, 2001), while the mtDNA data, reflecting maternal inheritance, has been used to argue that "Eve" was a Bushman—or woman (Vigilant et al. 1991; Watson et al. 1997; Chen et al. 1995, 2000). Popular accounts of this research follow on more than a hundred years of writing concerning the physical distinctiveness of the Bushmen, and have unfortunate echoes in the nineteenth-century classifications of Khoisan-speakers as less than human, and in the inordinate interest in their distinctive sexual organs and other features (Maseko 1998; Boonzaier et al. 1996). Early studies by Jenkins et al. (1970), and by Nurse, Weiner, and Jenkins (1995) demonstrated that the San populations of the Kalahari, especially the !Kung or Ju/'hoansi, were genetically very distinct from their neighbors, both Khoi and Bantu-speakers. More recent DNA studies (Harpending et al. 1993, 1998; Vigilant et al. 1991; Soodyall and Jenkins 1992; Soodyall et al. 2000) and others have confirmed the presence of distinctive mtDNA and Y-chromosome variants among the Ju/'hoansi; indeed most genetic trees of relatedness place the Ju/'hoansi sample near the root of the tree, reflecting the distinctiveness of this group. In addition, the amount of variability within the Ju/'hoansi sample suggests a long period of isolated population development, and the patterning of interindividual variation suggest that the Ju/'hoansi represent a contracting population that experienced a major bottleneck in the past (Harpending et al. 1993, 1998; Jorde et al. 1997, 1998). Jenkins et al. (1970) also published a map (reprinted as Fig 11.2 in Nurse, Weiner and Jenkins 1995) in which they reconstructed from genetic data the approximate amount of genetic contribution from the San in the various Bantu-speakers of southern Africa. The percentage of San admixture ranged from 60 percent among the Bakgalagadi and Xhosa, 53 percent in the Bechuana (Batswana), 37–49 percent among the peoples of Natal but only 0–5 percent among the Ovambo, Okavango, and Ndebele.

Further genetic data (Jorde et al. 1998; Chen et al. 1995; Spurdle and Jenkins 1992; Underhill et al. 2000; Ke et al. 2001) have demonstrated that this admixture is reflected more clearly in the mtDNA, passed through the maternal line, but less in the Y-chromosome data (Douglas Wallace, personal communication). In other words, the Y-chromosomes of different African populations are even more distinct statistically from each other than are the mtDNA data. The difference between the patterning of paternal and maternal inheritance suggest that the admixture was created by San women marrying into Bantu-speaker societies, and gaining full marriage rights in the father's society for the children of such unions. In the Dobe area, for example, the local Batswana (Tswana) chief in the 1960s had a Ju/'hoansi grandmother, and several Ju/'hoansi had married at least one of their daughters to a Yei, Hambukushu, or Tswana-speaker. I knew of only one case where the children were raised as Ju/'hoansi; rather they tended to be accepted by the father's people and have full inheritance rights. In my camp one evening, one of our unmarried Herero workers tried to convince the father of a Ju/'hoansi teenager to allow him to marry his oldest daughter. "You would be able to drink milk whenever you wanted, and I will pay you in cattle." The father replied "Yes, and when the cattle die I will have nothing, but if she marries a Ju/'hoansi, her husband will work for me for seven years, and look out for me always." This argument suggested how a father could maximize his chances, maintain flexibility and practice risk avoidance through strategic marriage both within and outside Ju/'hoansi society. His negative decision also indicated the degree of resistance to incorporation into farmer-pastoralist society prevalent at Dobe even in the 1970s.

Comparative genetic work with different Kalahari populations suggests that the peoples of the northwest are more genetically distinctive and variable than the peoples of the center and south, such as the G/wi, G//anakwe, or Nama (Jenkins et al. 1970; Spurdle and Jenkins 1992; Nurse, Weiner, and Jenkins 1995; Jenkins 1995; Soodyall and Jenkins 1992; Soodyall et al. 2000).

As in the Kalahari, biological studies of Pygmies and other Central African forest dwellers confirm the biological distinctiveness of some Pygmy groups, not only in their short stature but also in their response to disease and nutritional deficiency. Geelhoed (1996) for example, showed that many Pygmies of the Ituri Forest develop grossly enlarged thyroids (goiter) in response to severe iodine deficiency. These usually do not become life threatening until after the bearer has reached reproductive age. Among Azande farmers who filtered south of the Uele River and occasionally shared forest-margin environments with Pygmies, however, the response to iodine deficiency is more likely to be congenital and developmental cretinism, which effectively removes the most affected sufferers from the gene pool. The physiological difference in responses suggests that the forest-dwelling foragers have acquired genetic adaptations to the iodine-deficient environment of the forest over a considerable period, while the Azande have not.

Genetic studies of Pygmies, reviewed by Köhler and Lewis (Chapter 11), reveal interesting differences in patterning across the great distance of the Central African forest region. Ituri Pygmies studied by Cavalli-Sforza (1986) are highly distinctive from other Africans, especially in their Y-chromosomes. In particular, the frequency of one Y-chromosome mutation, M60, is very high in the Mbuti and Biaka Pygmies—this mutation is also common in Khoisan speakers but rarer elsewhere in Africa and absent outside the continent. Its distribution suggests a very ancient lineage (Mortensen 2000; Underhill 2000; Knight et al. in press; Ke et al. 2001). Twa Pygmies of the eastern regions and Aka and Baka Pygmies of the western forest are much more similar genetically to their nonforager neighbors. Köhler and Lewis explain this difference between the distinctive Mbuti and Biaka and the less distinctive Aka and Twa in terms of patrilocal and matrilocal residence respectively for the children of mixed forager-farmer unions. In most such cases, the father is a farmer and the mother a Pygmy, so that the genetic admixture moves patrilocally into the farmer community in the Ituri Forest, but remains in the forager community on the eastern and western margins (see also Peterson 1991; Bailey 1991).

Hadza genetic studies are just now underway (e.g., Knight et al. 2000, in press; Mortensen 2000; Tishkoff, personal communication) but preliminary results indicate the presence of high frequencies of the Y-chromosome haplotype containing the M60 mutation relative to the frequencies observed in the Hadza's neighbors: the Iraqw (Afro-Asiatic speakers), Datoga (Nilo-Saharan speakers), Sukuma and other Bantu-speakers. The Hadza mtDNA data are also distinctive relative to their neighbors but both types of data show greater similarity to the Sukuma than to other neighboring groups, suggesting that there has been significant gene flow from Hadza groups into the others, but especially the Bantu-speakers, via the incorporation of Hadza women and their mixed-descent children into groups of farmer-pastoralists.

Thus in both the Ituri and the Hadza region, as well as in the Kalahari, the genetic data suggest that the lineages represented by present-day African foragers are very ancient and reflect a long period of separate development. In addition, the contrasting patterning of maternal and paternal inheritance in African foragers indicates that a variable but significant portion of the genetic inheritance of their farmer-pastoralist neighbors is derived via gene flow from forager women, and the subsequent incorporation of mixed-heritage children, in some cases (but not on the eastern and western forest margins, or among the matrilineal Hadza), into the farmer-pastoralist group. Both independence and the great variety of social constructions of dependency or exchange that resulted when foragers and farmers came into contact are reflected in this data.

FORAGERS AND FARMERS: THE LINGUISTIC DATA

Many types of linguistic information bear on past histories of independence and incorporation, including phonology, lexicon and grammar, use of categories, place names, word histories, and aspects of linguistic practice. Traill, for example (2000) has argued that clicks are too unusual and difficult to produce as phonemes to have been invented more than once; hence all the click languages of Africa must derive from the same source, and reflect either common ancestry or borrowing. These include not only all the Khoisan languages, which are otherwise highly diverse but share the use of clicks, but also the Bantu languages of the southeast and southern coast of South Africa such as Zulu and Xhosa, in exactly the region that was shown to be most affected by genetic admixture with Khoisan-speakers. The use of clicks by these Bantu languages, which otherwise cluster closely with other Bantu languages, is further indication of a long history of assimilation and incorporation via intermarriage.

The patterning of diversity within the Khosan languages is also relevant to a discussion of independence among foragers. Khoisan languages are very difficult to compare, owing to their greater diversity in lexicon and grammar than any other language family in Africa or elsewhere. The earliest classification of the Khoisan languages by Bleek (1929) and Westphal (1962a, 1962b, 1963) divided them into three groups, the Northern Group of San languages (such as !Kung or Ju/'hoansi) the Central Group (including G/wi and G//anakwe) and the Southern Group of !Xo and several recently extinct South African languages. Khoi and Nama are most closely related to the Central languages, while the Northern Group is the most distinct from the others, suggesting a parallel to the diverse histories of incorporation observed in the genetic data, with the smallest admixture in the north (Traill 1978a, 1978b, 1986, 2000; see below for archaeological evidence bearing on this point as well).

The use of place names and word histories to reconstruct past population movements has been well developed only for the Central African rain forest, as a result of the work of Vansina (1986, 1990) and Klieman (1999). Although no true Pygmy languages have survived, linguistic analysis of place names and other word differences suggests a much older stratum of forest-dweller langauges (Bahuchet 1993). The evidence reviewed by Köhler and Lewis reflects a diverse and dynamic history of forager interaction with farmers. In this region, however, the differences between foragers and farmers are reflected not in language per se but in the use of categories and the values placed on them. Köhler and Lewis argue that the linguistic practices of the Yaka in particular, and the collective animal nouns they use to describe both Europeans and non-Pygmy Africans, reflect a worldview that does not envision a dichotomy between culture and nature. This practice contradicts the grammatical patterning of the Bantu languages, whose noun classes impose a set of nonoverlapping categories (e.g., animal, human, inanimate) on the things being named. It is an argument that could as well be made in the Kalahari among the Ju/'hoansi, where the Europeans are known as "Steenbok people," and the trance experience allows practitioners to transcend the boundary between the material self and the spirits of animals and ancestors. In Central Africa in addition, the use of collective nouns such as "Baka" or "Yaka" by particular Pygmy groups to refer to all Pygmies including those who speak Nilo-Saharan rather than Niger-Congo (Bantu) languages reflects a sense of collective identity that transcends particular relationships between specific forager and farmer groups.

In regard to collective nouns among Central Kalahari San, Sugawara (Chapter 4) points out that *contra* Wilmsen (1990), who argued that the San had no sense of collective identity before the word "Bushmen" came into vogue among Europeans, and were thus, as a group, an artifact of European domination, the G/wi and G//anakwe use a collective noun Kua, to refer to all Bushmen or San. The G/wi and G//ana practice of naming babies for events surrounding their birth is widespread among the

Bantu-speakers of the Central Kalahari, and may reflect the long history of interaction in this region. When I worked near Raikops in the Central Kalahari during the summer of 1980, I employed two local non-Bushman workers whose names meant respectively "It hurts" and "Waiting for death." The naming narratives recounted by Sugawara suggest feelings of subordination and inequality among the G/wi and G//anakwe relative to the Bakgalagadi, especially in regard to the presumed power of sorcery among the latter.

THE EVIDENCE OF ARCHAEOLOGY

Although archaeological evidence is difficult to mine for evidence of individuals, cultural ideals, or ethnic groups, it does reflect contacts and new influences coming into an area, in both material goods and subsistence practices. The spread of material goods often predates and overstates the degree of actual contact between peoples (e.g., Mercader, Garcia-Heras, and González-Álvarez 2000)—this is evident, for example, in the way that sheep-herding and ceramic manufacture spread initially into the earliest pastoral Neolithic groups of southern Kenya ca. 4,000–5,000 years ago (Ambrose 1998; B. Mbae, personal communication), as well as among Khoi populations of the Cape around 0 A.D.. (Deacon and Deacon 1999), and around the same time or slightly later to the southern edge of the Okavango Delta (Reid et al. 1998). Another example is the spread of European goods into the Seacow Valley in the Free State at sites such as Abbott's Cave, long before there is any record of European travel to that area (Garth Sampson and Glenn Goodfriend, personal communication). The record of Native North Americans' contact with Europeans suggests a parallel that supports some of Kent's ideas (Chapter 3)—in that European diseases, guns, and horses spread rapidly far beyond the actual European frontier into areas not visited by Europeans until much later.

As Sadr (Chapter 2) suggests, archaeological evidence supports many kinds of interactions between hunter-gatherers and farmer-herders in southern Africa. In South Africa itself, sheep-herding and ceramics arrived in the Cape Province by around 0 A.D. with an expanding population presumably of Khoisan-speakers from the north. The expansion itself is supported by genetic and linguistic data linking the historic pastoralist Khoikhoi with Central Bush speakers, although the route of the expansion, via the west or the east, is debated (Elphick 1977; Deacon and Deacon 1999; Boonzaier et al. 1996). Herders do not appear to have reached the Seacow Valley until the fourteenth century A.D., which would rule out an interior migration route across the Karoo (Sampson 1988; Boonzaier et al. 1996). Bantu-speaking peoples dependent on both cattle-herding and farming spread from both the northwest and northeast to the southeast as far as the Fish River in the eastern Cape by ca. 500 A.D. (Boonzaier et al. 1996; Deacon and Deacon 1999). By the time the Bantu-speaking farmer-herders reached the borders of the Cape Province and the Karoo, however, the Khoikhoi had adopted cattle-raising as well as sheep-herding and were organized enough to resist the expansion of Bantu-speakers for centuries (Elphick 1975). Indeed, only since the ascendance of the ANC and the lifting of apartheid restrictions have Xhosa and particularly Zulu peoples established significant populations along the dry Atlantic coast north of the Cape. Since, in any case, the dry climate of these western regions did not support rainfall agriculture, but was conducive only to relatively sparse populations and pastoral adaptations, the Xhosa and Zulu seem to have been less able to expand into them, and content to leave the Khoi in place. The Khoi themselves developed a series of complex state-like societies, with formal economic and social relationships between their clans and those of the Bantu-speaking groups. In this sense, the desert and semiarid regions of South Africa seem to have functioned like the Ituri Forest, to provide a space where Khoisan hunter-gatherers could explore a variety of subsistence practices, including a kind of clientship with Bantu-speaking agriculturalists to the east and southwest. In southern Africa, however, there is considerable evidence that these populations shifted, over time, from pastoralism back to hunting and gathering and then again to pastoralism, as circumstances and climatic conditions allowed (Elphick 1975; Boonzaier et al. 1996).

The Kalahari debate between Wilmsen and others and Lee and others over the long-term independence of foragers specifically at Dobe can be addressed from the perspective of past settlement patterns, subsistence, and technological systems recovered through excavation of the archaeological record of the Dobe region. This record was investigated through about 20 years of archaeological survey and excavation by John Yellen, myself, and Edwin Wilmsen, together with our students and collaborators.

Questions to be asked of this record, as presently known, include:

1. How ancient is the record of human settlement here?
2. What was the nature of the ethnographic past at Dobe "B.A."—before anthropologists? Were the Ju/'hoansi observed hunting and gathering there in the 1960s heavily involved in pastoralist activities prior to this date, for example, during the 1940s?
3. Can the archaeological past be tied to the ethnographic past? Does the archaeological pattern, at least in its most recent phases, conform to that observed ethnographically in this area?
4 How far back into the past does the recent pattern extend? and
5. Conversely, if southern African foragers may be considered to have existed in a forager's world *only* prior to 2,000 years ago, is there evidence for contact with Iron Age peoples as this demarcation line is approached in time? And, does the contact appear to be associated with other changes in the subsistence, settlement, or technological pattern?

NORTHWEST KALAHARI GEOGRAPHY

The Northwest Kalahari lies between the relict and present marsh terrains of the Okavango Delta, and the central Namibian highlands (Helgren and Brooks 1983; Yellen 1974). With the exception of bedrock projections such as the Tsodilo, Aha, and /Cwihabe hills, the entire region is covered with veneers of relict aeolian sands, often in the form of longitudinal dunes, oriented in a northwest-southeast direction. In the Aha hills, a southerly wind direction has banked the sands more heavily on the south side of the hills and more sparsely in the northern lee.

An unconformity in the Ahas between karstic limestones and underlying impermeable schists gives rise to underground springs that drain eastward toward the Okavango swamps. This has resulted in four river valleys: the !Kangwa to the north, the /Xai/Xai to the south, and two smaller valleys to the east of the Aha hills. Only in years of heaviest rainfall are these marked by surface flow. In both the !Kangwa and /Xai/Xai valleys, however, circular pans, or depressions, intersect groundwater tables and provide year-round water sources. While sands are abundant in the valleys also, the heavy concentration of carbonates derived from evaporites and precipitates of groundwater results in relatively consolidated to very consolidated sediments, both on pan margins and underlying the unconsolidated sands of valley margins. Most archaeological sites are distributed within 1 km of these pans.

On a vegetation map of the Kalahari published in 1972, the demarcation line between Okavango Delta and Northwest Kalahari sediments is paralleled by a vegetation line corresponding to the limits of mopane tree savanna. The Tsodilo Hills with their associated Iron Age sites, 34 km southwest of the Okavango River and 120 km ENE of Dobe, are located in a mopane area, whereas the Dobe-/Xai/Xai area is not. The Dobe-/Xai/Xai area is also distinguished from the rest of the northwest Kalahari south of the mopane line, by a relatively higher proportion of trees, termed "northwest Kalahari tree savanna" rather than "northern Kalahari tree and bush savanna."

ETHNOARCHAEOLOGY IN THE DOBE-/XAI/XAI AREA

Ethnoarchaeological studies that looked at where people were currently leaving debris on the landscape began with John Yellen's (1977; Yellen and Lee 1976) work on short-term rainy-season camps in 1968–71, and continued with his study in 1975–83 of successive dry-season camps at Dobe (Yellen 1987, 1991a, 1991b). In the latter study, he walked middle-aged informants back over their earlier lives to each long-term dry-season camp occupied by that informant, to the point where the informant, as a boy, had first moved from his parent's hut to a hut of adolescent boys. These camps were then selectively excavated to derive information both about prior subsistence patterns and long-term survival of faunal and other remains.

Faunal remains from the oldest ethnoarchaeological sites, dating to the early 1940s, clearly demonstrate that "B.A." subsistence was based entirely on hunting, and by inference, on gathering. Moreover, dry-season camps were located in the same general area as those of the 1980s but in nonoverlapping sites, so as to maximize the availability of firewood and bushfoods and minimize disease. Rainy-season camps from the distant past do not appear to be detectable archaeologically. From this, we learned that the key concept in translating the ethnographic pattern of Ju/'hoansi life to the archaeological record is redundancy. Rainy-season camps are invisible archaeologically because they are occupied by few people, for only a few days, and almost never in the same location. Dry-season camps are recoverable archaeologically, although over a very long period the remains of dry-season camps, all located about 0.5 km from each permanent water hole, tend to blend or smear into a single scatter of debris without distinguishable features.

Older archaeological material from the Dobe-/Xai/Xai area was first reported by Malan (1950). Beginning in 1968, and continuing through 1983, systematic programs of survey and excavation were carried out in the area by Yellen, myself, and Wilmsen. Within the region, archaeological sites were located through a variety of different strategies including foot surveys of fossil drainage ways, transect surveys across the region from south to north, interval surface and subsurface sampling, examination of known exposures, and use of aerial photos to locate further exposures and likely archaeological site areas. All sectors of the present (1968) range of the Dobe band were surveyed, as well as the !Kangwa Valley east to !Goshe, the northern sector of the Aha hills, the /Cwihabe Valley, and the /Xai/Xai area.

With the exception of a single artifact of probable late Middle Stone Age type, no sites were located or found through subsurface sampling in the region of longitudinal dunes north of Dobe. Nor were sites located in the Ahas, with the exception of a very minimal cultural scatter at /Dwichu rockshelter. Since these areas lack surface water today, the absence of past human occupation with enough redundancy to produce archaeological signatures is not surprising.

On the basis of the archaeological survey, 13 sites were selected for more-or-less extensive excavation to depths between 20 cm and 3 meters. These included:

1   a few, very rich, stratified sites in consolidated pan margin sediments (≠Gi, !Kubi, Mahopa 2) (Helgren and Brooks 1983; Brooks and Yellen 1987; Brooks, Crowell, and Yellen 1981; Brooks 1985; Yellen and Brooks 1988, 1990; Brooks et al. 1990);

2. a larger number of relatively rich sites in unconsolidated sand within 1 km of pans (above references and Wilmsen 1978, 1989a, 1989b); and

3. two rockshelter/cave sites—one in the Ahas and one in the /Cwihabe Valley near /Xai/Xai—each with a very limited archaeological inventory (Yellen et al. 1987).

One of the central problems of this record was that the richest sites were on the margins of pans. No one today (1960 to 1980s) lives at the margin of a pan, due to insect pests and danger from predators such as hyenas and leopards. In addition, human settlement scares away the game that might otherwise come down to drink there. Was this pattern different in the past?

In the course of our excavation of one pan site, ≠Gi, we accidentally discovered the answer. While Yellen and I were away for a week getting supplies, our two students continued the excavation by living with the crew on the pan margin. Several Ju/'hoansi crew members built a hunting blind out of the backdirt, and, at night, lay in wait for kudu and other animals. Subsequent studies of this activity showed that for obtaining meat it was five time more efficient than stalking (Crowell and Hitchcock 1978; Brooks and Yellen 1987), that it was only feasible at certain times of year (early in the dry season), that it was always carried out at dwindling water sources in exactly the same locations. Blinds and their buried hearths were rebuilt and reused over a period of centuries. Indeed blinds currently in use contained Later Stone Age debris and hearths below the surface.

The results of the archaeological excavations suggest the following general conclusions about the past of this area:

1. The first occupations, known only from derived contexts, were at least 200,000 years ago, while the first *in situ* occupations apparently congruent with modern landscape-use patterns were at least 65,000–85,000 years ago;
2. Later Stone Age adaptations with many parallels to the hunting technology, subsistence pattern, and land-use of the ethnographically documented Ju/'hoansi were established ca. 20,000 years ago;
3. This Later Stone Age continues possibly as late as the nineteenth century with little evidence of change in settlement pattern, subsistence strategy, or technological inventory, other than a few rare fragments of metal or ceramics; and
4. There is absolutely no evidence for Iron Age economies or pastoralist settlement in the western part of the !Kangwa Valley at any time before the "ethnographic" present.

≠GI AND THE EVIDENCE FOR LONG-TERM CONTINUITY OF LSA TECHNOLOGY AND LAND-USE AT PAN MARGINS

Three sites in particular may serve to illustrate and elaborate these points. The first site is ≠Gi, a stratified pan-margin site with three main cultural units from lower to upper: **Unit 4,** Middle Stone Age with finely made bifacial and unifacial points and scrapers, **Unit 2C,** an intermediate industry with blades but few formal tools, and **Units 2A and 1A-B,** at least two horizons of Later Stone Age material of "Wilton" type with crescents, small scrapers, ostrich eggshell beads, and bone arrow foreshafts or points (Brooks et al. 1990).

By a combination of radiocarbon, thermoluminescence, and amino acid racemization of ostrich eggshell (Brooks et al. 1990), the Middle Stone Age level has been dated to 65,000 to 85,000 years, the intermediate industry to 34,000 years, and the older of the two LSA units to 24,000 years at the very base. The younger LSA horizon falls within the last 800 years, and a hearth near the top is dated to 110 ± 50 B.P., well within the time depth of residential stability claimed by present-day Ju/'hoansi in the region, although the C^{14} calibration curve could place this hearth at several points in the last 300 years. Shallow pit-hearths within this unit are comparable to hearths constructed in modern-day hunting blinds at the site, and are often stratified below hunting blinds still in use. At the base of the later LSA horizon are a series of deep pits containing kudu horns, a rhinoceros jaw (*Ceratotherium simum*), and numerous crescents and bone arrow foreshafts.

When our archaeological excavations had deepened to the point where they paralleled the ancient deep pits in size and depth, the Ju/'hoansi used our archaeological squares as kudu traps. Butchery of the resultant carcasses left behind only horns and jaws. Other parallels between the Later Stone Age and the modern Ju/'hoansi, besides the particular use-patterns of the pan margin, include the arrow foreshafts themselves, which were virtually identical, and the size of the ostrich eggshell beads. The time interval between the age of the surface level and the memory of the oldest living Ju may be small or nonexistent. ≠Gi thus provides some of the best evidence for continuity between the Ju/'hoansi and the Later Stone Age, as well as evidence for a long history of occupation in the area. Although the two Later Stone Age industries at ≠Gi certainly span but may not actually represent the initial contact period, almost no differences in typological composition exist between them (Table 8.1), other than a few more thumbnail scrapers and crescent varieties in the earlier level, and a tiny sample of potsherds and metal objects in the later level. With the debitage, not tabulated here, each level contained about 10,000 artifacts.

MAHOPA 1 AND /XAI/XAI: PROBLEMS OF STRATIGRAPHIC INTEGRITY AND FAUNAL PRESERVATION IN UNCONSOLIDATED SAND

After the pan margin sites, the second category of archaeological occurrences in order of density are located in the area of present-day dry-season camps, generally about 0.5 km from the margins of permanent water holes. Yellen and Wilmsen excavated a series of these occurrences at Mahopa, !Kubi, and /Xai/Xai. A large series of radiocarbon dates (Yellen and Brooks 1988, 1990) shows that these sites span the period when Iron Age peoples were moving into the Okavango Delta. Did life at Dobe or /Kai/Kai change in any way detectable in the archaeological record in response to these events? Unlike at ≠Gi, where the sediments were quite consolidated, the

Table 8.1

Frequencies (as Percentages) of Selected Artifact Types at ≠Gi

Type	Recent Levels (1A, 1B)	Late Pleistocene Level (2A)
Backed bladelets	1.50	3.50
Pointed bladelets	0.40	0.30
Crescents	7.00	10.00
Backed blades	1.40	2.30
Scrapers	11.30	15.30
Perforators	3.10	2.20
Cores	14.30	19.20
Retouched bladelets	3.80	4.00
Retouched flakes	14.10	9.60
Notched/denticulate pieces	6.90	2.80
Miscellaneous points, burins	1.50	0.90
Outils ecailles	1.10	0.60
Bifacial pieces	5.20	5.70
Iron, pottery, buttons	0.80	<0.1
Total number of retouched pieces (without debitage)	910	1,025

dry-season area camps were located in deep unconsolidated sands, so one must first confront the problem of stratigraphic integrity.

The site of Mahopa 1 is located ca. 0.5 km northwest of Mahopa pan in a flat sandy area utilized today for aggregation camps and villages. Eight squares, each 5 feet by 5 feet (1.52 m by 1.52 m), were excavated in 2-inch levels in unconsolidated sand, underlain by impenetrable calcrete at depths varying from 28 to 48 inches (71 to 122 cm). No stratigraphic or archaeological horizons were visible in this Kalahari sand, which elsewhere has been shown by Cahen and Moeyersons (1977) to permit vertical movement of artifacts over 1 meter. All of the material was Later Stone Age, but one may well question whether there is any inherent stratification in these unconsolidated sands (Leigh 2001).

Eight charcoal samples from five of the squares that were contiguous were dated by radiocarbon (Yellen and Brooks 1988, 1990). These suggest that the sequence extends from the present back to at least 3270 B.P., and may be divided into three stratigraphic horizons. The top 16 inches (40 cm) yielded dates ranging from 0 to 600 B.P., the next 4 inches (10 cm) yielded two dates that were about 2000 B.P., and the lowest levels up to 28 to 48 inches provided one date of ca. 3270 B.P. The topmost level in particular appeared to represent a significant time span with some churning and admixture through its 40-cm depth.

The tripartite chronological division corresponds in squares 4 through 8 to a patterning of artifacts with depth that is *not* replicated in the other three squares. This implies that stratigraphic correlations between noncontiguous squares cannot be assumed a priori. Out of 1,587 numbered (i.e., secondarily retouched) pieces from Mahopa 1, 3 were metal fragments and 10 (0.63 percent) were tiny thumbnail-sized potsherds, of which 2 were of Early Iron Age type (Denbow, personal communication), and could have derived from unit 2. Their rarity and small size raises the possibility that they were introduced into the site as sherds rather than pots, a possibility that has been suggested in similar occurrences further north in Zambia (Musonda 1984).

Of 25,400 faunal remains from Mahopa 1, only 13, all individual teeth, were identifiable as to species. All these were of wild, not domesticated animals. Ethnoarchaeological work on bone taphonomy in unconsolidated Kalahari sand (Yellen 1989, 1990, 1991a, 1991b), has shown that bone does not preserve in this environment over a period of about 40 years unless it is either burned, or located in the more calcareous, higher pH pan-margin sediments. Since burning causes bone to break down into tiny unidentifiable fragments, the rarity and fragmentary nature of identifiable remains in this assemblage is not surprising. In fact, it is the recovery of large, relatively complete specimens that would be unusual in this environment, and would lead to questions of provenience for the specimens involved.

The final site to be discussed here is / Xai / Xai. Yellen excavated two areas at / Xai / Xai, which is located about 50 km south of Mahopa. / Xai / Xai 1 is southeast of the pan consisting of three contiguous 5-foot squares, and / Xai / Xai 2 is west of the pan consisting of a single 5-foot square.

Fifteen samples of burned bone and charcoal were dated by radiocarbon (Yellen and Brooks 1989, 1990). As at Mahopa, the charcoal dates cluster into three units, of which the upper two exhibit internal stratigraphic mixing.

Unit I, the top 16 inches (40 cm) includes dates back to 635 B.P.

Unit II, the next 20 inches (50 cm) to a total depth of 36 inches dates to between 1765 and 2260 B.P., just prior to the appearance of Iron Age peoples at Tsodilo; and

Unit III dates to between 3205 and 3645 B.P.

The collagen and humic acid dates were not consistent with each other, which reflects considerable ground-water resolution. Only the collagen dates are reliable.

The patterning of artifact concentration by depth in the two site areas does not correspond, although a rise in artifact percentage is noted in each site at around

Level 18, near the interface between Units II and III. Nor do bone and lithic concentrations for the same squares parallel each other. Concentrations toward the base of each unit may reflect patterns of downward transport of artifacts, with bones and stones differentially transported due to density variation.

As at Mahopa 1, less than 2 percent of the numbered artifacts were sherds or metal fragments—only 12 of the former and 1 of the latter turned up. As many as 7 of the sherds may be of Early Iron Age type, referable to Unit II and thus at least 1,765 years old. A metal bead may also derive from this level.

Faunal remains from /Xai/Xai are all burned and fragmentary. None of the 1,342 specimens from /Xai/Xai 1 and only two isolated teeth from /Xai/Xai 2, out of 11,173 faunal specimens from the latter site area, could be identified.

Wilmsen conducted excavations at /Xai/Xai in 1975 (Wilmsen 1978). As noted also by Sadr (1997), the various 1-m diameter pits that he excavated to depths of about 1 m also exhibit differing concentrations with depth in each unit, suggesting that correlation by depth across widely separated units would be unwise. His results also reflect in general the overwhelming dominance of lithics, the rare and fragmentary occurrence of pottery and metal, and the poor preservation of faunal remains. Curiously, in light of the latter, he later reports a large piece of a maxilla with several teeth that he attributes to domesticated cow. Although this piece is 60 cm below the surface, its excellent preservation suggests a recent intrusion. In Yellen's excavations, an extremely recent (post-bomb) charcoal sample was recovered from a depth of 16 inches (40 cm.) Wilmsen, however, correlates this "cow" (the identification is also questionable) with a charcoal date from the same depth in a noncontiguous unit 8 meters away. The resultant age of ca. 600 A.D. forms the basis of Wilmsen's claim for the existence of cattle pastoralism and direct and overwhelming Iron Age contact in the /Xai/Xai area from the early Iron Age on. Yellen and I feel that this claim is not justified on either taphonomic or stratigraphic grounds (Yellen and Brooks 1988). No other direct evidence of domesticated livestock in antiquity has been recovered from any site in the Dobe-/Xai/Xai area. Nor, as Denbow readily admits (1990) is there any evidence of old pastoralist settlement—these are readily visible on the surface owing to the vegetation changes engendered by the distinctive soil chemistry of old cattle kraals. The evidence of contact, in the form of tiny amounts of pottery and metal, suggests rather that it was minimal and probably not direct, and had little effect on daily subsistence or settlement patterns.

Despite the unconsolidated nature of the sediments at dry-season area camps, the radiocarbon dates suggest that mixing of levels only occurred to within 40 to 60 cm below a past or present land surface. Most excavations recovered remains from three distinct periods of occupation, each with internal mixing. The oldest of these dated to the mid-Holocene (3000–5000 B.P.), another to just before and during the advent of Iron Age peoples, and a final level to the last 600 or so years. Throughout these occupations, all the fauna that could be identified represent the remains of wild animals—percentages of identifiable remains were, however, small, as burned bone breaks down rapidly in these sands to nonidentifiable fragments, and unburned bone does not survive. The settlement locations were congruent with those of the Ju observed as hunter and gatherers in the 1960s. While crossing the "Stone Age / Iron Age" boundary of the Okavango sequence, the Dobe-area sequence remained "Stone Age" in the basic orientation of its technology. There was little or no change in lithic type frequencies across the sequence from prior to 600 A.D. to the present. Furthermore, only a tiny fraction of the material from the most recent levels—0.5 percent of the retouched pieces, or 0.005 percent of the total assemblage—consisted of tiny fragments of pottery (15 sherds) or iron (4 pieces). Using Sadr's index of acculturation, this would suggest a rather minimal level of contact and assimilation with farming peoples to the east.

To summarize the results of archaeological investigations conducted to date in the Dobe and / Xai / Xai regions:

1. There is more stratigraphic integrity to the sandy sites than we originally assumed, although admixture within and between units does occur. One cannot assume a priori that nonadjacent pits have equivalent stratigraphic horizons.

2. The poor preservation of bone in these sediments implies that relatively complete specimens are probably intrusive from recent levels unless otherwise demonstrated. There is no evidence, however, for domesticated stock.

3. In neither ≠Gi, Mahopa 1, or / Xai / Xai do lithic type frequencies change across the pre–Iron Age to Iron Age boundary of ca. 600 A.D., suggesting that whatever functions were being carried out at these sites did not change over the 3,000 to 20,000 years of intermittent occupation.

4. Although pottery and metal indicate contact with Iron Age pastoralists beginning at least as early as the Tsodilo Hills sites, these items continue to be very rare and fragmentary. Pottery, in particular, may even have been introduced as sherds rather than as whole vessels (Musonda 1984).

5. As we have argued elsewhere (Brooks and Yellen 1987), the site patterning is congruent with the patterning of ethnographically documented hunter-gatherer land-use in the Dobe region, viewed in long-term perspective. Pan margin ambush sites, used redundantly, are most prominent in the archaeological record, while the other major group of archaeological sites is located in areas used today for dry-season aggregation camps.

In conclusion, the archaeological record of the Dobe-/Xai/Xai region suggests that the ancient inhabitants of this area were little affected by the advent of iron-using and cattle-keeping peoples on their eastern periphery. While the absence of archaeological evidence for change might not prove the absence of change, it certainly cautions against the too-facile assumption that Iron Age pastoralists in the Okavango-Tsodilo region profoundly affected the lives of foragers at Dobe and /Xai/Xai.

THE RECORD OF OTHER REGIONS IN SOUTHERN AFRICA

While Lee and Smith's data (Chapter 7) reflect similar conclusions about the long-term unsuitability of the northwestern Kalahari for pastoral adaptations, and the consequent long-term independence of forager adaptations there, other regions of southern Africa have yielded quite different suites of archaeological data suggesting different outcomes. In the Tsodilo Hills at White Paintings Shelter, occupation continues through the nearby Early Iron Age occupations of Ngoma and Divuyu, and continues to reflect the predominance of stone artifacts and bone fishing and hunting technology that was present before the advent of Iron Age farmers along with small amounts of ceramics and iron beads, indicative of a reciprocal or perhaps a client relationship. With the exception of one sheep mandible, all the fauna from these levels appears to be from wild animals (Murphy 1999; Robbins et al. 2000). Occupation of the site by San hunter-gatherers during the rainy season apparently continued to within the last 50 years, with a continuing predominance of wild foods, especially mongongo nuts, in the remains, along with a maize cob and a carbonized field pea. Along the Botletle River, on the other hand, sites formerly occupied by LSA hunter-gatherers such as the Hippo Tooth site (Denbow 1984, 1986; Denbow and Wilmsen 1986), have early Iron Age occupations with masses of potsherds at the surface, suggesting that pastoralist farmers assimilated and/or replaced hunter-gatherers in the settlement system.

As Sadr demonstrates, the archaeological record of "encapsulated" hunter-gatherers, who would probably have regarded themselves as independent, following in the footsteps and material culture traditions of their ancestors, disappears from southeastern Botswana only in the nineteenth century. Similarly in the Seacow River Valley of the Karoo Desert, Free State, Sampson has used the patterning of grass-tempered ceramics at thousands of sites to delimit the territories of mobile hunter-foragers, who had adopted and used ceramics in the Free State since the eighth century (Sampson 1988) and who continued into the European contact period of the early 1800s before they died out. He argues that although questions remain as to whether the Seacow Valley foragers in his archaeological study briefly owned small stock before the arrival of Khoi ceramics and pastoralists around the fourteenth century A.D., or whether or not they themselves descended in part from earlier herders, the archaeological data indicate a population of mobile hunter-foragers, operating independently at relatively high densities in an arid landscape.

THE ARCHAEOLOGY OF EASTERN AND CENTRAL AFRICA

In the Hadza region around Lake Eyasi, the best-known and dated site in this area is Mumba, a large rockshelter just west of Mang'ola on the lakeshore, opening to the northwest. While much of the deposit contains a dense accumulation of small quartz tools and food remains, the upper 10–20 cm includes a level with abundant potsherds and larger stone tools. This level is dated to ca. 1600 B.P. In addition, Mumba yielded a large series of burials (Braüer 1983) associated with stone tools and ostrich eggshell beads. The human remains appear not to cluster with the modern Sandawe on most of the plots, but rather with Nilotic peoples such as the Maasai or Nubians. Mumba may thus testify to the antiquity of forager-farmer relations in this area, if not to the maintenance of independence. In general, pastoral Neolithic adaptations appear to supplant LSA ones gradually by ca. 3,000 years ago in much of East Africa south of the Lake Turkana region (Ambrose 1998), where the transition is as much as 2,000 years earlier. As in the Dobe area and the southern African record, goats and sheep are the earliest domesticates, other than the dog, and evidence for cultivation is initially lacking. This is perhaps because of all the domesticated species other than the camel, which was not yet available as a domesticate, goats and sheep were less vulnerable to climatic downturns, more adaptable to different forage, and generally easier to care for than cattle.

Finally there is beginning to be a well-excavated and dated archaeological record of tropical forest regions in Africa that might shed light on the origins and history of its forager inhabitants. Three regions are of particular interest—the Virunga National Park in eastern D.R. Congo presently inhabited by Twa Pygmies in some areas, the Ituri Forest, and the site of Shum Laka in Cameroon, close to the northern margin of the forest, near the present habitat of Aka Pygmies. The most important conclusions of these three studies, as well as of another study of materials from closed canopy forest regions of Equatorial Guinea and Cameroon (Mercader and Marti 2000a, 2000b, in press), are that forager-based occupation precedes the advent of agriculture in the forest by more than 30,000 years. In the Ituri study (Mercader 1997; Mercader, Runge, et al. 2000; Mercader, García-Heras, and González-Álvarez 2000), phytolith analysis has demonstrated the continuous presence of a forest environment throughout the latter part of the Pleistocene, albeit with a more open canopy than at present, in association with archaeological debris. A second conclusion from burials unearthed at both Shum Laka and one of the Ituri sites, is that individuals whose stature is consistent with modern-day Pygmies occupied both these regions in antiquity. In Shum Laka two such individuals are dated to the LSA/ Neolithic transition, between 3300 ± 90 and 2940 ± 60 B.P. (Orban et al. 1996; Ribot et al. 2001), and are associated with stone and bone tools. In the Ituri the date is closer to 800 B.P. (Mercader et al. 2001) and the associated artifacts include rouletted ceramics and iron objects (Mercader, Rovira, and Gomez-Ramos 2000), implying a later Iron Age date, and possibly the existence of the types of client and/or symbiotic relationships between modern farmers and foragers of the Ituri.

In the Virunga National Park, which is largely composed of savanna and montane forests, new human remains dating to ca. 20–25,000 B.P. (Brooks and Smith 1987; Brooks, Smith, and Boaz 1989; Boaz, Brooks, and Pavlakis 1990; Mercader and Brooks 2001; Brooks et al., in press) were recovered from the lakeshore site of Ishango. Like other remains recovered from LSA levels at this site in the 1950s (Twiesselmann 1958), the individuals were tall and robust, and exhibited features such as the universal presence of septal aperture in all six humeri. In addition to the tall stature, the high frequency of this septal aperture may signal an affiliation with present-day Nilotic populations, who have the highest frequencies of this trait in modern Africa. Yet the archaeological record of Ishango is most comparable to that of the Ituri sites, although both the human remains and the habitat are different. We have argued elsewhere (Mercader and Brooks 2001) that this likely represents contacts between forest and savanna woodland peoples at a time when both were foragers. Ceramic and metals analysis suggests that the contact continued into the Iron Age (Mercader, García-Heras, and González-Álvarez 2000; Mercader, Rovira, and Gomez-Ramos 2000).

CONCLUSION: POINTS OF VIEW

In a return to some of the points raised in the opening section, we might well ask what factors influence whether foragers become assimilated and incorporated into a technologically dominant society, whether they cooperate but retain varying degrees of cultural and social independence, or whether they maintain a firm to hostile boundary against all encroachment by farmer-pastoralists. Why did the Pygmies lose their languages, but not the Hadzabe, the Sandawe, or many of the San? Within southern Africa, why is the degree of admixture and assimilation greatest in the southeast, and least in the northwest?

One major factor is the ability to hold onto separate territory either through strong political organization, or because the territory itself was not desired by competing groups and economic systems. This applies to the tsetse-infested, semiarid, and irrigation-dependent farming region of the Eyasi basin. It also applies to the Ituri, where even today many of the densest forest sectors are beyond the utilization zone of farmers, as well as to the drier regions of southern Africa, where pastoralism was impractical prior to borehole drilling except in very good years. The particularly deep water table of the Central Kalahari makes it impossible to dig wells by hand that intersect the water table. Hence the pattern of pastoral adaptation that dominated the Sahara with its relatively shallow aquifers could not be repeated easily in the Kalahari except along permanent watercourses such as the Okavango and Botletle. Farmer pastoralists appear first along these rivercourses and quickly come to dominate them. Several authors (e.g., Elphick 1975) argue that livestock herders then moved from the Okavango/Botletle down to the Cape, spreading Khoi languages related to the Central Bush group. These were soon followed by two groups of Bantu-speakers who similarly expanded through the well-watered areas of eastern South Africa and the river systems of Namibia and Botswana, but stopped at the effective limits of rainfall agriculture near the Fish River in the eastern Cape. Beyond this ecological frontier, Khoi pastoralism was uncertain enough and sparse enough on the landscape to allow room for hunter-gatherer adaptations in their midst and on their periphery. Even where hunter-gatherers have moved around as documented by Barnard (Chapter 9) and Köhler and Lewis (Chapter 11) for the forest, territorial identity is reestablished after the move. Laden (1992; Brooks and Laden n.d.) has described how Ituri Forest hunters "improve" their territories through the maintenance of forest trails and campsites known only to themselves. Guenther's paper demonstrates that sometimes a strong individual at the right time can affect the course of history, but only for a time.

The fact that the remaining foragers have, in most cases, a collective name for themselves and others like them, as opposed to their farmer neighbors of differing ethnicity, also provides a basis for the maintenance of ethnic identity. What is also important in all the cases studied is a sense of a shared culture and history, different from those of the surrounding peoples. This concept is reflected in the collective names, in religious practices, especially the trance dance of the Kalahari San, in cosmologies, origin myths and the like, as well as in a sense of identity with the natural world rather than opposition to it.

African lineage practices, especially patrilineal ones, have also contributed to both assimilation and independence, by removing the mixed-heritage children to, in many cases, the dominant group of the father, where they appear to share equal status with the children of farmer mothers. It is also interesting that some presumably cultural features, perhaps the complex of brideprice, female labor, and female inheritance of cattle in some cases, among the pastoral societies of east Africa, has kept them from assimilating the Hadzabe to the same extent as their Bantu-speaking farmer neighbors did. Indeed the data suggest that assimilation, for some reason, is easier in a farming society, since except for the forest peoples, most surviving African foragers who have practiced foraging in their lifetimes live among pastoralists, not primarily among rainfall agriculturalists.

Another factor is the flexibility and risk management systems of foragers, who try to pile up social capital and obligations through many different types of exchange and sharing relationships: gift-giving, naming, food-sharing, marriage, and labor. In the economy of the forager, any of these stocks might be worth more at a given time, and should be the one to be cashed in for the benefit. The literature of both European and Bantu-speaking farmers is full of references to foragers who worked faithfully for years and then just disappeared one day into the bush, never to return. The long-term occupation record of Dobe contains a gap during an extremely dry period in the 1950s, when little water was available and the Dobe group scattered to exploit other resources—some to relatives by birth or by marriage in other foraging areas, some to cattle posts of Bantu-speakers, some to the mines of South Africa. Most returned to Dobe when the rains returned, and took up their foraging lifeways again. Does this make them less than independent? I would argue that it does not.

Yet as we have discussed elsewhere (Brooks, Gelburd, and Yellen 1980), this same flexibility makes it difficult for foragers to commit to long-term agricultural lifeways. The hoarding of livestock and seed goes against the deepest values of the social order, which require the individual to develop a risk management strategy through human relationships rather than through stockpiling. The need to appoint leaders to resolve disputes that can no longer be avoided through fission, the emergence of greater divisions of labor, ownership, and male dominance, and the need to limit inheritance to preserve capital, all go against the egalitarian values of foragers. Most Kalahari and Ituri foragers end up in what the farmer-pastoralists see as dependent relationships as farm laborers rather than owners; disputes are resolved by the farmer rather than by the former foragers. From this position it is easier to maintain the social relationships that make it possible to slip back into foraging. In Hadza country as well, a missionary complained to me about the Hadzabe's unwillingness to seize economic opportunity and transform their lives. They seemed unable, he said, to form a political or an economic unit and decide who should be in charge, who should negotiate. Without such a transformation, there is little hope that their interests can be represented in the Tanzanian government.

Finally, it must be recognized that much of the revisionist debate is fueled by ethnographic bias on the part of the observers—not their own cultural biases, which most anthropologists try to detect and make explicit or compensate for, but by the biases of the eyes through which they view their data. Anthropologists have been less conscious (but see Turnbull 1960) of the need to set aside the prejudices of their main informants in a multicultural system, or of the people with whom they feel most at home. This feeling may be due to use of informants from that culture, to language competencies of the anthropologist, to the use of interpreters, or even to the local cultural affiliations of the anthropologist. Anthropological views on the independence from or dependence on farmers by foragers can depend on whether or not the anthropologist is working in the farmer language or operating from the farmer perspective or from the forager one. Wilmsen was drawn to Herero pastoralist culture, and allied himself in the field primarily with Herero—he learned their language as much or more than he learned to speak Ju/'hoansi. Lee, on the other hand, is most comfortable with the Ju/'hoansi, who echoed his radical sense of how property should be shared. Turnbull explicitly rejected earlier ethnographies of the Pygmies as biased by a perspective derived from the farmer societies, while Grinker, a member of the Harvard Ituri project whose members had questioned the long-term habitation of tropical forests by hunters and gatherers on ecological grounds, set out to balance Turnbull's views of Ituri hunter-gatherer independence by explicitly representing the Lese view.

Farmers nearly always view the foragers as subordinate and often inferior in status—in the 1960s the Tswana noun prefix for the Bushmen or "Sarwa" was "Ma" rather than "Ba" in the plural, connoting less than fully human status. This is not necessarily reciprocated, however, by a forager's belief in the superior status of the farmer. Farmers may view foragers living near them as dependents because they come around to scrounge some food in exchange for casual labor, while the foragers believe they are independent economic players, cleverly using a range of social skills to extract subsistence from every possible source, without investing heavily in any of them. Hence the relationships are asymmetrical, and cannot be described from only one side of the fence.

nine

The Complexities of
Association and Assimilation

An Ethnographic Overview

Alan Barnard and Michael Taylor

The various patterns of association and assimilation documented in the present volume call for explanation in terms of a wider framework of the inherent diversity subsumed by the category of people now labeled "Bushman," "San," "Basarwa," or "Khoe." This paper focuses both on that wider framework and on the contextualization of issues raised by other authors in this volume. We shall draw particularly on the comparative theoretical approach Barnard has employed in earlier work (e.g., Barnard 1992a) and on our understanding of the more recent sociopolitical dimensions of association and assimilation.

Contact with other ethnic groups has historically displayed a range of implications for foragers in southern Africa. Total assimilation has occurred, for example, with groups absorbed into coastal Nguni cultures over the last millennium. Domination and slavery in some parts of the Kalahari reduced some Basarwa to a distinct underclass. Yet, in other parts of the Kalahari, relative isolation (though, of course, never total isolation) has been maintained until recent years. Some groups have accepted periodic contact for purposes of trade, and others have chosen to live alongside Bantu-speakers, yet have retained a distinct identity. In the colonial and postcolonial eras, social, environmental, and political pressures have resulted in new forms of interaction.

An understanding of such recent changes can shed light on earlier points of contact and styles of contact, such as those implicated in the "Kalahari debate" (see, e.g., Barnard 1992b). An understanding of earlier changes and long-standing relations of symbiosis and of subjugation might also be of value in the struggle of contemporary groups to maintain their identities and develop their livelihood opportunities. Certainly these historical relations play a prominent role in the way many Bushmen today speak about their present circumstances. Thus the present and the past merge, as contemporary problems and historical ones, the practical and the theoretical, shed light upon each other.

ETHNIC DIVERSITY

In order to understand the dynamics and the complexity of association and assimilation, an excursion into the ethnic diversity of southern Africa's Bushmen populations is necessary. Ethnic diversity is here conceived according to two main factors: cultural difference (including cultural features related to environment and long-standing outside influence) and linguistic difference.

With regard to cultural difference, a number of groups, for example G/wi and G//ana of Botswana's Central Kalahari Game Reserve, have been essentially desert-dwelling people who have hunted and gathered for the bulk of their subsistence until just a few decades ago. //Anikhwe and Bugakhwe—so-called "River Bushmen" of the Okavango River area—hunted, gathered, and fished, and many have lived for extended periods in close association with neighboring agropastoralists. Shua and other groups in eastern Botswana have long herded livestock, both others' and their own (see map, Fig. 9.1).

With regard to linguistic difference, many groups speak languages of the Khoe group. These include Kūa studied by Susan Kent, various groups in eastern Botswana such as Shua, "River Bushmen" of the Okavango River and Delta, and Nharo and neighboring groups in western Botswana. Hai//om speak not a "Khoe Bushman" language, but Nama-Damara or Khoekhoe—the same Khoe language as herding peoples in Namibia. Non–Khoe-speaking "Bushmen" include !Kung or Ju/'hoansi in the northern Kalahari, as well as !Xoõ, and Eastern ≠Hoã, /'Auni and ≠Khomani, and other southern groups. The Khoe-speaking/non–Khoe-speaking distinction is important in marking a number of cultural differences, notably in aspects of kinship (Barnard 1992a:passim).

!Kung or Ju/'hoansi

The terms !Kung and Ju/'hoansi are widely known. Usage varies, but !Kung is generally taken to be the wider label, referring to all those from southern Angola to

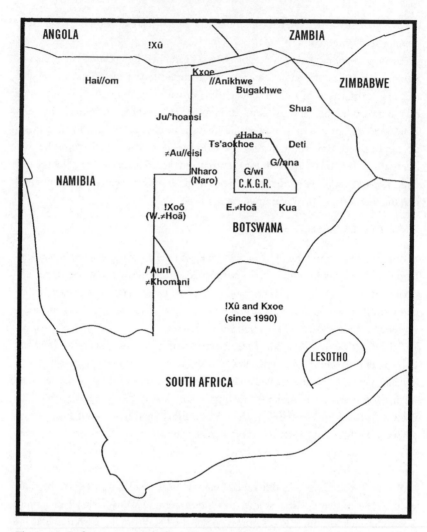

Figure 9.1. Bushman groups mentioned in the text.

central-western Botswana who speak !Kung or Ju/'hoansi dialects. In reality, this is the preferred term only of those who live in the far north, in Angola, while those commonly called !Kung in the works of writers such as Marshall (e.g., 1976, 1999) and Lee in his earlier works (e.g., 1979) tend to call themselves Ju/'hoansi or "real people" (cf. Lee 1993; and Lee's paper in the present volume).

It is useful to think of the population as a whole as consisting of three main ethno-linguistic groups—Ju/'hoansi proper or Central !Kung of northern Botswana and Namibia, !Xû or Northern !Kung of Angola, and ≠Au//eisi or Southern !Kung of the Ghanzi district of Botswana. The labels identify indigenously defined dialect areas, but they also correspond roughly to environmental zones. In total, the !Kung-speaking population may number as many as 25,000 or even 30,000. We shall concentrate here on Ju/'hoansi. ≠Au//eisi will de discussed below, together with Nharo whose former lands they now occupy. One migration worth noting here, however, is that of the !Xû soldiers, who, together with a number of Kxoe, had fought on the South African side in the Namibian war of liberation. In 1990 some 4,000 !Xû and Kxoe soldiers and their families were resettled at Schmidtsdrift, near Kimberley, South Africa. Since then a number of researchers have published academic articles on the challenges of this resettled community (see, e.g., Steyn 1994; Sharp and Douglas 1996), and with further resettlement and the recent development of new economic enterprises, academic interest in their situation is growing once again.

In many Ju/'hoansi areas there have been permanent water holes, and, until the 1960s, each band camped at one of these during the winter dry season. Often several bands, numbering on average some 25 people or more, shared the same permanent water hole and therefore the same winter location. Most water holes were, even then, also shared by Ovaherero and Batswana pastoralists apparently enjoying mutually beneficial relationships with resident Ju/'hoansi. Few permanent water holes remain, and most Ju/'hoansi today live all year round at the permanent water sources afforded by cattle-post and village boreholes. Band territories (termed n!oresi) overlapped, while areas without adequate resources were often unclaimed by any band. All this has changed greatly in many areas, first because of the disruption of the long Namibian war, especially in the 1980s (Marshall and Ritchie 1984), and later because of changes brought about by Namibian independence in 1990. Namibian independence brought about both beneficial new development efforts on the part of the government, and detrimental results of the return of Ovaherero pastoralists from their nearly 90-year exile in Botswana, as well as increased militarization in northern Namibia once again in the late 1990s.

While extensive social and environmental changes have affected Ju'/hoansi populations, there were also major changes in the perception of this Bushman group, in particular, brought about by the advent of the "Kalahari debate" which continues to this day. As Lee puts it so eloquently in his chapter: "Where earlier ethnographers saw bands, tribes, and chiefdoms, revisionists saw only peasants and proletarians enmeshed in the coils of merchant capital, or dominated by regional markets and states." Of course, both the images presented by the two sides, and the true situation of Bushmen themselves, are far more complicated than that. Were that not the case, the debate would never have generated either the number of publications it has or the interest in those publications among anthropologists, historians, and archaeologists across wide spectrums of these disciplines.

The extensive details from oral history that Lee (Chapter 7, this volume) provides give evidence that within living memory Ju/'hoansi were in far less contact with cattle-herders than in the 1960s when his own fieldwork revealed the presence of hundreds of cattle-herders using the same water holes as Ju/'hoansi. What is more, in the colonial period they felt themselves more autonomous than in recent history, in the sense that they could avoid the presence of other peoples and the authority of administrators and chiefs. It is often remarked that casual readers of some Ju/'hoansi ethnographies are left with the mistaken impression that these people live, or have lived until recently, in isolation both from other Bushman and from non-Bushmen. In fact, Lee does not suggest that this has been the case. As he notes, Ju/'hoansi have long lived in contact with Ovaherero, Batawana, and Bakgalagadi. They have shared their land, served as clients in patron/client relations, and traded with such people for centuries (see also, e.g., Tlou 1985:28–29, 52–54).

So where does this leave the "Kalahari debate"? At its simplest level, there are really two facets of understanding that are of relevance here. On the one hand, we have the consideration of historical fact, and on the other we have the matter of emphasis within ethnography, granting that all ethnography is by necessity always partial (cf. Strathern 1991). In reality, it is more complicated. Historical fact, like ethnography, is also a matter of interpretation. It could be that Lee's informants have misremembered. That does not mean that the "facts" necessarily go against him, but only that what may have been important to travelers or early ethnographers (such as the presence of cattle) is not so important to hunter-gatherers. There is indeed no reason for us to disbelieve either Lee's informants or the travelers and early ethnographers, which gives cause for rethinking the history of the area once again. The history of the Kalahari has not simply been an ever-increasing trend from isolation to assimilation, but one of both diversity and fluctuation as a result of warfare, cattle disease, environmental change, and a host of other factors. There is no doubt that Passarge's (1907) famous account, so important for Wilmsen's (1989) arguments, took place at an extraordinary and unrepeated time: that of the rinderpest epidemic of the late 1890s that decimated both the wildlife and cattle populations of Ngamiland.

Nharo and Related Groups and ≠Au//eisi

Nharo (Naro) live in the western part of Ghanzi district, mainly in the Ghanzi farms, and across the border in eastern Namibia. They number perhaps 9,000. In most Nharo areas there is a relatively good water supply, due partly to their locations along Ghanzi ridge. Bakgalagadi entered the territory in the early nineteenth century, and Afrikaners arrived to stay in the 1890s. To the northeast live Ts'aokhoe and some smaller groups, who are all closely related to Nharo. Natural water holes were very plentiful in the late nineteenth century, and were probably more numerous than in any other part of the Kalahari. Today, these have largely been replaced by farm and government boreholes. In the nineteenth century, Nharo generally spent the dry season camped at large permanent water holes and the wet season scattered among the seasonally filled pans. However, this pattern has changed as a result of the influx of ranchers over the past hundred years. Nharo settlements now are relatively permanent, although individuals often move freely from settlement to settlement within recognized territories that overlap the farm boundaries.

The first permanent white settlers arrived in Ghanzi in 1898, but the most drastic changes seem to have occurred since the early 1960s when the system of land tenure was changed from leasehold to freehold and the farms underwent a period of expansion. During this period farms were fenced, better-quality livestock were brought in, engine-pump boreholes were introduced, and for the first time, farm workers came to be paid in cash. The abundance of boreholes led to the formation of smaller bands—sometimes only a single nuclear family at each borehole (see, e.g., Barnard 1980; Guenther 1986a). Newer farmers increased the density of livestock, brought in high-velocity rifles (and killed off much of the game), and hired Bakgalagadi and Batswana herdsmen in preference to the indigenous Nharo. Thus many Nharo, who had by this time become part-time herdsmen, lost the opportunity to work, but also found hunting and gathering increasingly difficult because of the scarcity of vegetable resources or game animals in the area. As Guenther (Chapter 5, this volume) notes, this led to increasing dependence on farmers.

As Guenther also notes, many patterns associated with Nharo and ≠Au//eisi culture persisted into the second half of the twentieth century. This is despite contact with white farmers since the 1890s and with Bakgalagadi, Batawana, and Barolong pastoralists for much longer. Guenther's focus is mainly historical, concentrating on the general trajectory of change during and since the nineteenth century. Comparing his fieldwork with Barnard reveals the diversity within the western Ghanzi district. During his fieldwork in the 1970s, for example, Barnard found Nharo of the Hanahai Valley who retained distinct aspects of settlement, subsistence, and kinship. Barnard worked mainly on the southern edge of the Ghanzi farms, where during years of abundant resources (such as the mid-1970s) it was possible for Nharo to hunt and gather extensively even within the farming area. Guenther began work a few years before and his fieldwork was mainly at D'Kar, a mission-owned farm in the interior of the farming area, where there had even then been a closer association between Nharo and others, as well as a far greater dependence on nonwild foods.

Guenther also comments on the reports of Heinrich Schinz, Siegfried Passarge, Dorothea Bleek and others on the territoriality of the Nharo in the late nineteenth and early twentieth centuries. This is borne out in more recent times, even where Nharo groups have been resettled. Barnard (1986:48–50) has noted that Nharo from different band clusters settled at Hanahai (where they occupy separate settlements according to place of origin) were in 1980s buying and selling meat across historical band-cluster boundaries, whereas they shared meat within the confines of band clusters. The former large-scale territorial boundaries had become localized, and territoriality manifested as social (sharing) exclusion.

As Guenther says, foraging continued through the twentieth century, coupled with a transfer of the dependency relationship from Batswana and Bakgalagadi (and some Nama) overlords to white (mainly Afrikaans-speaking) ones. Yet this did not mark a greater degree of acculturation. Quite the contrary, the evidence for the Kalahari as a whole suggests that close association between Bushman and their black neighbors has led to greater social change than where the overlords are white (cf. Barnard and Widlok 1996). This contradicts earlier assumptions, such as that implicit in Silberbauer's *Bushman Survey Report* (1965:114–138), that suggest degrees of acculturation ranging from independent, to dependent on black agro-pastoralists, to dependent on white farmers. Not only is the situation more complicated than that, both historically and in the present (there are of course black farmers as well as white); there is no reason to assume that whites should bring any greater pressure for change. Perhaps the most telling note from Guenther's paper concerns the penchant for Bushmen to see "history" in terms of myths of origin, of racial and cultural differences in which animals represent *khoe* ("human" or especially "Bushman") pitted against Batswana or Afrikaners. This strikes us as an indication, on the part of Guenther's informants at least, of a vision of history in which primordial categories and great events are used to explain, or make sense of, the transitions that individuals observe in their own lifetimes.

Susan Kent (Chapter 6, this volume) points to several effects of contact between whites and foraging populations in southern Africa. What is striking is the diversity of white contact and the diverse effects that that contact had. While some whites killed Bushmen for sport, others tried to convert them to Christianity or assimilate them to Western ways. As European-introduced diseases spread, so too (albeit later) did Western medicine. The intolerance she reports has been rife throughout the history of whites in southern Africa, but some degree of symbiosis is to be found too even in cases where the economic domination of whites is obvious. What is striking about the writings on the Ghanzi farms is that where one author may emphasize conflict and marginality (e.g., Guenther 1986a) another, commenting on exactly the same time period, may emphasize benevolence and mutual respect (e.g., Russell and Russell 1979). Here again, the answer may lie in the great diversity of forms of interaction, even in such a relatively small area as the Ghanzi farms.

G/wi and G//ana

G/wi and G//ana are long-standing inhabitants of Botswana's Central Kalahari Game Reserve. Some who live in the Reserve also call themselves Kūa, an ethnic label more commonly associated with Basarwa to the south.

G/wi came to prominence in the 1960s through the work of George Silberbauer, who was then Ghanzi District Commissioner and Bushman Survey Officer. He served for six years in those posts, spending some three years, beginning in 1958, among G/wi at Xade (≠Xade) pan. This pan became the site of Silberbauer's borehole, in the south-central part of the Reserve. At least until the late 1970s, the Xade area was even known colloquially among Basarwa on the Ghanzi farms as "Silberbauer's farm." After Silberbauer, a number of ethnographers followed, notably Jiro Tanaka, Kazuyoshi Sugawara, Kazunobu Ikeya, and other Japanese scholars.

The Central Kalahari Game Reserve extends over more than 50,000 square kilometers and includes three diverse environmental zones: in the north, an zone of sand dunes with many species of trees and shrubs and large herds of migratory game; in the central area, a zone of flat bushveld; and in the south, a more heavily wooded zone. Only the southern and central zones contain enough edible plants to support permanent occupation. In the early 1960s G/wi band territory sizes were about the same as Ju/'hoansi ones, ranging in size from some 450 to 1,000 square kilometers, although their population size was somewhat larger, with an average of 57 people per band (Silberbauer 1972:295).

As studies by Tanaka (e.g., 1987) and others have shown, many changes have taken place in the Reserve since the time Silberbauer describes in his major publications. With the migration into the Reserve of several G//ana bands in the late 1960s, settlement patterns apparently became more flexible. Then with the drought of the late 1970s and early 1980s, many Central Kalahari Bushman bands migrated, at least seasonally, to areas outside the Reserve where borehole water and food distributed through Botswana's drought relief program were available. Despite legislation forbidding livestock in the Reserve, the number of donkeys and goats being kept by residents within the Reserve steadily increased through the 1970s and 1980s. Together with the increased human population, this put considerable pressure on the water and environmental resources around Xade. This is one of the reasons given as to why the Botswana government began in 1984 expressing its wish to remove the residents of Xade from the Reserve. Also of interest in this context are some of Ikeya's studies (e.g., 1993, 1996a, 1996b), which have shown that neither goat raising, nor handicraft production, nor attempts to cultivate melons and other crops have resulted in a transformation of the system of distribution or the value of sharing among G//ana and G/wi. Ikeya argues from detailed quantitative evidence that, in their eyes, wage labor is not a substitute for the maintenance of a flexible subsistence strategy; it is part of it.

Sugawara (Chapter 4, this volume) describes a number of changes that have taken place in the Reserve since the Botswana government's enforcement of the Tribal Grazing Land Policy in 1979. These often interrelated changes included the adoption of (illegal) equestrian hunting, the rapid increase in the number of goats, migration to and concentrated settlement around the borehole at !Koi!kom, and growing dependence on government handouts. Among G/wi and G//ana, even names have been changed to Setswana forms, though it must be said that naming customs among these people do not play a central role in kinship and social identity in the same way as among, for example, Nharo or Ju/'hoansi (cf. Barnard 1992a:48–50, 150–152).

Sugawara relates a number of narratives on relations between Kūa (G/wi and G//ana) on the one hand, and Bakgalagadi and ≠Kebe (people of mixed ancestry) on the other. It is important to note that the term Kūa is used here as a generic tem for "Bushmen" or "Basarwa" rather than specifically for the group from Khutse studied by Susan Kent. As Sugawara's narratives demonstrate, Bakgalagadi frequently exercise dominance over and even violence toward these Kūa in the Reserve area, in which both groups have lived for decades if not centuries (cf. Valiente-Noailles 1993:140–151).

The greatest changes have occurred since the resettlement of the majority of the population of Xade at Kx'oensakene (New ≠Xade or New Xade) in 1997. Sugawara notes with regret that the G/wi and G//ana strategy of "opportunistic subordination" involved in such a move is bound to fail, given the power of government and difficulty of understanding the intentions of this abstract alien entity—intentions which are indeed obscure even to its own agents.

Eastern and Northern Khoe Groups

The Eastern Khoe Bushmen comprise a number of groups scattered from the Kweneng District in the south to Ngamiland in the north. They may number as many as 50,000. Most live in the Central District, often as clients of Bamangwato, Bakgalagadi, Kalanga, and Ovaherero. The cultural (as opposed to linguistic) distinction between Central and Eastern Khoe Bushmen is a nebulous one, and in this regard it is useful to include among "Eastern" groups some G//ana who have migrated from the Central Kalahari Game Reserve to take up a more settled life among the cattle-herders to the south and east. The salient characteristics of "Eastern" groups, in this sense, are their association with herding people and their high degree of cultural and spatial association.

The Kalahari fringe area has drawn the attention of revisionist archaeologists (e.g., Denbow 1984, 1986). Of great significance is the fact that this archaeological work points to contacts between hunter-gatherer and herder-cultivator populations extending back over several centuries. This means that the Basarwa of the Kalahari fringe may be regarded not so much as recently acculturated, but as possessing a hybrid culture of some antiquity. Archaeological findings suggest a long period of contact and a clear association with the Great Zimbabwe culture, beginning over 1,000 years ago.

East of the Central Kalahari Game Reserve is a large population of mainly sedentary Bushmen who, like the Central Kalahari Bushmen, speak Khoe languages, but unlike the Central Kalahari Bushmen, are heavily integrated into the economies of Batswana and Kalanga (Hitchcock 1978). The Bushman groups there include the Shua, Deti, and others, who have lived in the area for centuries, and some G//ana who have migrated into the area in recent years. Estimates of Bushmen in this area vary from 8,000 to over 30,000, depending on, among other factors, whether individuals of Bushman descent who have lost either their original language or a predominantly hunting and gathering lifestyle are included.

In addition to their material difficulties, the Bushmen of eastern Botswana also face ideological ones. The cultural definition of Bushmen by Setswana society generally is that of low-status, poor, and marginal people. Bushmen own very few cattle, the most important prestige commodity in Setswana culture. Therefore, Bushman men in particular lack economic independence and their status tends to be defined accordingly. They are associated with the cattle post and the bush, and thus deprived of any significant role in village life (Motzafi 1986). The situation in the Kweneng District, immediately south of the Central Kalahari Game Reserve, is similar, although patron-client relationships are more recent in that region.

Bugakhwe, //Anikhwe, and Kxoe live on the riverine fringes of the northern Kalahari, and together number some 8,000 individuals (Brenzinger 1997). Although they have a long history of contact—even extensive intermarriage—with Bantu-speakers, this contact did not initially result in subordination to the extent experienced by many Bushmen elsewhere (Taylor 2000). In northern Botswana, most contact (in the eighteenth and nineteenth centuries) was with Bayei, characterized by Livingstone (1857:56) as "Quakers of the body politic in Africa." In contrast to the encounters between Bushmen and Bantu-speakers elsewhere, Bayei and Basarwa interacted on terms that were generally equal and amicable.

Stories of origin in the northern sandveld tell of an initial relationship of equality and mutual cooperation between Basarwa and Bayei. In most such stories told by Bushmen elsewhere, the separation between Basarwa hunter-gatherers and Bantu-speaking agropastoralists is spoken of as being due to the strength and trickery of Bantu-speakers (cf. Biesele 1986:321–323 [for Ju/'hoansi]; Guenther 1989:65–68 [for Nharo]; Widlok 1999:46–56 [for Hai//om]). In northern Botswana, however, Basarwa instead speak of a relationship of mutual cooperation between Khara/'uma, the first Mosarwa, and the first Moyei. Furthermore, many Bayei refer to Basarwa in a generic sense as their "uncles" (mothers' brothers) as an acknowledgment not only of Basarwa being "first people," but also of many Bayei having Basarwa ancestors.

Whereas most Bantu-speakers took Basarwa women whose subsequent offspring were then raised as their own, intermarriage took place in both directions between

Bayei and Basarwa, with Basarwa men taking Bayei wives and vice versa. The taking of non-Basarwa women by Basarwa men has not been common, but those examples documented have all involved (usually sedentary) northern Khoe: between Kxoe and Ovambo in northern Namibia (Gordon 1992:214); between Zama and Sekele / Mbukushu/Guangares/Mbuela in Angola (Almeida 1965); between Kxoe and Mbukushu/Mbwela (Köhler 1989b:395ff, 427ff); and between Ts'exa and Bayei (Taylor 2000:42). Following the predominant pattern of virilocal (patrilocal) residence, children from such relationships have usually been brought up in the father's social milieu, therefore regarding themselves as Bushmen.

In contrast to these generally amicable relations, the rise of the Batawana kingdom in Ngamiland in the second half of the nineteenth century was marked by severe forms of violence against local Basarwa populations. While this was not unusual in the very hierarchically organized Setswana-speaking kingdoms of the nineteenth century (see, e.g., Morton 1994), the degree by which Batawana were outnumbered in Ngamiland by the populations they attempted to subjugate prompted particular excesses (Taylor 2000:48, 52–54), with Basarwa receiving the brunt of such violence. The response of many Basarwa at this time was to simply move beyond the reach of the Batawana state, enabled by kinship networks extending over vast distances, and consequent fluidity in the membership of territory-based social groups. However, fleeing was tantamount to surrendering claim to the land on which they lived, a cost that many Basarwa did not want to pay for the opportunity to escape subjugation. Together with a combination of Batawana hegemony that to an extent naturalized a strong social hierarchy, along with the strategic use of terror, Batswana achieved a feat that Morton (1994:239) points out was almost unique in Africa: that of reducing their immediate neighbors to bondage.

As Sadr (Chapter 2, this volume) points out, a number of writers have touched on the question of how one might distinguish in the archaeological record between isolated or encapsulated foragers and those subjugated by agropastoralists. However, his is one of the few studies to concentrate specifically on the transition from precontact hunting and gathering, to postcontact hunting and gathering, to the subjugation of a hunter-gatherer community by a herding population. Interestingly, he points out that subjugation would seem to be a temporary condition. In the Kweneng district (where his main concern lies) and elsewhere, Bushmen accepted their status as serfs when it suited them, and engaged in independent livelihoods when that suited them. The situation is complicated in the Kweneng case, due partly to well-documented trade relations in the nineteenth century. Sadr's confirmation of a continuity of material culture in the area until definite signs of occupation by non–hunter-gatherers suggests that foraging culture may have endured long after first contact and simply been replaced in the twentieth century, perhaps even with Bantu-speakers taking over the caves occupied for millennia by hunter-gatherers.

!Xoõ, /'Auni, and ≠Khomani

!Xoõ are few in number and call themselves by a huge variety of different names. !Xoõ (!Xõ) is the most common, along with ≠Hoã in the east and Tshasi in the south. They are known to the outside world mainly through the linguistic work of Anthony Traill and the anthropological publications of the late H. J. Heinz, whose superb 1966 M.A. thesis detailed their social organization (published as Heinz 1994).

!Xoõ live in a poor environment, and for that reason have been in many respects less influenced by pastoralist expansion than groups elsewhere in Botswana. They live mainly at water holes and boreholes in the west-central Kalahari, west of the Central Kalahari Game Reserve and south of Ghanzi ridge. Thus they do come into considerable contact both with the sparse pastoralist populations of the area and—until the trans-Kalahari highway was finished in 1997—with those engaged in cattle drives across the Kalahari. The population numbers only about 3,000. Heinz (e.g., 1994:49–114) described them as being highly "territorial," as having clearly defined band cluster territories with strips of "no-man's-land" between them, and with all three levels of their social organization—the family, the band, and the band cluster—territorially based.

/'Auni and ≠Khomani are the tiny population groups of the Kalahari Gemsbok National Park in South Africa, near the Namibian and Botswana borders. They were long ago linguistically absorbed into other population groups, notably the Nama and the Afrikaans-speaking "coloured" population of the Northern Cape. They were the subject of intensive investigations by a number of scholars in the early part of the twentieth century, especially in the 1930s, and the journal *Bantu Studies* devoted two issues to the apparently dwindling population. However, in 1982 and 1983 H. P. Steyn visited the area and found a remnant population still hunting and gathering (see Steyn 1984). Some still identified themselves as ≠Khomani, though all members of the community then spoke Nama. They gathered *tsama* melons and hunted gemsbok and smaller, nonmigratory game. The continued existence of this group, in such a poor environment, shows the resilience and adaptability of Bushman populations.

Hai//om

Hai//om inhabit northern areas of Namibia, where they live in contact with white farmers and Ovambo agropastoralists. Thomas Widlok began intensive research on social change and economic relations among Hai//om in 1990. One of his findings is the discovery of what he calls an "inverse *mafisa*" system (Widlok 1999:113–118). In Botswana, the people who receive *mafisa* cattle to look after for others are generally less well off, often Basarwa. However, in the "inverse *mafisa*" system the poorer

Hai//om lend their livestock to wealthy Ovambo, who get to keep not only the milk but even the offspring of these animals. Why do Hai//om do it? It enables them to own livestock, but still to move about freely; and more significantly, it enables them to stave off traditional requests for sharing within their community, because their wealth in livestock is deposited elsewhere. Without this system, Hai//om would be under great pressure from relatives to slaughter their animals. The existence of both systems highlights the complexity of hunter/herder relations and draws attention to the fact that such relations can differ greatly across southern Africa.

Take another example. Whereas Sadr for the Kweneng district (Chapter 2, this volume) suggests the possibility of a radical and recent transformation from foraging to farming in one specific site, in other places gradual and even seasonal transformation would seem to be the norm. The latter is exemplified, for example, by G//ana of the eastern Central Kalahari Game Reserve, who for more than 120 years, and until very recently, spent the wet season in migrations within overlapping band territories in the reserve, and when necessary the dry season living on the more favorable water resources in Central district, east of the Reserve (Cashdan 1984). In an even more extreme case, some Hai//om live isolated in small groups, hunting small game and gathering mangetti nuts in the dry season, and living a farming lifestyle in the wet season (Widlok 1999:74–79; 165–170; Barnard and Widlok 1996:95–98). In this case, they frequently also commit themselves to seasonal labor for Ovambo—rather as in the classic style of Central African hunter-gatherers on the edge of agricultural villages (cf. the chapter by Köhler and Lewis).

POLITICAL RELATIONS AND BUSHMAN IDENTITY

As Kent (Chapter 3, this volume) suggests, there is a tendency in some revisionist writing to assume that hunter-gatherers not only borrowed from other cultures, but even abandoned their own cultures when they interacted with larger politico-economic units. She compares southern African hunter-gatherers in this regard to Efe Pygmies and to African American slaves of the eighteenth and nineteenth centuries. There can be no doubt that, of these three examples, Bushmen have been the least affected by the dominant forces that have over the last several centuries surrounded them. Kent maintains that changes in the archaeological record of southern African hunter-gatherer sites shows continuity, and not necessarily assimilation, enslavement, or extermination. Alison Brooks's pleas for a recognition of diversity in the archaeological record (Chapter 8, this volume) add further support to this assertion. There is also ample historical evidence that in some areas Bushmen and Bantu-speakers lived in close proximity, yet maintained distinct identities and patterns of living. This was commented upon, for example, on the peripheries of the Okavango Delta by Livingstone (1857:69), Selous (1893:141–143),

Gibbons (1904:202), and Hurwitz (1956). Contact has not necessarily entailed either assimilation or subjugation.

Although the different linguistic and cultural groupings into which Bushmen can be categorized remain pertinent today, they are more and more being drawn as "Bushmen" (or "Basarwa" or "San") into an overarching political economy that includes all citizens. Their place in these national contexts is often structured by their status as Bushmen. To take the example of Botswana, Basarwa have long been stigmatized by their pastoralist neighbors as "people of the bush," seen to be lacking in key attributes—particularly *molao* ("law" / "civilization")—that would give them social standing. In independent Botswana, a country that has prided itself on its rapid economic growth and social change over the last three decades, Basarwa are seen by many of their neighbors as an embarrassment, an inappropriate reminder of a past best forgotten. Their status therefore promotes a form of domination that attempts not to subjugate or enslave them as was common in the nineteenth century, but attempts to acculturate Basarwa into "mainstream" society. Comprehensive attempts are made by the Botswana government to discourage key cultural markers associated with Basarwa, such as hunting and gathering, and encourage Basarwa to adopt the norms and form of a dominant Setswana "culture." Behind this policy lies the assumption that the resultant assimilation will mark an end to the "Basarwa problem."

Derek Heater, a political scientist commenting on European nationalism, has commented that there were six ways in which, as he puts it, "the anomaly of minorities in a nationalist age" (Heater 1990:59) could be handled: toleration, conversion, discrimination, persecution, expulsion, or annihilation. Sadly, all of these have occurred with reference to foraging populations in southern Africa, though certainly annihilation has never been seen as a "solution" in Botswana. Since independence, toleration, and conversion have alternately been practiced in various branches of government, while discrimination has been common in the country at large, if not among bureaucrats. Today, persecution and (internal) expulsion are at least what the world sees when mention is made of Botswana's dealings with Basarwa. We are thinking specifically of the G/wi, G//ana, and others from the Central Kalahari Game Reserve. It is a peculiar irony that this reserve, established in the last few years of colonial rule for the protection of Basarwa, should over the last decade have been the subject of so much effort to exclude them. In terms of land, toleration has increasingly given way to attempts at cultural conversion in what, to Basarwa, is the most blatant possible way—removal and reestablishment in land which is not their own. There is, of course, nothing unique about Botswana here; this is a common way of treating minorities, especially poor minorities perceived as otherwise nonthreatening to the majority and the state.

By classifying populations as "Remote Area Dwellers," for over twenty years the

Botswana government has both denied those classified that way their several and distinct identities (G/wi, Nharo, etc.) and prevented them from forming effective political opposition. Botswana is one of the few African countries that is comparable to the archetypal European nation, with a numerical and culturally dominant majority and both economically advantaged and economically disadvantaged small minorities. In such cases, the crucial factor is whether one perceives one's primary identity as ethnic or national. The result of these differing perspectives of identity is a diametrically opposite understanding of the state, either as a protector of shared values of the larger society) or as a usurper of such values (of the indigenous minorities).

As early as 1986, it was predicted that the ethnic identity of Bushmen, both as members of a collective category of "Bushmen" and members of specific Bushman groups, would increase rather than decrease along with their incorporation into wider social structures (Barnard 1988:24). This prediction, especially with regard to collective Bushman identity, is gradually proving correct. What could not have been predicted is that that is equally true of the even wider category "Khoisan." This hitherto exogenous, anthropologists' label has become a mark of identity for people classified by governments and by themselves as members of several distinct groups, or even as members of no distinct cultural group at all.

DIVERSITY AND ADAPTATION

A prominent characteristic of Bushman cultures is adaptation, both to the natural environment and to changing social conditions. The latter form of adaptation is not as different from the former as it may at first appear. Foraging, as a subsistence technique, is by its very nature an adaptive process. Bushmen, like anyone else, change subsistence strategies to suit available resources. These changes can be relatively permanent, as when groups permanently migrate, or relatively temporary, for example because of seasonal or other short-term changes in the availability of resources. Adaptations to social changes can also be relatively permanent, or more commonly, at least until very recently, temporary ones. Seasonal labor and even long-term clientship of Bushmen among agropastoral peoples are common examples. These do not preclude the return to hunting and gathering, or necessarily destroy their social fabric, although the pressures for permanent change have been very strong indeed since the late 1970s when severe drought for nearly two decades threatened livelihoods throughout southern Africa. Coupled with increasing legal restrictions on hunting, this left an entire generation without the ability to gather wild food, as they had learned to depend on other sources and had neither the necessity nor the inclination to reply on the wild plants their parents and grandparents had lived on.

The most recent developments suggest that politics, rather than assimilation, will be the way forward. For example, the 1999/2000 report of the Working Group for

Indigenous Minorities in Southern Africa (WIMSA; 2000:23–25, 43) contains a list of 20 member organizations. Nine of these organizations are in Namibia, nine in Botswana, and two in South Africa. These organizations report on a number of issues, but two stand out as being overwhelmingly problematic: land and leadership (WIMSA 2000:15–17). There was some good news. The South African government had decided to recognize the ≠Khomani claim to their ancestral land in the Kalahari Gemsbok National Park. The same government had also purchased land for the exiled !Xû and Khoe communities living near Kimberley since 1990. The Namibian government had finally granted rights to land, under Namibia's Community Based Natural Resource Management (CBNRM) program, in the Nyae Nyae area. There was also bad news. The representative of First People of the Kalahari reported a negative attitude on the part of Botswana government officials on plans to map traditional areas of the Central Kalahari Game Reserve. The East Hanahai Naro (Nharo) representative reported on the desperate need for land to be restocked with game in order to reclaim the possibility of hunting. On leadership, details were not as forthcoming, but the long-standing squabbles within communities over financial matters and leaders' roles in them seemed to be continuing.

Taylor's recent research (Taylor 2000), alongside similar research by Twyman (1998) and Sullivan (1999), has indicated that struggles for land and resource rights by Bushmen are set to be increasingly conducted within the framework afforded by CBNRM programs. Initiated throughout southern Africa in the 1990s, these programs are aimed at enabling residents of rural areas to have a greater degree of management control over the natural resources in their vicinity. Although the extent to which management is actually decentralized is often decidedly limited in practice, CBNRM programs have provided a forum in which, for the first time in many places, debate on land rights is opened up on the local level between residents and government officials. Despite comprising a very small minority of southern Africa's overall populations, the fact that Bushmen generally live in remote areas means that they have a disproportionately high representation in such programs.

The importance of the nascent CBNRM programs, however, lies not only in the opportunity it presents to address resource rights. As participation requires the formation of local Community-Based Organizations, it encourages *political* organization on the local level, which then can become a channel for motivating for a broad range of political rights from the government. CBNRM also provides the opportunity for Bushmen to use their knowledge and local resources to engage in economic activities, particularly tourism enterprises—an issue that has aroused the interest of several commentators (e.g., Hitchcock 1997; ≠Oma and Thoma 1998; Guenther, in press). Undertaken on their own terms, involvement in tourism can provide an opportunity for not only financial reward, but also increased visibility and the expression and reformulation of history and identity in public arenas.

Ironically, far from marking the end of Bushman culture, the adaptation to new forms of economic activity could help some groups of Bushmen to compete against the pressures placed on them by drought, population expansion, and the encroachment of other groups. It is difficult to escape the reality that Bushmen will not always be pure hunter-gatherers. The survival of their cultures has, for thousands of years, depended on their ability to adapt, and the current trends toward livestock rearing and more intense involvement in economic activities are perhaps best seen in this light. The tragedy is that the current pressures on Bushman groups are much more serious than ever before, giving an urgency, as never before, that research with Bushmen must be oriented toward addressing these issues.

CONCLUSION

Marlowe (Chapter 10, this volume) makes an interesting point when he asks whether foragers cease to be "true foragers" when they have contact with nonforagers. As he suggests, some writers seem to think this is the case, in spite of evidence to the contrary. For example, among the Hadza and northern Khoe, long and extensive contact with outsiders has not affected the ability of such populations to keep a foraging ethos and lifestyle. Marlowe criticizes those on the revisionist side of the Kalahari debate, but it seems to us that both sides could be equally to blame. Anthropologists generally seem to expect a greater degree of cultural "purity" among foragers or hunter-gatherers than they do among other populations (see Barnard 1989). It is as if exposure to a nonforaging lifestyle should inevitably lead to cultural corruption and social instability.

Of course, this is not the case—as many of the chapters in this book show. Rather, what leads to social instability is the domination of outside forces, whether these be from the natural environment, from governments or nongovernmental organizations, traditional political authorities or military organizations, or more particularly from population groups whose lifestyle infringes on that of foragers or former foragers. It is not contact which is relevant or even trade; it is domination. Domination and subjugation come in different degrees, and have diverse affects when coupled with other factors such as the availability of water, of shops, or wage labor. Only by recognizing the complexity of the issue can we hope either to make new contributions to the now old "Kalahari debate" or to be of relevance to those former foragers caught up by these dominating forces.

ten

Why the Hadza Are Still Hunter-Gatherers

Frank Marlowe

For several years there has been a heated disagreement over the status of forag-ers in southern Africa, what has come to be called the Kalahari debate. One side argues that when first studied, the Ju/'hoansi (Dobe !Kung, or !Kung San) ap-proximated pristine foragers, "on the threshold of the Neolithic" (Lee 1972:352). The other side argues they were (along with other San speakers), dominated, enserfed, or enslaved by their Bantu pastoralist neighbors, possibly even ex-pastoralists them-selves, forced into foraging because they had lost their herds (Wilmsen 1989). Much of the debate turns on the issue of contact between the Ju/'hoansi and non-foragers (Wilmsen 1989; Wilmsen 1993; Wilmsen and Denbow 1990; Lee and Guenther 1995). From the perspective of the Hadza (also called Hadzabe, Hadzapi, Hatsa, Tindiga, Watindiga, Kindiga, Kangeju, Western Hadza: Wahi), a foraging society in East Africa with whom I work, this concern with contact seems exagger-ated. That is because the Hadza have had contact with nonforagers at least for the past century and yet they have persisted as foragers, in many respects I will argue, little changed. By examining the case of the Hadza, I hope to shed some light on the broader issues at stake in the Kalahari debate.

To one looking in from the outside, the most interesting question raised by the Kalahari debate is perhaps the extent to which foragers in the ethnographic record are useful models of preagricultural societies. Revisionists such as Wilmsen (1989, 1993) have argued that the picture of the Ju/'hoansi portrayed by Lee (1979), which has become such a standard model of Pleistocene life, is a myth. Based largely on arguments about contact with nonforagers, Wilmsen claims the Ju/'hoansi would be better described as the rural proletariat who are denied access to other means of production, than as pristine foragers. If contact with nonforagers is so important, perhaps only the earliest descriptions of some Australian, Andamanese, and Arctic societies would qualify as candidates for uncontaminated models of the past.

But how crucial is contact with nonforagers? Does even the slightest degree of contact with nonforagers mean a foraging society ceases to be 'true foragers'? This seems to be what revisionists imply. They claim, however, to be challenging the very notion of contemporary foragers as models of the past. Wilmsen and Denbow (1990) criticize Lee for describing the Ju/'hoansi as being "on the threshold of the Neolithic," saying, "Surely to remain among the few representatives of a way of life that everyone else gave up 10,000 years ago is to be a living fossil. If one has a history one is not on the threshold of an earlier time; one may forage and do nothing else without retaining an atavistic forager mentality and without being any more representative of foragers 10,000 years ago than are modern Bantu agropastoralists" (1990:503). That may well be possible, but it seems far more likely the Ju are more representative of foragers 10,000 years ago than are modern Bantu agropastoralists.

For one critical of the very notion of 'pristine,' Wilmsen seems to reify it. His insistence that contact with nonforagers invalidates Lee's picture of the Ju/'hoansi implies that lack of contact would at least be necessary, if not sufficient for contemporary foragers to be good models of the past. The importance of contact depends on what one wants to study. For example, even secondary foragers who once owned cows might be a valid society in which to study how individuals allocate their time when they must hunt and gather all their food rather than cultivate it. They may be less instructive regarding traits subject to strong cultural inertia. Certainly it is true, as the revisionists argue, that time has not stood still for foragers, even for those without contact, and the living-fossil idea has rightly been challenged. However, since some foragers like the Hadza have continued to forage long after they have been in contact with agriculturalists, we must entertain the possibility that many other aspects of their lifestyle have also remained unchanged. Often contact does spell the end of foraging but not always; when it does not, we must ask why not, and we must ask what other traits are conserved. Here, I use the case of the Hadza to explore those issues and answer the question, "Why are the Hadza still hunter-gatherers?"

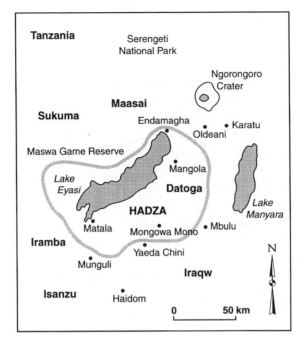

Figure 10.1. Map of Hadza area.

THE HADZA

The Hadza are hunter-gatherers who live in the eastern Rift Valley in northern Tanzania. In many ways they resemble the Ju/'hoansi of Botswana (Lee 1984) as they were until the 1970s. Not only do they have a similar tool kit, hunt many of the same animals and gather some of the same plants, live in almost identical huts, and have a similar mating system, but they speak a language with clicks. These clicks (and some etymologies) have caused many researchers to classify them together with southern African Khoisan speakers (Bleek 1931; Fleming 1986; Ruhlen 1991; but see Woodburn 1977; Sands 1995). Recent evidence suggests that unlike the click language of the Sandawe (who live a mere 130 km to the south of the Hadza), which is related to San languages, Hadzane (the Hadza language) may be a linguistic isolate, only very distantly related to San languages (Sands 1995). Hadzane is not at all related to any language of the immediate neighbors of the Hadza, a fact that suggests the Hadza have maintained a considerable degree of autonomy.

The Hadza population has been increasing slightly since 1900 and today is about 1,000 (Blurton Jones et al. 1992). The Hadza live around Lake Eyasi, a large salt-water lake that almost completely dries up in the dry season. About 250 live to the west of the lake and have been little studied. The other 750 live to the east of the lake in an area about 2,500 km² (Fig. 10.1). Although both groups come and go freely, it is the Eastern Hadza I will describe here since I know them best. Among the Eastern Hadza, about 200–300 still live almost exclusively from hunting game, collecting honey, digging tubers, and gathering berries and baobab fruit (Marlowe 1999). The remaining 450–550 Eastern Hadza shift between foraging and various other activities. Some Hadza guard the maize fields of their neighbors from animals, especially vervets and baboons, receiving maize in return, as well as eating the meat of the monkeys they kill. Some Hadza do labor on the two large European farms in the Mangola area. From time to time, a Hadza may work as a game scout or work for the game department. A few Hadza have paid government positions as community development officers. A growing number of Hadza depend on tourist money. Because I have been interested in studying foragers, I have spent most of my time with those Hadza least assimilated. Much of what I say is therefore biased toward the 200–300 most bush-oriented Hadza.

Virtually all Hadza, with the exception of very young children and some older women, speak Swahili fluently as a second language. Hadzane, however, is not in any immediate danger of being lost even though many words have been borrowed from Swahili and other languages in the area. This use of Swahili is fairly recent. According to Woodburn (personal communication), when he arrived in 1958 few Hadza knew Swahili. Instead, many knew Isanzu, the language of their Bantu neighbors to the south. The acquisition of Swahili appears to reflect an increase in its use as a lingua franca by all ethnic groups in Tanzania, rather than an increase in the degree of contact with non-Hadza. Swahili has simply replaced Isanzu as the second language of most Hadza.

The Hadza have acquired very little of their neighbors' religions. Their own religion is minimalist. They do have a cosmology and men can tell endless stories about how things came to be. They do not believe in an afterlife and there are few religious restrictions. There are few rules in general, and what few there are often go ignored with little consequence, except for the rules about eating the men's special *epeme* meat. Illnesses may be attributed to violation of these rules (Woodburn 1979). The most important ritual is the *epeme* dance. In camps with enough adults this takes place after dark on moonless nights. Men wear bells on their legs, a feather headdress, a cape, and shake a maraca as they sing and dance one at a time in a call-and-shout manner, inspiring the women to sing and dance around them. The other main ritual is the Mai-toh-ko, or female puberty initiation, which happens when the berries are ripening. Pubertal girls gather in a camp where they are covered with animal fat and adorned with beads, then chase boys and try to hit them with their fertility sticks.

NEIGHBORING GROUPS

Archaeological evidence shows that farmers and pastoralists have been in the general area of Hadza country for several centuries (Sutton 1992). The three groups of neighboring people with whom the Hadza interact most nowadays are the Cushitic Iraqw, the Nilotic Datoga, and the Bantu Isanzu. These three ethnic groups belong to three different linguistic phyla, and Hadzane belongs to a fourth, so none of the four languages is closely related (Ruhlen 1991).

The Iraqw (also called the Mbulu) are Cushitic speakers who migrated south from the region of Ethiopia. They have been in northern Tanzania for perhaps 3,000 years (Ehret 1974; Ochieng 1975; Ambrose 1982; Sutton 1992). The Iraqw live in the highlands where rainfall is plentiful and are primarily maize farmers. Remains of irrigation channels, probably built by the Iraqw (part of the Engaruka complex), have been found near Endamagha in the northern end of Hadza country (Sutton 1986). These fields were abandoned around 1700 A.D., possibly as a result of over-exploitation, or because the climate became drier (Sutton 1990). However, this was also at the same time the Maasai were expanding into the area. In the 1800s the Maasai expansion caused the Iraqw to take refuge in the Mbulu highlands flanking Hadza country to the east. During the past two decades the Iraqw population has been growing rapidly (3.5 percent per year) and is now over 230,000 (Meindertsma and Kessler 1997). Consequently, many Iraqw have moved down from the highlands into Hadza country, clearing trees and trying to make a go of maize farming in areas poor for cultivation but where hunting and gathering has in the past at least, been good for the Hadza.

The Datoga (also called Tatog, Barabaig, and Mangati) are Nilotic pastoralists who number 15–20,000 (Meindertsma and Kessler 1997). It is not clear when they arrived in Hadza country but they have probably been in the general area since the 1700s, when the Maasai expelled them from Ngorongoro Crater (Sutton 1990), which borders Hadza country on the north. Under German rule, Maasai expansion was checked and intertribal warfare and cattle raiding curtailed, causing Datoga herds to expand (Klima 1970). In response to Iraqw movement, the Datoga were also pushed out of current Iraqw areas. We know they have been interacting with the Hadza at least since 1917 (Bagshawe 1925). However, it was only in the 1930s and '40s that Datoga began moving into Hadza country (Tomita 1966; McDowell 1981). To-day, the most bush-dwelling Hadza interact more with the Datoga than any other group. The herds of the Datoga drink the scarce water in Hadza dry-season water holes and eat much of the vegetation needed to support wildlife, which poses one of the main threats to continued Hadza hunting. In addition, in the past according to the Hadza, Datoga would occasionally kidnap Hadza women. Even today, some Hadza women are afraid when they are out gathering and see Datoga men. From time to time, violent conflicts have occurred. For example, Hadza tell of cases in this century when Hadza who killed and ate cows were pursued and killed by posses of Datoga. Despite this conflict, Hadza individuals continue to trade with and beg from Datoga but do not work for them.

The Isanzu are Bantu agropastoralists who live to the south of Hadza country. They may have been in the general area since about 1500 A.D. (Nurse 1982; Soper 1982; Newman 1995), part of the continuing Bantu expansion into east and southern Africa. Hadza access to iron could possibly extend this far back, since the Bantu introduced iron to the Rift Valley area about 1500 A.D., though iron was used near Lake Victoria in Western Tanzania at least 2,000 years ago. Isanzu oral tradition tells of colonizing the area near Isanzu and Kirumi around 1850 (Cooper 1949). At least from the turn of the twentieth century until the 1960s, the Hadza interacted more with the Isanzu than with any other neighbors. Early European visitors used Isanzu guides and interpreters to communicate with the Hadza (Obst 1912; Bagshawe 1925; Bleek 1931) and there appears to have been much more intermarriage with Isanzu than with Iraqw or Datoga. The Hadza trace descent bilaterally and anyone with one Hadza parent is considered Hadza. There are perhaps 5 percent of Hadza today who have an Isanzu parent, and some Hadza live on and off with Isanzu at one spot called Numba Sita. The Hadza do not make alcohol but nowadays they often get beer from Isanzu, as well as Datoga. The Hadza do not practice witchcraft but often say they fear the powerful witchcraft of the Isanzu.

Other groups with which Hadza also have contact are the Sukuma, and Iramba, who are Bantu, and the Maasai, who are Nilotic. The Sukuma live west of Lake Eyasi and interact mostly with the Western Hadza. They have for a very long time been making trips in caravans to obtain salt from Lake Eyasi (Senior 1957). Today in the Mangola area the Hadza also have contact with a variety of "Swahilis," as the Hadza refer to generic Tanzanians (and here I do as well). These Swahilis have moved into the area to grow onions beginning in the 1940s, though there were very few until the 1960s and '70s. In 1962 there were about 900 taxpayers in Mangola (Woodburn 1962). Hadza also have contact with the three European families in Mangola, one of which settled there in the 1950s, though the first German plantation began there in 1928 (Tomita 1966). Researchers from Europe, Japan, and the U.S. have been studying the Hadza regularly since the 1960s and now there are increasing numbers of international tourists as well.

HISTORY

Hadza country is only about 50 kilometers south of Olduvai Gorge and the Laetoli footprints, where evidence of hominid occupation dates to 3.6 million years ago. On the eastern edge of Lake Eyasi, a few hominid remains and associated tools were discovered by Kohl-Larsen in the 1930s and recently estimated to be 130–200,000 years old (Mehlman 1987, 1988, 1991). Of course there is no way to know just how long Hadza ancestors have been there but, as evidenced by lithic materials, there has been continuous occupation of the Eyasi Basin at least since the Middle Stone Age

(Mabulla 1996). There is a consistent pattern of mobility and use of rockshelters right through to present-day Hadza campsites. Given the location of landmarks with Hadza place names, it appears the Hadza have long occupied all their current range and a bit more (Blurton Jones, personal communication), most of which they had largely to themselves as late as the 1950s (Woodburn, personal communication).

The earliest written accounts mentioning the Hadza are those of German explorers in the 1890s (Baumann 1897). However, these accounts are only secondhand descriptions of the Hadza as provided by guides, along with direct observations of Hadza huts and wooden pegs in baobab trees, which the Hadza use for climbing up to get honey (see references in Blurton Jones et al. n.d.). Presumably, the Hadza were hiding from these early European travelers, as they did originally in 1917 from Bagshawe (1925). The earliest written accounts of actually seeing Hadza are by Otto Dempwolff (1916) in 1910 and the German geographer Erich Obst (1912) in 1911, who spent eight weeks with the Hadza.

At the first camp Obst visited on the eastern edge of the Yaeda Valley, Hadza (Wakindiga) were living with Isanzu (Waisanzu). Obst said, "Of the fifteen men, eighteen women and twenty-two children who I met in the camp, barely half— seven men, as many women and eleven children—identified themselves as real Wakindiga. The rest were Waisanzu, who were too lazy to farm at home, or who had to escape the reach of the Boma because of some kind of misdemeanor." For this reason, Obst decided to move on to another camp in Mangola where he was told, "the inhabitants would be exclusively Wakindiga," and he hoped less influenced by Isanzu ways (Obst 1912:3).

Obst described the Hadza as strictly foragers who kept no animals, not even dogs. However, because they had words for some domestic animals and because Obst felt these were not borrowed words, he speculated that the Hadza might have once been pastoralists. Because Obst was told of wars between the Hadza and Maasai and because he figured that the Maasai would only be motivated to fight with other pastoralists, he took this also as an indication the Hadza may have been pastoralists who lost their herds. He notes, however, that the Hadza had no memory or stories of having ever been farmers or pastoralists. Perhaps Obst was influenced by those neighbors who, in their condemnation of Hadza backwardness, often say the Hadza are not a real tribe or culture, only an amalgam of the dispossessed, "who don't even have a real language" (Woodburn 1997). This view reflects ethnocentric bias rather than any evidence. Hadzane, for example, is certainly not a pidgin language.

The Hadza told Obst they always had to be ready for war with the Isanzu, Iraqw, and Maasai. They also told him that the Isanzu sometimes captured women and children. It is possible the Isanzu were capturing Hadza for the slave trade, since there was an Arab slave trade route up until the 1870s only about 250 kilometers to the south of Hadza country. Obst was told the danger from the Isanzu subsided once the elephants became rare, so presumably the Isanzu were also involved in the ivory trade. The Sukuma, he says, came from further away and gave old hoes which the Hadza pounded into arrow points in exchange for getting to hunt elephants, but he doesn't say whether it was only for meat or for ivory, nor does he say how they hunted them. Elephants are the only big game that Hadza do not hunt today because they say their poison is not strong enough to kill them. Obst mentions the Iramba, Maasai, Sukuma, Isanzu, and Iraqw but not the Datoga, suggesting interaction with them came later.

Obst described plentiful game of all sorts but said once the elephants became rare enough, the Isanzu began to interact peacefully with the Hadza. He said the Hadza took up the practice of circumcision and occasionally pierced their earlobes and inserted an Isanzu metal adornment. Men wore braided strings around their wrists and upper arms. Little girls wore a genital pendant of braided grass decorated with beads, which was exchanged at age eight to ten for a leather apron and loincloth. Women wore gigantic bead necklaces and brass spirals around their necks or lower arms, which he says they copied from the Isanzu. But in isolated camps, only leather ornaments were worn.

Obst said of the Hadza that he never saw such concerned mothers and active family fathers, even when a man had two wives. He also said a Hadza man would never marry his daughter off to any man she did not love. He noted they practiced the levirate (as they do today), but he also said that a man could marry anyone other than his mother or sister and that one man even married his granddaughter, something unknown today.

The next observer of the Hadza was F. J. Bagshawe, a district officer of the British government who made several trips to Hadza country soon after the Germans were defeated in World War I. According to Bagshawe (1925), a famine in 1918–1920 prompted some Isanzu to take up living and foraging with the Hadza. Although it is usually Hadza women who marry Isanzu men, he said, during the famine some Isanzu women married Hadza men. Bagshawe said the Hadza kept no domestic animals, not even dogs or fowl. He tells a story about their one and only experiment in pastoralism. Once the Hadza killed an elephant (which as I mentioned, they do not do now), and in exchange for the ivory received some goats from a native stranger. Next morning the goats strayed into the bush and no one bothered to follow them because they were feasting on the elephant meat. Then the Datoga attacked, declaring the goats had been stolen from them, and killed many Hadza. This shows that at least since 1917 there has been some hostile interaction with the Datoga.

Bagshawe said the old men and women circumcised boys and girls but no ritual was involved and he felt the practice had only recently been adopted from neighboring tribes. Based on my interviews, I suspect he was right. Linguist Dorothea Bleek (1931) visited the Hadza in 1930 and said that circumcision was unknown to the

Hadza. She also said they did not have tattoos, only small scars where medicine is rubbed in, as they do today, though these small lateral slits on the cheeks look almost more like aesthetic marks. She said two medicine men with slightly different dialects came from the far north wearing clothes of European stuffs with spears and bags of medicine to visit the Hadza at Dondu, west of Eyasi. Hadza danced in a circle all day with the medicine men in the center. That evening, two boys were tattooed and died from it. The next day two more were tattooed and also died. The third day only one Hadza medicine man was tattooed and the two visitors then left to visit other Hadza camps. These two visitors may well have been from another tribe (perhaps Datoga) or else were assimilated Hadza. Like Obst, Bleek found some Hadza who had large holes in their earlobes into which paper (rather than metal) ornaments obtained from neighbors were inserted. Bleek also found Hadza sometimes getting meal (presumably maize or millet) from the Isanzu. The early accounts may have been somewhat biased toward assimilated Hadza since the writers themselves note the lack of borrowed customs among the most isolated Hadza.

In 1945–47, the British colonial game officer B. Cooper (1949) visited the Hadza on two occasions for 10 days each time. He found there were some Hadza around an Isanzu village doing some cultivation. His guide was a Hadza whose father was an Isanzu who had lived in a Hadza camp to escape the hut tax. Cooper said that Hadza men sometimes cooperated in pairs or threes to drive game into ambush (which they rarely do today) and that men followed the honey-guide birds to find honey (just as they do today). He described the Hadza as having no tribal authority but said old men govern their own camp. He heard of some medicine men and said that those Hadza on the fringe of Isanzu country paid some allegiance to the Isanzu chief. He said the Hadza were peaceful, settling disputes without bloodshed, that monogamy was the rule, with a few beads as brideprice. Cooper said the Hadza had a primitive religion, while Bagshawe (1925) claimed they had no religion, but Obst (1912) said it was difficult to find out anything about their religion beyond the fact that the sun was God and that prayers were said over dead animals.

When Woodburn arrived in 1958, he found about 400 Eastern Hadza still foraging (1968a). At that time, the Hadza still had much of their area to themselves but there was an increasing influx of farmers into the Mangola area, and Datoga into Yaeda. Because there are many publications about the Hadza from this point on, I do not review them here (but see Table 10.1). Woodburn, and others since, have made a point of finding the best bush camps and spending more time with the Hadza. In some ways many of the later descriptions reveal less influence from outsiders, either because such influence actually subsided, or because Hadza further from any of their neighbors or villages had always been subjected to less outside influence. However, soon after Woodburn began work, it looked as if Hadza foraging would end as a result of a concerted attempt to settle the Hadza.

Table 10.1

Descriptions of the Hadza through Time

Year and Source	Population	Camps	Subsistence	Family	Trade and Interaction	General
1890s Baumann 1897		Saw houses	Baobab pegs in trees		Neighbors had name for Hadza	*Hadza hiding.*
1911 Obst (1912) 8 weeks German geographer	100	1–3 families 1st camp = 55, 25 were "real Hadza." Weeks, months at same place in dry season.	Don't recall herding or farming. Primary diet: tubers, berries, hyrax, baobab, gazelle, antelope, hartebeest, gnu, ostrich, giraffe. Night hunt in dry season. In wet, follow game many days, can go weeks without a big game kill. Watch vultures, scavenge from lion and leopard. Two kinds of poison.	Levirate. Can't marry mother, sister, *niece, granddaughter.* Doting mothers, fathers, 5–10 arrows for daughter if she loves man, polygyny often (two different huts).	Get tobacco, *brass neck rings from Isanzu* for lion, leopard fur, honey. Sukuma give beads, knives, old hoes. Isanzu captured women, kids until elephants rare.	Circumcision from Isanzu, only one man. Wars with Iraqw, Isanzu. No afterlife. Only old buried.
1917–23 Bagshawe (1925) several trips over 6 years British colonial district officer	5–600	2–3 men, wives and children	No farming, domestic animals, or dogs. Meat, honey, fruit, tubers, fish, *snakes, lizards,* carrion birds, eggs, *ants, insects,* all but hyena. *Kill elephant, scavenge rhino.* Had not tasted beef. Seldom lose wounded prey. Kill lions, match by day but eaten by lions when night hunting without fire. *Reed fish trap.* Running noose snare, no nets.	Brideprice 5–15 arrows. Easy divorce. During 1918–20 famine, some Hadza men married Isanzu women.	Get old spears as scrap iron, beads, tobacco for skins, honey, meat to neighbors on border. Attacked and killed by Datoga who claimed goats were stolen.	No spears or shields, one axe. Often hungry but happy. No religion, burial, magic, medicine or musical instrument. Cannabis.

Table 10.1 continued

Year and Source	Population	Camps	Subsistence	Family	Trade and Interaction	General
1930 Bleek (1931) 6 weeks Linguist		2–3 families of relations but one may move off by itself. Few weeks or months before moving.	No domestic animals or gardens. Roots, bulbs roasted in ashes, fruit, meat cooked on sticks or boiled, liver eaten raw. Seeds pounded then boiled. Giraffe, ostrich preferred meat. Honey is favorite dish, a treat for kids. Water only beverage. Get some meal from Isanzu. Hammer scrap into arrowhead with iron mallet.	*Most own 2 wives* in different camps but show children great affection. Girls marry at 16, boys a bit later, no ceremony, bride-price: beads to father. Take to groom's home.	Get tobacco, meal from Isanzu, iron scrap from Bantu, *paper ear ornaments; clay pots,* calabashes, beads, *copper rings,* stuffs for meat, skins, honey, beeswax (sell at a store).	Remember Maasai raids and famines. Dance in circle. Copper arm bands, both sexes wore beads. Medicinal scars. Lukucuko. Burial. No afterlife.
1931–38 Kohl-Larsen (1958) Many months Doctor, explorer	450 East, 100 West	From 1 extended family may grow to 60–80 in one camp	In photos— berries, baobab, tubers, klipspringer, ostrich, *killed rhino, hippos.* Native axe. Keep dogs.	Monogamy. Men kill adulterer and beat wife. Wife may leave husband if not good hunter, children stay with father.	Get beads maize, hemp, iron for furs, horns to Isanzu. Brass bracelets, some cloth. For tobacco, women take Isanzu lover.	Remember Maasai raids and famines. Dance in circle. Copper arm bands, both sexes wore beads. Medicinal scars. Lukucuko. Burial. No afterlife. Girl's fringed apron, tattoos, dancing, epeme items, firedrill. *Spear for hippos.*
1945-47 Cooper (1949) 10 days twice British colonial game ranger		5–12 huts, some camps >35, 2–3 men, wives, kids, grandparents. 7–10 days at one spot before deplete baobab.	Baobab main food 5 months. Roots, fruits. Follow honey-guide bird, smoke to stun bees and get honey. *Rhino,* buffalo, giraffe, wildebeest, hartebeest, zebra, impala, kudu, roan, birds, squirrel, tortoise, *some lizards,* hyenas when hard-pressed but not snakes, frogs, toads. 2–3 men may drive game.	Marriage after short engagement, bride-price few beads, monogamy the rule.	Get iron, millet for meat, skins but he stopped it. No punishment but ban on rhino hunting to sell horn. Love elephant he shot. *Few clay pots.*	No spears or shields, few native-made axes. One short camp stay: 2 impala, 2 warthog, 1 porcupine, 1 large bird.

Continued on next page |

Table 10.1 continued

Year and Source	Population	Camps	Subsistence	Family	Trade and Interaction	General
1950 Fosbrooke (1956)	Few hundred; <1,000	No fixed abode, small groups move in relation to food.	No herding or cultivation, roots, game, fruits, baobab, smoke native intoxicant plant.		Get cloth, clay pots, gourds. Would not take money so he gave cloth and beads.	Few make occasional visit to shop in outlying area.
1958–present Woodburn (1958, 1962, 1968a, 1968b, Barnicot et al. 1972) Many trips 1958 to present	750 (250 in West, 500 in East) 400 full-time foragers	18 (1–100) Large camps at water in dry, small, dispersed in wet. Few weeks in one spot, shorter than food dictates.	By weight, ~ 80% from vegetable matter, ~ 20% from meat and honey (but account for more calories than that). Berries, baobab, tubers. Usually hunt alone, lion, leopard, serval, wild cat, hyena, vulture, zebra, guinea fowl, jackal, impala, eland, giraffe, hyrax, (some of which is traded). Don't eat civet, monitor lizard, snake, terrapin.	Bilateral descent, Men marry in early 20s. ~60% marriages uxorilocal, few polygynous marriages, divorce rate = 49/ 1,000 years. Kids live with mother after divorce.	Some intermarriage. Proportions of Hadza ancestry = 79.8% Hadza, 17.3% Isanzu, 1.7% Sukuma, 1.2% Iramba (including grandparents, n = 437).	Lukucuko. Musical bow. Attribute disease to violation of epeme meat rules. No territoriality, fluid camp composition. Good health.
1961–64 Tomita (1966)	80 in Mangola	6–11	Hunt alone or in pairs. Berries, tubers, honey, baobab, catch eels and such fish in Eyasi by hand. Hunt impala, zebra, baboon, wart-hog, eland, guinea fowl, francolin, but not snakes, lizard, buzzard, and hyena.	Eland fat as brideprice.	Get corn for baobab. Aluminum pot.	Eland fat used in ceremonies. Small game to family, but larger than impala shared with all.
1980–81 McDowell (1981a, 1981b) Mangola area	800–1,000 Mangola = 165 (6 camps)	27.7 (22.6–31) Average distance between camps = 3 km 17.7 moves per year	8 roots, tamarind, baobab, fig, dates, 10 berries. Mostly small game but in calories, large game. Meat eaten 64% of days, honey 21% of days. Daily meat = .82 kg./person. Agricultural foods (maize, beans, sweet potato, especially in the late dry season).	All Hadza considered kin. Hadza women marry outsiders in outlying areas, men can't.	Witchcraft fears of neighbors in villages. Only ethnic group in Tanzania to escape tax shows autonomy.	Good diet and health relative to neighbors. Nonterritorial, egalitarian.

Table 10.1 continued

Year and Source	Population	Camps	Subsistence	Family	Trade and Interaction	General
1982–present Blurton Jones, Hawkes, O'Connell (1992) Many trips	1,000 (250 west, 750 E) density = .24/km², growth rate = 1.35/year	16.5 (2–48 in 36 bush camps)	Tubers, honey, meat, baobab, berries. Encounter hunt by day, intercept by night. Target large game and took one/29 hunter-days (4.9 kg/hunter-day). 5-year-olds forage at rate capable of meeting half their needs. 5% of calorie intake was agricultural foods.	Divorce rate = 60/1,000. TFR = 6.2. Infant mortality = 21%, juvenile = 47%. Life expectancy at birth = 32.5, women at 45=21.3	Some get maize for guarding fields, sweet potatoes for harvesting. Iron, cloth for honey. Cloth, nails, beads from researchers.	Frequent name changes. Epeme dance when no moon, Sun is god. Lobby researchers, negotiate gifts.
1995–present Marlowe (1999a, 1999b, n.d.) 17 months.	300 full-time foragers in east	29.1 (10–108 in 10 bush camps) 2 weeks to ~ once per month or 2 but 1 camp year round	Food brought into camp in order of importance: tubers, berries, honey, baobab, meat (large, medium, small game, birds) see Fig. 10.2 for %. No insects, snakes, or lizards. Fish killed by whacking with bows in new Yaeda Lake in 1998. In trade or gifts: maize, millet (see Figure 10.2 for %). Hunt in pairs at night in dry season. Hunt alone, occasionally in pairs. Take any bird or mammal, considerable scrounging. Women forage in groups of 3–8.	3% of full-time forager men (6% women) polygynously married. 1/3 young children are stepchildren, who receive less direct care. Men gave less care in camps with more fertile women. Total fertility = 6.1.	Get maize, millet, cow from Datoga, Iraqw, (iron from Isanzu) for meat, honey. Get clothes, matches, beads, nails from researchers. Money from tourists for crafts, singing, walkabout. Maize, millet from missionaries. When gathering, some women scared of Datoga men.	Epeme dance when no moon, girl's puberty ritual when berries ripen. More items more often shared in smaller camps. Scars on cheeks. Lobby researchers, negotiate gifts.

Italics indicate descriptions that differ from my observations of Hadza today.

SETTLEMENT ATTEMPTS

The first attempt to settle the Hadza, which lasted barely a year, was organized by the British colonial government in 1939 (McDowell 1981a). After the local scout in charge abused his authority, the Hadza left. In 1964 and 1965, soon after independence from Britain, the Tanzanian government (Mbulu district), with support from an American missionary, attempted to settle the Hadza at Yaeda Chini where a school and clinic were built. Hadza from even the most remote bush camps were taken to Yaeda in lorries, escorted by armed police. According to McDowell, "Many Hadza were taken ill and a significant number died, probably of respiratory and diarrheal infections" (1981:7). By early 1966, most Hadza left the settlement to return to foraging.

There was also a settlement established to promote agriculture among the Mangola Hadza at Endamagha from 1971 to 1975. A school, 12 houses, and a dispensary were built, water piped in, and seed provided. The village roll book listed 31 Hadza men in 1973. Then food aid was cut and the government told Hadza there they could not hunt in the area. After a drought and crop failure in 1975, the Hadza left the settlement and returned to foraging. Although Endamagha is still where many Hadza are sent to attend boarding school, Hadza account for only about one third of the students there today.

From time to time, missionaries have provided food and encouraged Hadza settlement. One Hadza man who allies himself with missionaries has several times tried to persuade other Hadza to abandon foraging in favor of farming, even using force at times. There was once a school at Munguli in the southern part of Hadza country, where many Hadza lived. When a missionary at Yaeda Chini provided food, many Hadza went there and stayed as long as the food lasted, which was only a few months. Meanwhile, the school and land in Munguli were occupied by Isanzu (Woodburn, personal communication). Likewise at Yaeda, the school and clinic built for the Hadza in the 1960s attracted various Swahilis who are still there. Another attempt at settlement in Yaeda began in 1979 and the number of Hadza rose from 30 to 300 (Ndagala and Waane 1982) but today there are no Hadza living there.

There is now a fairly permanent settlement at Mongo wa Mono, which was established as a Hadza village in 1988. The number of people there varies greatly from about 20 to 80 and at any given time there might be 5 to 10 people growing crops or tending beehives with very limited success, so most still also forage some. Many people float in and out, and while there, simply wait for food deliveries from missionaries or aid workers. Missionaries sometimes come to Mongo wa Mono and try to make converts. Usually, they do not last longer than a few months. Hadza children and teenagers often sing Christian songs, and the Hadza welcome the food provided by missionaries, but there has been little conversion to Christianity. Many observers felt the settlements would mean the end of Hadza foraging, but surprisingly, they did not. Even today, few Hadza practice any kind of agriculture. Although most adult Hadza have lived in a settlement at some point in time, such experiences have been short-term and have not prevented them from continuing their foraging lifestyle and maintaining much of their traditional culture.

STASIS AND CHANGE

Judging from photographs and descriptions, the Hadza visited by Obst in 1911 were remarkably similar to the Hadza I first met in 1995. They lived in the same houses in similar sized camps, used the same tool kit, foraged for the same foods, traded for the same items, and practiced the same sort of religion. In order to evaluate the degree of interaction with outsiders and the amount of change in Hadza culture, Table 10.1 provides a brief summary of descriptions of the Hadza from the earliest accounts to the present. Italics denote traits that today differ noticeably from what was described in the past. Table 10.2 lists probable influences from outsiders through time. Table 10.3 is intended to assess the extent of change over a much longer period and explore the relevance of contemporary foragers as models of the Paleolithic. It provides a list of Hadza possessions with estimated times of appearance either in the general Hadza area, or in the case of the earliest possible artifacts the earliest appearance anywhere.

The impression one gets from reading the historical record, as others have noted (Fosbrooke 1956), is that there is an overwhelming continuity in the descriptions throughout the twentieth century. While the population may have grown slightly, camp size, mobility, diet, and mating system are very consistent (Table 10.1). In 1960, Woodburn (1968a) found average camp population to be 18 (1–100). People camped at one spot for no more than a few weeks. In 1980, McDowell (1981) found the average camp population in the Mangola area was 27.7 (22.6 to 31), and camps moved about 17.7 times per year. In 1995–96, the average population of 10 camps for which I had numbers in various areas was 29.1 (10–108). However, I found that camps did not move so frequently. For example, even though people were constantly visiting other camps, there tended to be a camp at one spot for a month or two. Thus, it appeared camps might move only about 6–12 times per year though individuals moved more often than that and there was great variation. For example, the largest camp, which contained 108 people, was located in the spot with the most continuous water. While the composition of this camp changed with families moving in and out seasonally, there was always someone at this spot the year round. Although there were still people there the following year and it appeared to have become a permanent camp, it was abandoned in 1998. There may be a trend toward larger camps staying in one place longer in response to many areas being taken over by

Table 10.2

Influences from "Others"

Trait or Interaction	The "Others"	Source
Probably interacted with farmers on border	Engaruka complex at Endamagha (Iraqw) 1700 A.D.	Sutton 1986
Trade for iron, tobacco, beads	Isanzu, Sukuma	Obst 1912
Captured (maybe slave trade), ivory trade	Isanzu 1800s	Obst 1912
Warfare	Maasai 1900	Obst 1912
Maasai expansion halted	Germans 1890s	Obst 1912
Metal ear ornaments	Isanzu	Obst 1912
Brass neck ring	Isanzu	Obst 1912; Bagshawe 1925; Bleek 1931
Second language is Isanzu	Isanzu	Obst 1912; Bagshawe 1925; Bleek 1931
Killed for "stealing goats"	Datoga	Bagshawe 1925
Intermarriage	Isanzu	Bagshawe 1925
Male circumcision	Isanzu	Obst 1912; Bleek 1931 says none
Female circumcision	Isanzu or Datoga	Woodburn 1964
Trade for clay pots	Isanzu?	Bleek 1931; Cooper 1949; Fosbrooke 1956
Trade for cloth	Isanzu	Kohl-Larsen 1958
Studied	Europeans	Kohl-Larsen 1958
First settlement attempt	British 1939	McDowell 1981
Loss of range to Mangola village	Mangola European farmers 1950	Woodburn 1962
Loss of Mangola	Swahili farmers 1960	Woodburn 1962
Yaeda settlement	Tanzania government (Iraqw)	Woodburn 1968
Second language is Swahili	All neighbors	Woodburn, personal communication
Aluminum pots	Swahilis in Mangola	Tomita 1966
Sex to remove death pollution	Iraqwi widows seek out Hadza	Matthiessen 1972
Zeze (musical bow) *mbira*	Isanzu	Marlowe
Guard fields	Iraqw	Blurton Jones et al. 1992; Marlowe
Use of father's last name	Isanzu, Datoga, Iraqw, Swahili officials, missionaries	Blurton Jones, personal communication; Marlowe
Get beer	Isanzu, Datoga, Swahilis	Marlowe
Wells dug near waterholes	Datoga	Marlowe
Lion kill celebration	Datoga	Marlowe
Observed, get money	International tourists	Marlowe

Table 10.3

Hadza Possessions and Artifacts

Possessions and Artifacts	Earliest Possible Date (Years B.P.)	Earliest Citation	Pre-Neolithic	Post-Neolithic	Frequency Change in Twentieth Century
Pounding rock	>3 million		X		—
Anvil for pounding	>3 million		X		—
Dig stick	>3 million	1911	X		—
Firedrill	>300,000	1930	X		<
Hearth	>300,000	1890s	X		—
House		1890s	X		—
Skin shoes[b] (now tires)			X		<
Skin belt[b]		1930	X		<
Leather skirt[b]		1911	X		<
Leather kaross[b]		1930	X		<
Leather bags			X		—
Leather sheath		1930	X		—
Sleeping hide			X		—
Gourd container, dipper		1930	X		—
Organic jewelry		1911	X		<
Grass basket			X		?
Bow	10–35,000	1911	X		—
Arrow (6 types)	10–35,000	1911	X		—
2 poisons		1911	?		—
Shell (mixing poison)			X		—
Quiver		1931–38	X		—
Fertility walking stick			X		?
Medicine horn		1931	X		—
Wood toys		1960	X		?
Wood gambling chips		1930	X		<
Pegs for climbing		1890s	X		—
Stone pipe		1911	X		—
Wooden pipe		1930	X		?
Epeme items: feather or fur headgear, maraca, cape		1931–38	X		—
Twine noose snare		1917	X		?
Glass bead jewelry	700	1911		X	>
Epeme items: metal leg bands and bells	500	1931–38		X	>

Continued on next page

Table 10.3 continued

Possessions and Artifacts	Earliest Possible Date (Years B.P.)	Earliest Citation	Pre-Neolithic	Post-Neolithic	Frequency Change in Twentieth Century
Iron arrow point[c]	500	1911		X	—
Metal knife[c]	500	1925		X	>
Metal axe[c]	500	1925		X	>
Metal hammer[c]	500	1930		X	>
Metal chisel[c]	500			X	>
Metal needles[c]	500			X	>
Musical bow with wire	500	1960		X	>
Tobacco[c]	450	1911		X	>
Metal cooking pot[c]	500	1945		X	>
Previously clay pots	700	1930, 1945, 1950		X	<
Factory cloth	200	1911		X	>
Cloth dolls[c]	200			X	>
Plastic beads	12	1990s		X	>

[a]> = increasing frequency; < = decreasing frequency; — = no change in frequency; ? = uncertain

[b]Exist now but often made of different material.

[c]Likely made earlier but of different material.

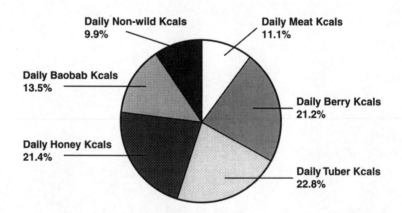

Figure 10.2. Hadza diet showing daily kilocalories brought into camp by type of food. Data collected over a 9-month period in 5 different camps in 1995–96 (2,733 person-days). All categories are foraged wild foods except "Daily Non-wild Kcals," which is mostly maize (5 percent) and millet (4.2 percent) gained as gifts from a missionary, or in trade with neighboring agropastoralists. This 9.9 percent of food entering camp equals about 6.93 percent of total diet, since about 30 percent of the diet is consumed while out foraging.

non-Hadza. However, large camps (e.g., 100) during berry season in certain areas also existed long ago (Woodburn, personal communication).

Just as Bagshawe (1925) and Cooper (1949) found, the Hadza today have no spears (but see Kohl-Larsen 1958) or shields and only a few native-made axes which are used to break open trees to get at honey. As found by all observers, hunting is done only with bow and arrow. As Obst (1912) and Woodburn (1968b) found, men today usually hunt alone in the wet season and many days may pass without any big game being killed. As Obst, Bagshawe, and Woodburn noted, in the dry season men often hunt in pairs at night around the few permanent water holes waiting for animals to come to them, which can be dangerous since lions employ the same strategy. As described by Obst and Bagshawe, meat is also obtained by scavenging. And as noted by almost all observers, women and children go foraging for tubers, berries, and baobab. In contrast to Bagshawe's observation, Hadza today do not eat insects or snakes, and I have never seen them eat lizards.

In 1985–86, Hawkes and O'Connell (Blurton Jones et al. n.d.) found that less than 5 percent of calorie intake (in one camp) was from agricultural food. In 1995–96 (in 2,733 person-days in 5 camps), I found 9.9 percent of all calories entering camps came from nonforaged food. Much of this was maize (5 percent) and millet (4.2 percent) delivered to one camp by one missionary during one month, the rest gained through trade with agropastoralist neighbors (Figure 10.2). Because I calculate the Hadza consume about 30 percent of their total calories while out foraging (Marlowe n.d.), what comes into camp is only about 70 percent of total consumption. This means that agricultural food received from non-Hadza represents only about 6.93 percent of total consumption (9.9 percent of 70 percent). Thus, the amount of food acquired from foraging in 1995–96 was not much less than in 1985–86.

I suspect that 50 or 60 years ago the 9.9 percent of food entering camp that is agricultural would have instead been from hunting, which would almost double the amount of calories from meat. It is clear that with so many people moving in and cutting down trees and herds eating the grass, the routes of migrating animals between the game parks have been affected. The Hadza say that there is less game than in the past, and Obst (1912) reported seeing large herds of big game in the Yaeda Valley in 1911. Not only were there many elephants (which are fairly rare today) but even rhino, which are now absent. In 1998, the El Niño rains created a new lake in the Yaeda Valley (which persisted for two years), and I found some Hadza fishing for large catfish by whacking them with their bows (even though the Hadza say that fish are not decent food). Before 1998, however, there were mostly herds of Datoga cows in the Yaeda Valley with only the occasional herd of antelope.

As Table 10.1 shows, the Hadza have been trading with their neighbors throughout the twentieth century. Just as they did at the time of Obst's visit, Hadza today give meat, skins, and honey in exchange for tobacco, marijuana, maize, millet, clothes, beads, cooking pots, and scrap iron for making their axes and arrowheads. They no longer get clay pots but rather metal pots and they no longer get brass neck rings. Nowadays, the Hadza also receive some beer from their neighbors, sell some crafts to tourists, and receive a variety of goods from researchers, especially clothes and nails for arrowheads.

Considering that the Hadza are surrounded by more powerful neighbors, a surprisingly small percentage of Hadza women marry non-Hadza men, perhaps less than 5 percent, though Kohl-Larsen (1958) says that in the 1930s, Isanzu men frequently stole Hadza wives. Often after a Hadza woman does marry an outsider and has a child, she leaves him and returns to raise the child in a Hadza camp. This may well be because Hadza women are too independent to put up with the sort of treatment they get from non-Hadza men. When they do return, they do not appear to be stigmatized. As described in virtually all earlier accounts, the Hadza are quite monogamous (serially) with occasional polygyny. There is no marriage ceremony, no arranged marriage, divorce is easy, and the levirate is practiced.

Despite the overwhelming impression of continuity in the historical record, there are a few exceptions and it is these that catch my attention precisely because they stand out in relief. Obst found some Hadza wearing brass neck rings, and making large holes in their earlobes, a practice they acquired from the Isanzu. Today, the Hadza do neither of these, though the Datoga do, even more so than the Isanzu. Obst said the Hadza adopted circumcision from the Isanzu but he saw only one circumcised man and he was an Isanzu living in a Hadza camp. Bagshawe (1925) said old men and women performed circumcision on boys and girls but without any elaborate ritual. Bleek (1931) said, unlike other tribes, circumcision was unknown to the Hadza. Hadza men are not circumcised today, although some women are. Given all these differences, it appears there may have been more influence from Isanzu then than now, at least along the margins of Hadza country.

Another difference between Hadza in the early 1900s and Hadza today is that they are less shy. These days Hadza will approach a visitor, at least a foreign visitor, rather than hide. Their second language is Swahili rather than Isanzu. They use metal rather than clay pots (there is usually at least one in every camp). In addition, many Hadza attend school, even if only for a year or less. I would say that about 20 percent of Hadza under 50 years old have attended some school and about 60 percent of those under 30 years old have attended some school. There is less gambling by men nowadays. I have seen Hadza men play their gambling game, *lukucuko*, only at one camp in one season. According to Woodburn (1970), in the 1960s they often played. My impression is that there may be less storytelling nowadays than in the past since all men can tell stories (for examples see Bala 1998), but only rarely do I observe them doing so. In some camps, there is now the occasional radio or flashlight (invariably lacking batteries). There are today more factory-made clothes, which researchers give as gifts.

Just in the last four years there have been developments that may well change

Hadza life. Even more than the ever-increasing number of Datoga, Iraqw, Isanzu, and Sukuma moving into the area, a threat to the foraging lifestyle is posed by the sudden influx of ethno-tourists. During my year in 1995–96 there was only about one van full of tourists per week visiting Hadza camps during the three or four months of tourist season in the Mangola area, where a Swahili village exists. In bush camps there was no tourism except for one company that brought very small groups of tourists once or twice a year. In most bush camps many people, especially women, much preferred gifts to money, since they did not ever go to a village and had no way to spend their money. During the dry season of 1998, there were several caravans of tourists, even at remote camps. The tourists come because they want to see foragers. Tourism may, therefore, keep the Hadza appearing to forage. In reality, at least during the dry season when tourist travel is possible, some Hadza receive enough money from the tourists that they can buy maize to live on, and only forage when the tourists show up and want to go on a walkabout. In one Mangola camp, Hadza have taken to making their traditional clothes of skins because tour guides tell them that is what the tourists want to see. In this respect, then, present-day Hadza in Mangola would appear even more like their ancestors a century ago. The only difference is that these new leather clothes have plastic beads sewn on, beads they make from bits of colored plastic they find around the village.

This tourism would not be troubling if the Hadza bought only maize, but after tourists pass through, their neighbors waste no time bringing them alcohol and leaving with all the money. During 1995–96 there was no drinking in remote camps, only in those close to the village in Mangola or the settlement at Mongo wa Mono. During 1998 there was much drinking in virtually all camps. Drinking leads to arguments and fights and injuries. It seems that for a while the Hadza may continue to forage during the wet season when the mud prevents tourists from coming. But it may not be long before tourism spells an end to foraging year round. It may be that Hadza culture, which has remained little changed despite long contact with more powerful neighbors, will now, with the arrival of tourists, finally succumb to outside influences, largely because the tourists are a source of money. The irony is, of course, that the tourists come because they want to see foragers and once they have completely eliminated real foraging they will no longer come, leaving the Hadza with no source of income.

Despite these changes, in the wet season at least, by and large, I would notice little difference were I to travel back in time to visit a camp in 1900. The continuity extends all the way to their bows and arrows being exactly the same mean length, the height of men and women being the same (Blurton Jones et al. n.d.), and their favorite colors of beads being blue and white (Kohl-Larsen 1958). Despite the fact that the Hadza have had contact with nonforagers continuously for many decades and perhaps centuries, they have changed little and conserved much.

WHY STASIS?

Why did the Hadza change so little in the face of contact? Woodburn (1979, 1988) argued that encapsulation was the result of the immediate-return organization of Hadza culture, which insulated them from the temptations of agriculture and the entanglements of extensive trade and serfdom. I agree. Yet Woodburn offers no explanation for why some, like the Hadza, are immediate-return while others are delayed-return foragers. The following are the best explanations I can offer for Hadza conservatism.

First, the habitat is rather marginal. It is poor for growing crops without irrigation. Second, although it is a good habitat for pastoralism, before a government eradication program in the 1940s and 1950s, the tsetse flies were very bad. This meant that pastoralists did not encroach too much. Thirdly, Tanzania has always been undeveloped. By embracing socialism with independence, development remained slow until recently. This lack of development and lack of infrastructure (e.g., roads) meant less change came to the Hadza area than would have occurred otherwise. Fourth, the presence of Ngorongoro Conservation Area, Serengeti National Park, Maswa Game Preserve, and Lake Manyara National Park, all of which border Hadza country, allowed wildlife to persist. Protected big game animals migrate through Hadza country allowing them to continue to hunt as well as gather. These game parks owe their existence, in part, to colonialism, since during British rule Serengeti and Ngorongoro were established by forcing the Maasai to move. Fifth, the Hadza have long adopted a low-key response to outsiders. As mentioned, they used to hide from strangers (Bagshawe 1925). This behavior may have helped avoid many confrontations that could have resulted in extermination at the hands of enemies. Even though the tsetse fly may have limited the potential for pastoralism, it also seems likely that, were it not for colonialism, when the Germans halted the Maasai expansion, the Maasai would have pushed the Hadza out of the area after pushing the Datoga out of Ngorongoro Crater.

It is possible that the interest of researchers beginning in the late 1950s and growing up to the present may have prolonged Hadza foraging (for reviews see Ndagala and Waane 1982; McDowell 1982). This might have occurred from the many gifts that researchers are expected to give. This may have made it less likely that some other tribe would subjugate the Hadza. Others also want outsiders to come and provide goods, and they recognize that the outsiders are coming to see or study the Hadza. For example, recently several villages have instituted fees for researchers and tourists just for passing through on their way to see the Hadza. It would hurt these neighbors if outsiders stopped coming because the Hadza were no longer foraging. On the other hand, it may well be research publications that have contributed to the awareness responsible for attracting tourists and hastening the end of foraging.

It certainly doesn't seem that the Hadza remained foragers because they were oppressed by their neighbors and denied access to other means of production, as revisionists might argue. On the contrary, Hadza have often refused to take up agriculture. Unlike some southern African Bushmen, Hadza labor has been in little demand by pastoralists. According to some informants, there has occasionally been a Hadza child kidnapped by Datoga and reared as a herder but it seems there would be little interest on the part of Hadza in working for Datoga even if there were any demand for labor. Why did some Bantu pastoralists have a demand for forager labor in southern Africa? Presumably, forager labor was so cheap it afforded an extra bit of leisure for the Bantu. Perhaps the Hadza remained independent simply because they could make a decent living foraging, in some respects a better living than their neighbors, many of whom eat a monotonous diet of maize only (Blurton Jones et al. 1996). The Hadza don't pass up any handouts of maize but they do not seem interested in working for Datoga or Iraqw agropastoralists, who may consequently find Hadza labor of little value, being so unreliable.

DISCUSSION AND CONCLUSION

Early anthropologists described cultural evolution as a unilineal process of development. Tylor (1871) believed in the psychic unity of all humans and felt that cross-cultural variation resulted from historical processes, not racial differences. Those least developed, like hunter-gatherers, were no different biologically but were, culturally, "living fossils." Morgan (1877) proposed a sequence of stages from hunter-gatherers (savagery) to complex states (civilization). Such a unilineal scheme implies that traits within a culture must change together, an extreme form of holism, and suggested some impetus toward complexity, often labeled progress. Such reasoning led some to speculate that foragers would have a primitive language to go along with their primitive technology. This is clearly not the case. In reaction, others argued against the living-fossil idea on the grounds that language or other traits may develop, even if technology does not. One could cite many examples to support this particulate view of culture, but it is an overreaction to dismiss completely an evolutionary sequence to cultural and ecological change. After all, all societies were foragers 12,000 years ago, and few have moved directly from foraging to industrial production.

Is the particulate view of culture responsible for the rejection of the living-fossil idea among so many today? It seems more likely they reject the idea because living fossils imply backwardness, which they wish to deny. In some ways, a forager culture may have changed greatly without technology changing much and if so, such foragers are only technologically living fossils. But it is also possible that in addition to technology, other cultural traits have changed little. In Tanzania, it is not only the

Hadza who have changed little but also their neighbors, the Datoga and Maasai pastoralists. The Maasai and Datoga are strikingly different from the general Tanzanian Swahili population and this difference is due to their strong conservatism. If they had sent their children to school and given up their traditional attire, they would now blend in. But they did not. In a sense, at least over the past century, they have approximated living fossils and, like the Hadza, appear little different than they did a century ago, even though they have been in contact with others.

Compared to most other ethnic groups in Tanzania, the Hadza, Datoga, and Maasai have been more conservative, more like living fossils than others groups. There is nothing mysterious about conservatism. It creates autonomy as much as it is caused by autonomy. It is wrong to think of foragers as living fossils if aspects of their cultures have changed appreciably. If that is what one wants to argue, one must present evidence of such change. But if one wants to reject the living-fossil idea in general, whether there is evidence of such change or not, I suspect it is because one equates conservatism and backwardness with inferiority. That equation is often made in Tanzania, where some people get angry or insulted that someone wants to come study the backward Hadza. They resent what they perceive as a foreign fascination with savages, and the portrayal of Tanzania as backward. Obviously they are right about the fascination with the Hadza, but it is virtually impossible to explain to them why this does not make the Hadza inferior.

Of course time does not stop for foragers who are isolated. It is revealing that my synopsis of Hadza history is a series of encounters with and influences from others. Few would be interested in reading a history that described how 100 years ago, the Hadza foraged for x, y, and z, then 90 years ago, they foraged for x, y, and z, while 80 years ago they foraged for x, y, and z. We tend to think of history as a series of changes, so it is understandable that a group experiencing little change is portrayed as frozen in time. The notion that what one sees when looking at foraging societies is a picture of what Pleistocene humans were like, has rightly been criticized. But just because the same amount of time has passed for all societies, does not mean the same amount of change has occurred. Obviously less change has occurred in the domain of subsistence and also fairly obviously in other domains as well. Even if foragers are not living fossils, surely they are the best living models of what life was like prior to agriculture. The pendulum has swung so far away from the view that contemporary foragers are living fossils that some people now dismiss them as models of anything like our Pleistocene ancestors, as the statement from Wilmsen quoted above illustrates.

Examining the case of the Hadza affords another perspective on the Kalahari debate. There is no question about whether the Hadza were, or were not, in contact with nonforagers before they were studied; they were. Clearly, they were also often dominated when they were in contact. There is no definitive evidence the Hadza were not enslaved or enserfed by their neighbors in the distant past, but there is no evidence that they were either. Nor is there evidence that they once were pastoralists or farmers. But suppose they were. What difference might that make? If they were secondary foragers we might be misled into thinking that certain traits, their religious beliefs for example, were the product of a foraging lifestyle when in fact, they may have evolved during an agricultural past and only persisted into the forager present through cultural inertia. If one is interested in studying foragers from an evolutionary ecological perspective it might not matter since many aspects of secondary foragers' lives would likely differ little from primary foragers. For example, time budgets, life history traits, and camp demographics should converge on values that are constrained by the foraging lifestyle, rather than cultural inertia.

Certain traits of ethnographic foraging populations may indeed be biased. This could result if only those foragers in marginal habitats survived long enough to be described, or if those societies described are those that survived because they went to extreme lengths to avoid conflict. Preagricultural societies may have engaged in much more warfare than those more peaceful societies that were spared precisely because they adopted a policy of hiding from more powerful strangers. In addition, perhaps ethnographic foragers are more egalitarian in response to their more powerful neighbors. Australian societies, who by and large were not in contact with nonforagers, or any state societies until Europeans arrived, were described as gerontocracies, with intense polygyny, and frequent warfare (Hart and Pilling 1979; Spencer and Gillen 1927). It is possible that preagricultural populations were more hierarchical, more polygynous, and more often engaged in war than most of the egalitarian foragers in the ethnographic record, but this will not be easy to resolve. The Kalahari debate will have proved worthwhile if it results in a closer examination of the archaeological record to identify pre- and postcontact forager traits (e.g., Sadr this volume).

The special place of foragers in anthropology has been challenged by the revisionists on the grounds that contemporary foragers are not primary foragers, or that they have been oppressed by outsiders, or that they are a creation of our need to view others as simple and primitive, as living fossils. But if we are interested in the past, surely foragers are the best models we have if we hope to actually observe and measure behavior. If the revisionists' criticisms lead to more careful scrutiny of those factors that make some contemporary foragers poor models of the past, this would be a valuable contribution of the Kalahari debate. For example, we can look for correlations that could improve our models, a correlation between say habitat and camp size, between diet, postmarital residence and social organization, between variance in food returns, hierarchy, and the mating system. We might discover that warfare is associated more with foragers in rich, wet environments that lead to high population densities, or conversely with foragers who live in such dry environments that water holes are defended. By using archaeological estimates of population density, we might be able to infer what rates of warfare would have been for various Pleistocene populations. By this method we may eventually arrive at an answer to the question of how representative some contemporary foragers such as the Ju/'hoansi or the Hadza are of the preagricultural past in southern and eastern Africa.

COMMENTARY ON OTHER CHAPTERS

Sadr's analysis (Chapter 2) of items that characterize known forager camps is the way to make progress on the question of past autonomy, assimilation, or enserfment. A study of the most bush-oriented Hadza camps would reveal a number of items acquired through trade or begging from agropastoralists even though such Hadza are certainly not enserfed. On the other hand, the degree of domination can rise without the number of items rising. For example, after a drought in 1997, some Hadza were forced to live close to Datoga who dug wells where there is normally surface water. Although there was no noticeable increase in trade items, there was an increase in the degree of domination by Datoga.

When I transpose Howell and Draper's analysis of bush-oriented and post-oriented Ju/'hoansi to the Hadza, I think of how those living in or near a village are often visited by their bush relatives. But why a Hadza moves away from the bush is not clear. Often, it will be a person who for one reason or another got more education than most. In fact, the two most assimilated Hadza of all have jobs from time to time, have traveled to Europe, and speak English. I know only three Hadza who speak any English at all. Some people move to a village because of a connection with a missionary. Others move because they have been hired to work on one of the three white farms in the Mangola area.

Lee found that the Ju/'hoansi perceived themselves as autonomous while at the same time could not imagine how they could have lived without pots they acquired from others. Trade has been important for a long time, but does not indicate the degree of oppression. The Hadza also have trouble imagining arrows and axes without metal or cooking without pots. But the trading they do with their neighbors does not make them subservient.

Kent (Chapter 3) notes that diffusion is not always one way. Foragers can influence pastoralists as well as be influenced by them. Hadza have had some influence on their neighbors. As mentioned, during an early famine, Isanzu took up living with the Hadza and took up foraging, and some Isanzu females even married Hadza men. I know one Maasai man who has a Hadza wife and claims Hadza raised him after his parents died. Another man, an Iraqw who owns a *boma* and herds, has married a Hadza, stays most of the time in her camp, and has become a skilled hunter. He now looks and acts more Hadza than Iraqw. Several authors in this volume have noted how environmental stress can increase forager dependence on others and that seems to be the case for the Hadza, as for example, after the drought in 1997. But under extreme stress, it seems the dependence runs in the opposite direction; foraging becomes the only viable strategy.

Kent also points out that the degree of assimilation or autonomy varies greatly across areas, and this is very true of the Hadza. I have described bush Hadza. There are many Hadza who have married out and live in villages, even a few who live far off in real towns or cities. A few have held local government posts. These Hadza are almost completely assimilated. On the other extreme, there are many Hadza women who have never been to even the smallest village, who are wary of any non-Hadza when out foraging, who still wear skin skirts, do not value money, and do not speak Swahili. The level of domination by non-Hadza does not necessarily correlate with the degree of assimilation either.

Ikeya describes three types of relationship between the Bakgalagadi and San. Among the Hadza, there is nothing like the first type, the *mafisa* system in which the San are allowed to take milk and calves from the cattle they tend for the Bakgalagadi. Like the second type, during part of the year some Hadza do some work for farmers, in exchange for some of the harvest. And like the third type, Hadza do trade skins and meat with their neighbors but, unlike the San, never borrow traps, dogs, or guns to hunt. In fact, one factor that may partially explain why the Hadza have not been enserfed like some San have is that there are virtually no guns in Tanzania, outside those held by the army and a few white farmers. Ikeya's portrayal of greater domination by Bakgalagadi in areas where they were more numerous and less where San were more numerous would also apply in the Hadza case.

Köhler and Lewis (Chapter 11) describe the patron-client relationship between Bilo farmers and Pygmies as one that is mutually exploitative, even though the Pygmies have less power. The Pygmy view of Bilo as gorillas shows that lack of power has not reduced the Pygmies to acceptance of Bilo superiority; quite the opposite. For most Hadza, there is nothing resembling the patron-client relationship and so, even though their neighbors largely look down on them, the Hadza do not go so far as to view others in quite such negative terms, because they have managed to maintain greater autonomy. But very much like the Mbendjele, the Hadza do not feel obligated to come through with their part of a deal with non-Hadza. The Hadza rarely make a deal involving repayment of a debt with labor, but often do so with the promise of meat or honey. Unless they are harassed seriously, they do not feel compelled to repay the debt because among Hadza, food can be demanded without incurring a debt. One thing that has made the Hadza a bit less vulnerable to indebtedness, and consequently subjugation by their neighbors, is the fact that they receive more gifts from researchers, and now tourists, than their neighbors do. For several years now, they have probably received enough big nails from us to meet their demand for arrowheads. Even when we are gone, the special attention they get from outsiders may help them achieve some measure of respect vis-à-vis their neighbors.

The Hadza are also similar to the G/wi and G//ana in their views of witchcraft practiced by their neighbors. Sugawara (Chapter 4) quotes Tanaka, who says, "The San are basically realistic and rational, having no systematic beliefs about supernatural powers." But Sugawara describes how the G/wi and G//ana reinterpret events through the lens of sorcery practiced by the Bakgalagadi. This description also applies to the Hadza. The Hadza do not practice witchcraft but do believe it gives their neighbors power and often interpret deaths and illnesses as the work of their neighbors.

According to Guenther (Chapter 5), the Nharo and ≠Au//eisi Bushmen in the Ghanzi veld experienced two phases in the nineteenth century. They went from first being autonomous hunter-gatherers, "politically complex, organized, centralized, militarized and able to assert their independence over agropastoral settler groups" with "an organizational pattern reminiscent of a tightly structured patrilocal band (*à la* Steward)" to being a "loosely egalitarian foraging band (*à la* Lee)." This happened because the incursion of outsiders led to a decline in game and in the Bushmen population due to outbreaks of malaria and smallpox. Their lower population, and the shift in emphasis from hunting to gathering, along with a new emphasis on commercial rather than subsistence hunting, weakened their resistance to settlers and caused changes in the social organization.

This same scenario may well apply to the Hadza in the past or may be underway at the present. It is difficult to say. There appears to be a decline in game over the past few decades and this could result in males losing some of their value to females. Hadza social organization is certainly loosely egalitarian (*à la* Lee) today, but it seems that it was in 1911 as well (Obst 1912). As noted, the Hadza were involved in warfare more around the turn of the century than now, but this seems to me to be less because they were more militaristic and capable of resistance than because their pastoralist enemies were making military assaults then. The issue raised by Guenther is the most important question about contemporary foragers raised by the Kalahari debate. The problem is that data with which to definitively answer it are lacking.

Finally, Kent raises the issue of how and why the foraging lifestyle came to an end in southern Africa (Chapter 6). Kent's argument that the arrival of Europeans was crucial may well be correct, though her reasoning does not convince me. Like Guenther, she notes that disease played a role. However, because contagious diseases introduced by Europeans would have hit the sedentary neighbors of the Bushmen more strongly, if anything, such diseases might only have stalled the decline of foraging by suppressing the numbers of agropastoralists. Her argument that there was something special about European ethnocentrism and racism which did in foragers more quickly or thoroughly than the Bantu arrival would have alone seems only partly convincing, and perhaps superfluous anyway. There may well have been a special flavor to European racism, which van den Berghe (1981) attributes to the consequence of a democratic ideology conflicting with old-fashioned ethnocentric discrimination. But isn't the military superiority of the Europeans enough to account for the rapid change they wrought?

In the case of the Hadza, Europeans were far fewer in number and as I noted, this may have stalled change in Tanzania. Their arrival did, however, curtail warfare, which likely would have done in the Hadza. The issue of cultural variation in outlook and attitudes seems far less relevant to me than technological, and hence, social organization. With the technological simplicity and mobility of foraging goes low population density and with that goes lack of power. All societies with other modes of production have imposed their will on foragers to a greater or lesser degree, which has resulted in the same basic outcome. Foragers are viewed as backward and inferior by their nonforaging neighbors, and this will inevitably result in their demise.

The equation of technological simplicity with backwardness might in subtler ways, even characterize many academics, despite their professed cultural relativism. It is that same view that makes the living-fossil notion so unappealing to them. The term *backward* has pejorative connotations, but if one does not think being conservative is a negative trait, then there is nothing abhorrent about being a living fossil. In many ways, contemporary foragers come close to being living fossils, and that is the reason they are so special and interesting. Those who think that is an insult might want to examine their own views. They likely think change equals progress, which equals good, and no change equals backwardness, which equals bad. I do not, and neither, I suspect, did Lee when he described the Ju/'hoansi as being "on the threshold of the Neolithic."

ACKNOWLEDGMENTS

I would like to thank the Hadza and their neighbors for being so accepting, Jeannette Hanby and David Bygott for all their help, the Tanzanian government (COSTECH) for permission to conduct research, and Sue Kent for her helpful comments.

eleven

Putting Hunter-Gatherer and Farmer Relations in Perspective

A Commentary from Central Africa

Axel Köhler and Jerome Lewis

P ygmy hunter-gatherers in Central Africa are similar to San people in that they include many different ethnic groups with different histories and experiences of contact with outsiders. This is briefly illustrated with the example of the Twa Pygmies. We discuss the way local people talk about ethnicity and introduce certain indigenous generic ethnonyms for people often referred to in the literature as hunter-gatherers or farmers, Pygmy or Bantu. The various models anthropologists have proposed to understand these relations are critically examined, as are 'revisionist' hypotheses. These models are considered with reference to the contemporary situation in Northern Congo and the models local people use to discuss their relations.

We argue that Pygmies and their non-Pygmy neighbors are interpreting the terms of their relations differently. Despite sharing words, they do not always share the same meanings. In different ways each thinks they are controlling the other. Rather than make judgments in a social situation that oscillates between extremes, we discuss how either side tries to manage the relationship and we elucidate some of the differences between the ways Pygmies and their neighbors talk about each other. Given the dearth of archaeological or other data to confirm or disprove the various historical hypotheses, we suggest this is one way of rethinking local histories from the perspectives of those involved.

> Almost everything about the Pygmies of Equatorial Africa is controversial, even their name. Their biology, their archaeology, their history, their past and present linguistic status, their uses of their environment, their relationships with their neighbours, their rights as citizens of the countries in which they live, their entitlement to live as they choose in the present and to work out their own future—all these and much more evoke vigorous differences of opinion. (Woodburn 2000:78)

The two largest groupings of hunter-gatherers and former hunter-gatherers in Africa are the San or Bushmen of Southern Africa and the Pygmies or Forest People[1] of Central Africa. Similarly to San peoples, there is great diversity among the peoples academics refer to as Pygmies. Today the generally accepted definition of Pygmies, by both academics and educated members of Pygmy groups,[2] encompasses virtually all the hunter-gatherers and former hunter-gatherers inhabiting the Central African equatorial forest belt and adjoining areas.

Pygmy people have specific names related to the areas of forest they inhabit. Significant natural features like mountains, rivers, lakes, marshes, and savannah often demarcate the boundaries between different groups. As can be seen on the map there are hunter-gatherer ethnic groups in many areas of the equatorial forest. Pygmy peoples live in at least ten Central African countries.[3] The majority inhabit forested areas and many remain heavily focused on forest life and activities.

The 'Kalahari Debate' that prompted the publication of this book has forced a careful reexamination of hunter-gatherer pasts and presents. This has had the positive effect of provoking an increasingly sophisticated understanding of hunter-gatherers' histories and interactions with other groups. Previous chapters attest to the diverse historical experiences of different San peoples of southern Africa. The Thamaga San discussed by Sadr appear to have gone from being autonomous hunter-gatherers to subjugated serfs in the last two or three centuries. The Ghanzi San, however, continued to trade independently, and fight and resist encroachers on their land despite encapsulation by farmers and pastoralists (Guenther, this volume). During the same period the Ju people were autonomous hunter-gatherers until Europeans began arriving in their area (Lee, this volume). San and Pygmy peoples' encounters with outsiders are similar for their diversity and not for any particular uniformity. The diversity of examples presented in this volume pays testimony to the great variety of situations that have arisen and the different solutions and accommodations hunter-gatherers have employed.

There are many different groups of Central African forest hunter-gatherers and

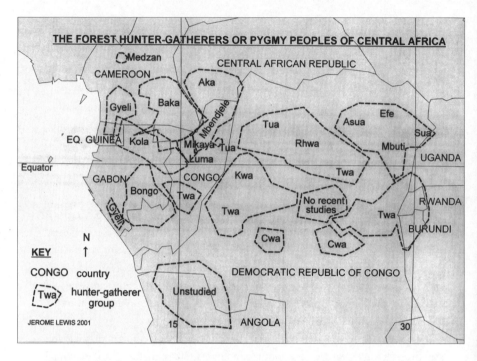

Figure 11.1. The forest hunter-gatherers or Pygmy peoples of Central Africa.

former hunter-gatherers that are referred to as Pygmies, but each has its own history, its own name, area of forest, and particular current situation, as well as high levels of intracultural variation. To illustrate our discussion we take some examples from our own research areas among two western Pygmy groups living in Northern Congo, the Baka and the Mbendjele (Aka),[4] and an eastern Pygmy group, the Twa of the Great Lakes Region, in addition to existing ethnography.[5] The history of the Twa Pygmies of the Great Lakes Region provides an illustration of the diversity of relations that can occur between the same Pygmy hunter-gatherer group and farmers and pastoralists migrating onto their land.

A BRIEF HISTORICAL SUMMARY OF SOME TWA ENCOUNTERS WITH INCOMING FARMERS AND PASTORALISTS

The Twa Pygmies of the Great Lakes Region are estimated to number between 70,000 and 87,000 people dispersed over approximately 100,000 square kilometers (Lewis 2000:5). The rich volcanic soils of their region have proved extremely attractive to incoming agriculturalists and today support some of the highest population densities in rural sub-Saharan Africa.

In what is known as Rwanda today, the ancestors of the Hutu and the Tutsi had colonized most of the best agricultural land by the fifteenth century, taking it over by gradual deforestation. The Twa were increasingly confined to forest areas considered inhospitable by farmers. By the seventeenth century the Tutsi monarchy was firmly established in Rwanda. During the nineteenth and twentieth centuries, according to Kagabo and Mudandagizi (1974), the majority of Twa were unable to live from hunting and gathering because of widespread deforestation. Deprived of land, pottery became their main occupation. Being a potter gave the Twa the right to build a house but not land rights, or an acknowledged or legal right to the clay they required. Many Twa ended up as impoverished clients or tenants paying with labor and pottery. Thus the occupation of potter became a symbol of low status and poverty.

Other Twa took refuge in high montane forests to avoid the farmers. However, as population pressures increased, these areas were increasingly encroached upon. There are several documented accounts of Twa resisting incoming farmers and pastoralists. Schumaker (1950:400) recounts that Twa groups in the Bushiva highlands fought long wars with agricultural peoples who attempted to clear their ancestral forest for farms. This fighting continued right up until the 1930s.

In precolonial Bufumbira (southwestern Uganda) the Twa were recognized by the Rwandan kings as owners of the high montane forests they occupied (Maquet and Naigiziki 1957). They paid tribute to the Rwandan king and were entitled to tolls from caravans passing through their forest as well as payment from Hutu farmers wishing to set up. From 1750 onwards the population of farmers increased greatly and inter-Hutu conflict intensified. The Twa were crucial in helping lineage heads protect their farms and population from attack. In the 1830s the Tutsi royal family, critically depending on Twa archers, conquered and incorporated Bufumbira into the Rwandan State. Some Twa established themselves as important personages at the royal courts. In eastern Bufumbira the Twa claimed tribute from the Hutu farmers around them and paid tribute to the Tutsi court at Busanza (Kingdon 1990; Mateke 1970).

However, during the twentieth century the increasing numbers of newcomers cutting down the forest for farms and pasture encapsulated the Twa in ever-diminishing areas of forest.

"Since the beginning we have always lived in the forest. Like my father and grandfathers, I lived from hunting and collecting on this mountain. Then the Bahutu came. They cut the forest to cultivate the land. They carried on cutting and planting until they had encircled our forest with their fields. Today they come right up to our huts. Instead of forest, now we are surrounded by Irish potatoes!" Gahut Gahuliro, Twa man, born c. 1897, Muhabura, Uganda, July 1999. (Lewis 2000:8)

PYGMIES AND THEIR NEIGHBORS

All contemporary Pygmy ethnic groups maintain some kind of relationship with village-dwelling people from farming, trapping, and fishing communities. The many languages they speak today attest to the diversity of Pygmy groups' histories and their relationships with others. This has caused a consensus to develop over the last three decades among scholars concerning a long and complex history of contact between hunter-gatherer and farming populations, and the debate has largely shifted from the discussion of isolated cultures to issues concerning their articulation. Even ecologists are looking for explanations of social phenomena in the history of specific interactions between the peoples concerned rather than in ecological or evolutionary models of systems adapting or in equilibrium.

The authors' fieldwork areas in Northern Congo provide interesting snapshots of some consistencies in the ways local people understand these relations. Mbendjele refer to all the Pygmy people they know of as Yaka (plural Bayaka or Baaka, and singular, Moyaka or Moaka) and consider them to be *bisi ndima* ("forest people") regardless of what language they speak. Thus even the Ubangian-language-speaking Ngombe (Baka) on the west side of the Sangha River are Yaka to the Bantu-language-speaking Mbendjele on the east side. And vice versa, Baka Pygmies living near Moloundou in southeastern Cameroon call themselves Baka and refer to other Pygmy groups—like the Mbendjele, Luma, or Mikaya—as Baka too. Despite the linguistic classification of the two languages as entirely different in structure and origin, Mbendjele (Aka) say they all used to speak Yaka and that when they go to stay with Baka they are able to understand and speak Baka easily after a short time.

All groups in this area either use the name Bayaka, Baaka, or Baka. They claim shared origins and ancestry with the first forest people, and claim that their slightly different ethnonyms are all versions of the same name—*yaka (what Bahuchet [1993] has referred to as the *baakaa). The differing pronunciations of this term reflect regional accents and the popular tendency to drop consonants in normal speech.

A similarly broad ethnic classification is made of non-Yaka farming or fishing peoples who have moved into Yaka forest and speak a wide variety of different languages. The Mbendjele term *Bilo* encompasses over 48 different ethnic groups, though currently Mbendjele maintain relations with only around ten of these. 'Bilo' are various Bantu- and Ubangian-language(s)-speaking, village-dwelling agriculturalists. These peoples have migrated into the Mbendjele forest where they make a living from farming, and fishing or trapping. For the Mbendjele they all fall into the category of *bisi mboka* ("village people"), who like to live in cleared and therefore hot and open spaces and who make aggressive claims to own rivers, forests, and other people.

In conversations, Mbendjele elders often remark that these groups of outsiders are transient: "they are passing by," "they have arrived but are not yet gone," and "they came into life but will go again." As examples of this movement they mention abandoned villages and logging sites and point to generally diminishing numbers of people living in rural Bilo communities. Indeed, none of the forest-dwelling Bilo groups claim to have been in the forest for long; in their oral histories they all talk of migrations occurring during the late precolonial period. In contemporary Mbendjele parlance, growing urban populations are also referred to as Bilo.

With the exception of immigrant Muslim traders from countries further north, Baka across the Sangha River from the Mbendjele summarily refer to all local and nonlocal Bantu as 'Kaka.' Kaka is the ethnonym of a particular group of Bantu speakers (A 90), who live in southeastern Cameroon and in Northern Congo-Brazzaville. In Li-Baka, their name has become a generic term for the 16 known different groups of Bantu- and Ubangian-language(s)-speaking neighbors and is used even in areas where there are no ethnic Kaka. In order to avoid confusion with the Kaka ethnic group, in this chapter we will use the term *Bilo* to represent both the Mbendjele and Baka use of this indigenous generic term.

Other anthropologists have attempted to capture this sense of a generic ethnicity using concepts such as 'Bantu' and 'Pygmies,' 'farmers' and 'hunter-gatherers,' or 'Grands Noirs' ("tall blacks") and 'Pygmées' (Bahuchet). Importantly the term *Bilo* does not make a distinction between Bantu- and Ubangian-language(s)-speakers or between distinct modes of subsistence. In this way it captures well a Yaka perspective on outsiders and a general sense of ethnicity.

There exists a developed oral tradition that elaborates and entrenches cultural stereotypes differentiating Yaka from Bilo through accounts of the past. These numerous and widely told stories attest to the enduring and elaborate nature of the opposition between Bilo 'village people' and Yaka 'forest people.' Similar ethnic distinctions are widespread among the peoples of Central Africa and have been commented on by other ethnographers of the region. Notably, in the Ituri Forest of the Democratic Republic of Congo by Turnbull (1966) for the Mbuti forest people, and more recently by Grinker (1994) for the Lese Dese village people.

Even where forest people no longer have access to forest, speak the same language, or have many similar cultural practices and beliefs as their farmer neighbors, these ethnic oppositions do not break down. Indeed, they can become more entrenched, when segregation and discrimination increase, as it becomes more and more difficult to gain an independent livelihood from the forest. This has happened to the Twa Pygmies in many parts of the Great Lakes Region (Lewis 2000).

MODELS OF PYGMY-FARMER INTERACTIONS

The most commonly held view on the history of these relations is that Pygmies and farmers have been engaged in ecologically and socioeconomically conditioned exchange relationships for thousands of years in some areas. The conventional view is that groups of Bantu, Adamawa-Ubangian, and Central Sudanic-speaking cultivators expanded southwards into the forest from about 5000–4000 B.P. onwards, and had settled most areas by 1000 A.D.[6] The archaeological evidence suggests a continuous presence of hunter-gatherers for 100,000 years, at least in some parts of the forest (Clist 1999). There is no conclusive evidence for the phenotype of these people since no skeletal remains have been found yet.

With the notable exceptions of Bailey et al. (1989, 1992) and Blench (1999), most researchers subscribe to the idea that the contemporary Pygmy groups are the descendants of these indigenous Central African rain-forest hunter-gatherers. As the farming groups arrived on the edges of the forest, Pygmies guided their migrations across the forest and showed them how to live in their new environment. In return farmers are believed to have provided cultivated food, iron, and salt—and more recently modern consumer items such as second-hand clothing, imported household goods, and radios—in return for labor, meat, and other forest products from Pygmies.

Over three decades ago, Colin Turnbull (1966) famously argued against a then-prevalent notion of the Mbuti Pygmies, as a degenerate and culturally inferior race that depended for their subsistence needs on their farming neighbors.[7] His ethnographic realism was driven by the humanistic intention to provide a critique of Western civilization and to counter the negative portrayals of a people then commonly seen as surviving vestiges of prehistoric human life.[8] Committed to the idea that Mbuti Pygmies had a high potential for complete autonomy, Turnbull emphasized their social and ideological distinctiveness and argued that their relations with neighboring farmers had to be understood in terms of economic exchange and mutual convenience. Since then, the status of Pygmies both as dependent, independent, or interdependent actors has been discussed in a variety of historical and geographical contexts. Their contemporary situation, however, is usually understood as resulting from a long-standing symbiosis or interdependency, which invariably appears to have led to their dependent status and often also to their exploitation by farmers.

A common assumption is that these relations are predicated upon material exchanges and result from complementary and specialized subsistence practices that exploit different ecological niches. Though rooted in symbiosis, a socioeconomic and cultural interdependency, they resemble patron-client relations that are politically biased in favor of the farmers (cf. Bahuchet 1985:546). It is within such a framework of materialist and behavioral ecology, with the assumption of standard categories of patron/client-type relations, that most of the current anthropological research is conducted.[9] In this approach, qualitative aspects of these relations tend to be gauged by the quantification of exchanges and a comparison between local subsistence technologies and resource management.

With some notable exceptions (Bahuchet and Guillaume 1982; Grinker 1990, 1994; Terashima 1987), little attention has been paid to the symbolic and cultural dimensions of these relations. Grinker most clearly criticized the material bias and the analytical primacy of economic factors for obscuring or ignoring ideas and beliefs underlying farmer/hunter-gatherer interaction. Focusing on the symbolism of exchanges rather than their economic content, his particular advance on conventional views was an analysis of Lese farmers and their Efe Pygmy exchange partners as mutually constitutive and interconnected subgroups participating in a larger social collectivity, indeed as one ethnically differentiated society (1990, 1994:4).

His 'two cultures—one society' model is, however, heavily biased toward the Lese farmers' perspective and analyzes Efe cultural distinctiveness as if it was the result of their subordinate incorporation into the Lese social system. From the Lese perspective, Efe are incorporated as children into their 'Houses' and thus figure as juniors in the relationship. Although Grinker extensively discusses ethnicity as a historically constituted process in which the Lese and the Efe have integrated themselves into a set of relations of inequality, he crucially omits the Efe perspective on this process. Grinker does not discuss whether Efe contest Lese views or how they interpret and respond to what he presents as an hegemonic system of cultural distinctions and an apparently unchallenged ideology of Efe subordination. The Efe virtually have no voice at all. The 'mutual constitution' of hunter-gatherers and farmers is thus highlighted through a focus on Lese representations of themselves, the Efe and their mutual relations, privileging a perspective that takes Efe subordination for granted.

The dual structure that is central to Grinker's approach, in terms of a dominant and a subordinate culture united in a single social system, resembles a reformulation of the patron-client model that is also implied in most subsistence-related analyses. The latter posit distinct, sometimes overlapping, but usually complementary modes of subsistence that characterize the interaction of farmer and hunter-gatherer groups.

However, a major problem with the orthodox 'symbiosis' view is its suggestion that hunter-gatherer/farmer relations were continuously maintained once they had been established out of a nutritional necessity. If this were the case all farmers and all hunter-gatherers would have to maintain close relations continuously in order to survive. Questions concerning historical contacts and the development and continuity of relations are, however, far from being answered. That all contemporary Pygmy groups speak languages related to those of non-Pygmy farmers points to prolonged and intensive social interaction. The historical divergence of their languages following the separation of former 'language communities' as well as various oral traditions indicate, on the other hand, that these relations have also been discontinuous both in space and time.

Grinker's study is important because it provides a very good example of the way agricultural groups attempt to legitimate their demands for Pygmy labor by an elaborate ideology that places specific Pygmy groups under their authority. These ideological constructions are typical of many farmer peoples throughout the forest that seek to denigrate Pygmy people and justify claims to authority over their labor and forest land.[10] The symbolic domination of Efe by their Lese partners has many similarities with the attempts of various Bilo/Kaka groups in the Congo to justify 'their' Pygmies' position as juniors and dependents. In our view this is because most farming groups face similar problems in obtaining necessary additional farming labor at key moments in the agricultural cycle and use similar strategies to secure it from their Pygmy neighbors. From a Yaka point of view, the categories of 'Bilo/Kaka' make additional sense because they group together all the different ethnic groups that share a demand for their labor and forest produce.

THE 'KALAHARI DEBATE' IN THE RAIN FOREST

A 'revisionist' debate on the historical origins of tropical forest hunter-gatherers began simultaneously with regard to the Mbuti Pygmies (Hart and Hart 1986) and the Penan Negritos of Borneo (Headland 1987). Bailey and his coauthors (1989) further developed the argument that is essentially based on the hypothesis that humans are unable to live in tropical rain forests without agriculture, and therefore hunter-gatherer groups could not have been in the forest prior to the arrival of farmers. Whereas the revisionists in the 'Kalahari Debate' introduced neglected historical sources and opened a discussion of the wider political economy of the area, Pygmy contacts with their agriculturalist neighbors have so far been discussed mainly in ahistorical terms focusing on subsistence economy and ecological relations.

The argument that autonomous rain-forest hunting and gathering was not viable was partly based on the ethnographic finding that contemporary rain-forest hunter-gatherers are almost universally engaged in exchange relationships with cultivators. The 'revisionists' further noted a lack of reports or data showing that forest dwellers could subsist exclusively and all year round by hunting and gathering[11] and inferred from a limited set of biological data that 'primary' rain forests produced low yields of energy-rich foods.[12] The Pygmy specialization in obtaining forest products—skills they are thought to have acquired in forest fringe zones, forest-savannah ecotones, or through seasonal forays into the forest—was thus a necessary condition for the joint colonization of the deeper forest in symbiosis with savannah cultivators (Bailey et al. 1989:63). Therefore, they argued that forest hunter-gatherers' relations with farmers come from necessity, not choice, and that this accounts for their domination by farmers.

These hypotheses provoked a strong reaction among researchers who had spent extended periods with 'independent' forest hunter-gatherers. Against the 'culti-vated calories hypothesis,' a range of comparative ecological, archaeological, ethno-historical, and linguistic data was rallied to support an alternative hypothesis. In particular, Bahuchet and his coauthors (1991:208) pointed out that the ecological studies by Hart and Hart (1986), on which the revisionists' hypothesis rested, were mainly concerned with the peculiar *Gilbertodendron* monospecific forest, rather than the more common 'mosaic forest' characteristic of the Congo basin and preferred by Aka people. Mbendjele Pygmies among whom Lewis worked prefer explicitly not to camp for extended periods with women and children in large areas of *Gilber-todendron* forest precisely because of the difficulty in finding wild yams. This over-sight on the part of the revisionists is related to the mythologizing of the Central African forests as a pristine wilderness of 'primary' rain forest. In fact, *Homo sapiens sapiens* has continuously inhabited the western Congo basin for 100,000 years (Clist 1999). Villages have existed in some parts of the forest for at least 2,500 years and the signs of past human occupation are present in the form of palm nut kernels in al-most every forest stream of reasonable size (M. Fay, quoted in Quammen 2000:16).

Ichikawa (1983 and 1991:135) made the important point that his own ecological re-search shows that a fully balanced wild plant food diet is available to the Mbuti of the Teturi region in D.R. Congo. However, Ichikawa suggests that the Mbuti today use only a limited number of these wild resources because, with their increasing specialization in the bush meat trade, they can secure an advantageous exchange for cultivated calories. On a similar theme Bahuchet and his coauthors (1991) and Bahuchet (1993a) have argued that under present conditions Pygmies have relatively easy access to cultivated food and make a correspondingly low use of wild plant foods, especially of wild yams. This situation does not, however, allow us to infer a low availability of wild plant food resources nor a similarly limited use of them in the past. Sato (2001) recently vindicated those who doubted the revisionist argu-ment by providing conclusive evidence to demonstrate the sufficiency of wild starch food plants for people in Baka forest. It is likely that similar results would be obtained in other areas of the Congo basin popular with Pygmy peoples.

The 'rain forest revisionist' claims have similar implications to the 'revisionist' argument in the 'Kalahari Debate,' as 'antirevisionists' have pointed out. They imply denial of the efficacy of hunter-gatherers' own intentions and cultural cre-ativity and that their unique skills were only developed as a consequence of the needs and activities of other, more powerful groups of farmers (or herders). Curi-ously, however, the first attempts at 'rain forest revision' in Central Africa (Bailey et al. 1989) did not question the status of Pygmies as the indigenous Central African forest people, nor the essential nature of their hunter-gatherer lifestyle.

Blench (1999), however, has made a radical attempt to revive this debate. He com-pares different types of evidence—subsistence and other technology, linguistic, archaeological, biological, and cultural data—and comments on crucial absences of information. In support of his main argument—that the African Pygmies are simply the same people as their farmer neighbors—Blench notes that there is no ancient Pygmy language, no archaeological traces are proven to have been left by Pygmy ancestors, existing genetic data are problematic, there are insufficient wild carbohydrates in the forest, no exclusive hunting technology, and no musical style or features common to all Pygmy groups. Since the forest cannot support a hunting-and-gathering lifestyle all year round, new arrivals settled ecotones on the edge of forest and other environments such as swamp or river. A specialized group of hunters developed who periodically went into the forest. Eventually they became endogamous and were regarded as another ethnic group. Their small stature was achieved through natural selection and by marrying out the taller women to their farmer neighbors (1999:51).

The fundamental problem with Blench's argument—which he acknowledges—is the absence of data to support his polemical hypothesis. The most significant weakness is its basis on the contention that the tropical forest cannot support hunter-gatherers all year round. Other issues also require clarification. The genetic research undertaken by Cavalli-Sforza (1986) shows Ituri Pygmy groups to have distinctive and unique genes whereas Aka and Baka Pygmies are genetically quite similar to their neighbors and Twa, Kola, Gieli, and Bongo Pygmies are even more so. Blench (1999:44–45) interprets this as showing Pygmies to be the same as their neighbors. Thus the Ituri results are simply anomalous and hence doubtful. However, both Blench, and previously Cavalli-Sforza (1986), fail to take social practices into account. At present, when Pygmy women in the Ituri Forest give birth to farmer children, these children are incorporated into farmer society and live in the village as a farmer, thus passing Pygmy genes into the farmer gene pool but not vice versa. In contrast, among farmer groups living around the Yaka (Aka and Baka) any child issuing from a union between Pygmy and farmer is left with the mother to be brought up a Pygmy. These different practices—observed in the twentieth century—are conditioned by particular forms of socioeconomic relations at a given time and we cannot project them into the past, but distinct patterns of social integration—absent in the interpretation of the genetic data referred to above—point to alternative ways of accounting for such data.[13]

In comparing Pygmies with the San, Blench comments that Pygmies no longer speak their own languages. However, in his comparison he fails to remark on the hugely different timescales between San groups' contacts with outsiders and Pygmy-farmer interactions. In the former case, interactions with incoming groups may only be a few hundred years old; in the latter these interactions are thought to have begun around 4,000–5,000 years ago. Over such lengths of time much can happen to languages. Bahuchet's (1992, 1993a) analysis of the shared vocabulary between Aka and Baka led him to argue that it represents an ancient shared language—an argument Blench contests as being possibly a "contact phenomenon" (1999:51). However, both contemporary Aka and Baka agree that they share the same ancestors and origins, and spoke the same language in the past.[14]

The Aka are in contact with 19 ethnic groups speaking different languages and the Baka with 16 (Bahuchet 1993a:68). The example of the Hadza hunter-gatherers of Tanzania is a useful comparison here. Woodburn (1988:40) describes how outsiders in Hadza country, even long-term immigrants into Hadza society, do not learn to speak or understand Hadza but expect Hadza to learn their languages. This is consistent with other social barriers imposed as a consequence of the negative stereotypes almost universally held of hunter-gatherer and former hunter-gatherer peoples by their agricultural, pastoral, or capitalist neighbors.[15] The behavior reported of outsiders in Hadza country is consistent with the behavior of most farmers in the Central African forests, and the reasons are very similar.

Quite widely in Africa, hunter-gatherers are seen as relatively politically impotent, and hence frequently labeled as inferiors by their neighbors. Their lifestyle contrasts in so many ways with the cherished values of a successful farmer that it is often represented as unintelligible, or as a 'bastardized form.' As Woodburn points out, this leads to two areas of stereotype construction: one in which the hunter-gatherers are seen as inferior, or another in which they may be portrayed as "outcasts or outlaws who are living as they do because other choices have been denied them" (Woodburn 1988:40). Blackburn (1971:144, cited in Woodburn 1988:41) describes as a gross misconception a similar notion held by unspecified outsiders that Okiek hunter-gatherers in Kenya are a group of criminals and runaways from diverse ethnic groups. Woodburn warns of caution before believing outsiders' views of stigmatized groups and notes that "much recent writing has, I believe, fallen into the trap of doing just that" (1988:42).

Following Vansina's lead (1990:56), Schadeberg (1999) presents the distribution and meanings attributed to the term Batwa in the Bantu languages of much of sub-Saharan Africa and confirms that it is an ethnic label for autochthonous people, including many Pygmy groups, who have a history of hunting and gathering or continue to practice it today. As Woodburn (2000:79) points out, the wide distribution of this term indicates that the category 'hunter-gatherer' is not a result of nineteenth-century European evolutionary theories but is a long-standing indigenous African category. This is further demonstrated by generic indigenous ethnonyms such as Yaka (hunter-gatherer) and Bilo (non–hunter-gatherer). The emphasis on subsistence practices in otherwise highly politically charged African self-categorizations is attested to by the observation that in some cases there are no obvious traits, such as language or culture, to make an ethnic distinction between those referred to as Batwa and their non-Batwa neighbors apart from the (former) Batwa mode of subsistence and associated 'immediate return' values (see Lewis 2000).

Pygmy peoples' adoption of Bantu and Ubangian languages may be better understood in this context. When cultural and ethnic difference is primarily defined by
mode of subsistence, those practicing the same mode of subsistence are more likely
to focus on markers of ethnicity such as language or culture in order to distinguish
themselves. When the groups concerned have radically different modes of subsistence, it may be that language is much less important as a marker of difference, and
hence much less significance is placed on maintaining different languages. Hunter-
gatherers are more likely to accommodate themselves linguistically to their neighbors than vice versa. This is for some of the reasons pointed out above but also, very
importantly, it derives from forest hunter-gatherers' own values of social and economic equality and inclusiveness.

It is the significance of the differences between groups that comes out of chapters
in the present volume and offers important alternatives to totalizing revisionist arguments. Just as it is now clear that there is no uniform or singular San or 'Bushman'
history, neither is there a single 'Pygmy' history. Bahuchet (1993b) charts how writers, philosophers, theologians, and later scientists and other academics created the
concept of 'Pygmies,' from Homer's *Iliad* to the nineteenth-century interest of
physical anthropologists in discovering other forms of humanity. He ends his article, entitled 'The Invention of the Pygmies' with the observation that *"To tell the
truth, the Pygmies do not exist.* The people who do exist have the names Baka, Ba-
Bongo, BaKola, BaAka, BaSua, Efe, Asua, BaTwa . . . who knows what they have in
common, apart from exciting the Western imagination"* (Bahuchet 1993b:175, original emphasis, our translation).

The generalizing of grand historical hypotheses and their tendency to ignore
and smudge over important and meaningful differences on the ground must be
avoided unless carefully qualified. It is the histories of these smaller groups that are
interesting, and it will only be through studying them individually that a more general picture will emerge.

The most detailed of these have been done by Bahuchet and Guillaume (1982),
Delobeau (1989), and Joiris (1998). In particular, Joiris's sophisticated synthesis of approaches provides an analysis of Baka-Bilo relations in southeastern Cameroon that
is both historically informed and anthropologically sensitive. Her ethnography and
examination of key terms is presented alongside an erudite historical analysis that
argues that in this case Baka-villager relations were established within the context of
interethnic and intergroup raiding, and the villagers' need for ivory to participate in
prestige economies prior to the colonial pacification. Villagers, fearing attacks by
Baka *mokelakela* ("elephant men"—see also Köhler 2000), sought alliances with Baka
elephant hunters to protect themselves from these attacks by other Baka transformed into elephants. Additionally, renowned Kwele, Konabembe, and Bangando
warriors sought initiation into Baka ritual associations such as Jɛngi or *mokela* (a

shape-shifting association) for the mystical powers these gave. Joiris convincingly demonstrates that establishing relations with Baka was a political decision by villagers, not one forced upon them by ecological limitations. Those influential villagers or feared warriors who could attract Baka would greatly enhance their clan's numbers, their ability to conduct raids, and increase their fame and prestige.

In short, Joiris shows that relations forming between Baka and villagers by the end of the nineteenth century were based on similar principles to the warrior alliances that had commonly been used in this area to unite villager groups during the nineteenth century (Joiris 1998:21–26). She elucidates three major ways that Baka-villager relations are symbolized and maintained: as ritual friendships between members of the same sex; as fictive kinship relations; and as the solidarity established between co-initiates during *beka* circumcision rites. These relations have been modified and adapted to changing contexts to produce the relations we can observe today. Joiris's overall formulation demonstrates the significance of political, social, and military considerations in creating Pygmy-villager relationships rather than concerns for carbohydrates and protein.

REGIONAL HISTORIES

Among the most interesting general studies of Central African history are those based on linguistic sources. These have emerged in the study of words, their distribution and pronunciation shifts. Some of these focus on limited historical regions and include Pygmy languages. Through the identification of loanwords and phonological analyses, such studies have been able to trace historical contacts between different language communities.

In Vansina's (1990:65) historical trajectory, hunter-gatherer Pygmy bands were gradually but inexorably drawn into dependent relationships with farmers, thoroughly lost their languages,[16] and had disappeared from large portions of the Central African rain forest long before 1900. Vansina has proposed that these developments had occurred with the diffusion of iron-working technologies and, much more importantly, with the spread of the banana from circa 200 B.C. to around A.D. 500, which allowed farmers to live in forest areas. The first process led to clashes between hunter-gatherers and immigrating farmers, the second to hunter-gatherer dependence and their increasing marginalization.

Contra Vansina, Klieman has suggested that neither the knowledge of metallurgy nor the advances achieved through cultivation—for instance of the banana—necessarily led to the development of hierarchical social systems in which agricultural societies wielded economic and social power over hunter-gatherers (1995:20). In her view, as trade networks expanded, peoples throughout the region took up economic specializations, most often turning to resources they had at hand. Thus autochthonous communities became specialist procurers of forest products (cam-wood, ivory, meat, etc.). In some cases this led to increased reliance of forest special-ists on neighboring agriculturalists, in others it led to more-or-less balanced social and economic relations. Linguistic evidence indicates that in entering into broader trade networks, some forest specialist groups even began lessening their contacts with people they shared a language with, eventually to develop their own version of that language.[17] The latter is evident in the delivery of hunting products directly to local sovereigns without the aid of agriculturalist middlemen. So there is no evi-dence for dating 'serfdom' or 'dependence' that far back (1995:15).

Just as for their agriculturalist neighbors, it simply cannot be upheld that the different Pygmy or hunter-gatherer groups have the same history, or that it was a linear or static history. Instead they experienced shifting periods of greater and lesser contact with agriculturalists over time and in different areas (Klieman 1995:20). Klieman (1995, 1997, 1999, in press) has focused mainly on the question of the socioeconomic autonomy and dependence of hunter-gatherers in relations with agriculturalists and their participation in trade systems. She has thus fruitfully advanced the debate by outlining the distinct 'histories' of some of these hunter-gatherer groups over the last five millennia as evidenced by data from archaeology and historical linguistics.

Klieman also points out that developments during the mercantilist era, a period spanning five centuries and characterized by social and economic upheavals un-precedented in African history, do not reflect realities before the Atlantic Trade. The effects of this trade from the late fifteenth century onwards may have been more profound on hunter-gatherer societies than they were on others, since those that had remained independent throughout the era of Bantu settlement had not developed the hierarchical social structures that would have allowed them to enter the markets on an equal basis. Therefore, if they wished to enter the trade they had to contend with an incorporation into the system at its lowest level, that of pro-duction. Only during this era does Klieman attribute relations of dependence or serfdom to hunter-gatherer populations (1995:18–19).

THE 'DOMINANT ACTOR' APPROACH TO BILO-YAKA RELATIONS

The above discussion has highlighted a more general problem in most authors' ap-proach, even those focusing on the Pygmy 'side' of interaction. There is a tendency to accord priority to the agency of farmers and to their strategies to bind Pygmies to them.[18] Although Pygmies are undeniably seen as actors in their own rights, the common assumption is that farmers are the dominant social (and economic) force and are able to impose their will on their Pygmy neighbors. Early missionaries and colonial officials in Northern Congo frequently described their association as a relationship between village 'patrons' and Pygmy 'clients' (for example, Hauser 1951:25–28), and later on Delobeau, among others, saw it as a feudal relation between sedentary peoples and their Pygmy 'serfs' (1984:121).[19]

Pygmies are thus usually cast not as victims but as subject to outside forces, primarily those of their natural environment but also to those of the immigrating farmers. The rain forest has widely been conceived as an essentially adverse and inhospitable environment for humans. Pygmies are one of the exceptions since they successfully 'adapted' to it, especially in biogenetic terms through 'dwarfing.' Concerning their human environment they are either experiencing subordination or they have been trying to 'resist' such attempts. Pygmy agency is thus either eclipsed by, or reduced to, an organic adaptation to environmental pressures or obscured by quantifying approaches to their contemporary interaction with farmers. When Pygmies finally enter the scene as social actors, their agency is ultimately compromised in avoidance strategies.[20]

Despite diversity in the ways different Bilo groups ideologically express their aspirations to dominate Pygmy people and to incorporate them into their social systems, there is a shared core of practices and claims that resemble anthropological concepts of patron-client relations. In Northern Congo, Bilo try to represent their Yaka partners to the state, claim rights over their labor, and describe their position as that of 'owner' or 'patron.' However, describing these attempts as patron-client relations ignores a rather resolute, and effective, opposition by Yaka groups to Bilo claims to authority, and the very limited ability of Bilo 'patrons' to coerce their 'clients' to obey their wishes. Classifying this complex ethnic interaction wholesale as a patron-client relationship is misleading because it carries inappropriate connotations. Above all, it results from not taking into account the Yaka view.

The misapplication of the 'patron-client' category is often the outcome of an unfortunately common habit of conducting research among Pygmies with the help of non-Pygmy interpreters and research assistants. Thus a formative input in the investigation of politically charged relations comes from a necessarily biased and partial party. In our experience, the context created by the presence of Bilo, even of those sympathetic to the Yaka, will always affect the way Yaka talk about their relations and respond to questions about them. Thus we agree with Vansina (1986:432, 1990:29) that it is a fatal flaw to study only parts of societies, and that it is important to examine both partners' conceptions of each other in order to understand their relations. But we would add that it is even more fatal to collect data about Pygmies through neighboring, often more accessible groups, or to treat Pygmies as an organic component of forest environments (see, for example, Bailey and Aunger 1990; or Sawada 1990) rather than as social actors producing their own history. In the interest of a less biased view, it is not only necessary to observe interactions as they unfold, but also to listen to both sides independently.

We are not claiming that there is a homogeneous, unchanging 'Pygmy world-view.' As for all people, such worldviews are historically and geographically situated. But we will concentrate on the Mbendjele case to elaborate what we believe are common threads in Yaka strategies to 'exploit' resources and to structure relations with outsiders. To do this we will focus on cultural stereotypes of their relations. This focus may obscure the slightly different ways different groups interact, and ignores the variety of possible interpersonal relations that can develop between individuals. But the strong similarities between Yaka communities in the ways they talk about their relations with members of various Bilo ethnic groups, justifies analyzing particular Mbendjele cultural stereotypes in an attempt to elucidate a more general understanding of these relations. This allows us to focus on the content of indigenous views, rather than on the question of how anthropological categories can be made to fit them.

THE SITUATION IN NORTHERN CONGO

The 'two cultures—one society' model and other dualisms of the farmer/hunter-gatherer type are abstractions that do not capture the complexity of our, and most other, regional contexts, neither now nor in the past. Interethnic social relations are usually embedded in 'multicultural' constellations. For the past, this has been substantiated by shared words for iron objects and other trade items across numerous groups. And in present-day Northern Congo, the Mbendjele maintain formal relations with over ten ethnically distinct Bilo groups and four other Yaka groups, and Baka in the Souanké and Sembé Districts interact with at least three other Bantu-speaking Bilo and one other Yaka group. The precolonial and early colonial corporate structure of 'Houses' likewise had a 'multicultural' history not only in our areas (cf. Vansina 1990:73–77). Under the leadership of 'big' men 'Houses' incorporated cognates, affines, friends, clients, and dependents from a variety of ethnic groups.[21]

At present, wider social configurations, not only in Northern Congo, usually include a number of Bilo and Yaka groups plus politically important minorities such as Muslim traders, nonregional administrators, foreign loggers, development agents, and even non-African researchers. Such complex configurations are better understood as multitier formations rather than being simplified into a dual structure. Locally, Bilo often understand the position and relation of the different groups to each other as a hierarchical configuration.[22] This is not the case for the Mbendjele. Rather, central to Mbendjele thought about outsiders is that they are temporary inhabitants of the forest, in contrast to Yaka peoples who are permanent. In normal speech the term *Bilo* is used to refer to any non-Yaka black people. *Mindele* is used to refer to all light skinned people—Caucasians, Chinese, and other

Asians alike. In conversation, unless people are Yaka, they are simply referred to as Mindele, Bilo, or by animal names.

According to elder Mbendjele informants, the ancestors called the Bilo 'Bamakaba.' This literally translates as "they will give." This usage probably coincided with the precolonial period, before 1870, and the early colonial period when the Bilo and Mbendjele in Lewis's research area claim they first began establishing relations. The Bilo recount how they used gifts to attract Mbendjele to them. This generosity seems to be implied in the term Bamakaba. Today the polite way to refer to Bilo is with the term *Bilo*. 'Bilo' literally means "uninitiated." Apparently the ancestors never initiated Bilo, but today most communities do. Nowadays 'Bilo' carries the connotation of 'village people' rather than 'the uninitiated.'

In every Mbendjele community visited, Bilo are more commonly called 'gorillas,' than by any other name.[23] This name is not always intended to insult, although it does when Bilo hear it. The Mbendjele consider it a factual statement about Bilo disposition and character. Bilo resemble gorillas because they are both large animals with abundant meat, or wealth in the Bilo case, but they are easily angered and dangerous to hunt. Both Bilo and gorillas are preoccupied with demarcating and aggressively claiming areas of forest as their own, to the exclusion of all others. In both cases Yaka oppose them.

White people are referred to by two animal names. Most often they are called 'red river hogs' and rarely today, but more frequently in the past, 'elephant of our ancestors.' Both these appellations refer to the economic value of white people. Elephants are a source of valuable ivory and abundant meat. This image conveys the potential of whites as sources of immense wealth. In the past, white men often came on their own, but were accompanied by Chadian or Senegalese soldiers. Large rogue elephants provide the biggest tusks and are fearfully powerful. The metaphor fits the early colonial administrators and traders well. Large elephants were more common in the past than they are today. Now red river hogs have taken over from elephants in terms of commercial value. These large, often very fat, wild pigs are in great demand for the bush meat trade with urban centers. Their habit of living in groups means that sometimes three or four may be killed at a time. These resemblances go further than purely economic criteria. Today most white people come in groups who live together, mainly as loggers, conservationists, or on scientific expeditions. Everyone lives in the same forest, yet Mindele are all unbelievably wealthy, just as red river hogs somehow have huge amounts of fat.

This use of animal names for Bilo and whites contrasts with how other Yaka groups are called. Mbendjele refer to them with the names Ngombe, Luma, Ngabo, or Mikaya, that have no physical referent. Nicknames for other Mbendjele groups refer to their Yaka qualities; 'people who fly,' referring to the Mbendjele of Ibamba and Indongo who are respected for being adept spirit controllers. The name 'children of the flowers' refers to the Mbendjele of Minganga, who are considered to be very forest-oriented, and so on. Both Bilo and Mindele are given animal names because they are cast as prey. They are transient resources with potential. But, like game animals, each requires particular strategies to be successfully exploited.

Each group, either Bilo or Mbendjele, has its own understandings and interpretations, applies different strategies in order to deal with the other, and uses different metaphors and symbolism when talking about these relations. Even a very similar use of metaphor can signal very different meanings. Bilo sometimes call Mbendjele 'chimpanzees,' and often refer to them as animals. However Bilo use of animal labels contrasts with the way Yaka use them. Yaka use animal names descriptively, many Yaka have animal nicknames, like 'chimp,' which are not value judgments and do not cause offense. However, for Bilo they are explicitly derogatory. Whereas Bilo denigrate the wild, Yaka value it. Bilo often liken the Yaka nomadic lifestyle to that of wild animals, and their physical appearance with that of great apes. Yaka are said to be dirty, smelly, ignorant, stupid, childish, gluttonous, and chimp-like. Bilo do not like to get too close to Yaka, they do not inhabit the same places. They will not marry, sit together, eat together, or share the same plates and cups.

The Bilo claim that Yaka are inherently inferior, and subjugated to them. Bilo express their ideal role, as 'owners' of Yaka, with the term *konja*. In this part of Northern Congo, a *konja* claimed absolute authority over war captives, his juniors, wives, and land. The labor force provided by captives was vital for the success of tropical horticulture and forest resource extraction from the times of the Atlantic Trade onwards. Bilo groups say that before they encountered the Yaka, their captives were from other Bilo groups. Bilo captives could not escape because they would get lost in the forest. Contemporary Bilo stories of their first encounters with the Mbendjele five generations ago claim that the latter were initially captured using force and then brought to the Bilo village. Here they were shown iron, fed, clothed, given tobacco to smoke, and in some cases even shown fire.

Capture crucially justifies incorporating Yaka as subordinates in Bilo clans. This status places them under the mystical authority of the Bilo *konja*. A *konja*'s ability to curse is feared by the Yaka. Most feel inadequate at protecting themselves from Bilo sorcery. Bilo encourage these beliefs by regularly and verbosely cursing Yaka they feel wronged by. The threat of Bilo sorcery creates a contradiction between the very negative way Yaka talk about Bilo in their absence, and the generally respectful and polite way they act when actually in the presence of Bilo. This skews data when research is conducted through Bilo interpreters.

In Grinker's (1990, 1994), and in most other representations of this relationship, only these or similar Bilo conceptions are considered. Bilo political domination is presented as mostly unchallenged and comprehensive. There is little space for some of the effective practices that Pygmy peoples employ to maintain their independence. From our own experience Yaka peoples think of themselves as living freely and properly in contrast to Bilo lifestyles and values, and employ a number of strategies, such as avoidance and mobility, that can render farmers' claims to authority over them rather ineffective.

Yaka not only contest farmers' claims to political dominance but also manage well to actively structure these relations according to their own goals. When away from Bilo, Mbendjele get visibly annoyed by questions that approach their relations with Bilo from the Bilo point of view—in terms of justifying myths of capture,[24] or of innate inferiority and subordination. Only with persistent questioning would two Mbendjele elders elaborate a little on how they defined the term *konja*.

"*Konja* really means 'friend.' Our fathers found them and gave them to us. If we need food he gives it to us. We give him things too. But he's a friend, not an owner . . . if your Bilo surpasses himself in wickedness, you must find another friend" (Minganga elder, January 1995).

Another man continued: "We say, '*Milo wamu*' ["my Bilo"], but all it means is friend. It's the Bilo who don't understand. They think they are all chiefs. He's only a friend, and if he stops being generous then trouble starts" (Minganga elder, January 1995).

The Mbendjele ideal of their relationship with Bilo is based on friendship, sharing, mutual aid, and support, and on equality and respect for one another. Bilo link generosity to status. Therefore, if a Bilo claims to be superior to a Mbendjele, he has to prove it by giving more than the Mbendjele could ever reciprocate. The Mbendjele use this attitude to their advantage and demand a lot from Bilo. Since the economic depression of the 1990s, Bilo have been less able to meet Mbendjele expectations. This has led to increasing conflict and rupture in relations. In the late 1990s, many Mbendjele who were with Sangha-Sangha Bilo abandoned them in favor of the Bongili and Bodingo. They explained that these new partners are more generous and respect them better than the Sangha-Sangha.

In contrast to the Bilo conception of Mbendjele as captives, the Mbendjele consider themselves free from commitment and binding ties. Able to leave and go whenever they like, they will find new 'friends' if they are not satisfied. This conflicts with Bilo claims to fixed, enduring ties with 'their' Mbendjele, who are supposedly subjugated to their dying breath. These very opposed ideals, and unrealistic expectations of what the relationship should be like, lead to a great deal of conflict in their everyday interactions.

Relations between Mbendjele and Bilo are not static, nor of one particular type. They are fluid, being continuously renegotiated, potentially on a transaction-by-transaction basis. Their relations produce a spectrum of possible outcomes: from the Mbendjele getting everything they want for nothing, to the Bilo treating the Mbendjele as unpaid servants. It is this inherent ambiguity and plethora of possible outcomes that have led to such divergent interpretations of Yaka relations with Bilo groups. Attributing comprehensive political dominance to the Bilo reflects a bias toward accepting Bilo discourse and an overall Yaka marginalization at face value, whilst depreciating the informal mechanisms and common-sense approach used by the Yaka. As already pointed out, both Bilo discourse and the 'village' situation are also more amenable to study.

Hunting and gathering in the forest involves hard work and often some degree of hardship. That Yaka should sometimes suffer in order to obtain goods from Bilo is considered normal. As Esakola, an elder Mbendjele man from Mobangui, explained in February 1995: "When you want to kill an elephant you must follow it. It is hard work and dangerous. You must smear its fresh excrement on yourself. It is the same for us with Bilo!"

The accomplished Mbendjele hunter has mastered all the strategies required to hunt successfully the main game animals in the forest. There is a predictability to hunting that comes with experience. Certain strategies in particular places produce relatively reliable results. Learning to hunt is both learning about these different places, and the appropriate strategies to use. For instance, in certain types of undergrowth duikers are common. Coming across a large junction of animal trails in such forest undergrowth, an experienced hunter squats and mimics a duiker call. Very often duikers will approach the hunter. Different forest environments contain specific resources that require particular adaptive strategies to extract them.

The village world of Bilo is one such environment from which goods can be extracted. Yaka have developed strategies to use with Bilo that are intended to get goods from them. But, as when they hunt, Mbendjele are practical and flexible, quickly improvising and adapting their strategies as a situation unfolds. In order to obtain Bilo goods, Mbendjele employ strategies designed for efficacy and safety. They adapt themselves to suit the human prey just as the elephant hunter adopts particular strategies to catch his animal prey. Bilo stigmatization annoys them, but they try and use it pragmatically to their advantage. Thus they strategically use the stereotypes Bilo hold of them to obtain goods from Bilo. They may evoke pity, or flatter, or shame to encourage Bilo to be generous, to forget their gorilla tendencies, and share as people should. These strategies are combined with mobility and the threat of avoidance to back up demands on Bilo.

The use of forest idioms, in particular 'models of predation' to describe strategies that engage with outsiders, has been reported among other Pygmy groups in Central Africa. Turnbull, talking of the Mbuti living almost 800 miles east of the Yaka, describes how they refer to the village as a place of good hunting, and consider villagers as animals. When hunting tricky animals like villagers Mbuti use appropriate tactics, like carrying wood for them or helping build their houses. Mbuti talk of eating the villagers (1966:82).

Another, more recent source suggests that the metaphor of predation is being used flexibly and expanded to encompass novel situations such as 'development' projects. In his synthesis of responses to, and the effects of development initiatives aimed at Pygmies in Central Africa, Beauclerk states: "Complex battles of wits can develop as Pygmies and their developers each pursue their separate aims. The process is, at its most innocuous, merely a game. . . . Some hunter-gatherers describe goods acquired in this way as 'meat' and the method of obtaining them 'hunting'" (1993:33).

There seems to be a common language used by many Central African forest hunter-gatherers to express and discuss their engagement with outsiders. The supra-ethnic self-ascribed category 'Yaka,' or forest people, is meaningful because of these and other similarities between linguistically diverse groups.[25] Yaka people use language flexibly depending on context. The most striking example of this is the use of an animal's 'language' to catch it. This is a common feature of Yaka hunting methods. Duikers or crocodiles are successfully called to the hunter by mimicking their mating calls. Monkeys are called out of the high branches by mimicking the screams of a fallen infant. Some men call buffalo. The adoption of their neighbors' languages by Central African hunter-gatherer groups in the past has readily been interpreted as a sign of their subordination. Maybe, rather than being universally a sign of subjugation, part of the explanation for the widespread use of Bilo languages by hunter-gatherers such as Yaka groups is that they use these languages to 'hunt' the Bilo too.

When examining the contemporary relations between Bilo and Yaka in Northern Congo it is not possible to talk about subjugation or domination without bias to either Bilo or Yaka. From an ideological or political perspective, Bilo could be seen to dominate the Yaka. However, from a practical perspective and in a very real sense, Yaka could be said to have the Bilo at their mercy, since they can come and go as they like, whereas the Bilo will risk destitution if they cannot get additional labor at the right moment in the agricultural cycle. Mbendjele recognize this and sometimes sing about it while performing ceremonies requested by the Bilo: 'Thanks to us the Bilo are what they are!'

THE DISTINCTIVENESS OF YAKA METAPHORS:
A WAY TO UNDERSTAND YAKA-BILO DIFFERENCE

In an Amazonian (Amerindian) context, Viveiros de Castro (1998) has elaborated an indigenous concept of 'perspectivism,' according to which the world is inhabited by different sorts of subjects or persons, human and nonhuman, who apprehend the world from distinct points of view. For the Yaka, such a different perspective is most obvious when they compare their own ways with how the Bilo view and interact with them. From a Yaka perspective, 'resource extraction' strategies employed in the natural and in the human social environment resemble each other; they are applied in a kind of 'single social field.'

Basically this means two things. First, human and nonhuman animals go about satisfying their needs in similar ways. Members of a 'family' or 'insiders' share most intimately with each other. The sharing of energies with 'outsiders' is equally necessary for the sustenance of life, but since they are 'outsiders' this form of sharing is often cast in metaphors of predation. Secondly, a 'single social field' implies that what goes on beyond the boundaries of human interaction is also understood as 'socializing.' And, indeed, Yaka employ similar strategies when they 'track,' 'look for,' or 'hunt' natural resources, for instance an animal or honey, as when they try to obtain commodities or services from a fellow human being.[26]

For Yaka it makes sense to apply imagery from a valued domain of livelihood strategies in which they excel, are proud of and reputed for, to other domains. Hunting tropes are thus easily mapped onto other 'nonhunting' settings such as the village, a logging town, the Bilo-run administration, or a European conservation or research project. But in line with other authors we suggest that this is not simply the transfer of ideas into other domains, but a fundamental characteristic of perceiving the world as a single social field (cf. Bird-David 1990, 1993; Ingold 1994, 1996).

Different perspectives may entail different approaches. From their own perspective, Yaka make a crucial ethnic and cultural distinction between 'insiders,' other forest people like themselves, and transient forest occupants or 'outsiders' like Bilo. Bilo difference is registered, for instance, in their angry, selfish, arrogant, and possessive approach to the rivers and forest, which from the Yaka perspective are for all to share. Bilo are commonly referred to as 'gorillas,' but this is a distinction that does not really question their humanity. It rests primarily on the common Bilo and gorilla approach to the forest, their competitive attitudes to others, their aggressive territorial claims, and their disregard for sharing more generally.

Our 'perspectivist' approach to understanding hunter-gatherer/farmer relations relies on Bird-David's seminal argument for a distinct hunter-gatherer perception of a 'giving environment' (1990), which is rooted in a particular kind of economy, a 'cosmic economy of sharing' (1992). The 'giving environment' of the forest is perceived as an 'ever-providing parent' and is distinct from the 'reciprocating environment' of agriculturalists who construct nature as a 'reciprocating ancestor' (Bird-David 1990:190). A 'cosmic economy of sharing' is distinct from both a commodity and a gift economy and implies a socializing of human beings and other constituents of the environment on an equal footing. People share with the nonhuman components of their environment just as they share with one another (Bird-David 1992:30). Both arguments are drawn from an analysis of the cultural metaphors that inform what Gudeman (1986) has called 'local economic models.'

There is a danger of misapplying such a metaphor-based model and to claim that

"what is literally true of relations among humans . . . is only figuratively true of relations with animals, [that] is to *reproduce* the very dichotomy between animals and
society that the indigenous view purports to reject" (Ingold 1994:19, original emphasis). One of our points here is precisely that Yaka root metaphors are based in the
perception of a shared forest world. They are interactive, that is, they go both ways
and do not necessarily prioritize the human body or human social institutions. They
are rooted in a perception that does not essentially distinguish between social and
natural relations.[27] As Bird-David herself comments on the interactive associations
of core or root metaphors, they generate insight into 'how things are,' evoke 'asso-
ciative commonplaces' which are 'active together' and thus result in 'interillumina-
tion.' Metaphors reorganize users' views both of their 'source domain' and their
'topic domain' (1993:112, footnote 1).

We suggest that the primary metaphors, which Bird-David interprets as a cultural projection of human social institutions upon the natural world (1992:28), are
in the Yaka case better understood as pointing to a level on which humans, animals, and plants share a common existential status, namely as living beings (cf. Ingold 1996:134) in a shared world. In particular, Yaka animal metaphors for human
beings point to qualities they share as a resource and/or in their behavior and attitudes to the forest and to others. Yaka neither confound a European and a bush
pig, nor a Bilo and a gorilla, but in both pairs they perceive properties or qualities
that distinguish them from other living beings. As Michael Jackson put it, "metaphor must be apprehended nondualistically . . . metaphor reveals, not the 'thisness
of that' but rather that 'this *is* that'" (1989:142, original emphasis).

In the Yaka-Bilo context it is important, however, to pay attention to who uses
the metaphor and where s/he situates herself in relation to both 'this' and 'that.'
Yaka animal metaphors for humans reveal the equivalence of both the 'source' and
the 'topic' with specific reference to shared behavioral qualities. From a necessarily
partial perspective, the Yaka metaphor also indicates how both are to be approached
as a potential resource or a partner. The emphasis remains on what both have in
common rather than on what distinguishes them from a Yaka. For Bilo this is not the
case. Distinctive meanings are discernible, for instance, in the 'children' metaphor.
Yaka perceive themselves as 'children' of the forest, but this refers to an existential
status that all living beings share in a forest cosmos, which provides for all. The Bilo
use of the metaphor, however, refers to an inferior Yaka status and their dependency on the nurturing capacity of Bilo 'parents.'

Bilo animal metaphors for Yaka are based in a perception of the world as divided
into a wild and rather unpredictable forest sphere, which is populated by animals,
Yaka, and ancestral spirits, and the civilized space of the human village and farms.
Bilo perception essentially discriminates between species and between social
agents, and it juxtaposes them in dialectical opposition. There are humans and there

are animals, Bilo and Yaka, patrons and clients, parents and children. What unites subjects and agents on one side of the structural divide is their affordance. Both animals and Yaka serve as 'meat' to be eaten or exploited by Bilo; both children and Yaka are dependent on their parents' nurture, education, and assistance (tutelage), and so on. Here the animal metaphor is used not as a reference to a shared world, but as a divisive instrument, a symbolic device to denigrate Yaka, to relegate them to animal status and to justify depriving them of basic human rights.[28]

Concerning Yaka cultural metaphors and their discourse on socializing and exploitation strategies, we can thus summarize that Yaka may conceptualize their own agency to obtain things as 'tracking' and 'hunting' a resource—be that a Bilo, an animal, a plant, or a commodity.[29] However, the exploitation of resources, and relations with and within the natural environment more generally, are not modeled in terms drawn from the sphere of human social and productive relations. Yaka metaphors of human exchange partners and nonhuman resources, and of their own strategies for communication and exchange, are truly interactive. Their experience with human and nonhuman animals, in particular, is such that neither serves as a model for the other. Rather, both serve as interactive models for each other.

CONCLUSIONS

Our contention is that Yaka make choices from a number of available subsistence strategies. Like other people, they value variety and quality in life. Yaka employ proactive strategies as much in human interaction as in natural resource management. Like their farming neighbors, they attempt to turn social contacts into advantageous relations and to profit from them as well as they can. 'Resource management' for Yaka translates as a walkabout in the forest or a visit to a Bilo village. It means meeting, communicating, and socializing with Yaka friends and relatives, or Bilo partners, by sharing talk, food, tobacco, or a drink, as well as communicating and socializing with nonhuman agents, sharing physical and spiritual energies by singing and dancing, or through herbal remedies and charms. In all domains the strategies involved in successful interaction and 'exploitation' imply ecological knowledge, social skills, and technological expertise. Characteristic of their perception of relational strategies, however, is the metaphorical integration of human and nonhuman domains.

Our attention has been on the active and strategic structuring of such relations. As we have argued, forest activities such as hunting and gathering, and village activities such as meeting Bilo, exploring new relationships, striking a work contract, and acquiring goods are described in terms that are commonly derived from experience in the forest. We contend that the apparent dissolution of such classic Western dualisms as the social and the ecological, the cultural and the natural, of human interaction and natural resource exploitation, are not signs of an incipient acculturation process nor the conceptual attempt to integrate the village into an essential forest existence. Rather, it is to do with a fundamentally 'egalitarian' perception of human relations that is governed by demand-sharing as the means of both recognizing equality and achieving it. The egalitarianism of hunter-gatherers—like most Pygmy and San peoples—is an orientation to the world that immediately renders claims by outsiders—such as Bilo—to authority or superiority both scandalous and preposterous. Overly explicit or assertive Bilo claims to power over Yaka are either ignored, countered on the spot with cutting humor, or later commented on in aggressive storytelling.

We have argued that the perceptual incorporation of new, nonforest experiences into an expanding Yaka experience of the world neither exhibits the workings of a local model (e.g., Bird-David 1990, 1992; Gudeman 1986) nor the other way round of a naturalist model. Rather it shows a truly interactive organization of metaphoric perception that distinguishes according to shared 'cultural' elements such as traits, properties, or qualities, in both human and nonhuman domains. The most prominent example has been the aggressiveness and territoriality of both Bilo villagers and forest gorillas. To substantiate the connection between social and economic practices and the way people talk about them, we have pointed out how recent shifts in metaphorical perception are linked to interrelated transformations in subsistence strategies and exchange relations. Thus Europeans have gone from rogue male elephants to red river hogs. Without archaeological or other data to confirm or disprove hypotheses about the terms of historical contacts, we suggest that this is one way of rethinking local histories from the perspectives of those involved. Its contribution to the debate is that it works with local metaphoric categories and through their reflexive use rather than through the fitting of established anthropological categories onto a given ethnographic situation.

To conclude, although not all groups of Pygmies are indigenous to the specific area of forest they occupy today, all Pygmy groups consider themselves, and are considered by their neighbors, to be the aboriginal people of the Central African forests. They are said to have lived independently in the forest before the arrival of the 'village people.' Until archaeological evidence can disprove or confirm whether the ancient forest dwellers were Pygmies or not, revisionist hypotheses will remain controversial, and caution is advisable. This chapter has also sought to show the difficulties that are evident when trying to judge or analyze Pygmy peoples' relationships with outsiders from non-Pygmy perspectives and the skew this gives to data. That such claims are contentious even in the present should act as a particular warning against attributing relations of dependency, subordination, or serfdom to their past relations.

ACKNOWLEDGMENT

We would like to thank Kairn Klieman for helpful comments on an earlier version of this chapter.

NOTES

1. Lewis (2001) describes Yaka Pygmy conceptions of themselves and other Pygmy groups as 'Forest People' in contrast to their non-Pygmy neighbors, the 'Village People.' These or similar concepts have been used widely in the literature as a convenient shorthand for a series of local bipolar oppositions epitomized in the 'forest' and the 'village' spheres respectively. But this has usually been done in an essentializing way and with the implication of a whole range of Western debates on loaded dualisms such as 'nature' and 'culture,' on social evolution, and the historical transition of hunting-and-gathering to farming, rather than in an explicit recognition of local conceptions.

2. Lewis (2000:3) explains how educated Twa activists use the term *Pygmy* to show solidarity with other Pygmy groups because of their shared problems of marginalization and discrimination.

3. Angola, Gabon, Republic of Congo-Brazzaville, Cameroon, Equatorial Guinea, Central African Republic (CAR), Democratic Republic of Congo (D.R. Congo), Uganda, Rwanda, and Burundi.

4. However the majority of Baka live in southeastern Cameroon, and Mbendjele (Aka) forest stretches into CAR.

5. Axel Köhler did his field research in the Souanké District, Sangha Region, during 1992–94 and was supported by a grant from the DAAD (Deutscher Akademischer Austauschdienst). Jerome Lewis's field research was undertaken in the Ndoki forest, Sangha and Likouala Regions, during 1994–97 with generous support from the Wenner-Gren Foundation for Anthropological Research, an Emslie Horniman Anthropological Scholarship and a Swan Fund Scholarship. Assistance for writing up the Ph.D. thesis has been provided by an Alfred Gell Memorial Scholarship. Additionally he has been conducting research with the Twa of the Great Lakes Region since 1993.

6. The dating of the forest fringe movements of Adamawa-Ubangian and Central Sudanic speakers is less clear than that of the so-called 'Bantu expansion,' but it may well have preceded the latter.

7. Concerning farmer/Pygmy relations more generally but with particular reference to the Mbuti and their neighbors, this line of argument had been developed by Schebesta (1933, 1936), Schmidt (1910), and Schweinfurth (1878).

8. In terms of the structuring meta-narrative, Turnbull's works on the Mbuti move from an early romantic optimism—the 'noble savage' as a humanistic ideal—to a kind of tragic nostalgia as he later envisions the almost inevitable loss of Mbuti forest lifeways (see Turnbull 1983).

9. For example, anthropologists from the Harvard Ituri Project, Japanese researchers working in the same area of D.R. Congo, and French ethnoecologists in CAR, Republic of Congo-Brazzaville, and Cameroon.

10. According to Klieman (n.d.:ch. 4), this ideology is rooted in religious beliefs that underlie what Kopytoff (1987) has called the 'principle of precedence,' a political-cultural notion concerning 'first-comers' and their ritual powers that is widespread at least among Niger-Congo peoples and which has deeply influenced the nature of interactions between Bantu 'late-comers' and autochthonous peoples in Central Africa. According to this principle, the religious and/or political authority of indigenous peoples, i.e., 'first-comers,' must be recognized and honored, because only they have access to the ancestral and territorial spirits of the land. In their initial dependency on indigenous societies the immigrants or 'late-comers' wholeheartedly subscribe to the formers' 'civilizing status.' In later phases of their settling-in, however, they attempt to establish political, economic, and sometimes religious hegemony, which leads to a lessening of status for indigenous peoples and others deemed 'outsiders' to the new rulers of the land. Klieman thus explains the contradictory coexistence of oral traditions in which Pygmies are talked about as the original 'civilizing beings,' yet remain subjected to various levels of discrimination.

11. Lewis met several Mbendjele groups in remote areas of forest who had not visited Bilo villages in several years. When Lewis visited the Ibamba area again in 2001, Ngbwiti and Ekwese's group had been living continuously in the forest since 1991. In 1997 Ekwese had explained: "We are here in the forest where we were born. Our fathers are gone so we look after the forest behind them. We fear Indongo [a Mbendjele village near some Bilo villages] because of the heat from fighting. . . . So we thought we'll just keep our eyes on our forest, where we are the owners, here at Bamba."

12. Taking into account a debate dedicated to the topic in volume 19 (2) of the journal *Human Ecology* (1991) and a number of subsequent publications, Headland (1999) recognized that various authors "have found serious deficiencies with the wild yam hypothesis, at least as we originally proposed it in the late 1980s. Solid criticisms have been put forth in the 1990s that bring the hypothesis into question." In our study area, Sato (2001) provides conclusive evidence for the sufficiency of wild yams to support Baka people independently from agriculture in all types of forest. Whether this was the case in the past remains unknown since Baka today practice the 'paracultivation' (Dounias 1993) of wild tubers and thus influence their growth in the wild. However, as Fairhead and Leach (1995 and 1998) and Guyer and Richards (1996) have pointed out, most, if not all forests today, no matter how 'pristine' or 'primary' they may appear, are anthropogenic, that is, they have a human 'resource management' history that has shaped their growth and affected their landscapes.

13. The problem of delimiting and classifying populations for genetic research in an unambiguous and consistent way has been pointed out by MacEachern (2000:364) in particular reference to the continental genetic tree of African populations generated by Cavalli-Sforza et al. (1994). Whereas the Saharan and Northern African populations in this book are only nationally identified (Algerians, Tunisians, etc.), the sub-Saharan population samples are denoted by (1) "traditional" ethnonyms (Amhara, Hausa, etc.), (2) geographical designations (Bantu, N.E., Bantu, S.W., etc.), (3) designations based on language affiliation (Nilotic,

Ubangian, San, etc.), or (4) designations based on particular physical characteristics (Pygmy/Pygmoid).

14. Interviews among both Aka and Baka by Lewis (1995–97, and 2001) confirmed their perception of shared ancestry and history followed by conflict around 250 years ago and the flight of the Baka out of Aka forest toward their present locations to the west.

15. Woodburn (1997) provides an excellent analysis of these issues.

16. It has been interpreted as evidence for the intensity and longevity of such interaction that Pygmies assimilated their neighbors' languages as *linguae francae*. A model of this language assimilation is that small bilingual hunter-gatherer groups lost or gave up their own languages in intense and durable socioeconomic relationships with farmers whose villages became a focus of sustained daily interaction (cf. Bahuchet 1993a:16–20; Vansina 1986:435–436). According to this model, linguistic assimilation was not accompanied by either physical or cultural assimilation, and social interaction must therefore have developed in such a way that ethnic distinctions and economic specializations were maintained.

17. Based on linguistic data, Klieman (1999, n.d.) argues that a number of hunter-gatherer groups—the ancestors of the Aka and Mbendjele among others—were actually severing close contacts with Bantu agriculturalists of the same language community over the last five hundred years. Apparently this was especially prevalent in regions on the peripheries of centralized states, such as the southwestern quadrant of the equatorial rain forest.

18. For a nuanced and historically informed view of Mbuti interaction with their neighbors and, in particular, with forest conservation projects, see Kenrick (1996).

19. More examples of the notion of Pygmy 'serfdom' exist among French economic anthropologists (Dupré and Guillot 1973:8; Vincent 1961:36–37). For an early notion of a 'free contract' between Pygmies and their chosen 'patrons,' see Bruel (1910:113) and Regnault (1911:285–286).

20. This is classically captured in titles such as 'Wayward Servants' (Turnbull 1966) and 'Elusive Persistence' (Wæhle 1989).

21. Vansina (1990) uses the term *House* to denote a residential unit encompassing both lineage and other forms of social organization as an alternative to the long-criticized term *lineage*. Vansina asserts that in Equatorial Africa "there were no lineages" (1990:75). The term *House* represents a widespread indigenous term for "a large household establishment often called 'the house' or the 'hearth'" (Vansina 1990:73), and reflects, far better than *lineage,* the historical realities of social groupings. Houses had recognized leaders who achieved rather than inherited their status, and who were capable of expanding their establishments by attracting kin, friends, clients, dependents, and followers. "The ideology of the House was based on the fiction that it was a family, that is, a bilateral group in anthropological parlance, or better yet, an 'undifferentiated' group. The 'big man' was the father of all the others" (Vansina 1990:75). Such 'Houses' thus integrated members from different ethnic groups speaking distinct languages and belonging to a number of distinct cultural groupings.

22. Robineau (1967:39), for instance, speaks of the recognition of a "civilizing current" (*courant civilisateur*) by the Njem, which originates with the Fang and the Bulu, passes via the Njem and the Bakwele, and ends with the Baka. Nowadays, most Bantu in Souanké

District think of the Muslim traders as superior, because they virtually control the import and export economy.

23. The following discussion of the mutual use of animals names by Mbendjele and their Bilo neighbors, and its connotations and implications—especially of the terms 'gorilla' and 'chimp'—applies equally to Congolese Baka, Mikaya and Luma, and their respective non-Pygmy neighbors.

24. We are referring here to the 'original' myths of capturing Yaka. In the colonial period, European exploitation often forced Bilo to pass the pressure on and to 'capture' Yaka in order to get them to help in fulfilling the required quota.

25. Bahuchet has commented on the great similarities in social organization between Aka and Baka Pygmy groups in widely separate areas (1993a:21–25). Hewlett (1996) also notes the high similarity of cultural traits between Pygmies across a vast area in Central Africa. And many others have commented, for instance, on the similarities in their unusual polyphonic singing style (Arom 1978; Kazadi 1981:836; Sawada 1990; Schebesta 1933:13; Thomas 1979:145; and Turnbull 1966:23).

26. By our focus on 'hunting metaphors' we may be seen to privilege the male view of social contacts and the male side to Yaka subsistence strategies. But a 'hunting' terminology is as much applied to immobile agents and objects—be they plants or modern consumer items—as to animals. This is well captured in the almost indiscriminate Baka use of two French terms that also happen to be phonetically very similar: chasser ("hunt") and chercher ("look for"). Among Mbendjele, hunting metaphors are particularly appropriate for discussing engagement with outsiders, since this is an area associated primarily with male activities. In a general sense, within the Mbendjele division of labor, men are oriented to the outside, women to the inside.

27. This may simply be "because social processes are experienced as natural" (Bloch 1992:130–132). But as our examples indicate, we may likewise say that natural processes are experienced as social.

28. In no way are we implying here a fixed Bilo use of such metaphors through time. The derogatory aspect of animal metaphors for autochthonous forest dwellers and nature/culture-type social distinctions probably developed during the Atlantic Trade era, when warfare and extreme competition for resources caused growing sociopolitical distance between autochthonous forest and immigrant communities. In the colonial period such metaphors then acquired new semantic layers with the introduction of European racial and other discriminatory categories.

29. This has many similarities with what Ingold (1996:129) has called 'interagentivity,' i.e., encounter, communication, and exchange, integrating the human and the nonhuman domain. The difference between 'interagentivity' and 'intersubjectivity' is that the latter only describes relations in the human sphere.

References Cited

Adas, Michael

1992   Comment. In *Colonialism and Culture,* edited by Nicholas Dirks, pp. 127–134. Ann Arbor, MI: University of Michigan Press.

Almeida, Antonio de

1965   The Black Bushmen (Zama or Kwenong). In *Bushmen and Other Non-Bantu Peoples of Angola: Three Lectures by Antonio de Almeida,* edited by Phillip V. Tobias and J. Blacking, pp. 13–22. Johannesburg: Witwatersrand University Press.

Ambrose, Stanley H.

1982   Archaeology and Linguistic Reconstruction of History in East Africa. In *Archaeological and Linguistic Reconstruction of African History,* edited by Christopher Ehret and Merrick Posnansky, pp. 104–157. Berkeley: University of California Press.

1998   Chronology of the Later Stone Age and Food Production in East Africa. *Journal of Archaeological Science* 25:377–392.

Amin, S.

1972   Underdevelopment and Dependence in Black Africa: Origins and Contemporary Forms. *Journal of Modern African Studies* 10:503–524.

Anderson, B.

1983   *Imagined Communities: Reflections on the Origin and Spread of Nationalism.* London: Verso Editions and New Left Books.

Andersson, Charles John

1857   *Lake Ngami or Explorations and Discoveries during Four Years' Wanderings in the Wilds of South Western Africa.* 2d edition. London: Hurst and Blackett Publishers.

Arom, Simha

1978   *Anthropologie de la Musique des Pygmées Aka.* Paris: Ocora.

Bagshawe, F. J.

1925   The Peoples of the Happy Valley (East Africa). The Aboriginal Races of Kondoa Irangi, Part II, The Kangeju. *Journal of the African Society* 24 (94): 25–33, 117–130.

Bahuchet, Serge

1985   *Les Pygmées Aka et la Forêt Centrafricaine. Ethnologie écologique.* Ethnoscience 1. Paris: SELAF/CNRS.

1992   *Dans la Forêt d'Afrique Centrale. Les Pygmées Aka et Baka. Histoire d'une Civilisation Forestière.* Vol 1. Paris: SELAF/Louvain Peeters.

1993a   *La Rencontre des Agriculteurs. Les Pygmées parmi les Peuples d'Afrique Centrale. Histoire d'une Civilisation Forestière.* Vol. 2, Ethnoscience 9. Paris: SELAF/Louvain Peeters.

1993b   L'invention des Pygmeés. *Cahiers d'Études Africaines* 129, XXXIII (1): 153–181.

1993c   History of the Inhabitants of the Central African Rain Forest: Perspectives from Comparative Linguistics. In *Tropical Forests, People, and Food: Biocultural Interactions and Applications to Development,* edited by C. Hladik, A. Hladik, O. Linares, H. Pagezy, A. Semple, and M. Hadley, pp. 37–54. Paris: MAB-UNESCO.

Bahuchet, Serge, and Henri Guillaume

1982   Aka-Farmer Relations in the Northwest Congo Basin. In *Politics and History in Band Societies,* edited by Eleanor Leacock and Richard B. Lee, pp. 189–211. Cambridge and New York: Cambridge University Press.

Bahuchet, Serge, Doyle McKey, and Igor de Garine

1991   Wild Yams Revisited: Is Independence from Agriculture Possible for Rain Forest Hunter-Gatherers? *Human Ecology* 19 (2): 213–243.

Bailey, Robert

1985   The Socioecology of Efe Pygmy Men in the Ituri Forest, Zaire. Ph.D. diss., Harvard University. Ann Arbor, MI: University Microfilms International.

1991   *The Behavioral Ecology of Efe Pygmy Men in the Ituri Forest, Zaire.* Anthropological Papers of the Museum of Anthropology No. 86. Ann Arbor, MI: University of Michigan.

Bailey, Robert C., and Robert Aunger, Jr.

1990   Humans as Primates: The Social Relationships of Efe Pygmy Men in Comparative Perspective. *International Journal of Primatology* 11:127–146.

Bailey, Robert C., Serge Bahuchet, and Barry Hewlett

1992   Development in the Central African Rainforest: Concern for Forest Peoples. In *Conservation of West and Central African Rainforests,* edited by Kevin Cleaver, Mohan Munashighe, Mary Dyson, Nicolas Egli, Axel Peuker, and François Wencélius, pp. 202–211. World Bank Environment Paper No. 1. Washington, D.C.: World Bank.

Bailey, Robert C., Genevieve Head, Mark Jenike, Bruce Owen, Robert Rechtman, and Elzbieta Zechenter

1989   Hunting and Gathering in Tropical Rainforests. Is It Possible? *American Anthropologist* 91 (1): 59–82.

Baines, T.

1864   *Explorations in South-West Africa.* London: Longman, Roberts, & Green.

Bala, G. G.

1998   *Hadza Stories and Songs.* Printed by Nicholas G. Blurton Jones and available through him.

Banks, Marcus

1996   *Ethnicity: Anthropological Constructions.* London: Routledge.

Barnard, Alan

1980   Basarwa Settlement Patterns in the Ghanzi Ranching Area. *Botswana Notes and Records* 12:137–148.

1986   Rethinking Bushman Settlement Patterns and Territoriality. *Sprache und Geschichte in Afrika* 7 (1): 41–60.

1988   Cultural Identity, Ethnicity, and Marginalization among the Bushmen of Southern Africa. In *New Perspectives on Khoisan,* edited by Rainer Vossen, pp. 9–27. Quellen zur Khoisan-Forschung 7. Hamburg: Helmut Buske Verlag.

1989   The Lost World of Laurens van der Post? *Current Anthropology* 30:104–114.

1992a   *Hunters and Herders of Southern Africa: A Comparative Ethnography of the Khoisan Peoples.* Cambridge: Cambridge University Press.

1992b   *The Kalahari Debate: A Bibliographical Essay.* Centre of African Studies, University of Edinburgh, Occasional Papers No. 35. Edinburgh: University of Edinburgh.

1992c   Social and Spatial Boundary Maintenance among Southern African Hunter-Gatherers. In *Mobility and Territoriality,* edited by Michael Casimir and Aparna Rao, pp.137–151. New York: Berg.

1996   Emic and Etic. In *Encyclopedia of Social and Cultural Anthropology,* edited by Alan Barnard and Jonathan Spencer, pp.180–183. New York: Routledge.

Barnard, Alan, and Thomas Widlok

1996   Nharo and Hai//om Settlement Patterns in Comparative Perspective. In *Cultural Diversity among Twentieth-Century Foragers: An African Perspective,* edited by Susan Kent, pp. 87–107. Cambridge: Cambridge University Press.

Barnicot, N., F. Bennett, James Woodburn, T. Pilkington, and A. Antonis

1972   Blood Pressure and Serum Cholesterol in the Hadza of Tanzania. *Human Biology* 44:87–116.

Barrow, John

1801–   *An Account of Travels into the Interior of Southern Africa in the Years 1797 and 1798.*
1804   2 volumes. London: Cadell and Davies.

Barth, Fredrik

1998   Introduction. In *Ethnic Groups and Boundaries,* edited by Fredrik Barth, pp. 9–38. Prospect Heights, Illinois: Waveland Press.

Baumann, Oscar

1897   Bevölkerung des bayerischen Schwabens in ihrer geschichtlichen Aufeinanderfolge. *Beiträge zur Anthropologie* 12:105–126.

Beauclerk, John

1993   *Hunters and Gatherers in Central Africa: On the Margins of Development.* Oxfam Research Paper No. 6. Oxford: Oxfam.

Beinart, William, ed.

1987   *Hidden Struggles in Rural South Africa: Politics and Popular Movements in the Transkei and Eastern Cape.* London: James Currey.

Biesele, Megan

1986   Aspects of !Kung Folklore. In *Kalahari Hunter-Gatherers: Studies of the !Kung San and their Neighbors,* edited by Richard Lee and Irven DeVore, pp. 303–324. Cambridge, MA: Harvard University Press.

1993   *Women Like Meat: The Folklore and Foraging Ideology of the Kalahari Ju/'hoansi.* Johannesburg/Bloomington: Witwatersrand University Press/Indiana University Press.

Bird-David, Nurit H.

1990   The Giving Environment: Another Perspective on the Economic System of Gatherer-Hunters. *Current Anthropology* 31 (2): 189–196.

1992   Beyond "The Original Affluent Society": A Culturalist Reformulation. *Current Anthropology* 33 (1): 25–47.

1993   Tribal Metaphorization of Human-Nature Relatedness: A Comparative Analysis. In *Environmentalism. The View from Anthropology,* edited by Kay Milton, pp. 112–125. London: Routledge.

Blackburn, Roderic

1971   Honey in Okiek Personality, Culture and Society. Ph.D. diss., Michigan State University.

Bleek, Dorothea Francis

1928a   Customs and Beliefs of the /Xam Bushmen. Part III: Game Animals. *Bantu Studies* 6:233–249.

1928b   *The Naron: A Bushman Tribe of the Central Kalahari.* Cambridge, England: Cambridge University Press.

1931a   The Hadzapi or Watindega of Tanganyika Territory. *Africa* 4 (3): 273–286.

1931b   Traces of Former Bushmen Occupation in Tanganyika Territory. *South African Journal of Science* 28:423–442.

Bleek, W. H. I.

1929   *Comparative Vocabularies of Bushman Languages.* Cambridge: Cambridge University Press.

Blench, Roger

1999   Are the African Pygmies an Ethnographic Fiction? In *Central African Hunter-Gatherers in a Multidisciplinary Perspective: Challenging Elusiveness,* edited by Karen Biesbrouck, Stefan Elders, and Gerda Rossel, pp. 41–60. Leiden: CNWS, Universiteit Leiden.

Bloch, Maurice

1992   What Goes without Saying: The Conceptualization of Zafimaniry Society. In *Conceptualizing Society,* edited by Adam Kuper. London: Routledge.

Blurton Jones, Nicholas G., Kristen Hawkes, and James F. O'Connell

1996   The Global Process and Local Ecology: How Should We Explain the Differences between the Hadza and !Kung? In *Cultural Diversity among Twentieth-Century Foragers: An African Perspective,* edited by Susan Kent, pp. 159–187. Cambridge: Cambridge University Press.

n.d.   *History and the Hadza: Lost in the Bottom of the Rift Valley?*

Blurton Jones, Nicholas G., L. C. Smith, James F. O'Connell, Kristen Hawkes, and C. Llwechungura Kamuzora

1992   Demography of the Hadza, an Increasing and High Density Population of Savannaforagers. *American Journal of Physical Anthropology* 89:159–181.

Boaz, N. T., A. S. Brooks, and P. P. Pavlakis

1990   Late Pleistocene-Holocene Human Remains from the Upper Semiliki, Zaire. In *Evolution of Environments and Hominidae in the African Western Rift Valley,* edited by N. T. Boaz, pp. 273–299. Virginia Museum of Natural History Memoir No. 1. Martinsville, VA: Virginia Museum of Natural History.

Bollong, C. A., and Garth Sampson

n.d.   Later Stone Age Herder-Hunter Interactions: A Ceramic Perspective. In *Technological Strategies of African Hunter-gathers and Herders,* edited by Britt Bouseman. Botswana National Archives HC. 144: "Correspondence on Ngamiland Affairs and the Proceedings of the Ngami Police Detachment."

Bollong, C. A., A. B. Smith, and Garth Sampson

1997   Khoikhoi and Bushman Pottery in the Cape Colony: Ethnohistory and Later Stone Age Ceramics of the South African Interior. *Journal of Anthropological Archaeology* 16:31.

Boonzaier, E., C. Malherbe, A. Smith, and P. Berens

1996   *The Cape Herders: A History of the Khoikhoi of Southern Africa.* Athens, OH: Ohio University Press.

Bousman, Britt, and Louis Scott

1994   Climate or Overgrazing?: The Palynological Evidence for Vegetation Change in the Eastern Karoo. *South African Journal of Science* 90:575–578.

Bräuer, G.

1983   *Die archäologischen und anthropologischen Ergebnisse der Kohl-Larsen-Expeditionen in Nord Tanzania 1933–1939,* herausgegeben von H. Müller Beck. Tübinger Monographien zur Urgeschchte Band 4, Nr. 4. *Die menschlichen Skelettfunde des 'Later Stone Age' aus der Mumba-Höhle und anderen Lokalitäten nahe des Eyasi-Sees (Tanzania) und ihre Bedeutung für die Populationdifferenzierung in Ostafrika.* Tübingen: Verlag Archaeologica Venatoria, Institut für Urgeschichte der Universität Tübingen.

Brenzinger, Matthias

1997   Moving to Survive: Kxoe Communities in Arid Lands. Khoisan Forum Working Paper No. 2, University of Cologne.

Brooks, Alison S.

1984   San Land Use Patterns, Past and Present: Implications for Southern African Prehistory. In *Frontiers: Southern African Archaeology Today,* edited by M. Hall, G. Avery, D. M. Avery, M. L. Wilson, and A. J. B. Humphreys, pp. 40–52. Cambridge Monographs in African Archaeology 10 (BAR International Series 207).

Brooks, Alison S., A. L. Crowell, and John E. Yellen

1980   ≠Gi: A Stone Age Archaeological Site in the Northern Kalahari Desert, Botswana. In *Proceedings of the Eighth Panafrican Congress of Prehistory and Quaternary Studies, Nairobi, 1977.* Edited by R. E. F. Leakey and B. A. Ogot, pp. 304–309. Nairobi: The International Louis Leakey Memorial Institute for African Prehistory.

Brooks, Alison S., Diane E. Gelburd, and J. E. Yellen

1984   Food Production and Culture Change among the !Kung San: Implications for Prehistoric Research. In *From Hunters to Farmers: The Causes and Consequences of Food Production in Africa,* edited by J. D. Clark and S. A. Brandt, pp. 293–310. Berkeley: University of California Press.

Brooks, Alison S., P. E. Hare, J. E. Kokis, G. H. Miller, R. D. Ernst, and F. Wendorf

  1990   Dating Pleistocene Archaeological Sites by Protein Diagenesis in Ostrich Egg-shell. *Science* 248:60–64.

Brooks, Alison S., and Greg Laden

  n.d.   Environmental Determinants of Site Formation: A Comparison of Ethnoar-chaeological Work in the Kalahari Desert and Ituri Forest, with Implications for the Emergence of Human Culture. Unpublished ms.

Brooks, Alison S., and C. C. Smith

  1987   Ishango Revisited: New Age Determinations and Cultural Interpretations. *The African Archaeological Review* 5:65–78.

Brooks, Alison S., C. C. Smith, and N. T. Boaz

  1991   New Human Remains from Ishango, Zaire, in Relation to Later Pleistocene Human Evolution. Abstract of presentation. *American Journal of Physical Anthropology* Supplement 12, Annual Meeting Issue, pp. 54–55.

Brooks, Alison S., and J. E. Yellen

  1987   The Preservation of Activity Areas in the Archaeological Record: Ethnoar-chaeological and Archaeological Work in Northwest Ngamiland, Botswana. In *Method and Theory of Activity Area Research: An Ethnoarchaeological Approach,* edited by S. Kent, pp. 63–106. New York: Columbia University Press.

  1992   Decoding the Ju/wasi Past. *Symbols* (9/92): 24–32.

Brooks, Alison S., J. E. Yellen, J. Verniers, E. Cornelissen, and A. Hauzeur

  in press Myth or Math: The Historical and Archaeological Background to the 'Baton Gravé' d'Ishango (RD Congo). In *Proceedings of the XI Congress of the Union International des Sciences Pre- et Proto-Historiques, Liège, Belgium, September 2–8, 2000.*

Bruel, G.

  1910   Les Populations de la Moyenne Sanga. Les Babinga. *Revue d'Ethnographie et de Sociologie* (Paris) 5-7:111–118.

Cable, Charles

  1984   *Economy and Technology of the Late Stone Age of Southern Natal.* British Archaeo-logical Reports International Series 201. Oxford: Archaeopress.

Cahen, D., and J. Moeyersons

  1977   Surface Movements of Stone Artifacts and Their Implication for the Prehis-tory of Central Africa. *Nature* 266:812–815.

Caister, D.

  1982   Archaeological Perspectives on Settlement Patterns in South East Kweneng District. In *Settlement in Botswana,* edited by R. Renée Hitchcock and Mary R. Smith, pp. 87–92. Gaborone: Botswana Society.

Campbell, Alec C., Gunilla Holmberg, and Catrien van Waarden

  1991   A Note on Recent Archaeological Research around Gaborone. *Botswana Notes and Records* 23:288–290.

Campbell, Alec C., Catrien van Waarden, and Gunilla Holmberg

  1996   Variation in the Early Iron Age of Southeastern Botswana. *Botswana Notes and Records* 28:1–22.

Campbell, John

　　1822　　*Travels in South Africa Undertaken at the Request of the London Missionary Society.*
　　　　　　London: London Missionary Society.

Carter, P. L., P. J. Mitchell, and P. Vinnicombe

　　1988　　Sehonghong: The Middle and Later Stone Age Industrial Sequence at a
　　　　　　Lesotho Rock-Shelter. BAR International Series 406. Oxford: BAR.

Cartmill, Matt

　　1998　　The Status of the Race Concept in Physical Anthropology. *American Anthro-*
　　　　　　pology 100:651–660.

Cashdan, Elizabeth

　　1984　　G//ana Territorial Organization. *Human Ecology* 12:443–463.

Cavalli-Sforza, Luigi Luca, ed.

　　1986　　*African Pygmies.* Orlando: Academic Press.

Cavalli-Sforza, Luigi Luca, Paolo Menozzi, and Alberto Piazza

　　1994　　*The History and Geography of Human Genes.* Princeton: Princeton University Press.

Chapman, James

　　1868　　*Travels in the Interior of South Africa.* 2 vols. London: Bell & Daldy.

　　1971　　*Travels in the Interior of South Africa, 1849–1863.* 2 vols., edited by Edward C. Ta-
　　　　　　bler. Reprint. Cape Town: Balkema.

Chen, Y.-S., A. Olckers, A. M. Kogelnik, K. Huoponen, and D. C. Wallace

　　2000　　mtDNA Variation in the South African Kung and Khwe- and Their Genetic
　　　　　　Relationships to Other African Populations. *American Journal of Human Genet-*
　　　　　　ics 66:1362–1383.

Chen, Y.-S., A. Torroni, L. Excoffier, A. S. Santachiara-Benerecetti, and D. C. Wallace

　　1995　　Analysis of mtDNA Variation in African Populations Reveals the Most An-
　　　　　　cient of All Human Continent-Specific Haplogroups. *American Journal of*
　　　　　　Human Genetics 57 (1): 133–149.

Childers, G. W.

　　1976　　Report on the Survey/Investigation of the Ghanzi Farm Basarwa Situation.
　　　　　　Gaborone: Government Printer.

Clastres, Pierre

　　1974　　*La Societe contre l'État. Recherches d'anthropologie politique.* Paris: Ed. de Minuit.

Cliffe, Lionel

　　1982　　Class Formation as an "Articulation" Process: East African Cases. In *Introduc-*
　　　　　　tion to the Sociology of Developing Countries, edited by H. Alavi and Teodor Sha-
　　　　　　nin. New York: Monthly Review Press.

Clist, Bernard

　　1999　　Traces des Très Anciennes Occupations Humaines de la Forêt Tropicale au
　　　　　　Gabon. In *Central African Hunter-Gatherers in a Multidisciplinary Perspective:*
　　　　　　Challenging Elusiveness, edited by Karen Biesbrouck, Stefan Elders, and Gerda
　　　　　　Rossel, pp.75–88. Leiden: CNWS, Universiteit Leiden.

Comaroff, John, and Jean Comaroff

　　1991　　*Of Revelation and Revolution,* vol 1. Chicago: University of Chicago Press.

　　1997　　*Of Revelation and Revolution,* vol. 2. Chicago: University of Chicago Press.

Cooper, B.

  1949   The Kindiga. *Tanganyika Notes and Records* 27.

Cronk, Lee, and D. Bruce Dickson

  2001   Public and Hidden Transcripts in the East African Highlands: A Comment on Smith (1998). *Journal of Anthropological Archaeology* 20:113–121.

Crowell, A., and Robert Hitchcock

  1978   Basarwa Ambush Hunting in Botswana. *Botswana Notes and Records* 10:37–51.

Cumming, Roualeyn Gordon

  1980   *A Hunter's Life in South Africa*, 2 volumes. Bulawayo: Books of Zimbabwe Pub-
  [1950]   lishing Co.

Curtin, Philip

  1998   *Disease and Empire.* Cambridge: Cambridge University Press.

Cusick, James

  1998   Historiography of Acculturation: An Evaluation of Concepts and Their Ap-plication in Archaeology. In *Studies in Culture Contact: Interaction, Culture Change, and Archaeology,* edited by James Cusick, pp. 126–145. Center for Ar-chaeological Investigations, Occasional Paper No. 25. Carbondale: Southern Illinois University.

Deacon, Hillary, and Jeanette Deacon

  1999   *Human Beginnings in South Africa: Uncovering the Secrets of the Stone Age.* Cape Town: David Philip.

DeCorse, Christopher

  1998   Culture Contact and Change in West Africa. In *Studies in Culture Contact: In-teraction, Culture Change, and Archaeology,* edited by James Cusick, pp. 358–401. Center for Archaeological Investigations, Occasional Paper No. 25. Carbon-dale: Southern Illinois University.

Delobeau, Jean-Michel

  1984   Les Pygmées dans la Colonisation. *Afrika Zamani—Revue d'Histoire Africaine* (Yaoundé) 14 & 15:115–133.

  1989   *Yamonzombo et Yandenga. Les relations entre les villages monzombo et les campe-ments pygmées aka dans la sous-prefecture de Mongoumba (Centrafrique).* Paris: Peeters/SELAF.

Denbow, James

  1981   Broadhurst: A 14th Century A.D. Expression of the Early Iron Age in South-eastern Botswana. *South African Archaeological Bulletin* 36:66–74.

  1984   Prehistoric Herders and Foragers in the Kalahari: The Evidence for 1500 Years of Interaction. In *Past and Present in Hunter-Gatherer Studies,* edited by Carmel Schrire, pp. 175–195. New York: Academic Press.

  1986   Patterns and Processes: A New Look at the Later Prehistory of the Kalahari. *Journal of African History* 27:3–28.

  1990   Congo to Kalahari: Data and Hypotheses about the Political Economy of the Western Stream of the Early Iron Age. *African Archaeological Review* 8:139–175.

Denbow, James, and Edwin N. Wilmsen

  1986   Advent and Course of Pastoralism in the Kalahari. *Science* 234:1509–1515.

DeVos, George

1995   Ethnic Pluralism: Conflict and Accommodation: The Role of Ethnicity in So-
        cial History. In *Ethnic Identity: Creation, Conflict, and Accommodation*, 3d edi-
        tion, edited by Lola Romanucci-Ross and George DeVos, pp. 15–47. Walnut
        Creek, CA: AltaMira Press.

DeVos, George, and Lola Romanucci-Ross

1995   Ethnic Identity: A Psychocultural Perspective. In *Ethnic Identity: Creation,
        Conflict, and Accommodation*, 3d edition, edited by Lola Romanucci-Ross and
        George DeVos, pp. 349–379. Walnut Creek, CA: AltaMira Press.

Dounias, Edmond

1993   Perception and Use of Wild Yams by the Baka Hunter-Gatherers in South
        Cameroon. In *Tropical Forests, People, and Food: Biocultural Interactions and Ap-
        plications to Development*, edited by Claude Marcel Hladik, Annette Hladik,
        Olga F. Linares, Hélène Pagezy, and M. Hadley, pp. 621–632. Paris: Unesco
        and the Parthenon Publishing Group.

Draper, Patricia

1975a   Cultural Pressure on Sex Differences. *American Ethnologist* 2:602–616.

1975b   !Kung Women: Contrasts in Sexual Egalitarianism in Foraging and Sedentary
        Contexts. In *Toward an Anthropology of Women*, edited by Rayna Reiter, pp.
        77–109. New York: Monthly Review Press.

Draper, Patricia, and Nancy Howell

1998   Historical Dynamics of the Socioeconomic Relationships between the No-
        madic San and the Rural Kgalagadi. Paper presented at the 297th Annual
        Meeting of the American Anthropological Association, Chicago.

Draper, Patricia, and M. Kranichfeld

1990   Coming in from the Bush: Settled Life by the !Kung and Their Accommoda-
        tion to Bantu Neighbors. *Human Ecology* 18 (4): 363–384.

Dunn, E. J.

1873   Through Bushmanland. *Cape Monthly Magazine* 6:31–42.

1931   *The Bushmen*. London: Charles Griffin.

Dupré, G., and Bernard Guillot

1973   *Projet de Développement de la Culture du Cacaoyer dans la Région de la Sangha.
        Études Géographiques et Sociologiques. Tome II, Sociologie*. Brazzaville:
        O.R.S.T.O.M.

Earle, T., and J. Ericson, eds.

1977   *Exchange Systems in Pre-History*. New York: Academic Press.

Ebert, J.

n.d.   The Later-Stone Age of the Dobe area. Paper presented at "The Kalahari De-
        bate" Symposium at the American Anthropological Association Annual
        Meeting, Chicago, November 1989. Co-organizers: Robert K. Hitchcock and
        Richard B. Lee.

Ellenberger, D. Fred

1912   *History of the Basuto: Ancient and Modern*. London: Caxton Publishing Com-
        pany (Reprinted 1992 by Morija Printing Works, Morija, Lesotho).

Elphick, Richard

    1977   *Kraal and Castle: KhoiKhoi and the Founding of White South Africa*. New Haven: Yale University Press.

Fahlbusch, M., M. Rössler, and D. Siegrist

    1989   Conservatism, Ideology, and Geography in Germany 1920–1950. *Political Geography Quarterly* 8:353–367.

Fairhead, James, and Melissa Leach

    1995   False Forest History, Complicit Social Analysis: Rethinking Some West African Environmental Narratives. *World Development* 23 (6): 1023–1035.

    1998   *Reframing Deforestation. Global Analyses and Local Realities: Studies in West Africa*. London and New York: Routledge.

Fernandes-Costa, F., John Marshall, Claire Ritchie, Susan van Tonder, David Dunn, Trefor Jenkins, and Jack Metz

    1984   Transition from a Hunter-Gatherer to a Settled Lifestyle in the !Kung San: Effect on Iron, Folate, and Vitamin B12 Nutrition. *The American Journal of Clinical Nutrition* 40:1295–1303.

Fischer, Hans

    1990   *Völkerkunde im Nationalsozialismus*. Berlin: Dietrich Reimer Verlag.

Fisher, John J.

    1986   Shadows in the Forest: Ethnoarchaeology among the Efe Pygmies. Ph.D. diss., University of California, Berkeley. Ann Arbor, MI: University Microfilms International.

Fleming, H. C.

    1986   Hadza and Sandawe Genetic Relations. *Sprache und Geschichte in Afrika* 7 (2): 157–187.

Fosbrooke, H. A.

    1956   A Stone Age Tribe in Tanganyika. *The South African Archeological Bulletin* 11 (41): 3–8.

Foster-Carter, A.

    1978   The Modes of Production Controversy. *New Left Review* 107:44–77.

Foucault, Michel

    1980   *Power/Knowledge: Selected Interviews and Other Writings*. New York: Pantheon Books.

    1983   Afterword: The Subject and Power. In *Beyond Structuralism and Hermeneutics*, 2d edition, edited by Hubert Dreyfus and Paul Rabinow, pp. 208–226. Chicago: University of Chicago Press.

Fritsch, G.

    1906   Die Buschmänner der Kalahari von S. Passarge. *Zeitschrift für Ethnologie* 38:71–79.

Gadibolae, M. N.

    1985   Serfdom (Bolata) in the Nata Area 1926–1960. *Botswana Notes and Records* 17:25–32.

Garman, James

    1998   Resistant Accommodation: Toward an Archaeology of African-American

Lives in Southern New England, 1638–1800. *International Journal of Historical Archaeology* 2:133–160.

Geelhoed, G.

1996   Metabolic Maladaptation: Individual and Social Consequences of Medical Intervention in Correcting Endemic Hypothyroidism. M.A. thesis, George Washington University.

Gellner, E.

1983   *Nations and Nationalism.* Oxford: Basil Blackwell.

Gibbons, Alfred St. Hill

1904   *Africa from South to North through Marotseland.* 2 vols. London: John Lane, the Bodley Head.

Gill, Stephen

1992   Introductory Essay. In *History of the Basuto: Ancient and Modern,* by D. Fred. Ellenberger. Morija, Lesotho: Morija Printing Works.

Gillett, S.

1969   Notes on the Settlement in the Ghanzi District. *Botswana Notes and Records* 2:52–55.

Gilman, S. L.

1985   Black Bodies, White Bodies: Toward an Iconography of Female Sexuality in Late Nineteenth-Century Art, Medicine, and Literature. *Critical Inquiry* 12:204–242.

Goffman, Erving

1963   *Behavior in Public Places.* New York: The Free Press.

Gopolang, S.

1997   The Impacts of Iron Age Populations on Late Stone Age Populations: An Archaeological Survey of Thamaga Area. B.A. research essay, Department of History, University of Botswana.

Gordon, Robert

1984   The !Kung in the Kalahari Exchange: An Ethnohistorical Perspective. In *Past and Present in Hunter-Gatherer Studies,* edited by Carmel Schrire, pp. 195–224. New York: Academic Press.

1992   *The Bushman Myth: The Making of a Namibian Underclass.* Boulder, CO: Westview Press.

Grinker, Roy Richard III

1990   Images of Denigration: Structuring Inequality between Foragers and Farmers in the Ituri Forest, Zaire. *American Anthropologist* 17 (1): 111–130.

1994   *Houses in the Rainforest: Ethnicity and Inequality among Farmers and Foragers in Central Africa.* Berkeley: University of California Press.

Gudeman, Stephen

1986   *Economics as Culture: Models and Metaphors of Livelihood.* London: Routledge and Kegan Paul.

Guenther, Mathias G.

1976   From Hunters to Squatters: Social and Cultural Change among the Farm San of Ghanzi, Botswana. In *Kalahari Hunter-Gatherers: Studies of the !Kung San and their Neighbors,* edited by Richard B. Lee and Irven DeVore, pp. 120–134. Cambridge: Harvard University Press.

1986a   *The Farm Bushmen of the Ghanzi District, Botswana.* Stuttgart: Hochschulverlag.

1986b   From Foragers to Miners and Bands to Bandits: On the Flexibility and Adaptability of Bushman Band Societies. *Sprache und Geschichte in Afrika* 7 (1): 133–159.

1986c   *The Nharo Bushmen of Botswana.* Hamburg: Helmut Buske Verlag.

1989   *Bushman Folktales: Oral Traditions of the Nharo of Botswana and the /Xam of the Cape.* Studien zur Kulturkunde 93. Stuttgart: Franz Steiner Verlag Wiesbaden.

1993/94   'Independent, Fearless and Rather Bold': A Historical Narrative on the Ghanzi Bushmen of Botswana. *Journal of the Namibian Scientific Society* 44:25–40.

1996a   Diversity and Flexibility: The Case of the Bushmen of Southern Africa. In *Cultural Diversity among Twentieth-Century Foragers: An African Perspective,* edited by Susan Kent, pp. 65–66. Cambridge: Cambridge University Press.

1996b   From 'Lords of the Desert' to 'Rubbish People': The Colonial and Contemporary State of the Nharo Bushmen. In *Miscast: Negotiating the Presence of the Bushmen,* edited by Pippa Skotnes, pp. 225–238. Cape Town: University of Cape Town Press.

1997   'Lords of the Desert Land': Politics and Resistance of the 19th Century Ghanzi Bushmen. *Botswana Notes and Records* 29:121–141.

1999a   Review of *The Kalahari Ethnographies (1896–1898) of Siegfried Passarge,* edited by Edwin Wilmsen. *Africa,* pp. 645–674.

1999b   *Tricksters and Trancers: Bushman Religion and Society.* Bloomington: Indiana University Press.

in press   Ethnotourism and the Bushmen. In *Self- and Other Images of Hunter-Gatherers,* edited by Henry Stewart and Alan Barnard. Senri Ethnological Studies. Osaka: National Museum of Ethnology.

Guyer, Jane, and Paul Richards

1996   The Invention of Biodiversity: Social Perspectives on the Management of Biological Variety in Africa. *Africa* 66 (1): 1–13.

Hall, Martin

1987   *The Changing Past: Farmers, Kings, and Traders in Southern Africa 200–1860.* Cape Town: David Phillip.

1988   At the Frontier: Some Arguments against Hunter-Gathering and Farming Modes of Production in Southern Africa. In *Hunters and Gatherers: History, Evolution, and Social Change,* edited by Tim Ingold, David Riches, and James Woodburn, pp. 137–160. Oxford: Berg Publishers.

Hall, Simon, and Benjamin Smith

1998   *Empowering Places: Rock Shelters and Ritual Control in Farmer-Forager Interactions in the Northern Province, South Africa.* Paper given at the American Anthropological Association Annual Meeting, Chicago, IL.

Hamilton, Carolyn, ed.

1995   *The Mfecane Aftermath.* Johannesburg: Witwatersrand University Press.

Handler, Jerome, with Michael Conner and Keith Jacobi

1989   *Searching for a Slave Cemetery in Barbados, West Indies: A Bioarchaeological and*

Ethnohistorical Investigation. Center for Archaeological Investigations, Research Paper No. 59. Carbondale: Southern Illinois University.

Harpending, Henry, M. A. Batzer, M. Gurven, L. B. Jorde, A. R. Rogers, and S. T. Sherry

1998   Genetic Traces of Ancient Demography. *Proceedings of the National Academy of Sciences* 95:1961–1967.

Harpending, Henry C., S. T. Sherry, A. L. Rogers, and M. Stoneking

1993   The Genetic Structure of Ancient Human Populations. *Current Anthropology* 34:483–496.

Hart, Charles William Merton, and Arnold R. Pilling

1979   *The Tiwi of North Australia*. New York: Holt, Rinehart and Winston.

Hart, Teresa B., and John A. Hart

1986   The Ecological Basis of Hunter-Gatherer Subsistence in African Rain Forests: The Mbuti of Eastern Zaire. *Human Ecology* 14 (1): 29–56.

Hauser, Andre

1951   *Les Babinga*. Brazzaville: Office de la Recherche Scientifique Outre Mer. Institut d'Études Centrafricaines. Sociologie. Reprinted in *Zaïre* (Bruxelles) VII (2), Février 1953:147–179.

Hayes, Alden

1981   *Contributions to Gran Quivira Archaeology*. Publications in Archeology 17. Washington, D.C.: National Park Service.

Hayes, Alden, Jon Young, and A. H. Warren

1981   *Excavation of Mound 7, Gran Quivira National Monument*. Publications in Archeology 16. Washington, D.C.: National Park Service.

Headland, Thomas N.

1987   The Wild Yam Question: How Well Could Independent Hunter-Gatherers Live in a Tropical Rainforest Ecosystem? *Human Ecology* 15 (4): 463–491.

1999   Could "Pure" Hunter-Gatherers Live in a Rain Forest? A 1999 Review of the Current Status of the Wild Yam Question. Electronic document. http://www.sil.org/sil/roster/headland-t/wildyam.htm

Heater, Derek

1990   *Citizenship: The Civic Ideal in World History, Politics, and Education*. London: Longman.

Heinz, Hans-Joachim

1994   *Social Organization of the !Kõ Bushmen*. Quellen zur Khoisan-Forschung 10. Köln: Rüdiger Köppe Verlag.

Helgren, D. M., and A. S. Brooks

1983   Geoarchaeology at Gi: A Middle Stone Age and Later Stone Age Site in the Northwest Kalahari. *Journal of Archeological Science* 10:181–197.

Hemphill, Brian, John Lukacs, and Subhash Walimbe

2000   Ethnic Identity, Biological History and Dental Morphology: Evaluating the Indigenous Status of Maharashtra's Mahars. *Antiquity* 24:671–681.

Henneberg, M., and M. Steyn

1995   Preliminary Report on the Paleodemography of the K2 and Mapungubwe Populations (South Africa). *Human Biology* 66:105–120.

Hermans, J.

1977   Official Policy towards the Bushmen of Botswana: A Review. *Botswana Notes and Records* 9:55–67.

Hesse, Hans

1997   Khoisan in Kannaland: Observation by the German Lutheran Missionaries from 1838 to 1938. Paper delivered at the Khoisan Identities and Cultural Heritage Conference, University of the Western Cape at the South African Museum, Cape Town, South Africa.

Hewlett, Barry

1996   Cultural Diversity among African Pygmies. In *Cultural Diversity among Twentieth-Century Foragers: An African Perspective*, edited by Susan Kent, pp. 215–244. Cambridge: University Press.

Hindess, Barry, and Paul Q. Hirst

1975   *Pre-Capitalist Modes of Production*. London: Routledge.

Hitchcock, Robert K.

1978   *Kalahari Cattle Posts: A Regional Study of Hunter-Gatherers, Pastoralists, and Agriculturalists in the Western Sandveld Region, Central District, Botswana.* 2 vols. Gaborone: Government Printer.

1997   Cultural, Economic and Environmental Impacts of Tourism amongst Kalahari Bushmen. In *Tourism and Culture: An Applied Perspective*, edited by E. Chambers, pp. 93–128. Albany: State University of New York Press.

1999   *Bushmen and the Politics of the Environment in Southern Africa.* IWGIA Document No. 79. Copenhagen: International Work Group for Indigenous Affairs.

Hitchcock, Robert. K., and John D. Holm

1993   Bureaucratic Domination of Hunter-Gatherer Societies: A Study of the San of Botswana. *Development and Change* 24:305–338.

How, M. W.

1962   *The Mountain Bushman of Basutoland*. Pretoria: J. L. Van Shaik.

Huffman, T.

1989   Ceramics, Settlements, and Later Iron Age Migrations. *African Archaeological Review* 7:155–182.

1998   The Antiquity of Lobola. *South African Archaeological Bulletin* 53:57–62.

Hurwitz, Hilliard

1956   Social and Cultural Anthropological Observation of the Bushmen and Other Indigenous Peoples of the Okavango Swamp. *The Leech* 26 (1), Witwatersrand University Medical School, Johannesburg.

Ichikawa, Mitsuo

1983   An Examination of the Hunting-Dependent Life of the Mbuti Pygmies, Eastern Zaire. *African Study Monographs* 4:55–76.

1991   The Impact of Commoditisation on the Mbuti of Eastern Zaire. In *Cash, Commoditisation, and Changing Foragers*, edited by Nicolas Peterson and T. Matsuyama, pp. 135–162. Senri Ethnological Studies 30. Osaka: National Museum of Ethnology.

Ikeya, Kazunobu
    1993   Goat Raising among the San in the Central Kalahari. *African Study Monographs* 14 (1): 39–52.
    1996a   Road Construction and Handicraft Production in the Xade Area, Botswana. *African Study Monographs,* Supplementary Issue 22:67–84.
    1996b   Dry Farming among the San in the Central Kalahari. *African Study Monographs,* Supplementary Issue 22:85–100.
    n.d.   Socio-Economic Changes among the San in the Central Kalahari Game Reserve, Botswana. Paper presented at 8th International Conference on Hunting and Gathering Societies, 26–30 October 1998. Osaka: National Museum of Ethnology.

Imamura-Hayaki, Kaoru
    1996   Gathering Activity among the Central Kalahari San. *African Study Monographs,* Supplementary Issue 22:47–65.

Ingold, Tim
    1994   From Trust to Domination: An Alternative History of Human-Animal Relations. In *Animals and Human Society: Changing Perspectives,* edited by Aubrey Manning and James Serpell, pp.1–22. London: Routledge.
    1996   Hunting and Gathering as Ways of Perceiving the Environment. In *Redefining Nature: Ecology, Culture, and Domestication,* edited by Roy Ellen and Katsuyoshi Fukui, pp. 117–155. Oxford: Berg.

Jackson, Michael
    1989   *Paths Toward a Clearing: Radical Empiricism and Ethnographic Enquiry.* Bloomington and Indianapolis: Indiana University Press.

Jenkins, Trefor, A. Zoutendyk, and A. G. Steinberg
    1970   Gammaglobulin Groups (Gm and Inv) of Various Southern African Populations. *American Journal of Physical Anthropology* 32:197–218.

Jerardino Wiesenborn, Antonieta
    1996   Changing Social Landscapes of the Western Cape Coast of Southern Africa over the Last 4,500 Years. Ph.D. diss., University of Cape Town, South Africa.

Joiris, Daou Veronique
    1998   *La chasse, la chance, le chant: Aspects du système rituel des Baka du Cameroun.* Ph.D. thesis, Université Libre de Bruxelles.

Jolly, Pieter
    1995   Melikane and Upper Mangolong Revisited: The Possible Effects on San Art of Symbiotic Contact between South-Eastern San and Southern Sotho and Nguni Communities. *South African Archaeological Bulletin* 50:68–80.
    1996   Symbiotic Interaction between African Rock Art Studies, Ethnographic Analogy, and Hunter-Gatherer Cultural Identity. *Current Anthropology* 37 (3): 277–305.

Jones, Sian
    1997   *The Archaeology of Ethnicity: Constructing Identities in the Past and Present.* London: Routledge.

Jorde, L. B., M. Bamshad, and A. R. Rogers
    1998   Using Mitochondrial and Nuclear DNA Markers to Reconstruct Human Evolution. *BioEssays* 20 (2): 126–136.

Jorde, L. B., A. R. Rogers, M. Bamshad, W. S. Watkins, P. Krakowiak, S. Sung, J. Kere, and
H. C. Harpending
  1997   Microsatellite Diversity and the Demographic History of Modern Humans.
          Proceedings of the National Academy of Sciences 94:3100–3103.

Kagabo, José, and Vincent Mudandagizi
  1974   Complainte des Gens d'argile, les Twa du Rwanda. *Cahiers des Etudes Afric-
          aines* 14 (1) Cahier No. 53, pp. 75–87.

Kaplan, Jonathan
  1993   The Archaeology of the Muela Rock-Shelter. Report for the Lesotho High-
          lands Development Authority, Agency for Cultural Resource Management.

Kazadi, Ntole
  1981   Méprises et Admires: L'ambivalance des Relations entre les Bacwa (Pygmées)
          et les Bahemba (Bantu). *Africa* 51 (4): 836–847.

Ke, Y., B. Su, X. Song, D. Lu, L. Chen, H. Li, C. Oi, S. Marzuki, R. Deka, P. Underhill, C.
          Xiao, M. Shriver, J. Lell, D. Wallace, R. S. Wells, M. Seielstad, P. Oefner, D.
          Zhu, J. Jin, W. Huang, R. Chakraborty, Z. Chen, and L. Jin
  2001   African Origin of Modern Humans in East Asia: A Tale of 12,000 Y Chromo-
          somes. *Science* 292:1151–1153.

Keita, S. O., and Rick Kittles
  1997   The Persistence of Racial Thinking and the Myth of Racial Divergence.
          American Anthropology 99:534–544.

Kelly, Robert L.
  1995   *The Foraging Spectrum: Diversity in Hunter-Gatherer Lifeways.* Washington,
          D.C.: Smithsonian Institution Press.

Kenrick, Justin
  1996   Mbuti Hunter-Gatherers and Rainforest Conservation in the Ituri Forest,
          Zaïre. Ph.D. thesis, University of Edinburgh.

Kent, Susan
  1990   Invisible Foragers: The Archaeological Visibility of Prehistoric Hunter-Gatherers.
          Paper given at the Society for Africanist Archaeology Conference, Gaines-
          ville, Florida.

  1992   The Current Forager Controversy: Real versus Ideal Views of Hunter-Gatherers.
          Man 27:45–70.

  1993   Sharing in an Egalitarian Kalahari Village. *Man: Journal of the Royal Anthropo-
          logical Institute* (NS) 28 (3): 479–514.

  1995a   Does Sedentarization Promote Gender Inequality? A Case Study from the
          Kalahari. *Journal of the Royal Anthropological Institute* (NS) 1:513–536.

  1995b   Unstable Households in a Stable Community: The Organization of a
          Recently Sedentary Kalahari Community. *American Anthropologist* 97 (2): 297–
          312.

  1996a   Cultural Diversity among African Foragers. In *Cultural Diversity among Twentieth-
          Century Foragers: An African Perspective,* edited by Susan Kent, pp. 1–18. Cam-
          bridge: Cambridge University Press.

  1996b   Hunting Variation in a Recently Sedentary Kalahari Community. In *Cultural*

Diversity among Twentieth-Century Foragers: An African Perspective, edited by Susan Kent, pp. 125–156. Cambridge: Cambridge University Press.

1998a   Do Flexible Cultures Equal Flexible or Oscillating Economies? Paper delivered at the 8th Conference on Hunters and Gatherers Society (CHAGS 8). Osaka, Japan.

1998b   Hunter-Gatherers or Pastoralists or Both during the Late Stone Age and Early Iron Age in Southern Africa? Paper delivered at the Society for Africanist Archaeology Conference, Syracuse, New York.

in prep   How Egalitarian Are Egalitarian Societies? Variation among Kalahari Foragers. Manuscript submitted to journal.

Kent, Susan, ed.

1996   *Cultural Diversity among Twentieth-Century Foragers: An African Perspective.* Cambridge and New York: Cambridge University Press.

Kent, Susan, and Richard B. Lee

1992   A Hematological Study of !Kung Kalahari Foragers: An Eighteen Year Comparison. In *Diet, Demography, and Disease: Changing Views of Anemia,* edited by Patricia Stuart-Macadam and Susan Kent, pp. 173–199. New York: Aldine de Gruyter.

Kingdon, Elenor

1990   Caught between Two Worlds: Moral Problems Relating to Conservation in South-West Uganda. *International Journal of Moral and Social Studies* 5 (3): 235–249.

Kirby, Percival Robson, ed.

1939   *The Diary of Dr. Andrew Smith, 1834–1836,* Volume 2. Cape Town: Van Riebeeck Society.

Kitamura, Koji

1990   Interactional Synchrony: A Fundamental Condition for Communication. In *Culture Embodied,* edited by Michael Moerman and Masaichi Nomura, pp. 123–140. Senri Ethnological Studies 27. Osaka, Japan: National Museum of Ethnology.

Klatzow, Shelona

2000   Interaction between Hunter-gatherers and Agriculturalists in the Eastern Free State. M.A. thesis, Department of Archaeology, University of the Witwatersrand.

Klein, Richard

1979   Paleoenvironmental and Cultural Implications of Late Holocene Archaeological Faunas from the Orange Free State and North-Central Cape Province, South Africa. *South African Archaeological Bulletin* 34:34–49.

Klieman, Kairn

1995   Hunter-Gatherers in the Agricultural History of the Western Equatorial Rainforest, c. 1500 B.C. to 1900 A.D. Paper presented at the 38th Annual Meeting of the African Studies Association, Nov. 3–6.

1997   Hunters and Farmers of the Equatorial Rainforest: Economy and Society, c. 3000 B.C. to 800 A.D. Ph.D. diss., University of California, Los Angeles.

1999   Hunter-Gatherer Participation in Rainforest Trade-Systems: A Comparative History of Forest vs. Ecotone Societies in Gabon and Congo, c. 1000–1800 A.D.

In *Central African Hunter-Gatherers in a Multidisciplinary Perspective: Challenging Elusiveness*, edited by Karen Biesbrouck, Stefan Elders, and Gerda Rossel, pp. 89–104. Leiden: CNWS, Universiteit Leiden.

in press Towards a History of Precolonial Gabon: Farmers and Forest Specialists along the Ogooué, c. 500 B.C.–1000 A.D. In *Culture, Ecology, and Politics in Gabon's Rainforest*, edited by Michael C. Reed and James F. Barnes. Boulder, CO: Westview Press.

n.d.   The Pygmies Were Our Compass: Bantu and Batwa in the History of West Central Africa, Early Times to c. 1800 C.E. Unpublished ms.

Klima, George J.

1970   *The Barabaig: East African Cattle Herders.* New York: Holt, Rinehart and Winston.

Knight, A., H. M. Mortensen, G. Passarino, A. A. Lin, L. L. Cavalli-Sforza, P. A. Underhill, and J. L. Mountain

2000   Out of the Rift: Genetic Diversity within and among Tanzanian Populations and Affinities with Other African and Non-African Populations. Paper presented at the Cold Spring Harbor Symposium on "Human Origins and Disease," October 25–29.

Knight, A., P. A. Underhill, L. Zhivotovsky. H. M. Mortensen, M. Ruhlen, and J. L. Mountain

in press African Y Chromosome and mtDNA Diversity and the Antiquity of Click Languages. *Proceeding of the National Academy of Sciences.*

Köhler, Axel

2000   Half-Man, Half-Elephant: Shapeshifting among the Baka of Congo. In *Natural Enemies: People-Wildlife Conflicts in Anthropological Perspective*, edited by John Knight, pp. 50–77. London and New York: Routledge.

Köhler, Oswin

1959   *A Study of Gobabis District.* Pretoria: The Government Printer.

1989a   *Die Welt der Kxoe-Buschleute. I Die Kxoe-Buschleute und ihre ethnische Umgebung.* Berlin: Dietrich Reimer Verlag.

1989b   *Die Welt der Kxoé-Buschleute im südlichen Afrika. Eine Selbstdarstellung in ihrer eigenen Sprache, Band 1: Die Kxoé-Buschleute und ihre ethnische Umgebung.* Berlin: Dietrich Reimer Verlag.

Kohl-Larsen, L.

1958   *Wildbeuter in Ostafrika, die Tindiga, ein Jäger- und Sammlervolk.* Berlin: Dietrich Reimer Verlag.

Konner, M., and M. Shostak

1986   Ethnographic Romanticism and the Idea of Human Nature: Parallels between Samoa and the !Kung San. In *The Past and Future of !Kung Ethnography*, edited by Megan Biesele, pp. 69–76. Hamburg: Helmut Buske Verlag.

Kopytoff, Igor

1987   The Internal African Frontier: The Making of African Political Culture. In *The African Frontier: The Reproduction of Traditional African Societies*, edited by

Susan Miers and Igor Kopytoff, pp. 3–86. Bloomington and Indianapolis: Indiana University Press.

Laden, G. T.
1992   Ethnoarchaeology and Land Use Ecology of the Efe (Pygmies) of the Ituri Rain Forest, Zaire: a Behavioral Ecological Study. Ph.D. diss., Harvard University.

Lamont, Michele, and Marcel Fournier, eds.
1992   *Cultivating Differences: Symbolic Boundaries and the Making of Inequality.* Chicago: University of Chicago Press.

Lane, P., A. Reid, and A. Segobye, eds.
1998   *Ditswa Mung: The Archaeology of Botswana.* Gaborone: Pula Press and Botswana Society.

Lau, Brigitte
1987   *Namibia in Jonker Afrikaner's Time.* Windhoek: National Archives.

Lebzelter, Viktor
1934a   *Eingeborenenkulturen von Südwestafrika Die Buschmänner.* Leipzig: Verlag Karl W. Hirsemann.
1934b   *Eingeborenenkulturen in Südwest- und Südafrika.* Leipzig: Verlag Karl W. Hiersemann.

Lee, Richard B.
1965   Subsistence Ecology of !Kung Bushmen. Ph.D. diss., University of California, Berkeley.
1976   !Kung Spatial Organization: An Ecological and Historical Perspective. In *Kalahari Hunter-Gatherers,* edited by Richard B. Lee and Irven De Vore, pp. 73–97. Cambridge: Harvard University Press.
1979   *The !Kung San: Men, Women, and Work in a Foraging Society.* Cambridge and New York: Cambridge University Press.
1984   *The Dobe !Kung.* New York: Holt, Rinehart and Winston.
1992a   Art, Science, or Politics: The Crisis in Gatherer-Hunter Studies. *American Anthropologist* 90 (1): 18–45.
1992b   The !Kung in Question: Evidence and Context in the Kalahari Debate. *Michigan Discussions in Anthropology* 10:9–16.
1993   *The Dobe Ju/'hoansi.* 2d edition. Fort Worth: Harcourt Brace College Publishers.
1997   Gumi Kwara: I Kwara: E Ba N//A Basi O Win Si !Kwana: Oral Histories from Nyae Nyae-Dobe and the Khoisan Renaissance. In *The Proceedings of the Khoisan Identities and Cultural Heritage Conference,* edited by A. Banks, pp. 67–73. Cape Town: InfoSource and the Institute for Historical Research, University of the Western Cape.
1998   Anthropology at the Crossroads: From the Age of Ethnography to the Age of World-Systems. *Social Dynamics* 24:34–65.

Lee, Richard B., and Megan Biesele
1994   A Local Culture in the Global System: The Ju/'hoansi Today. *General Anthropology Newsletter* 1 (1): 1–3.

Lee, Richard B., and Mathias G. Guenther

1991   Oxen or Onions? The Search for Trade (and Truth) in the Kalahari. *Current Anthropology* 32:592–601.

1993   Problems in Kalahari Historical Ethnography and the Tolerance of Error. *History in Africa* 20:185–235.

1995   Errors Corrected or Compounded? A Reply to Wilmsen. *Current Anthropology* 36 (2): 298–305.

Lee, Richard B., and Robert K. Hitchcock

1998   African Hunter-Gatherers: History and the Politics of Ethnicity. In *Transformations in Africa: Essays on Africa's Later Past,* edited by Graham Connah, pp. 14–45. London: Cassels.

Leigh, D.

2001   Buried Artifacts in Sandy Soils. In *Earth Sciences and Archaeology,* edited by P. Goldberg, V. T. Holliday, and C. Reid Ferring, pp. 269–293. New York: Kluwer/Plenum.

Le May, Godfrey Hugh Lancelot

1995   *The Afrikaners: An Historical Interpretation.* Cambridge: Blackwell Publishers.

Levine, Hal

1999   Reconstructing Ethnicity. *Journal of the Royal Anthropological Institute* 5:165–176.

Lévi-Strauss, C.

1949   *Les Structures Élémentaires de la Parenté.* Paris: Presses Universitaires de France.

Lewis, Jerome

2000   *The Batwa of the Great Lakes Region.* Minority Rights Group Report, Minority Rights Group: London.

2001   Forest People or Village People: Whose Voice Will Be Heard? In *Africa's Indigenous Peoples: 'First Peoples' or 'Marginalised Minorities'?* edited by Alan Barnard and Justin Kenrick, pp. 61–78. Edinburgh: Centre for African Studies.

Livingstone, David

1852   Latest Explorations into Central Africa beyond Lake Ngami. *Journal of the Royal Geographical Society* 22:163–173.

1971   *Missionary Travels and Researches in South Africa.* Reprint of 1857 edition
[1857]   originally published in London by John Murray. New York: Harper and Brothers.

Ludden, David

1992   India's Development Regime. In *Colonialism and Culture,* edited by Nicholas Dirks, pp. 247–287. Ann Arbor: University of Michigan Press.

Lye, William F., ed.

1975   *Andrew Smith's Journal of his Expedition into the Interior of South Africa, 1834–1836.* Cape Town: A. A. Balkema.

Mabulla, A. Z. P.

1996   Middle and Later Stone Age Land-Use and Lithic Technology in the Eyasi Basin, Tanzania. Ph.D. diss., University of Florida.

MacEachern, Scott

2000   Genes, Tribes, and African History. *Current Anthropology* 41 (3): 357–384.

Mackenzie, John
  1971   Ten Years North of the Orange River: A Story of Everyday Life and Work among the
  [1871]   South African Tribes from 1859–1869. Reprint of 1871 edition originally published
             in Edinburgh by Edmonston. London: Frank Cass and Co.
Malan, F.
  1950   A Wilton Site at Kai Kai, Bechuanaland Protectorate. South African Archaeolog-
             ical Bulletin 5 (20): 140–142.
Manhire, Anthony
  1987   Later Stone Age Settlement Patterns in the Sandveld of the South-Western Cape Prov-
             ince, South Africa. BAR International Series 351. Oxford: BAR.
Maquet, Jacques, and S. Naigiziki
  1957   Les Droits Fonciers dans le Rwanda Ancien. Zaïre 4:339–359.
Marlowe, Frank
  1999a   Male Care and Mating Effort among Hadza Foragers. Behavioral Ecology and
             Sociobiology 46:57–64.
  1999b   Showoffs or Providers: The Parenting Effort of Hadza Men. Evolution and
             Human Behavior 20:391–404.
  n.d.   What Explains Hadza Food Sharing? Under review, Journal of Anthropological
             Research.
Marshall, John, and Claire Ritchie
  1984   Where Are the Ju/wasi of Nyae Nyae?: Changes in a Bushman Society, 1958–1981.
             Communications No. 9. Cape Town: Centre for African Studies, University
             of Cape Town.
Marshall, Lorna J.
  1961   Sharing, Talking, and Giving: Relief of Social Tensions among !Kung Bush-
             men. Africa 31:231–249.
  1976   The !Kung of Nyae Nyae. Cambridge: Harvard University Press.
  1999   Nyae Nyae !Kung Beliefs and Rites. Peabody Museum Monographs No. 8. Cam-
             bridge: Harvard University Peabody Museum Press.
Maseko, Z.
  1998   The Life and Times of Sara Baartman: "The Hottentot Venus." New York: First
             Run/Icarus Films.
Mateke, Paul
  1970   The Struggle for Dominance in Bufumbira, 1830–1920. Uganda Journal 34 (1):
             35–48.
Matthiessen, Peter, and Eliot Porter
  1972   The Tree Where Man Was Born: The African Experience. New York: Dutton.
Mauss, Marcel
  1954   The Gift. London: Cohen and West.
Mautle, Gaontatlhe
  1986   Bakgalagadi-Bakwena Relationship: A Case of Slavery, c. 1840–c. 1920.
             Botswana Notes and Records 18:19–32.
Mazel, A. D.
  1986   Mbabane Shelter and eSinhlonhlweni Shelter: The Last Two Thousand Years

of Hunter-Gatherer Settlement in the Central Thukela Basin, Natal, South Africa. *Annals of the Natal Museum* 27:389–453.

McCabe, J.

1855   Journal Kept during Tour into the Interior of South Africa to the Lake N'Gami and to the Country Two-Hundred-and-Fifty Miles beyond by Mr. Joseph McCabe. In *History of the Colony of Natal, South Africa*, edited by W. C. Holden, pp. 413–434. London: Alexander Heylin.

McDowell, W.

1981a   A Brief History of Mangola Hadza. Mbulu District Development Directorate, Mbulu District, Arusha Region.

1981b   Hadza Traditional Economy and Its Prospects for Development. Report for the Rift Valley Project, Ministry of Information and Culture, Division of Research, Dar es Salaam, Tanzania, and District Development Directorate, Mbulu District, Arusha Region, Mbulu.

1982   Hadza Relations with Foreign Researchers. *Review of Ethnology* 8:103–105.

McKee, Larry

1987   Delineating Ethnicity from the Garbage of Early Virginians: Faunal Remains from the Kingsmill Plantation Slave Quarter. *American Archaeology* 6:31–39.

Megaw, J. V., and M. R. Megaw

1996   Ancient Celts and Modern Ethnicity. *Antiquity* 70:175–181.

Mehlman, M. J.

1987   Provenience, Age, and Associations of Archaic Homo Sapiens Crania from Lake Eyasi, Tanzania. *Journal of Archaeological Science* 14:133–162.

1988   Hominid Molars from a Middle Stone Age Level at the Mumba Rock Shelter, Tanzania. *American Journal of Physical Anthropology* 75:69–76.

1991   Context for the Emergence of Modern Man in Eastern Africa: Some New Tanzanian Evidence. In *Cultural Beginnings: Approaches to Understanding Early Hominid Life-Ways in the African Savanna*, edited by D. Clark, pp. 177–196. Bonn: R. Habelt.

Meindertsma, J. Donwe, and J. J. Kessler

1997   *Towards a Better Use of Environmental Resources: A Planning Document of Mbulu and Karatu District, Tanzania.*

Mercader, Julio

1997   Bajo el Techo Forestal: La Evolución del Poblamiento en el Bosque Ecuatorial del Ituri, Zaire. Ph.D. diss., Universidad Complutense, Madrid.

in press   Foragers of the Congo: The Early Settlement of the Ituri Forest. In *Under the Canopy: The Archaeology of Tropical Rainforests*, edited by J. Mercader. New Brunswick: Rutgers University Press.

Mercader, Julio, and A. S. Brooks

2001   Across Forests and Savannas: Later Stone Age Assemblages from Ituri and Semliki, Democratic Republic of Congo. *Journal of Anthropological Research* 57:197–217.

Mercader, Julio, M. García-Heras, and I. González-Álvarez

2000   Ceramic Tradition in the African Rain Forest: Characterisation Analysis of

Ancient and Modern Pottery from Ituri, D.R. Congo. *Journal of Archaeological Science* 27:163–182.

Mercader, Julio, M. D. Garralda, O. M. Pearson, and Robert C. Bailey

2001   Eight Hundred Year–Old Human Remains from the Ituri Tropical Forest, Democratic Republic of Congo: The Rock Shelter Site of Matangai Turu, Northwest. *American Journal of Physical Anthroplogy* 115:24–37.

Mercader, Julio, and R. Marti

2000a   Middle Stone Age Site in the Tropical Forest of Equatorial Guinea. *Nyame Akuma* 51:14–24.

2000b   Archaeology in the Tropical Forest of Banyang-Mbo, SW Cameroon. *Nyame Akuma* 52:17–24.

in press   The Hunter-Gatherer Occupation of Atlantic Central Africa: New Evidence from Equatorial Guinea and Cameroon. In *Under the Canopy: The Archaeology of Tropical Rainforests,* edited by J. Mercader. New Brunswick: Rutgers University Press.

Mercader, Julio, S. Rovira, and P. Gomez-Ramos

2000   Shared Technologies: Forager-Farmer Interaction and Ancient Iron Metallurgy in the Ituri Rainforest, Democratic Republic of Congo. *Azania* 35:107–122.

Mercader, Julio, F. Runge, L. Vrydaghs, H. Doutrelepont, C. Ewango, and J. Juan-Tresseras

2000   Phytoliths from Archaeological Sites in the Tropical Forest of Ituri, Democratic Republic of Congo. *Quaternary Research* 54:102–112.

Mielke, Andreas

1988   Hottentots in the Aesthetic Discussion of Eighteenth-Century Germany. *Monatshefte* (University of Wisconsin), 80:135–148.

Mitchell, Peter

1993   The Archaeology of Tloutle Rockshelter, Maseru District, Lesotho. *Navorsinge: Van Die Nasionale Museum Bloemfontein* (Journal of the National Museum, Bloemfontein) 9:4:77–132.

1996   Comment on Jolly's Article, Symbiotic Interactions in Southern Africa. *Current Anthropology* 37:291–292.

Mitchell, Peter, John Parkington, and Royden Yates

1994   Recent Holocene Archaeology in Western and Southern Lesotho. *South African Archaeological Bulletin* 49:33–52.

Moerman, Michael

1988   *Talking Culture: Ethnography and Conversation Analysis.* Philadelphia: University of Pennsylvania Press.

Moore, Sue Mullins

1981   The Antebellum Barrier Island Plantation: In Search of an Archaeological Pattern. Ph.D. diss., University of Florida. Ann Arbor, MI: University Microfilms International.

Mortensen, H.

2000   Evidence of African Prehistory: Y Chromosome and mtDNA Analysis of Four Linguistically Diverse African Groups (the Hadzabe, Datoga, Irawq, and Sukuma of Northeastern Tanzania). M.A. thesis, Stanford University.

Morton, Barry

    1994   Servitude, Slave Trading, and Slavery in the Kalahari. In *Slavery in South Africa: Captive Labor on the Dutch Frontier,* edited by Elizabeth A. Eldredge and Fred Morton, pp. 214–250. Boulder, CO: Westview Press.

Morton, Fred

    1987   Introduction: Seeing Botswana as a Whole. In *The Botswana: A History of the Bechuanaland Protectorate from 1910 to 1966,* edited by Fred Morton and Jeff Ramsay, pp. 1–10. Gaborone: Longman Botswana.

Motzafi, Pnina

    1986   Whither the True Bushmen?: The Dynamics of Perpetual Marginality. *Sprache und Geschichte in Afrika* 7 (1): 295–328.

Motzafi-Haller, Pnina

    1998   Beyond Textual Analysis: Practice, Interacting Discourses, and the Experience of Distinction in Botswana. *Cultural Anthropology* 13 (4): 522–547.

Müller, H.

    1912   Ein Erkundungsritt in das Kaukau-veld. *Deutsches Kolonialblatt* 23:530–541.

Murphy, Kimmarie

    1996   The Skeletal Elements of the Iron Age in Central and Southern Africa: A Bioarchaeological Approach to the Reconstruction of Prehistoric Subsistence. Ph.D. diss., Indiana University. Ann Arbor, MI: University Microfilm International.

Murphy, M. L.

    1999   Changing Human Behavior: The Contribution of the White Paintings Rock Shelter to an Understanding of the Changing Lithic Reduction, Raw Material Exchange and Hunter-Gatherer Mobility in the Interior Regions of Southern Africa during the Middle and Early Late Stone Age. Ph.D. diss., Michigan State University.

Musonda, F. B.

    1984   Late Pleistocene and Holocene Microlithic Industries from the Lusemfwa Basin, Zambia. *South African Archaeological Bulletin* 39:24–36.

Nakagawa, Hiroshi

    1996   An Outline of |Gui Phonology. *African Study Monographs,* Supplementary Issue 22:101–124.

Ndagala, D. K., and A. C. Waane

    1982   The Effect of Research on the Hadzabe, a Hunting and Gathering Group of Tanzania. *Review of Ethnology* 8:94–103.

Nettleton, G. E.

    1934   History of the Ngamiland Tribes up to 1926. *Bantu Studies* 8:343–360.

Neville, D. E.

    1996   European Impacts of the Seacow River Valley and Its Hunter-Gatherer Inhabitants, A.D. 1770–1900. M.A. thesis, Department of Archaeology, University of Cape Town.

Newman, James L.

    1995   *The Peopling of Africa: A Geographic Interpretation.* New Haven: Yale University Press.

Newton-King, Susan

1999   *Masters and Servants on the Cape Eastern Frontier.* Cambridge: Cambridge University Press.

Ngcongco, Leonard

1982   Impact of the Difaqane on Tswana States. In *Settlement in Botswana,* edited by R. Renée Hitchcock and Mary R. Smith, pp. 161–172. Gaborone: Botswana Society.

Nurse, Derek

1982   Bantu Expansion into East Africa: Linguistic Evidence. In *Archaeological and Linguistic Reconstruction of African History,* edited by Christopher Ehret and Merrick Posnansky, pp. 199–222. Berkeley: University of California Press.

Nurse, George T., J. S. Weiner, and Trefor Jenkins

1995   *The Peoples of Southern Africa and Their Affinities.* Research Monographs on Human Population Biology No. 3. Oxford: Clarendon.

Obst, E.

1912   Von Mkalama ins Land der Wakindiga. *Mitteilungen der Geographischen Gesellschaft in Hamburg* 26:1–45.

Ochieng, William Robert

1975   *An Outline History of the Rift Valley of Kenya up to A.D. 1900.* Kampala, Nairobi, Dar es Salaam: East African Literature Bureau.

Okihiro, G. Y.

1973   Resistance and Accommodation: baKwena BaGasechele 1842–52. *Botswana Notes and Records* 5:104–116.

1976   *Hunters, Herders, Cultivators, and Traders: Interaction and Change in the Kgalagadi, Nineteenth Century.* Ann Arbor, MI: University Microfilms International.

≠Oma, Kxao Moses, and Axel Thoma

1998   Does Tourism Support or Destroy the Indigenous Cultures of the San? Unpublished paper prepared for the Workshop on Tourism and Indigenous People, Geneva, 28th July 1998.

Orban, R., I. Ribot, S. Fenaux, and P. de Maret

1996   Les restes humains de Shum Laka (Cameroon), LSA–Age de fer. *Anthropologie et Préhistoire* 107:213–225.

Osaki, Masakazu

1984   The Social Influence of Change in Hunting Technique among the Central Kalahari San. *African Study Monographs* 5:49–62.

1990   The Influence of Sedentism on Sharing among the Central Kalahari Hunter-Gatherers. *African Study Monographs,* Supplementary Issue 12:59–87.

1996   A Historical Perspective on the Present Situation of |Gwi and ||Gana Bushmen. *Minzokugaku-Kenkyu (Japanese Journal of Ethnology)* 61 (2): 263–276. (In Japanese with English abstract.)

Otto, John

1984   *Cannon's Point Plantation, 1794–1860: Living Conditions and Status Patterns in the Old South.* Orlando, FL: Academic Press.

Parkington, John

1984   Soaqua and Bushmen: Hunters and Robbers. In *Past and Present in Hunter-*

Gatherer Studies, edited by Carmel Schrire, pp. 151–174. Orlando, FL: Academic Press.

Parkington, John, and Cedric Poggenpoel

1987   Diepkloof Rock Shelter. In *Papers in the Prehistory of the Western Cape, South Africa,* edited by John Parkington and Martin Hall, pp. 269–293. BAR International Series 332. Oxford: BAR.

Parkington, John, Royden Yates, Anthony Manhire, and David Halkett

1986   The Social Impact of Pastoralism in the Southwestern Cape. *Journal of Anthropological Archaeology* 5:313–329.

Parsons, Q. Neil

1977   The Economic History of Khama's Country. In *The Roots of Rural Poverty in Central and Southern Africa,* edited by Robin H. Palmer and Neil Parsons, pp. 113–144. London: Heinemann.

1985   The Evolution of Modern Botswana: Historical Revisions. In *The Evolution of Modern Botswana,* edited by Louis Picard, pp. 26–39. London: Rex Collins.

Passarge, Siegfried

1904   *Die Kalahari: Versuch einer Physisch-Geographischen Darstellung der Sandfelder des Südafrikanischen Beckens.* Berlin: Dietrich Reimer Verlag.

1906   Berichtigung zu der Besprechung über 'Die Buschmänner der Kalahari.' *Zeitschrift für Ethnologie* 38:411–414.

1907   *Die Buschmänner der Kalahari.* Berlin: Dietrich Reimer.

1997   *The Kalahari Ethnographies (1896–98) of Siegfried Passarge,* edited by Edwin Wilmsen. Köln: Rüdiger Köppe Verlag.

Peacock, Nadine

1985   Time Allocation, Work, and Fertility among Efe Pygmy Women of Northeast Zaire. Ph.D. diss., Harvard University. Ann Arbor, MI: University Microfilms International.

Penn, Nigel G.

1987   The Frontier in the Western Cape, 1700–1740. In *Papers in the Prehistory of the Western Cape, South Africa,* edited by John Parkington and Martin Hall, pp. 462–503. BAR International Series 332(ii). Oxford: BAR.

1996   "Fated to Perish": The Destruction of the Cape San. In *Miscast: Negotiating the Presence of the Bushmen,* edited by Pippa Skotnes, pp. 81–92. Cape Town: University of Cape Town Press.

Petersen, R.

1991   To Seach for Life. Ph.D. diss., University of Wisconsin, Madison.

Pieterse, Jan

1996   Varieties of Ethnic Politics and Ethnicity Discourse. In *The Politics of Difference: Ethnic Premises in a World of Power,* edited by Edwin Wilmsen and Patrick McAllister, pp. 25–44. Chicago: University of Chicago Press.

Quammen, David

2000   Megatransect: Across 1,200 miles of Untamed Africa on Foot. *National Geographic Magazine* (October 2000), pp. 2–29.

Quine, Willard V. O.

1960   *Word and Object*. Cambridge: MIT Press.

Ramsay, Jeff

1989   Some Notes on the Colonial Era History of the Central Kalahari Game Reserve Region. *Botswana Notes and Records* 20:91–94.

1991   The Batswana-Boer War of 1852–53: How the Batswana Achieved Victory. *Botswana Notes and Records* 23:193–209.

Raum, Johannes

2000   Review of *The Kalahari Ethnographies (1896–1898) of Siegfried Passarge*, edited by Edwin Wilmsen. *Current Anthropology* 102 (3): 668.

Reck, H., and L. Kohl-Larsen

1936   Erster Überblick über die Jungdiluvialen Tier- und Menschenfunde Dr. Kohl-Larsen's im Nordöstlichen Teil des Njarasa-Grabens (Ostafrika). *Geologische Rundschau* 27:401–444.

Regnault, M.

1911   Les Babenga (Négrilles de la Sangha). *L'Anthropologie* (Paris) 22 (3): 261–288.

Reid, A., K. Sadr, and N. Hanson-James

1998   Herding Traditions in Botswana. In *Ditswa Mung: The Archaeology of Botswana*, edited by P. Lane, A. Reid, and A. Segobye, pp. 81–100. Gaborone: Pula Press and Botswana Society.

Reitz, Elizabeth, Tyson Gibbs, and Ted Rathbun

1985   Archaeological Evidence for Subsistence on Coastal Plantations. In *The Archaeology of Slavery and Plantation Life*, edited by Theresa Singleton, pp. 163–191. San Diego: Academic Press.

Ribot, I., R. Orban, and P. de Maret

2001   *The Prehistoric Burials of Shum Laka Rock Shelter (North-West Cameroon)*. Annales Vol. 164. Sciences Humaines. Tervuren: Musée Royale de l'Afrique Centrale.

Robbins, Larry H.

1985   The Manyana Rock Painting Site. *Botswana Notes and Records* 17:1–15.

1986   Recent Archaeological Research in Southeastern Botswana: The Thamaga Site. *Botswana Notes and Records* 18:1–13.

Robbins, L. H., and M. L. Murphy

1998   The Early Late Stone Age and Evidence of Modern Human Behavior. Abstract of paper presented at the 7th annual meeting of the Paleoanthropology Society, Seattle, WA, March 24–25, 1998. *Journal of Human Evolution* 34 (3): A18.

Robbins, L. H., M. L. Murphy, G. A. Brook, A. Ivester, and Alec C. Campbell

2000   Archaeology, Paleoenvironment, and Chronology of the Tsodilo Hills White Paintings Shelter: Northwest Kalahari Desert, Botswana. *Journal of Archaeological Science* 27 (11): 1085–1113.

Robbins, L. H., M. L. Murphy, K. M. Stewart, A. C. Campbell, and G. A. Brook

1994   Barbed Bone Points, Paleoenvironment, and the Antiquity of Fish Exploitation in the Kalahari Desert, Botswana. *Journal of Field Archaeology* 21:257–264.

Robineau, Claude

1967   Culture Matérielle des Djem de Souanké. *Objets et Mondes* VII (1): 37–50.

Rogers, J. Daniel

1990   *Objects of Change: The Archaeology and History of Arikara Contact with Europeans.* Washington, D.C.: Smithsonian Institution Press.

Romanucci-Ross, Lola, and George DeVos, eds.

1995   *Ethnic Identity: Creation, Conflict, and Accommodation.* 3d edition. Walnut Creek, CA: AltaMira Press.

Roosens, Eugene

1995   Subtle "Primitives": Ethnic Formation among the Central Yaka of Zaire. In *Ethnic Identity: Creation, Conflict, and Accommodation,* edited by Lola Romanucci-Ross and George DeVos, pp. 115–135. Walnut Creek, CA: AltaMira Press.

Rosaldo, Michelle Z.

1980   *Knowledge and Passion: Ilongot Notions of Self and Social Life.* New York: Cambridge University Press.

Rossel, Gerda

1999   Crop Names and the History of Hunter-Gatherers in Northern Congo. In *Central African Hunter-Gatherers in a Multidisciplinary Perspective: Challenging Elusiveness,* edited by Karen Biesbrouck, Stefan Elders, and Gerda Rossel, pp. 105–116. CNWS, Universiteit Leiden.

Rudner, J.

1979   The Use of Stone Artifacts and Pottery among the Khoisan People in Historic and Protohistoric Times. *South African Archaeology Bulletin* 34:3–17.

Ruhlen, Merritt

1991   *A Guide to the World's Languages, Vol. 1: Classification.* Stanford: Stanford University Press.

Russell, Margo, and Martin Russell

1979   *Afrikaners of the Kalahari: White Minority in a Black State.* Cambridge: Cambridge University Press.

Sacks, Harvey

1972/   On the Analyzability of Stories by Children. In *Directions in Sociolinguistics,* edited by John J. Gumperz and Dell Hymes, pp. 325–345. Oxford: Basil Blackwell.
1986

Sadr, Karim

1997   Kalahari Archaeology and the Bushman Debate. *Current Anthropology* 38 (1): 104–112.

Sahlins, Marshall

1974   *Stone Age Economics.* London: Tavistock.

1994   Cosmologies of Capitalism: The Trans-Pacific Sector of "The World System." In *Culture/Power/History: A Reader in Contemporary Social Theory,* edited by Nicholas B. Dirks, Geoff Eley, and Sherry B. Ortner, pp. 412–455. Princeton: Princeton University Press.

Sampson, C. G.

1988   *Stylistic Boundaries among Mobile Hunter-Foragers.* Washington, D.C.: Smithsonian Institution Press.

1995   Acquisition of European Livestock by the Seacow River Bushmen between
        A.D. 1770–1890. *Southern African Field Archaeology* 4:30–36.

Sampson, C. Garth, Tim J. G. Hart, Deborah L. Wallsmith, and Jimmy D. Blagg

1989   The Ceramic Sequence in the Upper Seacow Valley: Problems and Implica-
        tions. *South African Archaeological Bulletin* 44:3–16.

Sandner, G.

1989   The 'Germania Triumphans' and Passarge's 'Erdkundliche Weltanschauung':
        The Roots and Effects of German Political Geography beyond 'Geopolitik.' *Po-
        litical Geography Quarterly* 8:341–351.

Sands, B.

1995   Evaluating Claims of Distant Linguistic Relationships: The Case of Khoisan.
        Ph.D. diss., University of California, Los Angeles.

Sartre, Jean-Paul

1943   *L'être et le Néant*. Paris: Gallimard.

Sato, Hiroaki

2001   The Potential of Edible Wild Yams and Yam-Like Plants as a Staple Food Re-
        source in the African Tropical Rain Forest. *African Study Monographs*, Supple-
        mentary Issue 26:123–134.

Saunders, Rebecca

1998   Forced Relocation, Power Relations, and Culture Contact in the Missions of
        La Florida. In *Studies in Culture Contact: Interaction, Culture Change, and Archae-
        ology*, edited by James Cusick, pp. 402–429. Center for Archaeological Investi-
        gations, Occasional Paper No. 25. Carbondale: Southern Illinois University.

Sawada, Masato

1990   Two Patterns of Chorus among the Efe Forest Hunter-Gatherers in North-
        Eastern Zaire—Why Do They Love to Sing? *African Study Monographs* 10 (4):
        159–195.

Schadeberg, Thilo

1999   Batwa: The Bantu Name for the Invisible People. In *Central African Hunter-
        Gatherers in a Multidisciplinary Perspective: Challenging Elusiveness*, edited by
        Karen Biesbrouck, Stefan Elders, and Gerda Rossel, pp. 21–40. Leiden:
        CNWS, Universiteit Leiden.

Schapera, Issac

1930   *The Khoisan Peoples of South Africa: Bushmen and Hottentots*. London: Routledge
        and Kegan Paul.

1941   *Married Life in an African Tribe*. New York: Sheridan House.

1942   *A History of the Bakgata-Bagakgafèla*. Cape Town: School of African Studies,
        University of Cape Town.

1970   *Tribal Innovators: Tswana Chiefs and Social Change, 1795–1940*. London: Athlone
        Press.

1976 [1953]   *The Tswana*. London: International African Institute.

1980   Notes on the Early History of the Kwena (Bakwena baga Sechele). *Botswana
        Notes and Records* 12:83–87.

1984   *The Tswana*. London: Routledge and Kegan Paul.

Schebesta, Paul

1933   *Among Congo Pygmies*. London: Jonathan Cape.

1936   *Revisiting My Pygmy Hosts*. London: Hutchinson & Co.

Schinz, Hans

1891a   *Deutsch-Südwest-Afrika*. Oldenburg und Leipzig: Schulzesche Hof-Buchhandlung und Hof-Buchdruckerei.

1891b   *Deutsch-Südwest Afrika: Forschungsreisen durch die deutschen Schutzgebiete, Gross-Nama-und Hereroland, nach dem Kunene, dem Ngami-See und der Kalahari, 1884– 1887*. Oldenberg: Schulzescher Hof-Buchhandlung und Hof-Buchdruckerei.

Schmidt, P. Wilhelm

1910   *Die Stellung der Pygmäenvölker in der Entwicklungsgeschichte des Menschen. Studien und Forschungen zur Menschen- und Völkerkunde*. Vol. 6/7. Stuttgart.

Schmidt, Sigrid

1989   *Catalogue of the Khoisan Folktales of Southern Africa*. 2 vols. (QKF 6.1 & 6.2) Hamburg: Helmut Buske Verlag.

1998   *Scherz und Ernst Afrikaner berichten aus ihrem Leben*. Köln: Rüdiger Köppe Verlag.

Schortman, Edward, and Patricia Urban

1998   Culture Contact Structure and Process. In *Studies in Culture Contact: Interaction, Culture Change, and Archaeology*, edited by James Cusick, pp. 102–125. Center for Archaeological Investigations, Occasional Paper No. 25. Carbondale: Southern Illinois University.

Schott, R.

1955   Die Buschmänner in Südafrika: Eine Studie über Schwierigkeiten der Akkulturation. *Sociologus* 32:132–149.

Schrire, Carmel

1980   An Enquiry into the Evolutionary Status and Apparent Identity of San Hunter-Gatherers. *Human Ecology* 8:9–32.

Schumaker, Peter

1950   *Expedition zu den Zentralafrikanischen Kivu-Pygmäen*. Mémoires de l'Institut Royal du Congo Belge. Section des Sciences Morales et Politiques, vol 5. Bruxelles: Institut Royal Colonial Belge.

Schweinfurth, Georg

1878   *The Heart of Africa: Three Years Travels and Adventures in the Unexplored Regions of Central Africa, from 1868 to 1871*. 2 vols. 3d edition. London: Sampson Low, Marston, Searle & Rivington.

Schweitzer, Franz, and M. L. Wilson

1982   Byneskranskop 1: A Late Quaternary Living Site in the Southern Cape Province, South Africa. *Annuals of South African Museum* 88:1–203.

Selous, Frederick Courteney

1893   *Travel and Adventure in South-East Africa*. London: Rowland Ward.

Senior, H. S.

1957   Sukuma Salt Caravans to Lake Eyasi. *Tanganyika Notes and Records* 46:87–90.

Serton, P., R. Raven-Hart, and W. J. de Kock, eds.

1971 *Francois Valentyn. Description of the Cape of Good Hope with Matters Concerning It.* Part 1, published 1726. Second Series, No. 2. Cape Town: Van Riebeek Society.

Setiloane, Gabriel

1976 *The Image of God among the Sotho-Tswana.* Rotterdam: A. A. Balkema.

Shanin, Teodor, ed.

1987 *Peasants and Peasant Societies: Selected Readings.* Oxford: Blackwell.

Sharp, John, and Stuart Douglas

1996 Prisoners of Their Reputation? The Veterans of the ?Bushman? Battalions in South Africa. In *Miscast: Negotiating the Presence of the Bushmen,* edited by Pippa Skotnes, pp. 323–329. Cape Town: University of Cape Town Press.

Silberbauer, George B.

1960 *The First Interim Report of the Bushman Survey.* Mafeking: Report to the Government of Bechuanaland.

1965 *Report to the Government of Bechuanaland on the Bushman Survey.* Gaberones (Gaborone): Bechuanaland Government.

1972 The G|wi Bushmen. In *Hunters and Gatherers Today,* edited by by M. G. Bicchieri, pp. 271–326. New York: Holt, Rinehart and Winston.

1981 *Hunter and Habitat in the Central Kalahari Desert.* Cambridge: Cambridge University Press.

1982 Political Process in G/wi Band. In *Politics and History in Band Societies,* edited by Eleanor Leacock and Richard Lee, pp. 23–35. Cambridge: Cambridge University Press.

1996 Neither Are Your Ways My Ways. In *Cultural Diversity among Twentieth-Century Foragers: An African Perspective,* edited by Susan Kent, pp. 21–64. Cambridge: Cambridge University Press.

Silberbauer, George, and Adam Kuper

1966 Kgalagari Masters and Bushmen Serfs: Some Observations. *African Studies* 25:171–179.

Silitshena, R. M. K.

1976 Notes on the Origins of Some Settlements in the Kweneng District. *Botswana Notes and Records* 8:97–103.

Silitshena, R. M. K., and G. MacLeod

1994 *Botswana: A Physical, Social, and Economic Geography.* Gaborone: Longman Botswana.

Singleton, Theresa

1998 Cultural Interaction and African American Identity in Plantation Archaeology. In *Studies in Culture Contact: Interaction, Culture Change, and Archaeology,* edited by James Cusick, pp. 172–1188. Center for Archaeological Investigations, Occasional Paper No. 25. Carbondale: Southern Illinois University.

Skotnes, Pippa

1996 *Miscast: Negotiating the Presence of the Bushmen.* Cape Town: University of Cape Town Press.

Slome, D.

    1929   The Osteology of a Bushman Tribe. *Annals of the South African Museum* 24:33–60.

Smiley, Francis E.

    1979/   The Birhor: Material Correlates of Hunter-Gatherer/Farmer Exchange. In

    1980   *The Archaeological Correlates of Hunter-Gatherer Societies: Studies from the Ethnographic Record,* edited by Francis B. Smiley, Carla Sinopoli, H. Edwin Jackson, W. H. Wills, and Susan Greggs, pp.149–176. Michigan Discussions in Anthropology, Vol. 5, Nos. 1 and 2. Ann Arbor: University of Michigan Press.

Smith, A. D.

    1986   *The Ethnic Origins of Nations.* Malden, MA: Blackwell Publishers.

Smith, Andrew B.

    1989   Khoikhoi Susceptibility to Virgin Soil Epidemics in the 18th Century. *South African Medical Journal* 75:25–26.

    1998   Keeping People on the Periphery: The Ideology of Social Hierarchies between Hunters and Herders. *Journal of Anthropological Archaeology* 17:201–215.

    2001   Public and Hidden Transcripts: A Response to Cronk and Dickson. *Journal of Anthropological Archaeology* 20:122–124.

Smith, Marvin A.

    1987   *Archaeology of Aboriginal Culture Change in the Interior Southeast: Depopulation during the Early Historic Period.* Gainesville: University of Florida Press.

Smith, Andrew B., and Richard B. Lee

    1997   Cho/ana: Archaeological and Ethnohistorical Evidence for Recent Hunter-Gatherer/Agropastoralist Contact in Northern Bushmanland, Namibia. *South African Archaeological Bulletin* 52:52–59.

Smith, Andrew B., and Roy Pheiffer

    1994   Letter from Robert Jacob Gordon to Hendrik Fagel, 1779. *Breuthurst Archives* 1 (2): 29–46.

Smith, Andrew B., Karim Sadr, John Gribble, and Royden Yates

    1991   Excavations in the Southwestern Cape, South Africa, and the Archaeological Identity of Prehistoric Hunter-Gatherers within the Last 2000 Years. *South African Archaeological Bulletin* 46:71–91.

Solway, Jacqueline S.

    1986   Commercialization and Social Differentiation in a Kalahari Village, Botswana. Ph.D. diss., University of Toronto.

    1994   From Shame to Pride: Politicized Ethnicity in the Kalahari, Botswana. *Canadian Journal of African Studies* 24:254–274.

Solway, Jacqueline S., and Richard B. Lee

    1990   Foragers, Genuine or Spurious? Situating the Kalahari San in History. *Current Anthropology* 31:109–146.

Soodyall, H., and T. Jenkins

    1992   Mitochondrial DNA Polymorphisms in Khoisan Populations from Southern Africa. *Annals of Human Genetics* 56 (4): 315–324.

Soodyall, H., B. Morar, and T. Jenkins

    2000   Human Origins and Continuing Evolution in Africa: The Place of the

Khoisan. Paper presented at the Cold Spring Harbor Symposium on "Human Origins and Disease," October 25–29.

Soper, Robert

1982   Bantu Expansion into Eastern Africa: Archaeological Evidence. In *Archaeological and Linguistic Reconstruction of African History,* edited by Christopher Ehret and Merrick Posnansky, pp. 223–238. Berkeley: University of California Press.

Spencer, B., and F. Gillen

1927   *The Arunta: A Case Study of a Stone Age People.* New York: MacMillan.

Sperber, Dan

1996   *Explaining Culture: A Naturalistic Approach.* Cambridge: Cambridge University Press.

Spielmann, Katharine

1982   Inter-Societal Food Acquisition among Egalitarian Societies: An Ecological Study of Plains/Pueblo Interaction in the American Southwest. Ph.D. diss., University of Michigan. Ann Arbor, MI: University Microfilms International.

Spurdle, A., and Trefor Jenkins

1992   Y Chromosome Probe p49a Detects Complex PvuII Haplotypes and Many New TaqI Haplotypes in Southern African Populations. *American Journal of Human Genetics* 50 (1): 107–125.

Stals, E. L. P., ed.

1991   *The Commissions of W. C. Palgrave.* Cape Town: Van Riebeck Society.

Stein, Gil

1998   World System Theory and Alternative Models of Interaction in the Archaeology of Culture Contact. In *Studies in Culture Contact: Interaction, Culture Change, and Archaeology,* edited by by James Cusick, pp. 220–255. Center for Archaeological Investigations, Occasional Paper No. 25. Carbondale: Southern Illinois University.

Steyn, H. P.

1971   Aspects of the Economic Life of Some Nomadic Nharo Bushman Groups. *Annals of the South African Museum* 56:275–322.

1984   Southern Kalahari San Subsistence Ecology: A Reconstruction. *The South African Archaeological Bulletin* 39:117–124.

1994   Role and Position of Elderly !Xû in the Schmidtsdrift Bushman Community. *South African Journal of Ethnology* 17 (2): 31–37.

Stoler, Ann

1992   Rethinking Colonial Categories: European Communities and the Boundaries of Rule. In *Colonialism and Culture,* edited by Nicholas Dirks, pp. 319–352. Ann Arbor: University of Michigan Press.

Strathern, Marilyn

1991   *Partial Connections.* Savage, MD: Rowan & Littlefield Publishers.

Stuart, Doug

1995   Images of the "Savage" in Southern African Missionary Discourse: Redemption. In *Shifting Cultures: Interaction and Discourse in the Expansion of Europe,* edited by Henriette Bugge and Joan Rubiés, pp. 115–129. Münster: Lit Verlag.

Sugawara, Kazuyoshi

1988   Social Relations and Interactions between Residential Groups among the Central Kalahari San: Hunter-Gatherer Camp as a Micro-Territory. *African Study Monographs* 8 (4): 173–211.

1990   Interactional Aspects of the Body in Co-Presence: Observations on the Central Kalahari San. In *Culture Embodied,* edited by Michael Moerman and Masaichi Nomura, pp. 79–122. Senri Ethnological Studies 27. Osaka, Japan: National Museum of Ethnology.

1991   The Economics of Social Life among the Central Kalahari San (G/wikhwe and G//anakwe) in the Sedentary Community at !Koi!kom. In *Cash, Commoditisation, and Changing Foragers,* edited by Nicolas Peterson and Toshio Matsuyama, pp. 91–117. Senri Ethnological Studies 30. Osaka, Japan: National Museum of Ethnology.

1996   Some Methodological Issues for the Analysis of Everyday Conversation among the |Gui. *African Study Monographs,* Supplementary Issue 22:145–161.

1997   A Name as a Mnemonic Device: An Ethnographic Study of Personal Names among the Central San (|Gui and ||Gana). *Bulletin of the National Museum of Ethnology* 22 (1): 1–92. (In Japanese with an English summary.)

1998a   Ecology and Communication in Egalitarian Societies: Japanese Studies of the Cultural Anthropology of Southern Africa. *Japanese Review of Cultural Anthropology* 1:97–129.

1998b   'Egalitarian' Attitude in Everyday Conversations among the |Gui. In *The Proceedings of the Khoisan Identities and Cultural Heritage Conference,* pp. 237–240. Cape Town: The Institute for Historical Research, University of the Western Cape/Infosource CC.

1998c   *Kaiwa no Jinruigaku (Anthropology of Conversation).* (In Japanese.) Kyoto: Kyoto University Academic Press.

2001   Cognitive Space Concerning Habitual Thought and Practice toward Animals among the Central San (|Gui and ||Gana): Deictic/Indirect Cognition and Prospective/Retrospective Intention. *African Study Monographs,* Supplementary Issue 27: 61–98.

Sullivan, Sian

1999   How Sustainable Is the Communalising Discourse of 'New' Conservation? The Masking of Difference, Inequality, and Aspiration in the Fledgling 'Conservancies' of Namibia. Paper presented at Displacement, Forced Settlement, and Conservation Conference, Oxford, 9–11 September 1999.

Sutton, J. E. G.

1986   The Irrigation and Manuring of the Engaruka Field System. *Azania* 21:27–48.

1989   Towards a History of Cultivating the Fields. *Azania* 24:98–112.

1990   *A Thousand Years of East Africa.* Nairobi: British Institute in East Africa.

Suzman, James

1995   *Poverty, Land, and Power in the Omaheke.* London: Oxfam UK.

Sylvain, R.

1998   Survival Strategies and San Women on the Commercial Farms in the Omaheke Region, Namibia. In *The Proceedings of the Khoisan Identities and Cultural Heritage Conference,* edited by Andrew Bank, pp. 336–343. Cape Town: InfoSource and Institute for Historical Research, University of the Western Cape.

Szalay, Mikkós

1979   Die ethnographische Südwestafrika-Sammlung Hans Schinz, 1884–86. *Ethnologische Zeitschrift Zürich* (special issue) 1.

1995   *The San and the Colonization of the Cape, 1770–1879.* Köln: Rüdiger Köppe Verlag.

Tabler, Edward C.

1973   *Pioneers of Southwest Africa and Ngamiland, 1738–1880.* Cape Town: A. A. Balkema.

Talma, A. S., and J. C. Vogel

1993   A Simplified Approach to Calibrating C^{14} Dates. *Radiocarbon* 35 (1): 73–86.

Tanaka, Jiro

1976   Subsistence Ecology of Central Kalahari San. In *Kalahari Hunter-Gatherers: Studies of the !Kung San and Their Neighbors,* edited by Richard B. Lee and Irven DeVore, pp. 98–119. Cambridge: Harvard University Press.

1980   *The San, Hunter-Gatherers of the Kalahari: A Study in Ecological Anthropology.* Tokyo: University of Tokyo Press.

1987   The Recent Changes in the Life and Society of the Central Kalahari San. *African Study Monographs* 7:37–51.

1989   Social Integration of the San Society from the Viewpoint of Sexual Relationships. *African Study Monographs* 9 (3): 55–64.

1991   Egalitarianism and the Cash Economy among the Central Kalahari San. In *Cash, Commoditisation, and Changing Foragers,* edited by Nicolas Peterson and Toshio Matsuyama, pp. 117–134. Senri Ethnological Studies 30. Osaka: National Museum of Ethnology.

1996   The World of Animals Viewed by the San Hunter-Gatherers in Kalahari. *African Study Monographs,* Supplementary Issue 22:11–28.

Tapela, M.

1998   An Archaeological Examination of Ostrich Eggshell Beads in Botswana. B.A. research essay, Department of History, University of Botswana.

Taylor, Michael

2000   Land, Life and Power: Contesting Development in Northern Botswana. Ph.D. thesis, Department of Social Anthropology, University of Edinburgh.

Templeton, Alan

1998   Human Races: A Genetic and Evolutionary Perspective. *American Anthropology* 100:632–650.

Terashima, Hideaki

1987   Why Efe Girls Marry Farmers: Socio-Ecological Backgrounds of Inter-Ethnic Marriage in the Ituri Forest of Central Africa. *African Study Monographs,* Supplementary Issue 6:65–83.

Thom, Hendrick Bernardus, ed.

1958   *Journal of Jan van Riebeeck, Vol. 3, 1659–1662.* Written by Jan van Riebeeck. Cape Town: Balkema.

Thomas, Brian

   1998   Power and Community: The Archaeology of Slavery at the Hermitage Plantation. *American Antiquity* 64:531–551.

Thomas, David, and Paul Shaw

   1991   *The Kalahari Environment.* Cambridge: Cambridge University Press.

Thomas, E. W.

   1950   *Bushman Folktales.* Cape Town: Oxford University Press.

Thomas, Jacqueline M. C.

   1979   Emprunt ou Parenté? A Propos des Parlers des Populations Forestières de Centrafrique. In *Pygmées de Centrafrique: Ethnologie, Histoire, et Linguistique. Études Ethnologiques, Historiques, et Linguistiques sur les Pygmées 'Ba.Mbenga' (Aka/Baka) du Nord-Ouest du Bassin Congolais,* edited by S. Bahuchet, pp. 141–169. Paris: SELAF/Louvain Peeters.

Thomson, Donald F.

   1949   *Economic Structure and the Ceremonial Exchange Cycle in Arnhem Land.* Melbourne: Macmillan.

Thorp, Carolyn

   1984   A Cultural Interpretation of the Faunal Assemblage from Khami Hill Ruin. In *Frontiers: Southern African Archaeology Today,* edited by Martin Hall, G. Avery, D. M. Avery, M. L. Wilson, and A. J. Humphreys, pp. 266–276. BAR International Series 207. Oxford: BAR.

   1996   A Preliminary Report on Evidence of Interaction between Hunter-Gatherers and Farmers along a Hypothetical Frontier in the Eastern Free State. *South African Archaeological Bulletin* 51:57–63.

   1997   Evidence for Interaction from Recent Hunter-Gatherer Sites in the Caledon Valley. *African Archaeological Review* 14 (4): 231–256.

Tlou, Thomas

   1975   Documents of Botswana: How Rhodes Tried to Seize Ngamiland. *Botswana Notes and Records* 7:61–65.

   1976   The Peopling of the Okavango Delta, 1750–1906. In *Proceedings of the Symposium on the Okavango Delta and Its Future Utilization,* pp. 49–53. Gaborone: Botswana Society.

   1985   *A History of Ngamiland, 1750 to 1906: The Formation of an African State.* Gaborone: Macmillan Botswana.

Tlou, Thomas., and Alec C. Campbell

   1984   *History of Botswana.* Gaborone: Macmillan Botswana.

Tomita, K.

   1966   The Sources of Food for the Hadzapi Tribe: The Life of a Hunting Tribe in East Africa. *Kyoto University African Studies* 1:157–171.

Tonkinson, Robert

   1978   *The Mardudjara Aborigines.* New York: Holt, Rinehart and Winston.

Traill, Anthony

   1978a   Research on Non-Bantu Languages. In *Language and Communication Studies in*

South Africa, edited by P. V. Lanham and K. P. Prinsloo, pp. 117–137. Cape Town: Oxford University Press.

1978b   The Languages of the Bushmen. In *The Bushmen: San Hunters and Herders of Southern Africa*, edited by P. V. Tobias, pp. 133–147. Cape Town and Pretoria: Human and Rousseau.

1986   Do the Khoi Have a Place in the San? New Data on Khoisan Linguistic Relationships. *Sprache und Geschichte in Afrika* 7 (1): 407–430.

2000   Khoisan Linguistic Prehistory. Paper presented at the Cold Spring Harbor Symposium on "Human Origins and Disease," October 25–29.

Truswell, A. Stewart, and John Hansen

1976   Medical Research among the !Kung. In *Kalahari Hunter-Gatherers: Studies of the !Kung San and Their Neighbors*, edited by Richard Lee and Irven DeVore, pp. 166–194. Cambridge: Harvard University Press.

Turnbull, Colin M.

1966   *Wayward Servants: The Two Worlds of the African Pygmies*. London: Eyre & Spottiswoode.

1983   *The Mbuti Pygmies: Change and Adaptation*. New York: Holt & Rinehart.

Twiesselmann, F.

1958   *Les Ossements Humains, Gîte Mesolithique d'Ishango*. Explorations du Parc National Albert. Fasc. 5. Brussels: Institut des Parcs Nationaux de Congo Belge.

Twyman, Chaska

1998   Rethinking Community Resource Management: Managing Resources or Managing People in Western Botswana? *Third World Quarterly* 19 (4): 745–770.

Tylor, Edward Burnett

1871   *Primitive Culture: Researches into the Development of Mythology, Philosophy, Religion, Language, Art, and Custom*. 2 volumes, 2d edition. London: John Murray.

Underhill, P., G. Passarino, P. Shen, A. A. Lin, L. Jin, G. Passarino, W. H. Yang, E. Kauffman, B. Bonné-Tamir, J. Bertranpetit, P. Francalacci, M. Ibrahim, T. Jenkins, J. R. Kidd, Q. Mehdi, M. T. Seielstad, R. S. Wells, A. Piazza, R. W. Davis, M. W. Feldman, L. L. Cavalli-Sforza, and P. J. Oefner

2000   Y Chromosome Sequence Variation and the History of Human Populations. *Nature Genetics* 26:358–361.

Underhill, P., G. Passarino, A. A. Lin, P. Shen, M. Mirazon Lahr, R. A. Foley, P. J. Oefner, and L. L. Cavalli-Sforza

2001   The Phylogeography of Y Chromosome Binary Haplotypes and the Origin of Modern Human Populations. *American Journal of Human Genetics* 65 (1): 43–62.

Valiente-Noailles, Carlos

1993   *The Kua: Life and Soul of the Central Kalahari Bushmen*. Rotterdam: A. A. Balkema.

Van den Berghe, P.

1981   *The Ethnic Phenomenon*. New York: Praeger.

Van der Ryst, M. M.

1998   *The Waterberg Plateau in the Northern Province, Republic of South Africa, in the Later Stone Age*. BAR International series 715. Oxford: BAR.

van Waarden, C.

in press   The Later Iron Age. In *Ditswa Mmung: The Archaeology of Botswana,* edited by P. J. Lane, D. A. M. Reid, and A. K. Segobye, pp. 115–160. Gaborone: Botswana Society.

Vansina, Jan

1985   *Oral Tradition as History.* Madison: University of Wisconsin Press.

1986   Do Pygmies Have a History? In *Sprache und Geschichte in Afrika* 7 (1), edited by F. Rottland and R. Vossen, pp. 431–445. Hamburg: H. Buske Verlag.

1990   *Paths in the Rainforest: Toward a History of Political Tradition in Equatorial Africa.* London: James Currey.

Vierich, H.

1977   *Interim Report on Basarwa and Related Poor Bakgalagadi in Kweneng District.* Gaborone: Ministry of Local Government and Lands.

Vigilant, L. M. Stoneking, H. Harpending, K. Hawkes, and A. C. Wilson

1991   African Populations and the Evolution of Human Mitochondrial DNA. *Science* 253:1503–1507.

Vincent, Jeanne-Françoise

1961   *La Culture du Cacao et son Retentissement Social dans la Région de Souanké.* Brazzaville: O.R.S.T.O.M.

Visser, Hessel, and Cobi Visser

1998   Analysis of Naro Names. In *The Proceedings of the Khoisan Identities and Cultural Heritage Conference,* pp. 225–231. Cape Town: The Institute for Historical Research, University of the Western Cape / Infosource CC.

Viveiros de Castro, Eduardo

1998   Cosmological Deixis and Amerindian Perspectivism. *Journal of the Royal Anthropological Institute* 4 (3): 469–488.

Voigt, E., I. Plug, and G. Sampson

1995   European Livestock from Rockshelters in the Upper Seacow River Valley. *Southern African Field Archaeology* 4:37–49.

Wadley, Lyn

1996   Changes in the Social Relations of Precolonial Hunter-Gatherers after Agro-pastoralist Contact: An Example from the Magaliesberg, South Africa. *Journal of Anthropological Research* 15:205–217.

2001   Who Lived in Mauermanshoek Shelter, Korannaberg, South Africa? *Journal of Anthropological Archaeology* 18:153–179.

Wæhle, Espen

1989   Elusive Persistence: Efe (Mbuti Pygmy) Autonomy Strategies in the Ituri Forest, Zaïre. M.A. thesis, Department of Social Anthropology, University of Oslo.

Walker, N.

1995   The Archaeology of the San: The Late Stone Age of Botswana. In *Speaking for the Bushmen,* edited by A. J. G. M. Sanders, pp. 54–87. Gaborone: Botswana Society.

Watson, E., P. Forster, M. Richards, and H. J. Bandelt

1997   Mitochondrial Footprints of Human Expansions in Africa. *American Journal of Human Genetics* 61 (3): 691–704.

Weber, W., L. White, A. Vedder, and L. Naughton, eds.

2001   *African Rain Forest Ecology and Conservation: An Interdisciplinary Perspective.* New Haven: Yale University Press.

Webster

1976   *Webster's New World Dictionary of the American Language.* Cleveland: Wm. Collins and World Publishing.

1997   *Webster's New World Dictionary and Thesaurus.* New York: Macmillan.

Westbury, William, and Garth Sampson

1993   To Strike the Necessary Fire: Acquisition of Guns by the Seacow Valley Bushmen. *South African Archaeological Bulletin* 48:26–31.

Westphal, E. O. J.

1962a   On Classifying Bushman and Hottentot Languages. *African Language Studies* 3:30–48.

1962b   A Reclassification of Southern African Non-Bantu Languages. *Journal of African Languages* 1 (1): 1–8.

1963   The Linguistic Prehistory of Southern Africa: Bush, Kwadi, Hottentot, and Bantu Linguistic Relationships. *Africa* 33:237–265.

Wheaton, Thomas, and Patrick Garrow

1985   Acculturation and the Archaeological Record in the Carolina Low Country. In *The Archaeology of Slavery and Plantation Life,* edited by Theresa Singleton, pp. 239–259. San Diego: Academic Press.

Whitelaw, G.

1994   KwaGandaganda Settlement Patterns in the Natal Early Iron Age. *Natal Museum Journal of Humanities* 6:1–64.

Widlok, Thomas

1999   *Living on Mangetti: Bushman Autonomy and Namibian Independence.* Oxford and New York: Oxford University Press.

Wiessner, Polly

1977   Hxaro: A Regional System of Reciprocity for Reducing Risk among the !Kung San. Ph.D. diss., University of Michigan. Ann Arbor, MI: University Microfilms International.

1990a   Comment to J. Solway and R. Lee, 'Foragers, Genuine or Spurious? Situating the Kalahari San in History.' *Current Anthropology* 31 (2): 135–136.

1990b   Comment on Paradigmatic History of San-Speaking Peoples and Current Attempts at Revision by Edwin Wilmsen and James Denbow. *Current Anthropology* 31:498–524.

1993   Hxaro. In *Im Spiegel der Anderen: Aus dem Lebenswerk des Verhaltenforschers Iraenaus Eibl-Eibesfeldt.* München: Realis.

Willoughby, William Charles

1912   *Nature-Worship and Taboo: Further Studies in "The Soul of the Bantu."* Hartford, Connecticut: Hartford Seminary Press.

Wilmsen, Edwin N.

1978   Prehistoric and Historic Antecedents of a Contemporary Ngamiland Community. *Botswana Notes and Records* 10:5–18.

1983   The Ecology of Illusion: Anthropological Foraging in the Kalahari. *Reviews in Anthropology* 10 (1): 9–20.

1988   The Antecedents of Contemporary Pastoralism in Western Ngamiland. *Botswana Notes and Records* 20:29–39.

1989   *Land Filled with Flies: A Political Economy of the Kalahari.* Chicago and London: Chicago University Press.

1990   Comment on 'Foragers, Genuine or Spurious?' *Current Anthropology* 31 (2): 136–137.

1993   On the Search for (Truth) and Authority: A Reply to Lee and Guenther. *Current Anthropology* 34 (5): 715–721.

1996   Introduction. In *The Politics of Difference: Ethnic Premises in a World of Power,* edited by Edwin Wilmsen and Patrick McAllister, pp. 1–23. Chicago: University of Chicago Press.

Wilmsen, Edwin N., ed.

1997   *The Kalahari Ethnographies (1896–1898) of Siegfried Passarge Nineteenth Century Khoisan- and Bantu-Speaking Peoples.* Köln: Rüdiger Köppe Verlag.

Wilmsen, Edwin N., and James R. Denbow

1990   Paradigmatic History of San-Speaking Peoples and Current Attempts at Revision. *Current Anthropology* 31 (5): 489–524.

Wilson, M. L.

1996   The Late Holocene Occupants of Die Kelders: Hunter-Gatherers or Herders? *Southern African Field Archaeology* 5:79–84.

Wolf, Eric R.

1982   *Europe and the People without History.* Berkeley and Los Angeles: University of California Press.

Woodburn, James

1958   The Hadza: First Impressions. East African Institute of Social Research, Kampala Conference. June, 1958, pp. 1–10.

1959   Hadza Conceptions of Health and Disease. In *One-Day Symposium on Attitudes to Health and Disease among Some East African Tribes,* pp. 89–94. Kampala: East African Institute of Social Research.

1962   The Future of the Tindiga. *Tanganyika Notes and Records* 59:268–273.

1968a   An Introduction to Hadza Ecology. In *Man the Hunter,* edited by Richard B. Lee and Irven DeVore, pp. 49–55. Chicago: Aldine.

1968b   Stability and Flexibility in Hadza Residential Groupings. In *Man the Hunter,* edited by Richard B. Lee and I. DeVore, pp. 103–110. Chicago: Aldine.

1970   *Hunters and Gatherers: The Material Culture of the Nomadic Hadza.* London: Trustees of the British Museum.

1977   The East African Click Languages: A Phonetic Comparison. In *Zur Sprachgeschichte und Ethnohistorie in Afrika,* edited by A. Tucker, pp. 300–323. Berlin: Reimer Verlag.

1979   Minimal Politics: The Political Organization of the Hadza of North Tanzania. In *Politics in Leadership,* edited by W. A. Shack and P. S. Cohen, pp. 244–266. Oxford: Clarendon Press.

1988   African Hunter-Gatherer Social Organization: Is It Best Understood as a Product of Encapsulation? In *Hunters and Gatherers, Volume I, History, Evolution, and Social Change,* edited by Tim Ingold, David Riches, and James Woodburn, pp. 31–65. Oxford: Berg.

1997   Indigenous Discrimination: The Ideological Basis for Local Discrimination against Hunter-Gatherer Minorities in Sub-Saharan Africa. *Ethnic and Racial Studies* 20 (2): 345–361.

2000   Elusive Pygmies. A Book Review. *Indigenous Affairs* (IWGIA) 2:78–83.

Working Group for Indigenous Minorities in Southern Africa (WIMSA)

2000   *Report on Activities, April 1999 to March 2000.* Windhoek: WIMSA.

Wright, J.

1971   *Bushman Raiders of the Drakensburg, 1840–1870.* Pietermaritzburg: University of Natal Press.

Yellen, John E.

1977   *Archaeological Approaches to the Present: Models for Interpreting the Past.* New York: Academic Press

1987   Optimization and Risk in Human Foraging Strategies. *Journal of Human Evolution* 15 (8): 733–750.

1990a   Comment on 'Foragers, Genuine or Spurious?' by Jacqueline S. Solway and Richard B. Lee. *Current Anthropology* 31:137–138.

1990b   Comment on 'Paradigmatic History of San-Speaking Peoples and Current Attempts at Revision,' by E. Wilmsen and J. R. Denbow. *Current Anthropology* 31:516–517.

1991a   Small Mammals: !Kung San Utilization and the Production of Faunal Assemblages. *Journal of Anthropological Archaeology* 10 (1): 1–26.

1991b   Small Mammals: Post-Discard Patterning of !Kung San Faunal Remains. *Journal of Anthropological Archaeology* 10:152–192.

1998   Barbed Bone Points: Tradition and Continuity in Saharan and Sub-Saharan Africa. *African Archaeological Review.* 15:173–198.

n.d.   The Transformation of the Kalahari !Kung. *Scientific American* 262 (4): 96–105.

Yellen, John E., and Alison S. Brooks

1988   The Late Stone Age Archaeology of the !Kangwa and /Xai/Xai Valleys, Ngamiland. *Botswana Notes and Records* 20:5–27.

1990   The Late Stone Age Archaeology in the /Xai/Xai Region: A Response to Wilmsen. *Botswana Notes and Records* 22:17–19.

Yellen, John E., A. S. Brooks, E. Cornelissen, M. H. Mehlman, and K. Stewart

1995   A Middle Stone Age Worked Bone Industry from Katanda, Upper Semliki Valley, Zaire. *Science* 268:553–556.

Yellen, John E., A. S. Brooks, R. Stuckenrath, and R. Welbourne

1987   A Terminal Pleistocene Assemblage from Drotsky's Cave, Western Ngamiland, Botswana. *Botswana Notes and Records* 19:1–6.

Yellen, John E., and R. B. Lee

1976   The Dode /Du/da Environment: Background to a Hunting and Gathering Way of Life. In *Kalahari Hunter-Gatherers: Studies of the !Kung San and Their Neighbors,* edited by R. B. Lee and I. DeVore, pp. 27–46. Cambridge: Harvard University Press.

Contributors

Prof. Alan Barnard
School of Social and Political Studies
University of Edinburgh
Adam Ferguson Bldg.
George Square
Edinburgh EH8 9LL
Scotland
A.Barnard@ed.ac.uk

Dr. Alison Brooks
Department of Anthropology
George Washington University
2110 G Street, N.W.
Washington,, D.C. 20052
USA
Office (202) 994-6079
Fax (202) 994-6097
abrooks@gwis2.circ.gwu.edu

Dr. Mathias Guenther
Sociology and Anthropology
Wilfrid Laurier University
Waterloo, Ontario N2L 3C5
Canada
Office (519) 884-1970
Fax (519) 886-9351
mguenther@sympatico.ca

Dr. Susan Kent
Anthropology Program
Old Dominion University
BAL 723, Hampton Blvd.
Norfolk, VA 23529
USA
Office (757) 683-3810
Fax (757) 683-5634
skent@odu.edu

Dr. Axel Köhler
CESMECA-UNICACH
Centro de Estudios de Mexico y Centroamerica
Avenida Diego Dugelay #4
Barrio Guadalupe
San Cristobal de las Casas
Chiapas, C.P. 29230
Mexico
axelkoehler@hotmail.com

Dr. Richard Lee
Department of Anthropology
University of Toronto
Toronto, Ontario M5S 3G3
Canada
Office (416) 978-4008
rblee@chass.utoronto.ca

Mr. Jerome Lewis
40 Dalberg Road
London, SW2 1AN
United Kingdom
Office [44] (171) 207-1225
Fax [44] (171) 274-3968
JINLewis@aol.com

Dr. Frank Marlowe
Department of Anthropology
Harvard University
Cambridge, MA
USA
fmarlowe@ucla.edu

Dr. Karim Sadr
Department of Archaeology
Private Bag 3
University of Witwatersrand
Wits 2050
Johannesburg
South Africa
107sadr@cosmos.wits.ac.za

Dr. Kazuyoshi Sugawara
Faculty of Integrated Human Studies
Kyoto University
Yoshida, Sakyo-ku
Kyoto 606-8501
Japan
Office [81] (75) 753-6610
ksugawar@ip.media.kyoto-u.ac.jp

Dr. Michael Taylor
Basarwa Research Programme
University of Botswana
P/Bag 0022
Gaborone
Botswana
taylors@botsnet.bw

Index

✖◯✖◯✖◯✖◯✖◯✖◯✖◯✖◯✖◯✖

Page numbers in **boldface** indicate illustrations